INVENTING AMERICA

INVENTING AMERICA

☆

Jefferson's
Declaration of Independence

GARRY WILLS

VINTAGE BOOKS
A DIVISION OF RANDOM HOUSE
NEW YORK

Library of Congress Cataloging in Publication Data

Wills, Garry, 1934-
Inventing America.

"The Declarations of Jefferson and of the
Congress": p.
Includes bibliographical references and index.
1. United States. Declaration of Independence.
2. Jefferson, Thomas, Pres. U.S., 1743-1826.
I. Jefferson, Thomas, Pres. U.S., 1743-1826.
Declaration of independence. 1979. II. United
States. Declaration of independence. 1979.
III. Title.
E221.W64   1979   973.3'13   78-11212
ISBN 0-394-72735-5

Manufactured in the United States of America

A la Natalia

Perchè? Perchè . . . essa la poesia
—Giacosa/Illica

Plan of the Book

The emphasis in the book's subtitle is on *Jefferson's* Declaration of Independence, which I mean to distinguish (as he did) from the congressional document. The heart of my analysis, in the book's central parts (Two, Three, and Four), is devoted to Jefferson's draft.

Preceding that study, Part One deals with the draft as Congress altered and established it. Following the central section, Part Five deals with the document as we have used, honored, and bent it.

I thus distinguish the Declaration of *Congress* (which is mainly political) from the Declaration of *Jefferson* (which is philosophical in the eighteenth-century sense, that is, scientific) and from *our* Declaration (which is symbolic, the thing we have reshaped even as it was shaping us). The three Declarations obviously overlap; but they are also different. Their differences have been both underrated and misstated. Whence this effort.

Table of Contents

Prologue

Americans like, at intervals, to play this dirty trick upon themselves: Pollsters are sent out to canvass men and women on certain doctrines and to shame them when these doctrines are declared—as usually happens—unacceptable. Shortly after, the results are published: Americans have, once again, failed to subscribe to some phrase or other from the Declaration of Independence. The late political scientist Willmoore Kendall called this game "discovering America." He meant to remind us that running men out of town on a rail is at least as much an American tradition as declaring unalienable rights. A good point; but *should* that be our heritage? Shouldn't we, as Americans, subscribe to the creed that (we are told) *made* us Americans?

Maybe. Still, do we really think we can find people, running around alive in the street, who believe in the psychology of Louis de Jaucourt, the contract theory of David Hume, the mechanics of benevolence as elaborated by Francis Hutcheson? And, if not, how can we ask people in good conscience to endorse a document of eighteenth-century science based on such beliefs? What are we asserting if we agree to the document? That it is eloquent, or part of our heritage, or noble in its aspiration? Or that it is *right?*

Obviously, to judge from the use made of the responses, good Americans are supposed to take the latter view. When many, or even most, refuse to agree with the Declaration's teaching, we are urged to fear that something has gone wrong with America; that it has ceased in part to be itself—i.e., to think as it ought. In 1975, the lieutenant governor of Pennsylvania wrote around to scholars for a list of appropriate modern leaders who might re-enact the signing of the Declaration on July 4, 1976. If he meant to re-enact what actually happened, he should have begun the signings on August 2 and continued them into November. But, even apart from that, the man was asking for the impossible, for a resurrection of the dead. Most of those brought in for such a ceremony would not know what on earth they were admitting to. And those who might know, and still wanted to sign, would have to justify their act in ways so devious as to defeat speculation on their motives.

It is not surprising that we should misunderstand the Declaration. It is written in the lost language of the Enlightenment. It is dark with unexamined lights. Besides, we have a very powerful document from the nineteenth century to help us along in our error. What the State of Pennsylvania was contemplating in 1975, the President of the United States had already accomplished in 1863—the recontracting of our society on the basis of the Declaration as our fundamental charter. This was accomplished by the principal political stylist of his day—indeed, of our entire history. Abraham Lincoln was a great and conscious verbal craftsman. The man who writes, "The world will little note, nor long remember, what we say here," has done his best—by mere ripple and interplay of liquids—to make sure the world will remember; as it has.*

Lincoln was a great artist of America's romantic period. The popular image of the man—pacing long corridors at night, moody, fearing madness—is Byronic in all but its American setting. And his literary kinship in America is established by the style itself: "The mystic cords of memory, stretching from every battlefield and patriot grave to every living heart and hearthstone, all over this broad land, will yet swell the chorus of the Union, when again touched, as surely they will be, by the better angels of our nature." That is purest Israfel; Lincoln's is the style of a soberer Edgar Poe, with touches of Emerson. It achieves a democratic-oracular tone.

He obviously gave some thought to the first six words of his most famous exordium: "Four score and seven years ago . . ." In the 1950s, a satirist rewrote the Gettysburg Address in Eisenhowerese: "About eighty-some years ago, I think—I'll have Sherm look that up for you if you need it. . . ." That was funny in its way. But so, in its way, is Lincoln's own exordium. "Four score and seven" is a very stilted way of saying eighty-seven. Lincoln himself, speaking at

---

* The phrase quoted has a musical pattern dear to Lincoln—preliminary eddyings that yield to lapidary monosyllables: "We shall nobly save, or meanly lose, the last best hope of earth."

Springfield in 1857, talked of the Declaration's passage "some eighty years ago" (which eerily anticipates the Eisenhower version). And later in the speech Lincoln cited the exact figure: "eighty-one years ago." That is the plain blunt way of counting back—and it is said (by those who have not given the matter much attention) that Lincoln's style charmed by its plainness.

Admittedly, "Four score and seven" rolls—it has less the accountant's style than the prophet's. You hear it and don't immediately start subtracting eighty-seven from 1863. ("Let's see, that gives us 1776.") And Lincoln had good reason to prefer that you hold off, for a while, on the computation till he made his case for it. It was not a necessary, or even obvious, number to choose for our date of national origin.

It is customary to settle for a vague justification of Lincoln's language as achieving dignity by periphrasis. But what, precisely, makes "four score" so dignified? One thing. The English Bible. That does the trick. Only in "three-score and ten" for the allotted life of man was "score" commonly used for twice-ten in the Victorian era. Lincoln is stirring biblical echoes in his opening phrase, and he keeps on stirring as he goes.

"Four score and seven years ago our fathers brought forth . . ." Fathers is another religious term. Faith of our Fathers. The language of the hymnal. Pilgrim Fathers. Washington as Father of his Country. "Fathers" of the Constitution. But Lincoln is not talking about the founders, in the sense of the framers, the men of 1787; if he were, he would have been forced to say "Three score and sixteen years ago" or "Four score minus four years ago," which is better history but inferior music.

"Our fathers *brought forth* . . ." Just what does that mean? Not simply that they introduced something onto this continent. If so, where was it before they brought it in? And how could it be called a *new* nation if merely transferred? No, "bring forth" cannot mean anything like "introduce from abroad." Lincoln is talking about generation on the spot. The nation is rightly called new because it is brought forth maieutically, by midwifery; it is not only new, but newborn. The suggested image is, throughout, of a *hieros gamos*, a marriage of male heaven ("our fathers") and female earth ("this continent"). And it is a miraculous conception, a virgin birth. The nation is conceived by a mental act, in the spirit of liberty, and *dedicated* (as Jesus was in the temple) to a proposition. The proposition to which it is dedicated forms the bridge back from Lincoln to Jefferson, from the Address to the Declaration—"the proposition that all men are created equal."

Lincoln was a master of the Bible's extraordinary hold on the Protestant imagination of nineteenth-century America. Edmund Wilson says that its patterns, already deep in his literary imagination, printed themselves ever more insistently on his mind as he grew into a Christic vision of his own office and the nation's ordeal. But earlier texts show how easily he thought of America as having been virgin-born. In his 1854 Peoria address, he had already used the Magnificat to describe America's special status among nations:

> Let us re-adopt the Declaration of Independence, and—with it—the practises and policy which harmonize with it. Let North and South, let all America, let all lovers of liberty everywhere, join in the great and good work. If we do this, we shall not only have saved the Union, but shall have so saved it, as to make and to keep it forever worthy of the saving. We shall have so saved it, that the succeeding millions of free happy people, the world over, shall rise up and call us blessed to the latest generation.

We shall, that is, be Mary of the Magnificat, guarding the thing born to us by a miracle. He picked up this theme again during the war, in his December 1, 1862, address to Congress: "The fiery trial through which we pass will light us down, in honor or dishonor, to the latest generation." The opening of St. Luke's Gospel is to the Gettysburg Address what the Book of Revelation is to "The Battle Hymn of the Republic."

That is why Lincoln chose his peculiar, his biblically shrouded, figure "four score and seven." The figure takes us back to 1776, the year of the Declaration, of the self-evident truth that all men are created equal. But there are some fairly self-evident objections to that mode of calculating. All thirteen original colonies subscribed to the Declaration with instructions to their delegates that this was *not* to imply formation of a single nation. If anything, July 4, 1776, produced twelve new nations (with a thirteenth coming in on July 15)—conceived in liberty perhaps, but more dedicated to the proposition that the colonies they severed from the mother country were equal to each other than that their *inhabitants* were equal.

So resistant to union were these colonies that their first experiment at it—the (articled) Confederation—failed. Still, that *was* an attempt upon single nationhood; so 1777, the date of the Articles, has a better claim to be the moment when a new nation was brought forth than does 1776. In that case, Lincoln would have to say, "Four score and six years ago . . ." But the Articles did not become a universally accepted instrument of government until 1781. So a better historian would amend to "Four score and two years ago . . ." And even then, as I say, the Confederation failed. It was more in the nature of a league between sovereignties than the creation of a new state. For that we have to wait not only six more years, to the drafting of the Constitution, a date that gives us "Four score minus four years ago . . ."; but, more properly, eight years—to the Constitution's final ratification, the seating of a Congress, and inauguration of a President. So Lincoln's best date would have been 1789—"Four score minus six years ago . . ." Those dissatisfied with the bicentennial celebrations of 1776 had only to wait thirteen years for a more appropriate date to be honored.

The mere idea of a sudden "birth" for America is very misleading. In the first place, the continent was not all that "virgin." It had not only Indians to be pitchforked toward the interior, but longstanding colonial governments which had reached a high degree of self-rule. Benjamin Harrison V arrived at the Continental Congress of 1774 as a member of the Virginia Assembly, in which Benjamin Harrison I had sat—and Benjamin Harrison II, *and* Benjamin Harrison III, *and* Benjamin Harrison IV. These were men with a century of governing behind them. America was already old before she got a chance to be "born" from an idea, as the myth of virgin birth demands.

The Declaration lends itself to that myth in ways the Articles or the Constitution could never do. They are messier enterprises, with the stamp of compromise upon them. To this the Articles add a note of failure and the Constitution adds a note of illegality. The convention that drew up our Constitution went far beyond its mandate; in effect, smuggled a new nation in upon the continent rather than bringing it forth by intellectual impregnation. The founding legend begins to look more like a case of Sabine rape than virginal conception.

Of course, to Lincoln—and to those progressive historians who fleshed out his insight—the compromises of the Constitution were a

natural struggling of the flesh, unable to live up to the pure spirit of
the nation's Idea. The Church may at times not live up to the
demands of Faith, but Faith was given us entire at the outset. We
move, here, from nineteenth-century Fundamentalism to liberal
Protestantism, to the idea of a development in the Church's living
of doctrinal truth. At Springfield, Lincoln put it this way:

> They [the Declaration's signers] meant simply to declare the right, so
> that enforcement of it might follow as fast as circumstances should per-
> mit. They meant to set up a standard maxim for free society, which
> would be familiar to all, and revered by all; constantly looked to, con-
> stantly labored for, and even though never perfectly attained, constantly
> approximated, and thereby constantly spreading and deepening its
> influence and augmenting the happiness and value of life to all people of
> all colors everywhere. The assertion that "all men are created equal" was
> of no practical use in effecting our separation from Great Britain; and it
> was placed in the Declaration not for that, but for future use. Its authors
> meant it to be—as, thank God, it is now proving itself—a stumbling block
> [like St. Paul's preaching at Galatians 5:11] to all those who in after
> times might seek to turn a free people back into the hateful paths of des-
> potism.

The *new* nation was not conceived in blood and conquest, like
other nations, nor by mere accident or legal convenience. There
was a necessity in its conception. But does this extraordinary birth
of itself make the nation too etherial to survive in our real world?
"Now we are engaged in a great civil war testing whether that nation, or any nation so conceived and so dedicated, can long en-
dure." We move from St. Luke to St. John, to the hour and the
power of darkness. Lincoln hints here, as he did elsewhere, at the
Civil War as the nation's crucifixion. The country set apart by miraculous birth undergoes its supreme test and achieves—resurrection: "that this nation under God shall have a *new birth* of freedom." The nation must be twice-born, according to the gospel
pattern, to become a sign for the nations, a pledge that "government of the people, by the people, and for the people shall not per-
ish from the earth."

Well, now, that is a very nice myth. It flatters us with our special
status, our central importance to all men's aspirations. If we tried to

live up to its implications, we might all be better human beings. So what's the matter with keeping the myth?

Useful falsehoods are dangerous things, often costing something down the road. We can already tot up some of the things this myth has cost us. To begin with, the cult of the Declaration as our mystical founding document led to a downgrading of the actual charter that gives us our law. The Constitution has often been treated as a falling off from the original vision of 1776, a betrayal of the Revolution—a compromising of the *proposition* to which (after being conceived in liberty) we were dedicated. That view of things was bad history and has been revealed as such. (I shall discuss it a little in chapter Twenty-seven.) But the surprising thing is that even scholars held and taught that view for so long—long enough for it to persist in the popular mind. That shows the power of our favored myth to distort facts.

There are subtler and more important results of the myth. A belief in our extraordinary birth, outside the processes of time, has led us to think of ourselves as a nation apart, with a special destiny, the hope of all those outside America's shores. This feeling, of course, antedated Lincoln. It was part of the Puritan ideal, of the city set on a hilltop. It turned George Washington into a Moses during the revolutionary period. It arose from Protestant America's strong feeling of kinship with the chosen people of its Old Testament. It returned in visions of manifest destiny at the beginning of this century. But Lincoln's was the most profound statement of this belief in a special American fate. His version of it was not pinned to a narrow Puritanism or imperialism, but simply to the Declaration itself. Its power is mythic, not sectarian. Lincoln did not join a separate religion to politics; he made his politics religious. And that is why his politics has survived the attack on less totally fused forms of "civil religion."

After his election in 1860, Lincoln said on his way to Washington: "It [the Revolution] was not the mere matter of separation of the colonies from the motherland, but [of] that sentiment in the Declaration of Independence, which gave liberty not alone to the people of this country, but hope to all the world, for all future time. It was that which gave promise that in due time the weights would be lifted from the shoulders of all men, and that all should have an equal chance. This is the sentiment embodied in the Declaration of Independence."

One way we felt we should save the world was to stay pure of it. If we were set apart, we should stay apart, to influence others precisely because we would not join them in the ruck of things. On the other hand, *when* we intervened in the affairs of the world, it would have to be for the highest and most total reasons—to save and transform the world, to give it a new life patterned after ours; to make the world safe for democracy, to free the captives, to bring self-determination to others. In 1960, John F. Kennedy adapted a phrase from Lincoln—who was, in turn, adapting the Bible—to say that the world cannot exist half-slave and half-free. The possession parable of the house divided against itself was used by Lincoln to show that the North must prevail over the South's demoniac "possession" by slavery. Kennedy expanded that to make us willing to throw Communist devils out of Russia, China, Cuba, or Vietnam.

Since we had a special mission, we could assume special powers. President Woodrow Wilson, invading Mexico because its electoral arrangements displeased him, said that our bayonets would teach the country to elect good men—men, say, like Woodrow Wilson. The virtue of our aims sanctified the means—so we could indulge in a righteous Hiroshima or two, in napalm and saturation bombing, in a Diem coup, or a Chile *putsch*. Lincoln spoke of shed American blood as expiatory and cleansing, as a washing in the blood of the Lamb; and if we shed even our own blood, might we not shed that of others for their salvation?

This touches only one manifestation of our messianic sense, our willingness to redeem men in blood. The heart of that urge comes from our dedication to a *proposition*. In 1921, when Gilbert Chesterton applied for entry to America as a visiting lecturer, he was amused by the questions he had to answer. Was he an anarchist? A polygamist? Did he advocate the overthrow of America by force? "I have stood on the other side of Jordan, in the land ruled by a rude Arab chief, where the police looked so like brigands that one wondered what the brigands looked like. But they did not ask me whether I had come to subvert the power of the Shereef; and they did not exhibit the faintest curiosity about my personal views on the ethical basis of civil authority." Only America, the land of the free, asked him what he thought about the kind of freedom it was peddling—and asked him not as a settler or possible immigrant, but merely as a visitor. He especially loved the idea that subverters of the nation would serenely declare, on a question form, their intention to subvert.

Chesterton, being as generous as he could to this odd inquisition, granted that America, with its ambition of combining the most disparate ingredients in one republic, had to have a mold of some kind: "The experiment of a democracy of diverse races has been compared to a melting pot. But even that metaphor implies that the pot itself is of a certain shape and a certain substance; a pretty solid substance. The melting pot must not melt." Chesterton rightly called the mold religious, and looked for the source of our religion in the Declaration of Independence (as that was understood by Lincoln): "America is the only nation in the world that is founded on a creed. That creed is set forth with dogmatic and even theological lucidity in the Declaration of Independence, perhaps the only piece of practical politics that is also theoretical politics and also great literature."

Certainly Lincoln felt that the Declaration's importance was doctrinal, a test of virtue and citizenship: "All honor to Jefferson—to the man who, in the concrete pressure of a struggle for national independence by a single people, had the coolness, forecast, and capacity to introduce into a merely revolutionary document, an abstract truth, and so to embalm it there, that today and in all coming days, it shall be a rebuke and a stumbling block to the very harbingers of reappearing tyranny and oppression" (Letter to H. L. Pierce, 1859). America is the American *idea* for Lincoln, and that idea is contained in the Declaration: "I have insisted that, in legislating for new countries where it [slavery] does not exist, there is no just rule other than of moral and abstract right. With reference to those new countries, those maxims as to the right of people to 'life, liberty, and the pursuit of happiness' were the just rules to be constantly referred to" (1858). Again, after being elected President, he said in Philadelphia: "I have never had a feeling politically that did not spring from the sentiments embodied in the Declaration of Independence. I have often pondered over the toils that were endured by the officers and soldiers of the army, who achieved that Independence. I have often inquired of myself what great principle or idea it was that kept this Confederacy so long together." Speak-

ing to the New Jersey Senate at the same period, he said: "I am exceedingly anxious that this Union, the Constitution, and the liberties of the people shall be perpetuated in accordance with the
original idea for which the struggle was made." These assertions
are inoffensive to most Americans—which explains why things like
the House Un-American Activities Committee were inoffensive for
so long.

If there is an American *idea*, then one must subscribe to it in
order to be an American. One must sort out one's *mental* baggage
to "declare" it on entry to the country. To be fully American, one
must adopt this idea wholeheartedly, proclaim it, prove one's devotion to it. Unless we know what our fellows *think*, we do not know
whether they are American at all, much less whether they are *truly*
American. Indeed, since the idea is so pure and abstract, we must
all be constantly striving toward it, trying to become *more* American. A Chesterton might well be shocked to find himself put under
inquest before touching these religious shores; he had never been
accused, at home, of "un-English activities." But here, to tell some-
one "That is not the American way" is to say, in effect, that the person addressed is not entirely American—not worthy of citizenship; a kind of second-class American or disguised interloper.
Uncovering heresy under such disguises was the aim of America's
loyalty oaths, security tests, black lists. Even the questions asked by
pollsters who quiz Americans on their dedication to the Declaration
are a politer kind of loyalty oath. The implication is that those who
answer "wrong" prove that we are not inculcating our creed well
enough. This very activity leans back toward the tradition Willmoore Kendall described. It rides the unorthodox out on a rail, of
ridicule at least, if not of actual violence.

This whole way of thinking would, on many grounds, have been
alien to Thomas Jefferson. He was not, like Lincoln, a nineteenth-
century romantic living in the full glow of transcendentalism (that
school of faintly necrophiliac spirituality). He was an eighteenth-
century empiricist, opposed to generalizations and concentrating on
particular realities. With Locke, he had rejected innate ideas. He
considered Plato's self-existent Ideas the great delusion of Western
history. He did not believe one could "embalm" an idea in a text,
lay it away in some heaven of the mind, for later generations to be
constantly aspiring after. He denied that a spiritual ideal could be

posed over-against some fleshly struggle toward it. He did not
material circumstances an obstacle to Reality. They, and they
alone, *were* reality for him. He would not have accepted Lincoln's
mystique of national union as a transcendentally "given" imperative.

He would never encourage people to yearn back toward some
ideal of perfection delivered to their forebears. He opposed "entailing" opinions on a later generation; he wanted constitutions revised often, since accumulated knowledge must make later generations wiser than that which drew up *any* old document. Even when
trying to placate John Adams, he would not yield on this vital
point:

One of the questions you know on which our parties took different
sides, was on the improvability of the human mind, in science, in ethics,
in government, etc. Those who advocated reformation of institutions,
pari passu, with the progress of science, maintained that no definite
limits could be assigned to that progress. The enemies of reform, on the
other hand, denied improvement, and advocated steady adherence to the
principles, practices and institutions of our fathers, which they represented as the consummation of wisdom, and *akmé* of excellence, beyond
which the human mind could never advance. Altho' in the passage of
your answer alluded to, you expressly disclaim the wish to influence the
freedom of enquiry, you predict that that will produce nothing more
worthy of transmission to posterity, than the principles, institutions, and
systems of education recieved from their ancestors. I do not consider this
as your deliberate opinion. You possess, yourself, too much science, not
to see how much is still ahead of you, unexplained and unexplored. Your
own consciousness must place you as far before our ancestors, as in the
rear of our posterity (Cappon, 332).

To the extent that Chesterton read the Declaration as "dogmatic
and even theological," he was misreading it. Jefferson would take
such terms as an insult if applied to his draft. He thought most
theology an enemy to man's freedom, and he opposed any religious
tests for holding office or citizenship.

The dry intellectual formulae of the eighteenth century were
traced in fine acids of doubt, leaving them difficult to decipher
across the intervals of time and fashion. When the Declaration is
read in Lincoln's romantic glass, darkly, its content becomes entirely a victim of guess and bias. Proof of this is easily obtained:
Lincoln congratulates Jefferson for not being "merely" practical, for

laying up a timeless truth, usable in future ages, though his own contemporaries could not recognize it. That praise includes almost everything Jefferson opposed. For him, the highest test of a thing was its immediate practicality to the living generation.

I have concentrated, here, on misreadings that derive from Lincoln, or are strengthened by his views, not because I think all our errors traceable to Gettysburg. Far from it. My point is that this is only one of *many* intervening filters that distort the text. The Declaration is not only part of our history; we are part of its history. We have cited it, over the years, for many purposes, including the purpose of deceiving ourselves; and it has become a misshapen thing in our minds. Jefferson never intended it for a spiritual Covenant; but it has traveled in an Ark that got itself more revered the more it was battered.

The best way to honor the spirit of Jefferson is to use his doubting intelligence again on his own text. Only skepticism can save him from his devotees, return us to the drier air of his scientific maxims, all drawn with the same precision that went into his architectural sketches. The pollster on the street wants us to "endorse" Jefferson's Declaration. But Jefferson would be the first to ask what such an exercise could mean. Despite his hostility to Plato, he liked Socrates and thought the unexamined life not worth living. Even more, the unexamined document is not worth signing. The Declaration has been turned into something of a blank check for idealists of all sorts to fill in as they like. We had better stop signing it (over and over) and begin reading it. I do not mean seeing it. I mean reading it.

That is a more difficult task than one might at first suppose. The Declaration is constantly invoked but rarely studied. There have, in fact, been only three important books on the document written in this century—John Hazelton's in 1906, settling the outstanding historical problems of the paper's passage and signing; Carl Becker's in 1922, enshrining the Lockean interpretation of its content; and Julian Boyd's first volume of the Jefferson *Papers* in 1950, establishing the text with magisterial thoroughness. Other books have done little but recast, popularize, or misquote these seminal works in three different fields connected with the Declaration.

Why such exiguous scholarship around a paper so loved, so often put to questionable political use, so omnipresent at the merely verbal level? A preliminary hint or two may be given here, to be explored more fully later. For one thing, the Declaration is not a legal instrument, like the Constitution. Each phrase of the latter document has been tested in courts and in legal classrooms, under strict rules of interpretation, with consequences of the most serious kind riding on the results of such inquiry. Men go free or go to jail, depending on the reading of a phrase. The Declaration, having no such force of law, has not undergone this discipline of "construction," strict or loose.

Besides, for the Constitution we have the long drafting process recorded in Madison's notes, the arguments of the framers voiced in protracted debate, the records of ratifying conventions in each state, along with the authoritative exposition of federal doctrine by "Publius." There are no notes from the drafting or acceptance of the Declaration, which was by comparison the work of a few days. Nor did the Declaration call forth early attack or exposition of a fruitful sort. It had, indeed, astonishingly little immediate effect in the world of ideas, and quickly sank into an obscurity not fully dispelled for almost half a century. When serious scrutiny did begin, it was occasioned by distorting acrimony. As the document grew in importance, so did the myths and partisan uses. The time of obscurity yielded to almost a century of blinding glare and misrepresentation, until Hazelton began the scholarly reclamation of the paper.

To the special hazards of the Declaration must be added more general problems connected with Jefferson's intellectual background. In chapter Eleven, I deal with the odd logjam formed around this subject, even in Jefferson's lifetime. Some have claimed, recently, that the ideas of Jefferson are well known and only his personal life is left for fresh exploration. The truth is almost exactly the reverse of that contention, as Douglass Adair realized when he concluded his important effort to trace the ideas of Jefferson to their source. He wrote in 1946 (in *WMQ*):

An exact knowledge of Jefferson's ideas . . . is still lacking. . . . We know relatively little about his ideas in the context of the total civilization of which he was a part. . . . Until all of Jefferson's ideas and projects are carefully examined against the background of contemporary European developments, and until his theories are appraised as part of the great tradition of Western social thought, we will be unable to take the true measure of the man.

Things have not changed since 1946—because they have not changed since 1922. Earlier I named the three important books on the Declaration to be published in this century. Of these, Hazelton's trailblazing historical work is over seventy years old; but its main points stand. The same is true of Boyd's work on the text, which incorporated his preliminary monograph of 1945. But Carl Becker's little book, over half a century old, remains for most scholars the beginning and the end of investigation into the *ideas* of the Declaration. As such, it has been the most broadly influential of these three major books. Yet it, alone of the three, is increasingly vulnerable. Put simply: If Adair is right, Becker is wrong. And if Becker is wrong, we have a lot of work ahead of us.

INVENTING
AMERICA

PART ONE

REVOLUTIONARY CHARTER

ONE

"... our sacred honor ..."

The haughty sultans of the South juggled the whole conclave of the delegates.
                    —*Rivington's Quarterly*, February 9, 1775

The Virginians clattered into Philadelphia with the glitter, almost, of Magi. Tall outdoorsmen, they came riding splendid horses and attended by liveried slaves. Rumor had exaggerated their wealth; but their bearing, on arrival, seemed to confirm the rumors. A man from the North called this delegation "the orators," and a Quaker who sent letters of introduction for three of the delegates called them "great speakers in our House of Assembly." Caesar Rodney of Delaware wrote his wife: "All the seven delegates appointed from Virginia are here, and more sensible [i.e., spirited] fine fellows you would never wish to see." Something of their style is suggested by the fact that Richard Henry Lee, who had blown off the fingers of one hand in a hunting accident, wrapped that hand in a black silk handkerchief, for gesturing, when he rose to speak.

They came in two groups, the first four men arriving September 2, 1774. Richard Henry Lee conducted his countrymen to the home of his brother-in-law, William Shippen, Jr. Dr. Shippen, a famous lecturer on anatomy, the founder of scientific obstetrics in America, had met and married Lee's sister in England, after completing his studies at Edinburgh. Nine years before this, young Thomas Jefferson had come up from Virginia to be inoculated by Dr. Shippen (Randall, 1:46). Now a regular invasion of Virginians would increase the influential doctor's role in anti-Quaker politics at Pennsylvania.

The arriving Lee relative, third of six ambitious sons, was grand but chilly—a visiting Frenchman later mistook him for a Presbyterian! He had the military face (all eyes and bone), the long forehead and delayed thick plume of hair, of an earlier Andrew Jackson. Lee was forceful but devious, with an almost childish earnestness. Flammable himself, he had the gift of inflaming others —a good man for dramatizing crises, even when there was no crisis. After entering the House of Burgesses in 1758, he had no equal as an orator until, seven years later, his superior arrived. Now men tactfully sorted out forensic skills by calling Lee Virginia's Cicero, and Patrick Henry its Demosthenes.

Lee's companions at the Shippen table were two huge country-squire types and an incongruous scholar. The squires were among the most affable and powerful men in their province, by right of birth, wealth, and offices—all skillfully used. They were brothers-in-law, one a grandson of Robert ("King") Carter and one the successor to John Robinson in the powerful Speaker's chair of the House of Burgesses. The Carter grandson, Benjamin Harrison, was six feet four inches tall, obese in a majestic way—"uncommonly large," Silas Deane of Connecticut described him. He was the fifth Benjamin Harrison to live in Virginia and hold office there. His son and great-grandson would become Presidents of the United States. Two descendants would follow him in the governor's office of the State of Virginia (an office he held the legal maximum of three terms running). In longevity of sway, in variety of high offices held, the Harrisons surpass all other political families in America, including that upstart line represented in Philadelphia by the "brace of Adamses," Samuel and John.

John Adams, in a typically ferocious description, called Harrison a lazy man; but he was one of those huge easygoing men who gets things done. As chairman of the Congress when it met in "committee of the whole," he presided over tense secret debates, like that on independence (July 1, 1776)—meetings the secretary could not record. Then, when Congress ventured into foreign relations, it was under Harrison's direction on other secret committees. In 1777, he returned to his state, to its House of Delegates, where he served the rest of his life, excepting his terms as governor. From age twenty-three to his death at sixty-five, he had never been out of elective office.

If Benjamin Harrison was a respected parliamentarian, his Virginia countrymen nonetheless preferred Peyton Randolph in that role. Randolph, another florid giant, had been the attorney general for Virginia, like his father and grandfather before him, and his brother afterward. In that capacity, he regularly foiled and taunted the colony's royal governors. The whole continent knew of his work in defeating Governor Dinwiddie's special tax ("the pistole fee") in 1754. A year later, when Virginians fell with Braddock at Fort Duquesne, he formed a volunteer band of lawyers to fight with the regular militia at their own expense. Popular from his youth, he succeeded to Speaker Robinson's legislative supremacy at Robinson's death and disgrace. With the help of Edmund Pendleton (handling the financial scandal of Robinson's recycled scrip), Robert Carter Nicholas (as treasurer), George Wythe (as clerk), his own brother John (as king's attorney), and Harrison (on key committees), he rescued the Robinson "machine" for new circumstances. His prudence and rectitude were such that his young cousin, Thomas Jefferson, made them touchstones for measuring his own actions. His boisterous large affability was not the style of Jefferson, who nonetheless paid tribute to the "attic pleasantry" animating Randolph's "heavy and inert" body (Ford, 10:59). One of the easiest tasks for the Continental Congress was its very first one, the unanimous election of Randolph as its president.

The odd man out in this company was Richard Bland, "staunch and tough as whitleather [parchment]—has something of the look of musty old parchments, which he handleth and studieth much," as Roger Atkinson wrote of him. He, too, was of old family, and famous outside his province. His pamphlets on the Two-penny Act and Stamp Act had earned praise at home and abroad. Jefferson would call him "the most learned and logical of those who took prominent lead in public affairs, profound in constitutional lore," and one of the Burgesses' "oldest, ablest, and most respected members." But like other pamphleteers of the sixties (Daniel Dulany and John Dickinson for instance), Bland seemed to be shying from later consequences of his own arguments, and his fellow delegates in Philadelphia would come to suspect his real intentions (Mays, *Pendleton*, 2:22). Even the moderate leaders of his own delegation were more adventurous than he by 1774.

All four of these men were "cousins" in the loose Virginia sense. Harrison and Randolph, besides being brothers-in-law, shared other Carter ties. Bland's mother was a Randolph. Lee's mother was a Ludwell, related to the Harrisons; and Lee had Carter and Bland in-laws. But kinship did not keep Virginians from fighting. Lee's family had circumvented the local oligarchy through London agents when it set up the Ohio Company for western land speculation. Richard Henry upheld the family interest against the rival Loyalist Company set up by Speaker Robinson, and was one of the first to demand an investigation of Robinson's finances. This made him a troublemaker to be "handled" by Robinson's successor, Peyton Randolph. These men were, of necessity, allies on foreign ground at Philadelphia; but that fact was tempered by memory of old disputes at home—disputes John and Samuel Adams were quick to hear about and put to use.

The day after the first four arrived, three other Virginians reached Philadelphia, completing the delegation. They came mounted, and matched with personal qualities the inherited power and experience of the party led by Randolph and Harrison. These men were younger as a group, with less impressive family ties. In fact, all three were "new men" by the standards of James River grandees and "King" Carter's Northern Neck empire.

Sometimes, of course, a *novus homo* becomes the best apologist for aristocracy. That was clearly the case with Edmund Pendleton, who even looked the part. An orphan taken up by a member of Speaker Robinson's family, he had educated himself while performing the duties of an office boy and legal clerk. Hugh Blair Grigsby preserved a tradition that he was "the handsomest man in the province," slim, tall, with silverpoint-fine features and a natural grace. But under his ease he retained the resourcefulness of a climbing office boy. Thomas Jefferson found him the most agile and frustrating debater he ever met. George Wythe, Virginia's first professor of law, was not its most successful practitioner, because everyone knew an infallible way of beating him at the bar—simply hire Edmund Pendleton.

Pendleton was not as learned as Wythe, but his sinuous way with an argument could hypnotize, distract, and lead a jury as no other man's. Even the oratory-inured lower house of Virginia could be baffled, and turn submissive, under his quiet arts. Jefferson would discover that in 1777, when he introduced his bill for disestablishing religion in Virginia—why recognize allegiance to Canterbury after renouncing Westminster? The Anglican ministry in Virginia had been largely discredited anyway. But Pendleton, the serpentine legal strategist, was sincere as a dove in his piety, so art and principle joined in a dazzling lost-cause effort that delayed the inevitable. Jefferson wrote in old age that his disestablishment measure "brought on the severest contests in which I have ever been engaged," and he retained afterward a stunned awe for his adversary. The best description of Pendleton's method is contained in Jefferson's account of another fight in that same session with an equally foreordained outcome—the repeal of entail:

> This repeal was strongly opposed by Mr. Pendleton, who was zealously attached to ancient establishments; and who, taken all in all, was the ablest man in debate I have ever met with. He had not indeed the poetical fancy of Mr. Henry, his sublime imagination, his lofty and overwhelming diction; but he was cool, smooth, and persuasive; his language flowing, chaste and embillished; his conceptions quick; acute and full of resource; never vanquished: for if he lost the main battle, he returned upon you, and regained so much of it as to make it a drawn one, by dexterous manoeuvres, skirmishes in detail, and the recovery of small advantages which, little singly, were important all together. You never knew when you were clear of him, but were harassed by his perseverance, until the patience was worn down of all who had less of it than himself. Add to this, that he was one of the most virtuous and benevolent of men, the kindest friend, the most amiable and pleasant of companions, which ensured a favorable reception to whatever came from him.

Pendleton's wariness of attack from all sides made him so skilled in framing judgments after he assumed the bench that no decision of his was reversed but one—and that by himself, after he entered the state's supreme court. Poor George Wythe was also on the bench by then, and his learned opinions were so regularly overturned that he was reduced to anonymous pamphleteering against his old nemesis. Pendleton and Jefferson remained mutual admirers, despite a general opposition in their politics, They were both aristocrats by nature. Pendleton lived in harmony with achieved position; his later politics were all a matter of supporting George Washington. Jefferson, by contrast, lived a paradox—élitist in his practice, egalitarian by principle. Jefferson might agree more with Patrick Henry, or even Samuel Adams; but he preferred to dine with Pendleton.

Patrick Henry—he was the second man in this trio. If Pendleton was a natural aristocrat, Henry was a deliberate maverick—what passed for a "democrat" in the society he joined while maintaining some pose of the outsider. He was as usefully dishabille as Pendleton was immaculate. This meant, in a flamboyant world of gambling horsemen, not so much real squalor (the charge of his enemies) as just the right provoking touch of the preacher. Edmund Randolph, himself a rhetorician, was the best-equipped observer of Henry's skills, and he realized that the orator "transferred into civil discussions many of the bold licenses which prevailed in the religions. If he was not a constant hearer and admirer of that stupendous master of the human passions, George Whitefield, he was a follower, a devotee of some of his most powerful disciples at least" (*History*, Shaffer ed., 179).

But Henry played his civil "revivalism" off against easy tavern ways and a readiness to be not very good upon his violin. Nothing could be less like Jefferson's chamber music with Governor Fauquier. Jefferson remembered, years afterward, their first meeting, when both were staying at a plantation's great house for the twelve days of Christmas. Jefferson was only sixteen, and Henry twenty-three; but the older man had all the teen-ager's mischievous energy and power to catch the eye, while we glimpse the younger man primly clearing his throat in Jefferson's later observations on Henry's antics. These "had something of the coarseness of the society he had frequented; his passion was for fiddling, dancing and pleasantry. He excelled in the last, and it attached everyone to him" (Ford, 11:415).

It is not just any man who can play Everyman. That takes a special discipline, of which Henry was the master. He was a jester with a dark sour look, which his preacher's clothes made more intriguing. He seemed to lounge through court trials, and through life —which made hearers consistently forget or underestimate his power, till he chose the right moment to display it. Though he was about six feet tall, he slouched on a horse, or in a chair; looked rather curved in and crumpled on himself. But he had the actor's trick, in his oratory, of lifting his whole body up toward climaxes, along with his voice, as if he *could* add cubits by wanting to. Edmund Randolph says Henry began to speak in public with an indolent manner, awkward, as if not fully adverting to his own words; but then some phrase would serve as spark to his own tinder, and he came to fiery life—making men realize "that a gesture at first too much the effect of indolence may expand itself in the progress of delivery into forms which would be above the rule and compass but strictly within the promptings of nature" (*History*, 179—and see the memories reported in Tyler's *Henry*, 147–49, Wirt's *Sketches* of 1818, 25, Randall's *Jefferson*, 101–2). No one who beheld him incandescent with a Cause ever forgot the experience—not Jefferson, looking in on the House of Burgesses as a law student and standing rooted to the doorsill; not Edward Carrington, who asked to be (and was) buried at the exact spot where he looked through St. John's church window and heard Henry spur the Virginia Convention on toward liberty or death.

Henry was a master of timing, of musical "rests." Randolph put it this way: "His pauses, which for their length might sometimes be feared to dispel the attention, riveted it the more by raising the expectation of renewed brilliancy. . . . His lightning consisted in quick successive flashes, which rested only to alarm the more" (180–81). And the timing of his speeches was used, on a greater scale, to pace political activity. He moved in a series of checks and charges, and brought into American councils the popularity and unpredictability of a Wilkes without the atheism. The eighteenth century was, after all, the age of Garrick, who was considered the voice of Nature—a time when the theater judged life. Thus Henry contrived to seem most natural when most calculating. He could shock with awkward lunges, yet be welcomed back to shock again. After rattling the House of Burgesses with the speech Jefferson overheard in 1765, Henry whistled his way out of town, leading his horse like a farm boy off on vacation. Critics say he left his radical proposals undefended. They do not notice how the tidiers-up made his essential points respectable once he was gone. He realized lightnings cannot be scattered out as cheap as daylight.

The economy of his technique is suggested by Hugh Blair Grigsby in his *Virginia Convention* (83): "Mr. Madison, in his latter days, told Governor Coles that when he had made a most conclusive argument in favor of the Constitution, Henry would rise to reply to him, and by some significant action, such as a pause, a shake of the head, or a striking gesture, before he uttered a word, would undo all that Madison had been trying to do for an hour before."

Patrick Henry's most famous line may have come, indirectly, from the theater. By the time William Wirt pieced together the speech in St. John's church, forty years after the event, a line from Voltaire's 1730 play, *Brutus,* had become a famous cry of the French Revolution: *"Dieux! donnez-nous la mort plutôt que l'esclavage!"* It will be seen how much closer this stands to Henry's reported speech than does the other source suggested for Wirt— Addison's 1713 play, *Cato* (ii, 4): "It is not now a time to talk of aught/But chains or conquest, liberty or death." Of course Henry may have said in 1775 what Wirt attributed to him—which only shows how close to theater was that time's politics.

Jefferson and Pendleton thought Henry worked most of his wonders by pure music without logic. Peyton Randolph had been on the board of examiners that found Henry barely qualified for entry to the bar. But some men of considerable intellect admired Henry, including George Mason. Mason lived near the third traveler in this company of delegates (he dined with them on the eve of the journey) and was Henry's ally on most issues that would be facing Congress. Henry no doubt tried to score points off the more conservative Pendleton as the three men rode north the next day, and no doubt failed. A contest to win over their companion was inevitable —it would, in fact, be the central task of American politicians through all the next two decades. For they rode out, after sleeping one night in Mount Vernon, with George Washington.

It was clear at once to those in Philadelphia that Virginians were hyperbolical gentlemen. Benjamin Harrison said, his first night there, he would have *walked* (all the lumbering poundage of him that had grown up on a horse) to reach this Congress. And even Richard Bland, with the face of learned parchment, would have gone to Jericho, he assured John Adams. But the tallest tale had preceded its subject into town: Colonel Washington of the Virginia militia—so delegates confided to their correspondents—had sworn to raise an army at his own expense, if need be; and he would fight the British with that army, though no others joined him. Actually, there is nothing less like Washington than such rodomontade. But his very presence was eloquent, and men tried to convey its force by inventing a rhetoric he never used. Parson Weems was just continuing a trend well developed in Washington's own lifetime when he put fluent oratory into the mouth of his superhuman child. Without indulging it himself, Washington inspired such extravagance. Even shrewd Abigail Adams was a bit swoony after meeting him, and wrote her husband:

> You had prepared me to entertain a favorable opinion of him, but I thought the one half was not told me. Dignity with ease and complacency [i.e., solicitousness]—the gentleman and soldier look agreeably blended in him. Modesty marks every line and feature of his face. Those lines of Dryden occurred to me:

> > Mark his majestic fabric; he's a temple
> > Sacred by birth, and built by hands divine.
> > His soul's the deity that lodges there.
> > Nor is the pile unworthy of the god.

Part of the charm was unquestionably physical. He was tall and red-haired, like Thomas Jefferson—each was two or three inches above six feet. But Washington *inhabited* his height, *seemed* tall to those who thought Jefferson rather collapsible, all wrists and elbow. In a land where horsemanship was often men's touchiest point of pride, Jefferson had to admit he never saw Washington's like for grace and control in the saddle. A frontier runner and Indian wrestler—his friend George Mercer described his frame as "padded with well-developed muscles"—Washington had by 1774 refined mere energy down to a grace of least movement, the higher athleticism of the dance. And he danced well. He had a square face, with defining corners to it, and features large but harmonious—worn to a unity like that of a knobbed cane handle. By this time, in his early forties, he looked young for one so old (as Silas Deane noted), or old for one so young; he had stepped through some warp or time-seam in the normal aging process—was already deferred to by old men, though the young still wanted to ride with him. The red tints now fading from his hair and skin had left their traces—an Indian summer.

It is hard to exaggerate his impact on others, even before his great deeds were accomplished. Solomon Drowne of Rhode Island wrote home from Philadelphia:

> With manly gait,
> His faithful steel suspended by his side,
> Passed Washington along, Virginia's hero.

Washington's subsequent legend has not magnified, but reduced him; turned his massive composure to insensitivity, his air of great power reined-in to mere languor. Some animal vitality, conveyed we don't know how, baked off him with few words. This self-assurance was to simple cockiness what an oak is to an acorn. He had, of course, made his mistakes—once. His care not to err the same way twice was perhaps his greatest weakness—ruling out alternatives, once unsuccessfully tried, though they might be applicable in new circumstances. But even that fault was disguised in his general restraint from hasty purpose. In the shadow of his mystery, other men's opinions grew. He was always being wooed to vast designs because he was so rarely won. There was a sense that, once set in motion toward any goal, he would be undeflectible—and so it proved. His powers exercised some weird attraction by their suspension, as if they grew in secret. When he left Mount Vernon with Henry and Pendleton, Martha is reported to have said: "I hope you will stand firm. I know George will." Everyone knew that, even when they did not know exactly where he stood; and those who did not succumb to admiration for him (which most people instantly felt) were doomed to an endless exasperation with the man. He was like a statue firm and unbreakable in itself, but hovering some distance off the ground.

This was no ragtag band of revolutionaries. The chariest investor would feel safe backing an endeavor led by the dignified Washington or Pendleton. And even Henry's democratic rhetoric bolstered Virginia interests of the established sort. People remember his denunciation of royal semidespotism in the Parsons' Cause (1763) but rarely emphasize the fact that he was helping large planters cut back on their payments to poor local churchmen. In Philadelphia, Henry startled the Congress with prophetic hints when he concluded: "The distinctions between Virginians, Pennsylvanians, New Yorkers, and New Englanders are no more. I am not a Virginian, but an American." But he was opposing the one-colony/one-vote rule, since representation by populace would give Virginia the heaviest influence. He had discovered a way to help Virginia by *not* being a Virginian. Debaters on the Constitution's ratification would later find out how ready he was to form a supra-Virginian America.

These seven men made up the Virginia delegation to the first Continental Congress. Not till the second Congress was held in

1775 were they joined—late—by an eighth man. Mr. Jefferson attended the Revolution in his finest coach and pair. Riding postillion was his slave Jesse, while Richard attended his person. A third may have cared for baggage and the other two horses in Jefferson's train. (Lodging the horses would cost him twice as much, in Philadelphia, as he paid for his own quarters in a cabinetmaker's home.) He rode up alone, since he had not been part of the delegation chosen in May. He came to substitute for Peyton Randolph, who was needed in Williamsburg to preside over the reconvened House of Burgesses.

This marginal first appearance of the man is somehow typical. He moved oddly in and out of his own life, keeping a shy but observant distance between himself and his surroundings. His surveyor father, rising by energy and charm, had married into the Randolph family, and Jefferson himself was brought up at Tuckahoe, the Randolph mansion on the James River. But he took no pride in this family connection, and got along ill with most of his cousins after the death of Peyton Randolph in 1775. (Some of his fiercer later enemies were relatives on his mother's side—John Marshall, for instance, and John Randolph of Roanoke.) But if Jefferson was not quite at home with the Tidewater barons, neither was he a frontiersman. Orphaned at his father's Piedmont plantation (Shadwell) when he was fourteen, he soon yearned back toward James River amenities (and libraries). At the College of William and Mary, Jefferson became the protégé of the most powerful man in the province, whose plantation was in the Williamsburg area and whose house contained the library Jefferson used during Randolph's lifetime and bought after his death. Thus Jefferson linked Peyton Randolph with his other principal tutors: "Under temptations and difficulties, I would ask myself what would Dr. Small, Dr. Wythe, Peyton Randolph do in this situation?" (Ford, 9:231). Jefferson also became the friend of Peyton's younger brother, John Randolph of Tazewell Hall, who was a violinist and gardener as well as king's attorney for the province—Jefferson coveted his fine violin and bought it from him when John, remaining loyal to the King, left Virginia in 1775.

Jefferson was a disciplined student, admitted already in his teens to the learned conversations of Governor Fauquier (a Fellow of the Royal Society)—though he was an Anglophobe even at this early age. After completing his college and law training, he lingered on in Williamsburg to converse with William Small, the one serious scholar of the college, and George Wythe, his law preceptor. He was like a modern graduate student loathe to get his degree and leave the campus. As a lawyer Jefferson was competent, but not devoted to his calling. By the age (late for colonials) of thirty, he had written nothing public, conducted no famous case, gained no eminence in the legislature, founded no family fortune. Yet he was familiar to all the Burgesses who rode into Williamsburg twice yearly for their sessions. He haunted the governor's mansion and Tazewell Hall, the mansion of Robert Carter and the laboratory of Dr. Small. He said little, but saw everything—men probably thought he would grow into another Richard Bland, a bookish aristocrat collecting historical documents. Our first vivid glimpse of Jefferson finds him at the door, not fully part of the scene, as he watched Patrick Henry in the Stamp Act crisis. Jefferson was twenty-two years old then, still lingering out his studies with Dr. Wythe. It would be another four years before he entered the House himself, representing Albemarle County along with his former guardian, Dr. Walker.

Even before Jefferson's life was well begun, he seemed ready to retire from it. After delaying his law practice as long as he could, he cut it off by 1774, to live in a Palladian temple of learning on his private mountaintop. He had spent most of his adult life as a single man in Williamsburg, a student not a businessman. Even when he entered the House, he spoke rarely if ever. In France he would have been one of those abbés without an abbey who drifted about in the best society wondering if that society did not need dismantling. Jefferson would always be quietly at odds with his surroundings, softly angular, not fitting in. His very bearing suggested this. Despite the discipline of his violin, he had a rather loose and awkward way of moving. His diffident, abstracted manner was easily mistaken for haughtiness. The best description of his bearing comes from middle age, when he made his nervous single appearance, as Secretary of State, before a Senate committee. William Maclay, on the committee, entered photographic details in his diary:

Jefferson is a slender man, has rather the air of stiffness in his manner. His clothes seem too small for him. He sits in a lounging manner, on one hip commonly, and with one of his shoulders elevated much above the other. His face has a scranny [i.e., scrawny—Maclay was a Scot] aspect. His whole figure has a loose shackling air. He had a rambling vacant look, and nothing of that firm collected deportment which I expected would dignify the presence of a Secretary or Minister. I looked for gravity, but a laxity of manner seemed shed about him. He spoke almost without ceasing. But even his discourse partook of his personal demeanor. It was loose and rambling, and yet he scattered information wherever he went, and some even brilliant sentiments sparkled from him.

Maclay must have thought Jefferson's clothes too small because his thin wrists were so prominent. Except for a brief time of affected plainness in the White House (meant as tacit criticism of George Washington), Jefferson was fastidious about his clothes. As for his "scranny" face, Jefferson was prognathous like Voltaire; but bright eyes and a pointed nose kept both men from looking sullen or feral. Jefferson's sandy-red hair and complexion must have seemed the standard Virginian color in Philadelphia, where Jefferson kept to himself while others engaged in rather feverish politicking and socializing.

If we ask where he fit in his own delegation, the answer is not easily given. He was not active with Randolph in the sessions nor with Richard Henry Lee in "out of doors" maneuver. Much later, he represented himself as making up the radical faction with Henry and Lee, as opposed to a conservative trio that roomed in the same house—Randolph, Harrison, and Washington. But there is no contemporary evidence of that, and all his views of the Congress were colored by later developments in his relationship with each of the men involved. Chosen in 1775 to stand in for Peyton Randolph, Jefferson was still known as Randolph's protégé. The relationship is suggested in a 1770 letter Jefferson wrote to Randolph on behalf of his friend James Ogilvie, who was seeking ecclesiastical preferment (*Papers*, 1:49–51). Jefferson's own early ties—of blood, locale, and money—were with the Robinson-Randolph circle. His father had been one of those who profited from Speaker Robinson's clandestine loans, and Jefferson still owned an interest in the Loyalist Company, which competed with the Ohio Company of Richard Henry Lee and other planters on the Potomac. Jefferson's property lay upland from the James, on which he had been raised and where he found his wife (the daughter of another man given money from Robinson's till). Jefferson first asserted his leadership in Albemarle by opening the Rivanna River as a conduit of tobacco into the James.

It is true that Jefferson was already, in 1775, an ally of Lee and Henry in some provincial matters. He had just voted with Henry for mobilizing the local soldiery, but so had Washington. A year earlier, Jefferson had worked with Henry and Lee in "cooking up" a day of fast and prayers, out of English Civil War precedents, to protest the closing of Boston's port after the "tea party." (John Quincy Adams was shocked at the "irreligious levity" of that cooking up—*Memoirs*, 8:278.) But the interesting point is that Jefferson, who probably found the precedents from his own or George Wythe's books, presented them to Robert Carter Nicholas, the treasurer of the province and a respected part of the House leadership, who published the resolution with a proper weightiness. Jefferson, alone of the group, had the right ties for this.

One reason for considering Jefferson a "radical" in Philadelphia is the uncompromising tone of his first published work, the pamphlet *A Summary View of the Rights of British America*. But this was written (unsolicited, so far as we know) as an instruction to the first delegation going to Philadelphia. Jefferson, who was averse to arguing his own views in public, fell conveniently ill when the convention met to choose and instruct its delegates. Still, he had two fair copies ready to send on. One went to Patrick Henry; but Jefferson must have pinned his real hopes on the copy sent to Peyton Randolph, who was bound to be chosen the leader of the delegation. Jefferson saw his instruction as an application and completion of Richard Bland's Stamp Act pamphlet, which had spoken for the leadership of Virginia. Besides, the Randolph circle would have most influence with the printer of the pamphlet, Mrs. Clementina Rind, who seems to have printed the 1774 Association for that leadership (*Papers*, 1:109). Furthermore, Jefferson tells us that only George Wythe espoused the whole doctrine of his *Summary View* (Ford, 1:12—cf. Grigsby, 122, 128). It is likely that the two men had discussed these matters before, in connection with Bland's pamphlet, and Jefferson's old law teacher would be a natural champion for the pamphlet. As a prominent member of the Randolph circle, and clerk of the House of Burgesses, Wythe had often seen to the printing of material released by the House: and since he was not going to Philadelphia in this first delegation, he would have had the time, as well as opportunity and motive, to see the paper through the press. This accords best with Jefferson's own account. He said "the members" did not accept his instruction, but that "*they* printed it*" (ibid., 1:13). This looks to something more official than a private effort by Lee or Henry.

The assumption that Jefferson's real friends were the radicals has led many to suppose that Henry's copy was the one Mrs. Rind first printed. Julian Boyd even supposes that Henry had the pamphlet reprinted in Philadelphia (*Papers*, 1:676). This is hard to reconcile with Jefferson's own supposition that Henry never read the copy he sent him (Ford, 1:12) and that he would not have agreed with it even if he had read it (Randall, 1:90). No doubt this reflects later disagreements between the men; but it would be too deliberately malicious for him to say these particular things if Henry had seen his first major piece of writing into print.

Nor can we suppose that Jefferson, in the small world of Williamsburg, never found out who published the work for him. When he says "they" (the delegation's members) printed it, he is giving his work as much official standing as possible—and Peyton Randolph was head of the delegation, the man with authority to say what "they" wanted. The normal procedure would be for Randolph to turn over to Wythe, as clerk, any documents he wanted printed. As for the Philadelphia edition of the work, the chances for publication there would be much greater if the document emanated from the household of the president of the Congress, not simply from a member like Patrick Henry.

Wythe and Randolph were, respectively, the teacher and the patron of young Jefferson. It was appropriate for them to launch his literary career. Two years later, when Wythe was in Philadelphia, Jefferson chose him to carry back his draft of a Virginia constitution, and Wythe championed that draft in Williamsburg debate (*Papers*, 1:336, 345, 355, 364–65). This probably continued a partnership founded not only on their studies together, but on the publication of Jefferson's *Summary View*.

John Adams preserves indirect evidence that Jefferson was seen, in Philadelphia, as a follower of Randolph and Harrison. He misapplies his own memory, saying Harrison put Jefferson on the com-

mittee for drafting the Declaration in order to deprive Richard
Henry Lee of the credit for it (JA, *Papers*, 3:336). We shall see that
this cannot explain the politics of drafting the Declaration—Lee
was on more important business in Virginia, and inclusion on this
committee was not the great honor it would later appear. But
Adams, guided by his cousin Samuel, was a careful student of in-
tradelegation stresses, and he worked particularly closely with Lee.
He probably remembers a more general resentment voiced by Lee
against the delegation leadership, which had passed to Harrison
after Randolph's death in 1775.

We get a further indication of this when Adams expresses his
grudge that the printed records of the Congress credited neither
Lee with making the motion for independence nor Adams himself
with seconding it. Adams claims this was because he and Lee had
offended the leadership of Congress, and he expressly names Harrison in that small leaders' band (ibid., 3:392).

Jefferson did not scheme with the Adamses—John says he was not
very active in the Congress (ibid., 3:335)—but he did socialize with
Harrison, who returned to Virginia in Jefferson's phaeton after the
summer session of 1775. Adams admits Jefferson was conscientious
in attending committee meetings, and Harrison chaired the most
important committees. When Adams says Jefferson was perceived
by Lee's Virginia critics as a safe man for drafting the Declaration,
he is preserving some more general memory of the factional lineup
within his particular fantasy of grievance. He works from a general
impression of the time that was probably accurate: Jefferson in
Philadelphia looked like a rising star of the James River oligarchy.
Fastidious, youthfully grave in his powdered hair, his slaves attending at the State House door, he must have suggested a younger Edmund Pendleton, studious of his elders and patrons, preparing himself to replicate their achievements. If, as seems likely, men of the
Congress thought that way, then they were wrong about Jefferson—
as Americans soon got into the habit of being.

TWO

". . . manly spirit ·bids us . . ."

Samuel Adams [is] the Cromwell of New England, to
whose intriguing arts the Declaration of Independence
is in a great measure to be attributed. . . .
   "Decius" in the London *Morning Post* (1779)

No one in Philadelphia appraised the arriving Virginians with
cooler eyes than Samuel Adams of Boston. Though he was feared
and distrusted by many delegates, Adams became the most influential man at the first two Congresses. Yet his name is connected with
few measures in Congress, with no documents, and with few
speeches. He made sure of that. Even in Massachusetts, people wondered, without knowing, how much he had to do with the Boston
Massacre, the Massacre trial, the Tea Party, the first shots at Lexington. But all knew he had hovered near them—fomenting, managing, publicizing—without becoming a public actor at any one of
them.

How did he achieve his great impact? Not by wealth or position.
He was not an impressive man. With the appearance of a stoutish
parson (lacking the complacency), he had a perpetual slight nervous palsy. Neither his prose nor his oratory was distinguished. A
failure in business, he had reached his forties in debt and some disgrace before the Stamp Act crisis launched him on a dozen or so
years of brilliant accomplishment. Suddenly he fused the highest
religious zeal with the lowest political tricks. He was the truest
Cromwellian on this continent, one who united Protestantism's war-
ring absolutes—the free conscience and the binding Word. His political "scripture" was the Massachusetts Charter. Copley painted
him in awkward mid-debate gesturing down toward that. Near the
Charter, he was Moses with his tablets, Luther with the Epistles.
When Caroline Robbins describes the Commonwealth tradition in

America, she is writing about him. He not only appealed to that tradition; he embodied it.

Yet he brought to this grand vision a curiously modern arsenal of weapons—street theater, surgical rioting, leaked documents, staged trials, managed news. He even had his own "wire service"—the committees of correspondence, serviced by Paul Revere. The greatest gift of Adams, however, was for that distinctive American contribution to politics: the caucus. In a century that fought high theoretical battles over the nature of "instruction" to delegates, New England held the extreme positions simultaneously. On the one hand, local town meetings sent instructed delegates to the provincial General Court—why conduct serious debate at the local level if its results are not to be registered at the higher council? On the other hand, town meetings were supposed to be open for every member's contribution—why send on binding instructions if they do not reflect the opinions of the community? As so often happens, maximum freedom prompted the most ingenious manipulation. The unscheduled nature of town-meeting debate led those with overlapping concerns to plot, ahead of time, their response to all contingencies. The plotting went on, so far as Boston was concerned, in the Caucus (originally "Caulkers") and other Clubs. Caucusing involved the widest prevision of problems that might arise and the narrowest choice of response to each possibility—who would speak to any issue, and what he would say; with the clubmen's ~neral assent guaranteed, ahead of time, to both choice of speaker and what the speaker's message would be. It was an early form of "war gaming" future situations, one denied in theory to English parliamentarians, who were still baffled by the demands of older whig doctrine—the doctrine that permanent opposition to the Crown was disloyal on its face and that parliamentary debate made no sense at all if prior instruction made a change in the participants' views impossible. Bostonian caucusing was neither opposition nor instruction in the strict sense. It went along with the town meeting's demand for debate, with its assumption that a royal governor could be challenged. Yet it managed debate with a foreknowledge that certain issues could be anticipated and that they were best handled by concerted strategies rather than formal instruction.

The Congress in Philadelphia seemed made for the skills of Adams, since delegates had only the loosest instructions from their

home province, with informal ways of interpreting those instructions among themselves. This made each group susceptible to
influence "out of doors." Let Randolph run general sessions, and
Harrison conduct committee hearings. Adams would try to penetrate the informal prior meetings that decided who went on committees or spoke in sessions. He could do this because he had been
plotting, even before his arrival in Philadelphia, with a Pennsylvania faction that meant first to use Stamp Act resisters (like John
Dickinson) and then to replace them. This faction was made up, at
the outset, of men like Thomas Mifflin, Joseph Reed, and Charles
Thomson. Reed and Mifflin had already visited Adams in Boston;
and Thomson had been writing to him for the Pennsylvania committee of correspondence. These three had staged an elaborate cha-
rade to get Dickinson's backing for the formation of that committee
of correspondence, raised in response to a call from Adams in 1774
(Ryerson, 134–40). Now members of that group came out to meet
Adams on the outskirts of Philadelphia, to inform him of their
schemes and make him part of them.

They meant to (and did) present the Congress with a series of
faits accomplis—the removal of the Congress from the State House
(turf of Joseph Galloway and the conservative Pennsylvania Assembly) to Carpenters Hall (turf of the Mechanics Association);
the election of one of their own, Charles Thomson, as congressional
secretary, though he had been excluded from the Pennsylvania delegation by Joseph Galloway; and the proposal of a currently left-
leaning pastor to give the opening prayer in Congress. Adams was
deep in all this plotting from the outset—he and John went with the
Pennsylvanians to look over Carpenters Hall on their first full day
in town (JA, *Papers*, 2:115), and Samuel himself brought forward
the Reverend Jacob Duché for the opening prayer (at a time when
he could only have found the right candidate with help from his in-
formants on the scene). This last action had the same dramatic
effect as his bolder strokes in Massachusetts: The zealot of the puritan North had shown compromise as well as control in his choice of
a respectable Anglican priest to hurl psalm verses at the British.
John Adams moved in his cousin's wake, and heard the cabal gloat-
ing at its coup: "[Joseph Reed] says we never were guilty of a
more masterful stroke than in moving that Mr. Duché might read
prayers. It has had a very good effect &c. He says the sentiments of

people here are growing more and more favorable every day"
(ibid., 131).

There is little record of most things done by Samuel Adams in
Philadelphia. Adams left even fewer traces there than in Boston.
His cousin later described his penchant for secrecy: "The letters he
wrote and received, where are they? I have seen him at Mrs. Yard's
in Philadelphia [where John roomed with him], when he was about
to leave Congress, cut up with his scissors whole bundles of letters
into atoms that could never be reunited, and throw them out of the
window, to be scattered by the winds. This was in summer, when
he had no fire. In winter he threw whole handfuls into the fire. As
we were on terms of perfect intimacy, I have joked him, perhaps
rudely, upon his anxious caution. His answer was, 'Whatever becomes of me, my friends shall never suffer by my negligence'" (Letter to William Tudor, June 5, 1817).

Joseph Galloway, who thought he could manage this Congress
held in his own back yard, soon heard vague scurryings all around
him and knew things were drifting out of his control—as the
Congress had itself come loose and drifted off from State Hall before anything could be done about it. And he knew who was doing
this, though he could not quite see how. He wrote of Samuel
Adams: "He eats little, drinks little, sleeps little, thinks much, and
is most decisive and indefatigable in the pursuit of his objects"
(Burnett, 55). When David Hawke analyzed the overthrow of
Pennsylvania's Assembly in 1776, he could trace the role of Adams
only by noting, from diaries, how often and at key times the plotters had met with their Boston mentor and friend (Hawke, 112–13,
cf. Ryerson, 549–60). That is as close as we can come to following
the tracks Adams covered so well. (The popular Broadway musical
1776 told amusingly how Congress managed to declare independence, and Samuel Adams never came on stage or was mentioned. He would have liked that.)

What role did the Virginians play in the Samuel Adams revolution? His cousin John later remembered Virginia as the key to Samuel's whole strategy: New Englanders would give the popular
Southerners credit for what was done, while the Adamses pulled
strings behind the scene. This claim is obviously colored by the bit-
terness Adams felt at the response to his presidency, as opposed
to the reign of the Virginians (Washington, Jefferson, Madison). He

exaggerates the effect of that first day's meeting with Pennsylvania radicals to begin the scheming (JA, *Papers*, 2:114, 115 n. 2). Yet, though he credited the meeting with too much later influence, it is significant that he pinned his feelings to this incident rather than another. He was doubtless very impressed by his cousin's "contacts" and ability to take control from the outset. John was always excited by the thought that he had been admitted to the real sanctum of power. He had grown up with the town-meeting system, but was astonished when he learned, at age thirty-four, how his cousin helped manipulate this open debate from a secret center—secret, anyway, to John Adams: "This day learned that the Caucus Club meets at certain times in the garret of Tom Dawes, the adjutant of the Boston regiment. He has a large house, and he has a movable partition in his garret which he takes down, and the whole Club meets in one room. There they smoke tobacco till you cannot see from one end of the garret to the other. There they drink flip, I suppose, and there they choose a moderator who puts questions to the vote regularly, and selectmen, assessors, collectors, wardens, fire wards, and representatives are regularly chosen before they are chosen in the town" (ibid., 1:238).

Seven years after that first glimpse into the smoke-filled room, Samuel made John part of his operation. This was during the trial of British soldiers for the Boston Massacre. Adams later presented this as an unpopular move in which, urged by duty, he risked the anger of his countrymen. John F. Kennedy, accepting this claim, placed Adams first among those American leaders offering a "profile in courage." But Hiller Zobel has demonstrated that Samuel put both his cousin John and Josiah Quincy up for the job, to keep the trial under control. John, for instance, blocked any effort to introduce material unfavorable to the city of Boston. And, far from risking his popularity, he ingratiated himself with Samuel's men—so much so that he was first elected to the General Court while he was preparing the trial (Zobel, *Massacre*, 220–21, 231, 259).

Although Samuel had worked principally with Joseph Warren, William Molineux, and John Hancock in Boston, John too could feel himself part of his cousin's faction—at this point, it was his principal claim to importance in the resistance movement. Only much later would he resent people's noticing he was not "*le fameux Adams.*" His impression of Samuel's importance must have been heightened when Philadelphia radicals, including Dr. Benjamin Rush, came out to meet him on the outskirts of their town. Samuel, barely arrived, already had an apparatus in place for directing affairs. Indeed, one of the Pennsylvania radicals, Dr. Thomas Young, had earlier been an agent of Samuel in Boston, serving on his committee of correspondence and allegedly taking part in the tea destruction.

Most delegates traveled to Philadelphia with apprehension about the unknown men they must deal with. John felt he had a sure guide in his cousin and followed his direction eagerly. He was not good at hiding anything; but his egotism could be played on and used—just as Hancock's was at Lexington and elsewhere. John's pride in his "machinations" shines through his letters to Abigail: "We have been obliged to act with great delicacy and caution. We have been obliged to keep ourselves out of sight, and to feel pulses, and to sound depths; to insinuate our sentiments, designs and desires by means of other persons, sometimes of one province, and sometimes of another" (*Family Correspondence,* 1:158). And, on the eve of independence, "when I consider the great events which are passed, and those greater which are rapidly advancing, and that I may have been instrumental in touching some springs and turning some small wheels which have had and will have such effects, I feel an awe upon my mind which is not easily described" (*Abigail,* 129). Charles Thomson, much closer to the crucial schemes in Philadelphia, would look back with similar complacency on "the secret springs and reality of action," at odds with what most men saw or thought was happening (Ryerson, xvii).

John grasped the importance of Virginia to Samuel's plans (though Pennsylvania was always *more* important). But even the Virginia strategy was partly mistaken by John, who talks of the southern delegates as unwitting "front men" for the shrewd New Englanders who used them. Samuel flattered John on his own ascendancy over Hancock among the plotters, convincing him that Washington was advanced as Commander in Chief, among other things, to keep Hancock in line. (John exaggerates even the vain Hancock's visible disappointment at not getting the post.) So convinced did John finally become that he and Samuel did all the *real* work that he could dismiss Benjamin Harrison, who chaired key committees, as a blustery do-nothing.

It is impossible to believe that Samuel took the same view of Virginia. He had begun his continental propagandizing with that province, since Arthur Lee (Richard Henry's brother), acting as the Boston radicals' counteragent to Benjamin Franklin in London, was the node of Samuel's larger network for half a dozen years before the Congress met. It was through Arthur that Samuel's intraprovincial committees of correspondence were meshed with an interprovincial scheme proposed by Richard Henry Lee. Richard Henry had even practiced an Adams kind of theatrical warfare, nine years earlier, when he dressed his slaves up in "Wilkes costume" and marched them to a solemn hanging of the stamp minister and stamp collector in effigy, Lee giving the dramatic last speeches of the condemned. He also used his militia to harass an unco-operative merchant, mobilizing his whole county against the Stamp Act.

Adams expected to work with Lee at the Congress, and his expectation was satisfied—John and Samuel saw much of Lee's brother-in-law and host, Dr. Shippen, during their first days in Philadelphia (JA, *Papers*, 2:114–17), and Samuel would keep in touch with Lee when the latter returned to Virginia (SA, *Writings*, 3:296–99). But the best proof of Lee's importance to Adams was later supplied by Jefferson, who remembered well the Adams method: "He was constantly holding caucuses of distinguished men, among whom was Richard Henry Lee, at which the generality of the measures pursued were previously determined on, and at which the parts were assigned to the different actors who afterwards appeared in them" (Randall, 1:182).

But there was tension between Lee and the Randolph-Harrison center of gravity in Virginia's delegation. The two elders, like Washington (who roomed with them in the same house), were used to giving, not taking, orders; and they were proud of work done *within* the legislature, not out of doors. The Virginians were military men—most (including Jefferson) held the title of colonel in their local militia; and some, like Harrison, invariably used it. They were not to be engaged in private schemings. But their pride could be publicly engaged. Since all the other first moves of Congress were managed by Adams's Philadelphia friends—including the choice of Thomson as secretary—it is hard to believe these men did not actively concur in, if not inspire, the choice of Randolph as president. Some have expressed surprise that a "conservative" like Harrison would serve on the secret committees making contact with foreign governments, one of the most radical undertakings of the Congress. But Randolph and Harrison, Washington and Pendleton, once committed to a course of resistance, would use their military pride and experience, along with their legislative skill, to supply the army—the most urgent congressional task after its very first session.

Patrick Henry, temperamental anyway, decided during the second Congress to stay in his theater of maximum effectiveness, Virginia, leaving Lee alone to deal with Adams—unless, of course, Jefferson could be engaged. But there is no direct evidence of Jefferson's caucusing with the Adamses, and John later denied this took place. That is the more surprising since one of Jefferson's heroes, the Philadelphia scientist David Rittenhouse, joined in the schemes of Pennsylvania's radicals. Besides, Jefferson had already been engaged, without knowing it, in one of Samuel's more energetic propaganda efforts. Adams realized it was not enough to arrange an event; one must control the impressions formed of that event. After each development in Massachusetts, he fired off his own letters, with accounts by others, news stories, and clippings, to England and the other colonies. In this way he inflated the Massacre (Zobel, *Massacre*, 211–15) and painted in muted colors the Tea Party. Relying on early reports sent to England and Virginia by Samuel's rapid system, Jefferson wrote a sincere but wildly inaccurate account of the tea incident in his first public work, *A Summary View of the Rights of British America* (1774).

The tea "party"—trivialized by that name, as the earlier riot had been expanded into a "massacre"—took elaborate organization of the very sort Samuel had mastered in Boston. It was an arduous undertaking, full of military risk and sheer physical problems. There were three docked ships laden with tea—340 chests of it, each weighing three hundred pounds. Simply to winch up and unload these chests would have been a good job for Boston teamsters, moving the chests off in wagons as they were unloaded on the wharf. To hoist up the chests and dump them overboard, from the loading area where the winches were, posed several problems. With no wagons carrying off the earlier chests, one hundred boxes would pile up on the water side of each ship's loading area in the shallow harbor, rising above the water, making it necessary to lift the later chests up off the deck onto the pile. Tea in the top chests would not even be spoiled. So it was planned, ahead of time, to undertake an even more time-consuming operation: The chests would be raised with block and tackle, broken up, the tea shoveled overboard, the wreckage of chests cleared away. Armed guards were posted at the wharf's end while volunteer "Mohawks" labored three hours in the cold December night. The teams on each ship worked efficiently under a designated leader. So huge was the destruction that even the loose tea shoveled overboard rose above the gunwales and had to be toppled outward—ninety thousand pounds of the stuff going in at low tide. In the morning, tea was islanded in windrows over the water, and rowboats had to be sent out to unmush a way for larger ships to pass through.

Samuel had given the agreed-on signal for his trained crew of "Indians" to run toward the ships, and he went immediately to work spreading his version of the incident (SA, *Writings*, 71–79). He tried to create the impression of a comparatively mild response to an uncompromising governor, and one of those he first deceived was Thomas Jefferson. Here is the version of the tea's destruction that appeared in *A Summary View* (1774):

'The East India company, who till that time had never sent a pound of tea to America on their own account [*only because they had in the past been forced to route it through England, to pay duties there*], step forth on that occasion the asserters of parliamentary right [*on the contrary, whigs in the Parliament objected to Crown intrusion in charter rights*] and send hither many ship loads of that obnoxious commodity. The masters of their several vessels however, on their arrival in America, wisely attended to admonition, and returned with their cargoes [*not in South Carolina, where the tea was landed*]. In the province of New England alone [*sic*] the remonstrances of the people were disregarded [*but the people, under Samuel's leadership, had insisted on the docking, which prevented a return without paying duty, as from Philadelphia*], and a compliance, after being many days waited for, was flatly refused. Whether in this the master of the vessel was governed by his obstinacy or his instructions, let those who know, say. [*Francis Rotch, in charge of the principal ship, tried to clear harbor but could not get a pass since the duty was unpaid.*] There are extraordinary situations which require extraordinary interposition. An exasperated people, who feel that they possess power, are not easily restrained within limits strictly [*sic*] regular. A number of them assembled in the town of Boston, threw the tea into the ocean and dispersed without doing any other act of violence. If [*sic*] in this they did wrong, they were known [*they had disguised themselves in "war paint" so they would not be known*], and were amenable to the laws of the land [*on the contrary, they had closed down the Superior Court because the judges were in the King's pay*], against which it would not be objected that they [*i.e., the laws*] had ever in any instance been obstructed or diverted from their regular course in favor of popular offenders. [*He probably refers to the soldiers' acquittal after the Massacre, neglecting unpunished acts of the popular offenders who sacked Governor Hutchinson's house and threatened the stamp collectors and tea consignees.*] They [*i.e., the destroyers of the tea*] should therefore not have been distrusted [!] on this occasion. But that ill-fated colony had formerly been bold in their enmities against the house of Stuart [*Massachusetts had resisted the Restoration and had its charter taken away*], and were now devoted to ruin by that unseen hand which governs the momentous affairs of this great empire. On the partial representations [*far less partial than the ones Jefferson was relying on as he wrote*] of a few worthless ministerial dependants, whose constant office it has been to keep that government embroiled, and who by their treacheries hope to obtain the dignity of the British knighthood [*he compares Hutchinson to Francis Bernard, the ex-governor knighted four years before this*], without calling for a party accused [*searches were made and one man arrested, but no one would give evidence against him*], without asking for a proof [*one witness was found, but would testify only in England, where it was safe*], without attempting a distinction between the guilty and the innocent [*a hopeless task, where the innocent were sheltering the guilty and the guilty threatening the innocent*], the whole of that antient and wealthy town is in a moment reduced from opulence to beggary. Men who had spent their lives in extending the British commerce [*often by smuggling with the Dutch and others*], who had invested in that place the wealth their honest endeavors had merited, found themselves and their families thrown at once on the world for subsistence by it's charities. Not the hundredth part of the inhabitants of that town had been concerned in the act complained of; many of them were in Great Britain and in other parts beyond sea; yet all were involved in one indiscriminate ruin, by a new executive power unheard of till then, that of a British parliament. A property of the value of many millions of money was sacrifised to revenge, not repay [*which Boston refused to do*] the loss of a few [*i.e., nine*] thousands [*of pounds*] (*Papers*, 1:127–28).

Jefferson must not have known how successfully the perpetrators were resisting trial and discovery even as he wrote. In the words of the Tea Party's best modern student, Benjamin Labaree: "Just who took active roles in the Boston Tea Party remains one of the mysteries of American history. A half-century later John Adams wrote that he did not know the identity of a single participant. The unparalleled secrecy . . . enshrouded their names." Yet a laundered version of the "party," much like Jefferson's, perdures in American memory. Martin Luther King even made the Tea Party a type of his own nonviolent form of protest, which must be undertaken "openly, lovingly, and with a willingness to accept the penalty." That describes Jefferson's tea party, but not the real one. We are still affected, unawares, by Samuel Adams's skill at managing the news.

John Adams knew most of the facts about the tea incident. He is forced to a more ingenious explanation than Jefferson could be content with. He poses the issue as one of direct conflict with royal troops, to force the ship back toward England: "An army and navy was at hand, and bloodshed was apprehended." So the "Indians" delivered a pre-emptive blow, to make such conflict unnecessary: "At last, when the continent, as well as the town and province, were waiting the issue of this deliberation with the utmost anxiety, a number of persons, in the night, put them out of suspense by an oblation to Neptune" (Novanglus, 87). The anger building up between men is vented on tea leaves instead—a euphemistic "oblation." The contrast between John Adams and Jefferson, in the period of the Continental Congress, has often been misstated in the light of their later dealings. John knew what tricks his cousin was up to, yet went along with him—just as he had defended the soldiers while Samuel was making sure they would be defamed annually in Massacre orations. Jefferson did not join in such maneuvers, even though he had not seen through the distortions in Samuel's account of the tea incident. "Conservative" and "liberal" are misleading terms in most cases, but rarely as misleading as when the former is applied to Adams and the latter to Jefferson. Adams had a theoretical caution but a headlong, informal, risk-taking manner in person. He was quick to trust or suspect, to take or give offense, to act on a moral "feel" for any situation. He felt a confidence in his cousin's basic integrity and high goals and did not hesitate to follow his example in using illegal means to reach them. He even planned with him the overthrow of the legitimate Pennsylvania legislature. Many historians attribute the Revolution to a growth of power in the provincial lower houses. Yet Adams, later a critic of

Pennsylvania's radical constitution, helped make that constitution possible when he joined in the overthrow of the last and most democratically elected lower house on the continent.

Jefferson, by contrast, was rather quick to spill literary blood, but slow to the point of timidity in facing actual violence. The title he gloried in least was that of colonel, and few thought he was very good at wearing it. His later calls for revolution have an oddly idyllic note to them, as when he tells us the tree of liberty must be periodically "manured" with blood. It is a voice from the Georgian manor talking a kind of remote and georgic poetry about the right "seasons" for madness and bloodshed. This is not a question of physical courage. Jefferson withdrew even from *legislative* conflict when it became too intense, though the issue was vital to him and he had a good chance of winning. There was loud dissatisfaction with his performance as governor of Virginia, not because his loyalty was suspect—only his diligence. He seems, in retrospect, to have been more interested in collecting material for his *Notes on the State of Virginia* than in making sure there would *be* a state of Virginia to be analyzed. He exasperated others by seeing inevitability where they saw only crisis, by a long-range vision that treated day-to-day struggles as already settled in their outcome. He brushed troubles aside as distractions from the main point or large pattern.

This tendency showed up most astonishingly when Jefferson advised David Rittenhouse, during one of the darker moments of the Revolution, to give up his work for the Pennsylvania government and get back to astronomy. It is important to dwell on this attitude toward Rittenhouse, since Jefferson tried to model his own efforts on that self-taught scientist's achievements. It is clear that Jefferson met Rittenhouse in 1775, and just as clear that he did not join in the political maneuvers that brought Rittenhouse into collaboration with the Adamses. Jefferson knew, and honored, only one side of Rittenhouse's life—a side that was in temporary abeyance during the crisis of 1775–76, when the Pennsylvanian was devoting all his time to the cause of independence.

By late 1775, it was clear that the Revolution was taking place in Philadelphia on three levels—physically, as well as symbolically, after the second Congress convened in the State House (present Independence Hall). Pennsylvania's Assembly, the proprietary legislature, vacated its quarters and moved upstairs for its sessions (stalling the proprietary governor with hopes that it could control the Congress sitting below in its own chambers). Meanwhile, down on the street, new committees had sprung up to handle the militia and the merchants, maintaining defenses and the boycott. In theory, there was a neat hierarchy: The legislature, above, had the right to instruct its delegates to the Congress, below, whose policies were implemented out on the street. But in fact the committees were doing more and more of the actual governing. This was obviously true in provinces where the legislature had been prorogued or dissolved. But even in Pennsylvania, where the Assembly still sat, the Committee of Safety (nominally an executive arm of the Assembly) was unable to stand up against the city's Committee of Inspection and Observation, backed as it was by local committees of correspondence throughout the province (which gathered at periodic conventions). Only the authority to instruct delegates in Congress gave the Assembly real power now, and John Dickinson was using that power to marshal all the remains of old proprietary or Quaker influence in a last stand for "moderation."

Rittenhouse was familiar with each level of this struggle back and forth toward revolution. In fact, he had to climb up past both Congress and the Assembly to maintain the State House clock, one of his salaried duties for the city. Beyond that, he was (from March of 1776) a member of the Assembly; he was intimate with the Adams faction in Congress (all of whose delegates had received complimentary copies of his great address on astronomy); and he had served both the main city committees, as a member of the Committee of Inspection and Observation and as the military engineer appointed by the Committee of Safety. He was trusted by the radicals and stood against the Dickinson faction within the Assembly (Hindle, *Rittenhouse*, 123–40).

Rittenhouse was part of a new wave of radicals that had succeeded the band led by Mifflin, Reed, and Thomson (who were now caught up in Congress or the army). The new group, led by men like James Cannon, decided to "pack" the Assembly with radicals and had the committees call for an election on May 1, 1776, giving broader representation to the city of Philadelphia and the back country. But three of the four new seats from the city were captured by moderates, and even the returns from the back country

were not entirely favorable to the radicals. So Cannon's group decided to break the Assembly.

These moves were carefully co-ordinated with the Adamses in
Congress. At the State House, the middle was playing the street off
against the top. John Adams introduced a resolution calling for the
provinces to adopt committee government if that was necessary to
implement the policies of Congress. John Dickinson let that resolution pass on May 10, arguing that Pennsylvania did not need an
"interim" government since its permanent one still sat, its validity
just reasserted by a broad and democratic election. Stymied, the radicals returned with a preamble to the resolution calling oaths of loyalty to the crown "irreconcileable to reason" during the crisis—a direct hit at Pennsylvania's Assembly, which still took the oath.
(Rittenhouse had been forced to take it just two months earlier.)
The preamble was voted through on May 15, by a six-to-four majority. Georgia was absent, Maryland walked out, and Pennsylvania
abstained. The radicals had their tool. Richard Ryerson deduces
from the event that "Adams's preamble was obviously well known
to Philadelphia's radicals even before it reached the floor of
Congress" (553). On the night of the fifteenth, radicals mobilized
the committees for a mass meeting on May 20, to use the resolution
of Congress against the Assembly's legitimacy. That meeting, held
in the rain with four thousand present, broke the will of the Assembly. It would now drag out a half-life of lessening resistance, right
up to the crucial vote for independence on July 2, when Dickinson
let the motion pass by withdrawing from the Pennsylvania delegation. The street had won.

Jefferson not only had no part in this dramatic struggle, he chose
the very time when it gathered toward a climax to absent himself
from Congress. He was gone from December of 1775 to May 13 of
1776. By accident he arrived back in time to write the Declaration
that commemorated the radicals' victory. But even during the tense
latter days of May and the whole month of June, when the excite-
ment at the impending vote for independence filled the letters of
other delegates, he was working out his own ideas on a new constitution for Virginia. At that point Rittenhouse was plunging into the
constitutional struggle in Pennsylvania; and John and Samuel
Adams had begun work on the foreign alliances that were supposed
to follow on independence. But Jefferson was anxious to be off for

Virginia, and soon was. Except for the luck of his reappearance just as the radicals' work was coming to fruition—and when Lee had gone to Virginia to co-ordinate calls for independence from that province—Jefferson would not have made his single important contribution to the events in Philadelphia.

His distance from the kind of machinations that made independence possible is reflected in his letter, written two years later, to a Rittenhouse still wrapped up in Pennsylvania's cause:

> Your time for two years past has, I beleive, been principally employed in the civil government of your country. Tho' I have been aware of the authority our cause would acquire with the world from it's being known that yourself and Doctr. Franklin were zealous friends to it, and am myself duly impressed with a sense of the arduousness of government, and the obligation those are under who are able to conduct it, yet I am also satisfied there is an order of geniusses above that obligation, and therefore exempted from it (*Papers*, 2:203–4).

Jefferson would never rank himself with Rittenhouse, in terms of genius; but he obviously felt his contribution to the cause in Philadelphia should be theoretical and literary, not political in the narrow or tactical sense. Yet even to make that contribution he had to write words that others would respond to, beginning with the Congress. Jefferson was as quiet and retiring in Philadelphia as he had been, for years, in Williamsburg. He found time to read and correspond and study constitutional law while others' days and nights were consumed in plot and counterplot. But those pale blue eyes missed little. He was an observer of all nature's order and oddities, and he had some very strange human specimens to study in Philadelphia. It was a difficult enough task to find pattern, some necessity of nature, behind all these scurryings and schemings. He would attend, vote with his delegation, and write when commissioned by his fellows. And even these minimal tasks called for a prior discipline, one he had acquired: He must *see*. All America was assembled, in symbol, at the Congress—and for the very first time. He saw a unified people there, despite appearances; so that he could speak of "one people" dissolving the bond with another (an alien) people. It took discernment to find such unity beneath divided factions.

THREE

"... former systems of government ..."

> Fifty gentlemen meeting together all strangers, are not acquainted with each other's language, ideas, views, designs. They are therefore jealous [suspicious] of each other—fearful, timid, skittish.
> —John Adams, at the Continental Congress

The delegates gathering in Philadelphia wrapped their deliberations in secrecy. In fact, to make doubly sure they were protected, defeated motions and votes were expunged from the record. The eraser followed close behind the pen, fear traveling with courage—a long-term fear of royal troops; but daily fear, as well, of homelier masked danger. They were afraid of each other. "Here is a diversity of religions, educations, manners, interest, such as it would seem almost impossible to unite in one plan of conduct," wrote John Adams (Burnett, 74)—even as he and Samuel labored to decipher "the character and connections, the interests and views" of men within the various delegations (ibid., 64).

Their fears were justified. The head of their host delegation would end up on the British side and write an unfavorable account of their deliberations—without being able to confirm what he said from the record. The first congressional chaplain remained loyal to the King. Even within individual delegations, trust fluctuated, had to be bargained for, was all too easily withheld. Richard Bland's suspect status in the Virginia delegation was not unique. Silas Deane had tried to keep Roger Sherman out of the Connecticut contingent. The Pennsylvania slate was packed by Joseph Galloway, whose foes, nonetheless, used the Congress to bring him down.

Even Benjamin Franklin, on his return from Europe, would be feared at the Congress as a spy. Letters from England convinced some that John Jay was an informer to the British in their midst. The New York delegation represented one of several factions in that province, each of which was trying to use the Congress against the others. Georgia did not even send delegates at first. (Lyman Hall, present as a volunteer, could speak only for his parish.)

Most of these men were used to political conclaves and scheming —but not on this scale, or in this company. The government of each colony was a relatively closed affair, indeed, a family affair. That fact is suggested in the replication of names among those at the first Congresses—not only Lees from Virginia, and Adamses from Massachusetts, but Livingstons from New York. South Carolina outdid the rest, sending two each of the Middletons, the Lynches, and the Rutledges—no Pinckneys, to be sure, but Edward Rutledge was married to one. Connecticut elected two Wolcotts, sons of the ex-governor, though only one attended. And last names, of course, are just indicators of the dense network of in-laws and cousinhoods. John Jay of New York was attending with his father-in-law. Of the twelve men who rode up to the first two Congresses from Virginia, nine were interconnected by blood or marriage. Leadership down to the lowest offices was stable and inbred. John Adams could write, in the next decade, "Go into every village of New England, and you will find that the office of justice of the peace, and even the place of representative, which has ever depended only on the freest election of the people, have generally descended from generation to generation, in three or four families at most" (*Defence of the Constitutions*, 1:110–11).

Each colony was a world in which men knew and were known, with marked places in society. That fact was reflected in the assignment of church pews by social rank. Every student in a Harvard College class was listed according to his family's prominence, not by alphabet or academic grades. The relative standing of the Boston and the Braintree Adamses is instantly established by noting that Samuel was sixth in his class (out of twenty-three) and John was fifteenth (out of twenty-four). Regions were delineated almost as much by family names and local traits as by geographic landmarks. Jonathan Boucher, the Maryland clergyman, wrote about his travels in colonial Virginia:

Certain districts come to be settled by certain families; and different places are there known and spoken of, not as here [the loyalist Boucher had returned to England at the Revolution], by any difference of dialect for there is no dialect in all North America, but by their being inhabited by the Fitzhughs, the Randolphs, Washingtons, Carys, Grimeses, or Thorntons. This circumstance used to furnish me with a scope for many remarks, such as do not so often occur here. The family character both of body and mind may be traced through many generations: as, for instance, every Fitzhugh has bad eyes, every Thornton hears badly, Winslows and Lees talk well, Carters are proud and imperious, and Taliaferros mean and avaricious, and Fowkeses cruel.

When Captain John Parker called out his Minutemen to confront the British troops at Lexington, over a quarter of those responding were his blood relatives or in-laws.

Of course, some loyalist families would not be represented at the opening Congress—Hutchinsons of Massachusetts, DeLanceys of New York, Allens of Pennsylvania, or Dulanys of Maryland. But in general the colonies' finest sent their emissaries; if for no other reason, to cope with potential colonial rivals. The very call for a Congress had been backed by certain "conservative" forces, to stall the demand for an immediate embargo in response to the Coercive Acts. And for this occasion even Samuel Adams put on respectable airs—he arrived with a brand-new wardrobe, provided him by the Sons of Liberty, as armor against foreign criticism.

Some delegates (nine of the fifty-six) had met at the Stamp Act Congress in 1765, or knew men from neighboring provinces; others had corresponded or heard of each other. But most were meeting for the first time. At Hartford, and again at New York City, the Massachusetts delegates were extensively briefed on the New York delegation before actually meeting it (JA, *Papers*, 2:106). When John Adams reached Philadelphia (after a three-week journey), he described strange men from very strange places. Cockfighting was as unthinkable in Boston as the stop-action sylvan frames of a New England sabbath would have been in Williamsburg, where preachers were drunk in their pulpits and militiamen drilled to cow the slaves on their one day of rest. In eighteenth-century Philadelphia, Smollett jostled Bunyan, as "Friend" Anthony Benezet lectured a submissive Patrick Henry on the evils of black slavery, gambling, and war. Adams, attending a popish Mass, a Quaker dinner, a modern surgery, a madhouse, was like a tourist to Cathay. London would have been more familiar than Philadelphia to most of these congressmen—at least there were no papist officials there.

Nor were mutual doubts dispelled by long association. After two years' sitting, a delegate would observe: "We do not treat each other with that decency and respect that was observed heretofore. Jealousies, ill-natured observations and recriminations take the place of reason and argument" (Burnett, 401). John Adams knew, as time went on, that other colonies did not fight for Massachusetts out of pure love: "They have their reasons, some plausible, some whimsical. They have a secret fear, a jealousy [suspicion], that New England will soon be full of veteran soldiers and at length conceive designs unfavorable to the other colonies" (ibid., 213). Even before Adams reached the Congress, one of New York's delegates had expressed these suspicions to him: "Says if England should turn us adrift, we should instantly go to civil wars among ourselves to determine which colony should govern all the rest. Seems to dread N. England—the leveling spirit &c. Hints were thrown out of the Goths and Vandals—mention was made of our hanging the Quakers &c." (JA, Papers, 2:107). Edward Rutledge would maintain this theme at the Congress: "The idea of destroying all provincial distinctions and making everything of the most minute kind bend to what they call the good of the whole is, in other terms, to say that these colonies must be subject to the over-ruling influence of the Eastern Provinces. The force of their arms I hold exceding cheap, but I confess I dread their overruling influence in council. I dread their low cunning, and those leveling principles which men without character and without fortune in general possess, which are so captivating to the lower class of mankind, and which will occasion such a fluctuation of property as to introduce the greatest disorder" (Burnett, 517–18).

These suspicions were natural. Each delegate was in Philadelphia to protect his country, province, people, or government—"colony" or "proprietary," the legal terms, were not much used in this context. Stressing the mode of dependence, these words were not dwelt on except for King's or governor's consumption. A subtle distortion colors all our efforts to look at these men as they judged

one another. It seems clear to us that they were brokering our own
"birth," initiating a history. They stand at the beginning. But they
saw themselves as defenders of a history accomplished; taking risks
that might end, rather than launch, a noble experiment. They were
speaking for deliberative assemblies of great antiquity—some nearly
a century old; one that had held its sessions in unbroken sequence
for over one hundred and fifty years. And each of these provincial
legislatures traced its patent overseas, and back in time, to Magna
Carta at the latest. Freedom, for whigs of the eighteenth century,
always had a pedigree. It was a child of paper, a *chartered* liberty.

Yet in Philadelphia this shared doctrine divided men. Each colony traced its freedom's lineage through separate documents and
cherished its particular descent. William Allen, chief justice for
Pennsylvania, stated the problem when he asked John Adams for
the ground of men's rights in Massachusetts. He meant: How have
the rights been assured by particular charter? As recently as 1764
Pennsylvanians had petitioned the King for a royal charter, to take
possession of the colony away from the Penns. That, indeed, was
the business that took Benjamin Franklin to London in time for the
Stamp Act controversy. The principal colonies had developed, defended, and interpreted their charters in such a way that they were
regularly referred to as "our constitutions" (*Respect*, 28, 41, 43,
119).

An interest in the diverse establishments of each colony would
continue during and after the Revolution, at a time when the Articles of Confederation made the thirteen *separate* establishments the
real government. The interest in these constitutions, at home and in
Europe, is symbolized by a work like Adams's *Defence of the Constitutions* (1787). Colonies had defended their charters, sometimes
against Parliament (e.g., Virginia during England's civil war),
sometimes against royal troops (e.g., Connecticut refusing to turn
its charter over to Governor Andros). The charters were conduits of
British freedom, derivable from Magna Carta by way of the Declaration of Rights. Thus Samuel Adams's father could describe, in
1731, "the great privileges we enjoy by the English Constitution
and the Royal Charter"; and he called impressment of colonial citizens "breaches of Magna Charta, the Charter of this Province, and
an Act of Parliament"—the proper order of basic, incorporating, and
applied rights. Daniel Dulany argued in 1766 that Maryland's char-

ter, even though a proprietary one, was derived from the Great Charter and therefore based on "the unalienable rights of the subject" (*Considerations*, 30). When Americans from different provinces used similar arguments, they did so to protect their own *different* channels of appeal to the British constitution.

Emphasis on the charter, on the written sign of men's legal standing, was taken—in America, as in England—to authorize all the standing liberties men had experienced under their charters. In England itself, the practice of whig government did not much resemble theories used to justify it. One result of this was colonial confusion over where to place the blame for incursions on men's rights—on King, or Parliament, or that *tertium quid*, "the Ministry." Still, the governing devices of Walpole arose within the matrix of whig theory justifying the Glorious Revolution; so even its "unwritten rules" were felt to be based on the Declaration of Rights.

Americans felt the same way about practices allowed—therefore, they argued, endorsed—within each colony's history of constitutional development. John Robinson, the powerful Speaker of Virginia's House of Burgesses, ran a loan service that was almost a native "civil list" to rival, on its small scale, Walpole's use of pensions and "places." Samuel Adams used a systematic laxness in his tax collector's office to curry favor with his followers; by the time the law caught up with him, he was too popular for its agents to collect the sums or punish him. James Otis and John Adams wove high moral doctrine around the recognized practice of smuggling (from which, in great part, John Hancock's adoptive father had derived his wealth); they could move from Magna Carta to the rum trade in the twinkling of an argument. Adams dated the Revolution's inception from the Otis defense of paralegal smuggling in the Writs of Assistance case. Boston became notorious for its independent trade outside the Empire (defended by native juries when rare cases came to trial). Thomas Pownall, despite his sympathy with American rights, described "how difficult (if ever practicable) it is in any of their courts of common law to convict any person of a violation of the laws of trade or in any matter of crown revenue" (*Administration*, 109). Faced with the charge that Boston whigs smuggled, John Adams's rather lame reply was that tories did it too (*Novanglus*, 88).

The illegal fur trade with Canada was bargained for by rival families through New York's agents in London. Virginians knew whose house to roll "lost" hogsheads of tobacco to in each port town. Back in the seventeenth century it was said that not one planter in ten paid his plantation duties. Virginia land speculators used every channel of ministerial influence in England. Edmund Morgan has pointed out (*WMQ*, 1967) how adept some Americans, like George Croghan, became at lamenting the corrupt ways of England even while profiting from them. In 1775, Benjamin Franklin sighed that London was corrupted beyond redemption; though he had been tempted, shortly before, to abandon his native land and live in England. And Franklin was glad enough to use "influence" when American agents brought all their force to bear on merchants during the Stamp Act crisis. What grieved Franklin in 1775 was the decline of American access to that influence. It is true that Americans thundered against corruption, as England's own politicians did. The literary model for this was, in America, the Puritan jeremiad—accusation as an instrument of reform; and the accusing continued, after the Revolution; redirected, now, at the native governments.

Nor can we say that Americans totally lacked what Bernard Bailyn has called England's rule by paragovernment, by the "private constitution" of patronage and influence. The lower houses of colonial legislatures had worked out complex ways of circumventing most royal governors, establishing their own "private constitution." William Byrd could say complacently, as early as 1735: "Our government is so happily constituted that a Governor must outwit us before he can oppress us, and if he ever squeeze money out of us he must first take care to deserve it."

Since the assemblies had acquired so much power, contact with the home ministry could not be maintained solely, or even mainly, through formal channels of the "public constitution"—governors' reports to the Board of Trade and Secretary of State for America, King's instructions sent back from the Council on Plantations. Instead, a large supply of American agents, formal and informal—hired residents of London, commissioned visitors from America, families divided by the ocean, business partners, fellow religionists—swarmed through the approaches to colonial secretary, Board of Trade, royal councillors, and the two houses of Parliament. Even Bailyn, who denies a paragovernment to America, must admit: "By the mid-eighteenth century, a stable pattern of informal communications had emerged, linking political forces in America directly to the political forces in England capable of overturning decisions taken in the colonies by the resident executive" (*Origins,* 70). The result was that the lower houses in a colony could reach centers of influence in England through "more permanent and reliable channels of influence in England than the governors" maintained. Bailyn, of course, is arguing that governors in America did not have the resources available to a British prime minister. But the fact that the lower houses had such influence vitally affects the moral claim that America was entirely lacking in the kind of corruption that focused political debate in England.

Self-government in America had, paradoxically, grown up by way of legislative influence in England. This would affect everything the delegates did at the first Congress. The pressures for colonial self-rule had hitherto been exerted in London, not directly *between* colonies. Colonial agents, except for their high period of concerted effort in 1765, were more often rivals than allies. Those agents who held multiple commissions were suspected of conflicting interests: Samuel Adams, opposing Massachusetts' use of Pennsylvania's agent in London (Benjamin Franklin), did his own business through an unregistered counteragent, Arthur Lee. Contending factions within a state had to maintain different troops of agents—e.g., the Morris family countering the DeLancey ties with London society. Or a special task might be farmed out to a specific lobbyist—e.g., by Thomas Lee in setting up the Ohio company.

If even single colonies often had contending agents, one can imagine the kind of rivalry that existed *between* colonies. This was true of provinces bound together by a single crop or other interest. North Carolina and Virginia were at odds over tobacco standards; Maryland and Pennsylvania over use of Baltimore's harbor by Western Pennsylvanians; Connecticut and Pennsylvania over control of the Wyoming Valley; New Hampshire and New York over what would later become Vermont; the Delaware counties over full independence from Pennsylvania, and so on. Georgia, denied slaves under its first charter, called for shipments of them just as Virginia, not wanting to drive down the price of homebred slaves, opposed further importation. Southern slave interests were united with the

New England sugar trade, but only to compete with powerful agents and representatives of the West Indies. Colonial agents were in London to undo each other's work, this colony using its powers with the Ministry against that colony—a process hard to reverse, all at once, in Philadelphia.

Although the delegates to the Congress voted, for convenience's sake, by geography (the New England, Middle, and Southern provinces), economic and social divisions cut, also, north and south through the colonies, dividing seacoast trade and tidewater farming from the mountain and frontier West. Those to the west were usually later arrivals, poorer, more exposed to nature and the Indians and (until recently) the French. Many were Scotch-Irish Presbyterians or German quietists, as opposed to the established churches or original dissenting groups (Congregationalists in New England, Quakers in Pennsylvania, Catholics in Maryland). But the umbilical tie, even for these fringe groups with their common interests and perils, ran back to the sea through the provinces' separate capitals, just as all those capitals' ligaments ran over the sea to Whitehall or Westminster. Defense against Indians meant money for weapons and men, to be collected by each area's Assembly. Westerners in New York had to call for British troops to handle the Six Nations. Those in Pennsylvania had to overcome Quaker pacifism by marching on Philadelphia. The western regions had, many of them, the same foes, needs, and grievances; but they had to seek redress back along the closest water route to the Atlantic, not through common action with their neighbors to the north or south. A frontier rebellion like that of the Regulators in the Carolinas had little chance of spreading north. Indeed, the western regions often fought each other or later settlers—and the voting from the "back country" was less distinct from eastern patterns than progressive historians assumed it must be.

What we find, then, is a grid of common interests plotted on latitudinal lines, countered by a grid of economic and political energies working on a longitudinal plan. In retrospect, the tension between these opposing lines of force gives the separation from England a natural air—the difficulties of the continent could only be worked out when its institutions came into better accord with its needs. But long patterns of thought are hard to break; and men felt bound together, not divided, by the sea. It was the world's high-

way. Prosperity looked outward from each coastal line, not up or
down the shore. And inland towns on rivers existed to get things to
the ocean ports. Plantations ran down toward the wharf, where produce could be loaded onto barges. (The principal exception, Monticello, is an economic blasphemy, perched on a mountain as if to
trade with Nephelococcygia.) Much intercolonial travel was by sea
—it was quicker, safer, and more comfortable than braving the
rough, unpoliced, and largely unmarked roads, where horses were
easily tired or hurt (like their riders), carriages battered and needing repair along the way (like their occupants). Even on the comparatively well-traveled roads from Fredericksburg to Philadelphia,
Jefferson had to hire guides twice on his way to the Second
Congress (Randall, 1:112). The Marquis de Chastellux, despite detailed directions from Jefferson, got hopelessly lost looking for the
Natural Bridge.

Inland, men used boats and ferries whenever they could, not only
for shipping goods but for carrying themselves and resting their
horses. The second contingent of Virginians made excellent time to
Philadelphia in 1774 by spelling its horses at ferries over the Chesa-
peake Bay and the Delaware. Adams, in his more leisurely trip
down from Boston, could avoid frequent "blowing" of his horses
only on legs of the journey like this: "At nine o'clock we cross
Powlus Hook ferry to N. Jersey—then Hackinsack ferry, then New-
ark ferry, and dined at Elizabethtown. After dinner we rode
twenty miles, crossed Brunswick ferry and put up at Farmers in the
city of Brunswick" (JA, Papers, 2:111).

Those who had seen most of the colonies were men engaged in
sea trade, touching in at different ports from Portland to Savannah
—or, rather, from Halifax to Kingston, since the unity of the land-
contiguous colonies was not yet established; nor even the separation from adjacent areas like Quebec and the Floridas. A man from
seagoing Boston could, like Samuel Adams, go half a century without mounting a horse. Fashionable society, if unable to go abroad,
sailed up to Newport, where plantation owners from "Charles
Town" and prosperous merchants from Philadelphia mixed with
Boston traders. It was on such a vacation, in 1773, that Thomas
Mifflin met the Massachusetts Sons of Liberty, plotting resistance at
a gentlemen's resort. Men did not travel about inland for pleasure.
Of Virginia's delegates, only Washington and Jefferson seem to

have gone to Philadelphia before 1774—Washington on royal army business and Jefferson to be inoculated.

We may have difficulty reconstructing a seaboard where the ties between "Charles Town" and Williamsburg, or between Boston and New York, ran all the way over to London and back—but so it was. England had arranged it thus, for her own advantage. All trade must look to the Empire's good, materials coming in, manufactures going out; the spokes meant to deal with each other always through mediation of the hub. Thomas Pownall had been one of the more popular and enlightened governors of Massachusetts, and he defended the rights of colonials when he returned to England; but he warned the central government to be unyielding in its demand for dependence from each colony:

Great Britain . . . must be the center of attraction to which these colonies, in the administration of every power of their government, in the exercise of their judicial powers, in the execution of their laws, and in every operation of their trade, must tend. They will remain under the constant influence of the attraction of this center; and cannot move but that every direction of such movement will converge to the same. And as it is not more necessary to preserve the several governments subordinate in their respective orbs than it is essential to the preservation of the whole empire to keep them disconnected and independent of each other, they must be guarded by this union against having or forming any principle of coherence with each other, above that whereby they cohere to this center, this first mover. They should always remain incapable of any coherence, or of so conspiring amongst themselves, as to create any other equal force which might recoil back on this first mover (*Administration,* 34–35).

Seen in these terms, the imperial strategy was precisely to keep the colonies declaring their independence—of each other.

The colonies needed little encouragement to nurture their separate ways. Culture, knowledge, hardware, religion, politics—all were imported goods. Each province had cultivated its own ties to the high European culture of the eighteenth century. Schooling abroad was the ideal for most wealthy families—except dissenting believers, barred from Oxford and Cambridge. We owe early Yale and Harvard and Princeton to the Thirty-nine Articles. Pinckneys, Lees, DeLanceys were educated in England, Carrolls and Dulanys in France. The closest thing delegates at the First Congress had to "old school ties" was a memory of the Inns of Court—twelve of its twenty-two lawyers had prepared for the bar in London. Doctors throughout the colonies studied at Edinburgh, or learned from compatriots who had. Some intercolonial marriages came from shared European experience, like Dr. Shippen's to Mary Lee. Colonials, meeting in England, sometimes made the grand tour of the Continent together, and formed a distinct circle in Rome.

Even the early revolutionaries came to each others' attention through London sources. Till almost the eve of the Revolution, resistance to imperial policy was better schemed at in London than in the colonies. Writing of the 1760s, H. James Henderson says: "Actually, if a center of communication existed for the proponents of radical existence at the end of the decade, it could be found not in New York where the Stamp Act Congress was held, but in London, where policy was made and colonial protests directed, where colonial agents were located and a community of Americans from the whole continent resided, and where a controversy over constitutional liberties within England already raged. In this sense London supplied what was lacking in the colonies—a location where opposition to innovations in British policy could be given continuous expression by Americans and colonial agents, where intercolonial contacts could be established and sustained both directly and indirectly." Many Americans first took up radical ideas while defending John Wilkes, participating vicariously in his ordeal through their agents, friendly travelers, or the London press. New arrivals to America like Paine and Priestley were instantly welcomed because they had been part of the American "interest" in England's radical circles.

When an artist showed promise, he was sent to Italy and France, like Benjamin West; or followed his patrons to London, like John Singleton Copley. A DeLancey of New York might go to Cambridge, but not to William and Mary—any more than the normal Virginian would go to Harvard. Most intercolonial school experiences arose from religious factionalism—Massachusetts strict observers bypassing Harvard for the "New Light" Yale, Presbyterians leaving their native state for the College of New Jersey. Maryland, without a college of its own, sent on the average two men per year (neither of them Catholic or wealthy) to the University of Pennsylvania in its formative stages. Only rarely—e.g., when James

Madison sought out Dr. Witherspoon at Princeton, on advice of his pastor—did a man go to another province because it offered academic excellence.

Indeed, with the exception of those delegates (from Pennsylvania and its lower counties, or parts of Maryland) for whom Philadelphia was the natural port city, more of those assembling in the early Congresses had been to London than to Philadelphia. None of the Massachusetts men had seen Philadelphia, but Robert Treat Paine in the first delegation, and Hancock in the second, had spent considerable time in England. Dyer from Connecticut had been an agent there. Smith of New Jersey and Lewis of New York had been abroad. All but one of the five South Carolina delegates had been educated in England—like Lee in the Virginia delegation. Peyton Randolph had been his colony's agent in the pistole-fee affair. Carter Braxton and Thomas Nelson had been in London for extended periods. In the later Congresses, returning agents would serve—men like Benjamin Franklin and Arthur Lee. H. James Henderson has noticed the high number of delegates who were in England during the controversy surrounding the Stamp Act. In a sense these men imported the Revolution from its first breeding ground to a secondary location in Philadelphia. Thus, between the two largest cities in the British Empire, London and Philadelphia, Americans knew the more distant one better than the one on their own continent.

Many things set colony apart from colony on their shared "home ground"—among them, religion, a subject intimately bound up with men's politics. Joseph Galloway feared the "congregationalist presbyterian republicans" flooding into his city. Others feared doing business with the Quakers, who would not stand firm where fighting was involved. Samuel Adams, who denounced even a Congregationalist like Thomas Hutchinson as papistical, now sat down to meals with the genuine article in Charles Carroll. New Yorkers, who had barred an Anglican bishop from the Continent, found in Carroll a man working to set up a Roman episcopate here. Edmund Pendleton, who had prosecuted dissenting preachers, was forced to smile at a tough puritan like Roger Sherman, who would not let Silas Deane's carriage travel on the sabbath during their trip from Connecticut. Congregationalists, who thought even Harvard was "deist," sat with graduates from dissolute William and Mary. An unfrocked clergyman (Lyman Hall) ate with the zealous Dr. Witherspoon. Even those from different colonies who shared the cultural tie of one religion had worked out a degree of tolerance or maneuver in their native provinces by entirely local devices. Quakers in Virginia had their favored lawyers and legislators (Patrick Henry among them); those in Pennsylvania knew their allies (like Joseph Galloway) and enemies (like John Dickinson) and how to use both in long struggles with the proprietors—when they needed help, they looked to Friends in London, not in other colonies. In the same way, Presbyterians looked first to the Dissenting Deputies, and only afterward (if at all) toward fellow believers on American ground. John Adams was not much exaggerating when he said men from the different colonies spoke entirely different languages. The American Revolution was not born from a Pentecost of mutual understanding, but from a Babel. That is why one of the best students of America had predicted, in the 1760s, that no force but massive stupidity in England could draw the colonies together. Thomas Pownall wrote:

No one colony can by itself become [independent]—and no two, under the present state of their constitutions, have any possible communion of power or interest that can unite them in such a measure; they have not the means of forming such; they have neither legislative nor executive powers that are extended to more than one; the laws of one extend not to the other; they have no common magistracy, no common ground, in short, no one principle of association amongst them. On the contrary, as I have said elsewhere, the different manner in which they were settled, the different modes under which they live, the different forms of charters, grants, and frame of government which they possess, the various principles of repulsion that these create, the different interests which they actuate, the religious interests by which they are actuated, the rivalship and jealousies which arise from hence, and the impracticability, if not impossibility, of reconciling and accommodating these incomparable ideas and claims, will keep the several provinces and colonies perpetually independent of, and unconnected with, each other and dependent on the mother country (*Administration*, 93–94).

Pownall urged the British to honor the particular charters of each province as an exclusive tie to Westminster, setting each colony off against the other. The colonies could find no common legal ground if they adhered with great loyalty to their charters. That argument seemed to make sense. But in Samuel Adams we find the paradox of a man who, out of love for his charter, destroyed that charter; while in Jefferson—who had a low opinion of colonial charter law, and wanted to sweep away all arrangements after the original "expatriation"—the same mystery works itself out backward: Jefferson would end his life appealing to the Declaration of Independence as America's "great charter," the Magna Carta of a new continent (Hazelton, 155, 200—cf. Ford, 10:131). The colonies, so at odds one with another, could separate from England only by imitating her, pretending (on rather exiguous grounds) to re-enact the history of her liberties derived from charter.

FOUR

"...right of the people to alter..."

> REVOLUTION: Change in the state of a government or
> country. It is used among us κατ' ἐξοχήν, for the change
> produced by the admission of King William and Queen
> Mary.
>
> —Johnson's Dictionary

At the first Continental Congress, everyone realized that alliance
could only be ventured if exits were kept open at every turn. Most
colonies meant to preserve as long as possible the option of renewed good relations with London. It was a congress very interested
in egress. That explains its prolonged eighteenth-century punctilio,
which can surprise a modern reader. Long after British and colonial
troops were fighting each other, the forms of loyal petition to the
mother country were maintained. These delegates were soon provi-
sioning an army, seizing forts, and besieging camps, while they kept
up humble address to the King as loyal subjects. There were several
reasons, legal and political, for observing these forms—not the least,
to keep each colony separable from the rest, in case the allied
stranger at hand became more menacing than the familiar but distant enemy. Delegates saw or suspected wild things going on in
other colonies—near at hand, they would witness a coup in the very
province where they sat.

Besides, each colony had reason to fear a strong reaction within
its own borders. The size of the loyalist and apathetic camps was
the more fearful for being interdeterminable. And we must not be
anachronistic in posing the loyalist problem. These were not men
choosing (or quietly preferring) England over America. They did
not think of the former as separate from themselves, or of the latter
as including themselves. They were choosing their own "country,"
with its traditional ties to London, over a set of new ties with an

unmanageable collection of foreigners. In Maryland, a Dulany did not choose London over Baltimore, but Baltimore-cum-London over Boston, New York, and Philadelphia. The continental "traitors" were yesterday's local patriots; they did not reject their own colony—just the twelve other ones.

Until very late in the game—more than a year after fighting had begun—it was possible for a New York, or Maryland, or Pennsylvania to withdraw from its fellow consultors, to say quite truthfully that it had been out of sympathy with many things done by the Congress, and to put down native radicals in favor of loyalists who still held respectable positions around (even in) the Congress as well as on home committees. The sessions in Philadelphia, as meetings of an informal committee, were secret. The only things delegates' names had appeared on up to August 2, 1776, were petitions, protests, and explanations of their acts in terms of continued allegiance. Even the dangerous resolution of May 10, 1776, recommending that each colony set up governmental structures of its own, could be endorsed as a way of maintaining separation from *each other* as much as from the King. This fact did not elude John Adams, who was running everywhere, at his cousin's direction, trying to seal up avenues of colonial escape from the defense of Boston. That is why he added the compromising preamble that passed narrowly on May 15. Even here there was a loophole for single colonies, which could argue that the preamble was a committee addendum to the resolution, not a considered opinion of the deliberating body. In fact, heated opposition to the preamble showed it was *not* a necessary corollary of the motion, which had passed unanimously.

Only after three years of each others' exasperating company, and after drastically increased signs of intransigence in London, and even then by a narrow margin, did most (not all) colonies and most (not all) delegates agree, on July 2, 1776, to seal off the channels of withdrawal they had maintained. This careful regard for legal forms may seem unconvincing if we think of it as the *joint* body's hope for reconciliation with the King. But it allowed the participants to take out thirteen separate insurance policies for negotiated restoration of royal government—perhaps, if the King should be in need of help against other colonies, a restoration that would win all the first points of protest. After all, separate colonies had opposed trade laws, and even engaged King's troops, in the past; yet they had been restored to favor, one by one. For a long time the safest course would remain one, not of union, but of keeping to themselves.

In retrospect, even startling changes acquire an air of inevitability. We wonder how the colonists could walk so far down this path and hope to retrace their steps. Yet the evidence is clear that many did have this hope. Down to the last debates in June of 1776, men like John Dickinson and James Duane, or Edward Rutledge and John Jay, held out the promise (to themselves and others) that relations could be both restored *and* improved. And these were the very men with close ties to London, who should have known best what the prospects were. How could men in the company of admitted *revolutionaries* claim they had remained so loyal as to be not only welcomed back but rewarded?

There was no "overturn" of a central government in the American Revolution, no decapitated king in Paris, no basement execution of a czar. George III ruled for another four decades, and Lord North's career continued despite his voluntary resignation. But Americans were willing to call their action a revolution precisely *because* it was an orderly and legal procedure. The first English meaning of "revolution" had been astronomical—the revolving of the heavens, an exchange of planetary positions; or the "period" (which is simply "revolution" in Greek) covered by such alterations. Hooker used "the Christian revolution" to mean the Christian *era* (*Ecclesiastical Polity*, v, 70, ix). The accepted word for violent withdrawal from allegiance was "revolt," not revolution. Revolt was synonymous with rebellion. The English Bible spoke of a people's "revolting and rebellious heart" (Jeremiah 5:23), and Milton wrote:

> Arm'd with thy might, rid heav'n of these rebell'd . . .
> That from thy just obedience could revolt.
> —*Paradise Lost*, vi, 737, 740.*

In 1775, John Adams expressly denied that the Continental Congress was engaged in rebellion, since "the people of this conti-

* For the connection of "revolt" with the fall of man, see Shakespeare *Henry V* 2, ii, 141–42—and 2 *Henry IV* 4, v, 65–66, *Troilus* 5, ii, 141–42, *Cymbeline* 1, vi, 111–12, *Merry Wives* 3, ii, 39.

nent have the utmost abhorrence of treason and rebellion"
(*Novanglus*, 32).

But in that same work Adams constantly appeals to "the principles of the Revolution" to justify American acts as nontreasonable
(55, and 16, 17, 33, 35, 65, 114). He means, of course, the Glorious
Revolution of 1688—the English Parliament's own proudest boast.
By that act, one king was replaced with another (as bodies change
position in celestial revolutions). So affected is Adams by this usage
that he can use "revolution" to mean *only* a change in the order of
royal inheritance (*Novanglus*, 175); but more often he means the
right of representative bodies to decide the legitimacy of executive
acts. In either case, the model is *the* Revolution, which even a tory
like Johnson called revolution "in its highest sense" (κατ' ἐξοχήν).
The Chambers Cyclopaedia (1741) had this separate entry: "The
REVOLUTION, used by way of eminence, denotes the great *turn*
of affairs in England in 1688. . . ." (Italics added.) It was easy for
the British to use this word for the installation of William and
Mary, since a nice regard for etymology had led them to apply the
term to the Restoration of Charles II—the revolving of the Stuarts
back into power (OED, s.v. #8a). But after 1689, the term was
used so regularly of the Glorious Revolution that a new word was
invented to describe those who took part in that act—"Revolutioners."

Revolution was such a respectable term in eighteenth-century
English that Edmund Burke tried to save it from French capture.
In his *Reflections,* he regretted that "zeal toward the Revolution"
had misled some Englishmen into sympathy with the Jacobins. He
reminded them that "the Revolution was made to preserve our ancient indisputable laws and liberties." True revolution is a constitutional development—the extraordinary act that is needed to
maintain the flow of ordinary ones: "This is the spirit of our
constitution, not only in its settled course, but in all its revolutions."
As the 1741 Cyclopaedia said, "There are no states in the world but
have undergone frequent revolutions." But six years after the *Reflections*, in his *Regicide Peace,* Burke had to concede the term to
French innovators; and since then revolution and revolt have
changed places in the "revolutions" of our vocabulary, revolution becoming the more drastic word for rejection of authority.

In colonial America, however, the word was still a glorious one with law-abiding men. Of the 1764 petition to the King, asking that Pennsylvania be made a royal, instead of a proprietary, colony, so conservative a gentleman as Joseph Galloway could say that "nothing would save [us] but a revolution" (Speech on the Petition, May 24, 1764). Another Pennsylvanian, Joseph Reed, wrote in the next decade, "All the principles of the Revolution show that there are certain cases wherein resistance is justifiable." To speak to the King of revolution was not a form of threat but of appeal, since the Hanoverians' own legitimacy was established by the Revolution. Thus Adams speaks of "the Revolution and the present Establishment" to describe the British Government of Protestant succession (*Novanglus*, 16, 17). And Charles James Fox, in his Address to the People of England (1788), reminds the heir of his "having been bred in those principles which had placed his illustrious House on the throne." "Junius," of course, could twist the appeal back into a threat, as when he concluded his famous Letter 35 by urging King George to "remember that, as it [the crown] was acquired by one Revolution, it may be lost by another."

Americans had undergone their own smaller revolutions while adjusting to the expulsion of James in 1688. The Dominion of New England was dissolved, and Governor Andros imprisoned, while a committee of safety governed Massachusetts. In New York Jacob Leisler seized power, and in Maryland John Coode. For all the colonies, the change in home government involved, like the Commonwealth and the Restoration, a renewal or redrafting of charters or other administrative links. That is why Adams wrote "It ought to be remembered that there was a Revolution here, as well as in England, and that we, as well as the people of England, made an original express contract with King William" (*Novanglus*, 114). America's appeal to the Revolution was to something it had experienced along with the English Parliament. Even an opponent of American developments compared conditions after the 1770 Massacre with those "at the time of the Revolution" (Bailyn, *Ordeal*, 162). But men like Adams argued that the home Parliament had not extended all the fruits of the Revolution to its partners in that experience. Revolution was not a new thing for such men, but an old thing left for too long uncompleted.

The members of the Continental Congress felt a special affinity with seventeenth-century Revolutioners since their actions, too,

were inspired by fear of despotic Roman Catholic regimes. The exclusion controversy of the 1680s (the real occasion for Locke's work
on government) had centered on the denial of a Catholic heir's
right to the throne. The Revolution ousted a Catholic incumbent
from that throne. Now Americans feared the spread of Catholic
religion and French law, as authorized by the Quebec Act. Richard
Henry Lee called this "the worst grievance" (Burnett, 78), and it
was mentioned prominently in official petitions and declarations of
the Congress (*Respect*, 11, 29, 44, 56, 76, 79, 92, 102). The continuity between the two Revolutions was so easily assumed that
Congress, from the outset, called its own statement of principle "A
Bill of Rights"—modeled after Parliament's 1689 document. (Parti-
sans of John Wilkes had advanced his cause, in 1769, by founding
the Society of the Supporters of the Bill of Rights.)

Americans set about making their Revolution much as the British
had—by the petition process. In the fifteenth and sixteenth cen-
turies, proposed bills submitted by Parliament for the King's
ratification were called petitions to the King. After Parliament's legislative role became more thoroughly established, the petition was
used to clarify constitutional relationships. Such was, for instance,
the 1628 Petition of Right, spelling out "the rights and liberties of
the people" in the struggle with Charles I. Again, in the exclusion
crisis, a group thereafter known as *the* Petitioners *par excellence*
sent an Address to Charles II with the petition that he reconvene
the Parliament (1681). Petitions were the recognized way of
addressing or defining what the seventeenth- and eighteenth-century Englishmen called "fundamental law." Even during Cromwell's protectorate, "constitutional" matters were settled by the
amended Humble Petition and Advice of 1657.

Of course the American Congress did not speak as a legislative
body (though neither did the Petitioners of 1681). But even private
citizens had the right of petition, which Adams called a basic right
in British law (*Novanglus*, 60) and part of the machinery of consent (ibid., 139) in governments that rule by the freemen's will.
Blackstone wrote in his 1765 *Commentaries* (1:143) that "the right
of petitioning the king, or either house of parliament, for the
redress of grievances" is "appertaining to every individual." The
antiquity of the formulaic connection between *petition* and *redress*

and *grievance* is such that Shakespeare can play variations on the cluster as a familiar reference point.*

Recourse to petition was the proper response to "such public oppressions as tend to dissolve the constitution and subvert the fundamentals of government" (Blackstone, 1:244). This is true even—indeed especially—when "the positive laws are silent" (ibid., 1:245); a point demonstrated for all time by the Revolution, when "King James II invaded the fundamental constitution of the realm":

> And so far as this precedent leads, and no farther, we may now be allowed to lay down the law of redress against public oppression. If therefore any future prince should endeavor to subvert the constitution by breaking the original contract between king and people, should violate the fundamental laws, and should withdraw himself out of the kingdom —we are now authorized to declare that this conjunction of circumstances would amount to an abdication and the throne would be thereby vacant (ibid.)

For almost three years, by petitioning the King, the American Congress attested that it did not believe the throne vacated. But Adams and others did claim that the Townshend duties raised points not of statute or positive law, but of the constitution itself, a matter for settlement outside the normal court procedures: "It was an attack upon a fundamental principle of the constitution, and upon that supposition was resisted, after multitudes of petitions to no purpose, and because there was no tribunal in the constitution from whence redress could have been obtained" (*Novanglus*, 88).

It is often asserted, in modern treatments of the Revolution, that all gatherings after the dissolution of any provincial legislature were illegal. If so, then the Congress was itself illegal, since most of its delegates had been chosen by such informal committees. That would reduce to absurdity the two petitions addressed to the King by Congress—how can men profess devotion to the law while openly defying it? We know that the protestations of loyalty were

---

* See for instance *Lucrece*, 1603, *Julius Caesar* 1, iii, 118; 2, i, 56–58; 3, i, 31–32; 2 *Henry IV* 4, i, 167–68; 4, ii, 36, 59, 66, 113–14. The last scene referred to contrasts what the people in arms did as petitioners (i.e., legally) and what they did as rebels (lines 116–17). This accords with Blackstone's warning: "Care only must be taken lest, under the pretence of petitioning, the subject be guilty of any riot or tumult" (1:143).

sincere in men like Joseph Galloway, who remained loyal to the
King after 1776; and there is no reason to doubt the original sincerity of most, if not all, those who later severed their ties to England.
Jefferson himself wrote, at the time of the *second* Congress, that he
"would rather be in dependance on Great Britain, properly limited,
than on any nation upon earth, or than on no nation" (*Papers*,
1:242). With even the "radicals" protesting their loyalty, what
could basically conservative men like Dickinson and Jay hope for in
a patently illegal venture? All the delegates signed the petitions
and declarations of Congress—in fact, Dickinson wrote most of
them. The Congress established the legal basis for its own existence
in its 1774 Bill of Rights:

> *Resolved*, N.C.D. [*nemine contradicente*] 8. That they have a right
> peaceably to assemble, consider of their grievances, and petition the
> King; and that all prosecutions, prohibitory proclamations, and commit-
> ments for the same, are illegal.

It is clear that these men did not *think* they were breaking the law.
Among other things, the votes of Washington and Pendleton give
us assurance on this point.

The committees that chose the delegates to Congress, in provinces where the assembly was dissolved, were not illegal sessions of
the legislature. Jefferson describes how the dissolved Burgesses met
at Raleigh tavern and "formed ourselves into a Meeting," an exercise of peaceable assembly, in which the men did not act as a legislature. Instead, they appointed a committee of correspondence to
help call another kind of meeting (con-gress) "to deliberate on
their common interests." They also proposed a "convention" to receive the letters elicited by the committee of correspondence
(*Papers*, 1:670). This latter convention, when it gathered, also
specified that it was not acting as the House of Burgesses: "Thinking that the people could not be legally represented under the ancient constitution, which had been subverted by the king, lords,
and commons, they unanimously dissolved themselves" as a legislature (Virginia *Gazette*, May 6, 1776). The assemblies that led to the
Congress were, variously, committees of correspondence, committees of safety, or committees for petition of redress (which latter
the Continental Congress itself became). For all these kinds of
spontaneous meetings, there was ample precedent. A committee of

safety had ruled the Massachusetts Bay Colony at the break-up of
the Dominion during the Glorious Revolution—and King William's
government dealt with it as legitimate. Such committees had also
been formed to deal with Indian threats or war necessities. The
committees of correspondence, violently attacked by American
tories (*Novanglus*, 94–95), were modeled on committees long established to deal with colonial agents when assemblies were not in
session. It was the conservative John Dickinson who denied the
Massachusetts governor's authority to disband such committees—
and he based his argument on the right, "deemed innocent even in
slaves, of agreeing in *petitions* [italics in original] for redress of
grievances" (*Respect*, 43).

As early as 1768, Richard Henry Lee had criticized the billeting
act in New York and proposed raising a constitutional question
about this sister colony's treatment:

> To obtain redress, sir, on these points, and to inform posterity what
> were our sentiments on them, it seems indispensibly necessary that a du-
> tiful, decent, but firm address should be presented to his majesty by the
> Assembly, requesting his royal interposition for the repeal of these acts.
> This method, you know, my friend, is constitutional. The subject, when
> aggrieved, has a right to appeal to the sovereign for redress (*Letters*,
> 27).

Obviously he would not consider this right abrogated by dissolution of the legislature. Men could peaceably assemble as private citizens for making petition when aggrieved in their own persons. On
the constitutionality of such provincial committees Dickinson
grounded the actions of the first Congress. He opens the Memorial
to the Inhabitants of the Colonies this way: "We, the delegates appointed by the good people of the above colonies to meet at Philadelphia . . ." (*Respect*, 35).

It is too often forgotten that the entire *raison d'être* of the
Congress, assembled in Philadelphia, was to petition for redress. No
more striking proof could be given for this than the instruction
Jefferson submitted beforehand for the Virginia delegation's consideration. Jefferson assumes, even in this "radical" document, that the
whole business of the Congress is to petition, and instructs delegates only on the form of that plea—"that an humble and dutiful
address be presented to his majesty begging leave to lay before him

as chief magistrate of the British empire the united complaints of his majesty's subjects in America. . . ." (*Papers*, 121). He concludes his suggested petition with a hope that the King "will be pleased to interpose with that efficacy which your earnest endeavors may insure to procure redress of these our great grievances" (ibid., 135). Almost three decades later, such phrases would be twisted from their legal setting to charge Jefferson with toadying to King George (ibid., 669). Actually his "instruction" was too harsh to be adopted by the Virginia delegation. The point here is that even so direct a challenge had to be placed within the legal context of a petition for redress.

The aim of the Congress was spelled out in the commissions to the various delegates—those instructions presented as credentials to the secretary and reproduced in the journals. Delaware sent its delegates to confer with the men from other colonies "for the redress of our general grievances" (*Journals*, 1:22). Virginia sent its "to procure redress" (ibid., 23), South Carolina to obtain "a redress of those grievances" (24), Pennsylvania to take part in the "general congress now sitting . . . on American grievances" (74).

Some modern writers describe the first petition to the King as an afterthought to the embargo set up by the Association, or the second petition as an intrusion on the effort to vote independence. This misconception is admittedly fostered by some of the participants' later recollections, and even by the original timetable. The Congress first assembled September 5, 1774, and issued its embargo decree on October 20, one day before it considered even a first *draft* of the Petition to the King. It finally agreed on that Petition only after passing five public documents and printing three of them. (The other two would be published before the Petition was "leaked" to an English publisher.) There is a natural inclination, then, to think that the real business of the Congress was the Association, a practical step taken to counter the Coercive Acts with commercial pressure; and to consider the Petition, sent off in the final days of the Congress, as a rationalization of, or protective cover for, that "real" business.

Yet we cannot have it both ways. We find, even three summers later, the movement for independence in heavy trouble, treated by some delegates as an aberration. We must fight off our knowledge of the goal to which in fact men's efforts were tending, if we are to judge their own hopes and fears as they made those efforts. The men in Philadelphia were feeling each other out as they addressed their formal business. It was their very care to make the Petition solid and well-grounded that delayed its composition.

The principal committee of the Congress—which came to be known as the Grand Committee and contained at least two representatives from each province—was established "for stating rights, grievances, and means of redress" (Burnett, 20). This is the order of a petitionary action. Before a petition can be drawn up, two prior steps are necessary. The colonies, each with different histories of conflict with the mother country, had to settle on a list of their *joint* grievances. This was not an easy task, because "grievance" had a technical meaning for the purpose of petition. It meant the denial of a constitutional right. Adams glosses the word as "a violation of an essential British right" (*Novanglus*, 129). It was therefore distinguished, on the one hand, from an offense against positive law, for which redress must be sought in the proper court; and, on the other, from irritations or generally unjust treatment that did not reach to a constitutional issue.

Typical of such *constitutional* rights would be that to free trial, to representation before taxation or military exaction, to observance of charters, and to separation of governmental branches. The List of Grievances finally agreed on by the 1774 Congress contains six heads and cites thirteen specific British acts passed in Congress; but all of them are reducible to one or other of these constitutional rights. Historians have noticed that many other matters were proposed for this List and rejected. Some explain this as an attempt by the delegates to preserve harmony: They adopted only the most *obvious* complaints. But the delegates pruned their list for legal reasons as well as political ones. None but constitutional infringements could be listed in a petition. Other things would not be grievances in the strict sense. A sensitivity on this point is registered in the debates over the Quebec Act. How could the American colonists speak for other people, with a different constitutional connection to England? A grievance had to be an infringement on the rights of the men seeking redress, a cause of complaint within their governmental system. So James Duane of New York argued: "Will it not be said that we go beyond our sphere and, while we contend for an exclusive internal legislature, intermeddle with the police of other governments?" (Burnett, 78).

The solution found for this problem was to cite the Quebec Act as posing an immediate peril to the very colonies that helped bring Quebec within the Empire—"to the great danger, from so total a dissimularity of religion, law, and government, to the neighboring British colonies, by the assistance of whose blood and treasure the said country was conquered from France" (*Respect*, 56). The argument was tortuous: Using the resources of the colonies to institute a foreign set of laws upon their borders amounted to military and tax exactions without proper representation of the taxed people's interests. The stress on colonial "treasure" used to gain Quebec derives from the same legal viewpoint that made the Congress insist that American colonies were established without expense to the mother country (*Respect*, 41, 91, 141).

The tortured nature of the argument used on the Quebec Act shows how even the most resented measure had to be cast in terms of a constitutional issue before it could be put in the list of grievances. Most colonials probably feared the long-term consequences of the Quebec Act even more than the Townshend duties or the Coercive Acts. And fear of Catholicism made for continuity between the American and the Parliamentary Revolutions. Yet only after long debate was a way found to include the Quebec Act in the congressional List.

The constitutional test for grievances meant that, even before drawing up the list, delegates had to agree on a statement of basic rights. How were they to decide that a right had been violated if they could not draw up a bill of rights that would apply to *all* the colonies, whatever their separate charter histories? This opened up the most basic kinds of question. Should the delegates rest their argument on natural rights, on English law, on their charters, or on all three? If they tried to distinguish between the three, would they not be admitting that these had *not* accorded in the past? The solution was to rest the Bill of Rights on all three sources: "The inhabitants of the English colonies in North-America, by the immutable laws of nature, the principles of the English constitution, and the several charters or compacts, have the following rights . . ." (*Respect*, 53). The Congress had already endorsed the Suffolk Resolves, dedicated to "the unalienable and inestimable inheritance, which we derived from nature, the constitution of Britain, and the privileges warranted to us in the charter of the province" (ibid., 1:32–33).

It is no wonder, then, that the Petition to the King had to wait on debate over rights and grievances. As late as October 18, the full list of grievances had not been agreed to (cf. James H. Hutson's notes to the Bill of Rights, *Respect*, 50–52). So, far from being an afterthought of the first Congress, cobbled up during the last days of its session, the Petition was the end product aimed at in the Bill of Rights and List of Grievances. Only on them as a foundation could the Petition be solidly grounded.

One might object to this interpretation of the Congress's work that the Association was announced before the first draft of the Petition was even submitted. Why state that trade is being withheld until grievances are redressed when one has not even submitted those grievances in a formal way? There are two answers to this objection, one legal and one practical.

In legal terms, the petitioning process normally began with noncompliance. This was the sign that a right was being asserted. Since "grievance" often meant an irregular tax-exaction (cf. Shakespeare, *Henry VIII* 1, ii, 20, 56, 104), nonpayment of an unjustified tax was the first step in the challenge that barons or legislatures had presented to kings. Congress was well aware of this practice, whi i was included in the preliminary list of rights mailed to the inhabitants of Quebec. John Dickinson, of the conservative wing in Congress, wrote: "If money is wanted by rulers who have in any manner oppressed the people, they may retain it, until their grievances are redressed; and thus peaceably procure relief, without trusting to despised [i.e., disregarded] petitions, or disturbing the public tranquillity" (*Respect*, 62–63). Dickinson refers to earlier petitions sent by individual provinces, without implying that the *joint* Congress would neglect the petitioning process that worked for the Stamp Act Congress.

Later, in its reply to Lord North, the Congress would take the same position (this time as worded by Thomas Jefferson), asserting:

That the colonies of America are entitled to the sole and exclusive privilege of giving and granting their own money; that this involves a right of deliberating whether they will make gift, for what purposes it shall be made, and what shall be it's amount; and that it is a high [i.e., constitutional] breach of this privilege for any body of men, extraneous to their constitutions, to prescribe the purposes for which money shall be levied on them, to take to themselves the authority of judging of their conditions, circumstances and situations; and of determining the amount of the contribution to be levied. (*Respect*, 119).

The justification for the Association is contained in that passage. It was not feasible to refuse duties on stuff actually going through the King's customs; so the only way to avoid payment of this tax was to stop the passage of such stuff to or from the American continent. It should be remembered that the colonies had twice before used this means of protest, and met with success—in the boycotts that followed on the Stamp Act and the Townshend Acts. Although English response had not formally recognized the legality of the means employed, the grievances in both cases were redressed, and there was no retaliation for the boycotting. In the eighteenth-century atmosphere of seizing commercial rights-by-usage, the colonists had set precedents they could appeal to.

In practical terms, the Congress had to cope with the prior appeal of Massachusetts for a continent-wide embargo, and the action of various counties, towns, and provincial committees undertaking voluntary restrictions. (Jefferson had drawn up the nonimportation resolution for Albemarle County and a draft for the provincial ban —*Papers*, 1:117–20). Unless Congress took immediate steps to co-ordinate these efforts, and to adjudicate local exceptions, the embargo effort would collapse, leaving Congress no means to put pressure on London merchants (as the Stamp Act Congress had). Besides, certain colonies argued over the starting date for various provisions (Virginia urging delay of nonexportation until the 1774 tobacco crop could be sold) or the range of trade exclusions (South Carolina arguing for sale of rice and indigo to Europe but not to England). The Congress was a forum for compromising these differences and for setting up a co-ordinated schedule of nonimportation (in 1774) and nonexportation (in 1775). This not only improved the embargo's chances for success, but gave a better legal basis for it. The announcement of the embargo ahead of time put the English on notice that noncompliance and petitioning had begun; but nonimportation would not go into effect until December (when the Congress expected the Petition to be placed before the

King) and nonexportation would not take place at all if the grievances were redressed by September 10, 1775 (*Respect,* 12–13).

In scheduling and completing its very complex business, the first
Congress showed a clear grasp of its legal and practical tasks, and
great skill in reconciling the two. For this, John Dickinson deserves
a degree of credit that would be obscured by later attacks on him
from congressional "radicals." Congress signed Dickinson's documents, despite the competing interests and cultures of its delegates,
because everyone agreed on the nature and legitimacy of the petitioning process. There was never any internal challenge to that. Nor
would Dickinson and the Adamses disagree on the nature and
justification of constitutional Revolution. The Congress sailed into
its conflict with England, securely guided by English stars.

The order of Revolution, enacted in the public documents of the
first Congress, established a structure for the Declaration that announced independence as the final response to unredressed grievances. The first Petition had relied, of necessity, on two prior steps
—the formulating of a Bill of Rights and a List of Grievances—and
it was backed by a mutual pledge (the Association for the embargo). The Declaration concludes with a mutual pledge to support
the step of independence; but that is preceded by a preamble stating the rights at issue, and a list of grievances infringing those
rights.

The Committee of the Whole made only six slight changes in
Jefferson's preamble. It must have read this as a more general description of those rights enumerated in the 1774 Bill of Rights. That
Bill spoke of "*indubitable* rights," just as Jefferson based his unalienable rights on *self-evident* truths. The Bill opened its list with
"life, liberty, and property," and then listed more specific rights
under ten heads. By inserting "certain" in the Declaration before
Jefferson's "inalienable rights," the Congress further emphasized
(what "among these" already said) that Jefferson's short list was
offered *exempli gratia,* and stood for the longer one already agreed
to by Congress.

The list of grievances is the longest part of the Declaration, and
it underwent the most changes from Congress—twenty-four (Boyd,
Evolution, 32–33). The most intense debate no doubt centered on
this section, since it was at the heart of the petitioning process that
had led, by way of unredressed grievances, to the great step of independence. Men had argued these matters in their own prov-

inces, drawn up lists of grievances, pared them down and rephrased them, giving them apter legal form. When Jefferson said he articulated an American mind in the Declaration, he was probably referring to this much-disputed list, rather than to the preamble (on which later generations would fix their attention). The question of basic rights, obscure to their descendants, seemed clear to men like John Dickinson, who felt themselves the heirs of the Revolution, of the glory derived from 1688. Americans of the 1770s felt they were approaching a "centennial" of their own, reliving memories of the English Bill of Rights. The points of conflict were not, in their eyes, doctrinal—they assumed their English mentors could read Blackstone as well as they did. The differences arose over application of "fundamental law" to particular acts, listed one by one, as part of a system at odds with the whole ethos of the British constitution.

The original petitioners of Congress expressed their resolution in a mutual pledge: "And we do solemnly bind ourselves and our constituents, under the ties aforesaid, to adhere to this association. . . ." Those ties were to bind until rights were redressed. The Declaration of 1776 signaled the end of further hopes for redress, and led to a new pledge of the "united states" to support each other in the final course of jointly declared independences: "And for the support of this declaration . . . we mutually pledge to each other our lives, our fortunes & our sacred honour."

The Declaration of 1776 signaled the failure of the petitions of 1774 and 1775 in terms that declared the continuity of the three documents. The Congress declared its independence in terms not basically at odds with its "dutiful petitions"—in fact, as a logical culmination of them. The same thing had happened before, Americans claimed—in 1688. Jefferson, the Declaration's author, had already described in his 1774 *Summary View* "the establishment . . . of the British constitution at the glorious Revolution on it's free and antient principles" (*Papers*, 1:131). The delegates to Congress began this most serious venture looking resolutely backward, claiming better memories than the English maintained for what *the* Revolution was all about. And some inheritors of that Revolution agreed with them: Charles James Fox said, "The Americans have done no more than the English did against James II" (Hazelton, 237).

FIVE

". . . assemblage of horrors . . ."

> In taking a general review of the charges brought
> against his Majesty, and his Parliament, we may ob-
> serve that there is a studied confusion in the arrange-
> ment of them. It may therefore be worthwhile to reduce
> them to the several distinct heads, under which I
> should have classed them at the first, had not the order
> of the answer been necessarily prescribed by the order—
> or, rather, the disorder—of the Declaration.
>
> —John Lind, 1776

The Declaration of Independence announced the failure of reform
by petition. Even to conclude the petitioning process, Congress had
to restate the grievances for which redress had been sought through
constitutional channels. Thus the attention of Congress was focused
on the listed grievances in Jefferson's draft, and rightly so. Only two
major answers to the Declaration were published on the English
side, and the bulk of both was given over to the list of grievances.
All points of law and fact turned on these assertions. Thomas Hutchinson, the ousted governor of Massachusetts, wrote a thirty-page
pamphlet, his *Letter to a Noble Lord*, meant for the King's eyes.
Nineteen pages deal with the grievances, and only four address the
preamble to the Declaration.

John Lind, a pamphleteer for the North administration, had written an answer to the 1774 petition of Congress, rejecting its claim
that the colonies had any grievance in the proper sense. In 1776, he
repeated his major points in *An Answer to the Declaration of the
American Congress*. He spent 110 of his 129 pages considering the
claimed grievances, first one by one (pp. 13–117), then by legal categories of his own devising (pp. 123–30). Only four pages (119–22)
discuss the preamble. Lind obviously thought this the proper divi-

sion of his labors: "Of the preamble I have taken little or no notice. The truth is, little or none does it deserve" (119).

It is not surprising that the grievances, felt to be actual in America, rejected as feigned in England, absorbed men's attention at the outset. After all, the preamble merely states the "self-evident" norms against which the justice of the various grievances must be tested; and the list of putative wrongs took up the bulk of Jefferson's document, even before Congress cut away some material. Yet almost all later treatments have reversed the proportions observed in the two first books on the Declaration. The preamble is quoted and discussed at length, the grievances rarely examined. Even the few extended discussions in this century—Herbert Friedenwald's in 1904, Sydney Fisher's in 1907, and Edward Dumbauld's in 1950—add little but pro-American bias to Lind's full discussion of the list.

The only grievance that has received great attention in recent years is one that could not be directly treated by Hutchinson or Lind, since it did not appear in the list as Congress issued it. This is the famous attack on slavery, the longest of the grievances, written with a rhetoric some have called inflated and some think expressive of deep feeling. Indeed, the exclusion of this grievance is enough, in the eyes of many, to justify Jefferson's reported anguish at changes made in his draft. They feel that this single omission explains his effort to keep the original draft before men's eyes, despite the official document's expanding authority.

But there are serious reasons for doubting this view of the matter. I shall mention three minor ones now, and come to two major ones later. First, if the important contrast between Jefferson's Declaration and that of the Congress was restricted to this passage, Jefferson could simply have sent the slavery grievance around to his friends and stressed that in his later notes and *Autobiography*. Instead, he copied out the whole Declaration for at least five friends, right after the congressional document was passed, and invented a scheme of underlinings and marginal insertions to present visually the contrast between the whole of each document in his later notes and autobiography. In chapter Twenty-three I shall discuss his reasons for this course of action more fully; but here, at the very least, it makes unlikely the claim that he regretted only, or even principally, the exclusion of the grievance based on slavery.

Second, Jefferson was unlikely to fret at the withholding of this item when he himself suspended publication of his *Notes on the State of Virginia* because its manumission plan might offend his "countrymen" in Virginia.

Third, he must have known that the motives for Virginia's attempt to slow the slave trade were questionable, and were bound to be seized on for satire by critics of the paper. We must look at the exact terms of his introduction to this long grievance:

He [the King] has waged cruel war against human nature itself, violating it's most sacred rights of life and liberty in the persons of a distant people who never offended him, captivating & carrying them into slavery in another hemisphere or to incur miserable death in their transportation thither. This piratical warfare, the opprobrium of *infidel* powers, is the warfare of the *Christian* king of Great Britain. Determined to keep open a market where *Men* should be bought & sold, he has prostituted his negative for suppressing every legislative attempt to prohibit or to restrain this execrable commerce (*Papers,* 1:318).

The "prostitution" of the King's negative refers to the repeated vetoing of Virginia's attempts to slow the slave trade with a colonial tariff. These efforts, begun with the century, led to bill after bill, all of them defeated (E. Donnan, *Documents,* 1969 ed., 4:66, 91–93, 112, 127–42, 153–58). The aims of the tariff were to limit the volatile slave population, equalize the balance of trade, sustain the price of slaves already arrived, and create revenue. It is true that by 1772 the colonists were also alleging humanitarian motives (ibid., 154); but one of the most outspoken members in this vein was Richard Henry Lee—and he was simultaneously negotiating for slave consignments himself (Chitwood's *R. H. Lee,* 1967, p. 20). The tariff schemes all failed. They were up against powerful counterpressures. The poorer landowners in Virginia would like to keep an open market; the British administration did not want to grant colonies the right to impose their own tariffs against the empire's trade; and the rice colonies were still understocked with slaves and petitioning the King to keep the trade open. Jefferson's own notes admit to this pressure *from the colonies* even while regretting that the King forced slaves upon America: "The clause too, reprobating the enslaving the inhabitants of Africa, was struck out in complaisance to South Carolina & Georgia, who had never attempted to restrain the importation of slaves, and who on the contrary still wished to continue it" (*Papers*, 1:314). Jefferson admits, in effect, that his claim was false—that colonies were still calling for the trade he represented as forced upon them against their will.

It has been remarked from 1776 on that Jefferson put the Congress on weak ground when he reproached the King for depriving slaves of their "rights of life and liberty" without showing any sign that those rights would be restored once the King's power was cast off. But these reasons pale beside two others still to be examined. For I have only quoted the long rhetorical "wind-up" to the grievance as Jefferson composed it. The actual "pitch" puts the grievance in such a compromised light that the wonder is not how Congress could reject it, but how Jefferson ever thought he could get it past that body of sharp-eyed lawyers.

To understand the real point of the slave-trade grievance, we must see where it stands in the Declaration's list of constitutional aberrations. Despite John Lind's polemical dismissal of the list as shapeless, it has a logical order, one that relies on former claims and then goes beyond them. It is often said that the earlier petitions of Congress, and even Jefferson's own *Summary View*, attacked the Parliament, while the Declaration changed emphasis and centered on the King's own faults. This is not a just representation of the Declaration's strategy, even if we look only to the paper as Congress passed it (as opposed to Jefferson's draft—which, as we shall see, gives even greater attention to a *third party* in the dispute). In earlier petitions, the legislative wrongs were stressed, the King's offenses only alluded to by implication, because the King was being asked to interpose his authority between Parliament and the colonies, righting a constitutional encroachment. But even in those earlier pleas, some of the grievances were based on acts of the ministry (presumed to be exercising the King's authority). In the Declaration, Congress recognizes that the King has not redressed earlier grievances and makes his refusal to do so the crowning and final reason for separation. Jefferson's list is made up of four distinct parts, three of which draw on earlier lists of grievances.

1) The first twelve counts refer to executive enactments. These are modeled on three other documents—Jefferson's own list of grievances which became the preamble to the Virginia constitution, composed shortly before his draft of the Declaration (*Papers*,

1:338–39); his *Summary View,* offered as a list of grievances for the first Congress (ibid., 121–35); and the actual grievances mentioned in that first Congress's petition to the King (*Respect,* 75–76). To correlate these four documents, I put each count from Jefferson's Virginia draft in parentheses after the listed counts of the Declaration. The items from the petition are also given by number (preceded by P), since they are easily distinguished as separate counts; but the *Summary View* lists grievances discursively, not by number, and page numbers after SV are the only easy mode of reference:

Declaration Counts:

1	(1) Disallowance	SV129–30	
2	(2) Suspension	SV130	
3	(3) Extending representation		
4	Moving assemblies		
5	(4) Dissolving assemblies	SV130	P10
6	(5) No elections	SV130–31	P[7][9]*
7	(6) Naturalization restrictions		
8	Courts not held		P5
9	Judicial salaries		P6
10	Excise officers		P4
11	(7) Standing armies		P1
12	(8) Civil supremacy		P2, 3

There are some other relations that could be traced, e.g., number 10 on the Declaration list was mentioned as number 6 in the formal list of grievances after the 1774 Bill of Rights (*Respect,* 55); but the main ones are indicated in this little chart, and we see how the misapprehension arose that no earlier rebuke was directed at the King himself. Admittedly, all the counts so far mentioned are directed at executive abuse: The King or his ministers (including local governors) have allowed change in the charters, laws, procedures of courts or assemblies. But the first Congress neatly separated these from the formal list of grievances directed at *legislative* encroachment, by tactfully including them in the personal petition to the King as mere *allowances* of the direct aggression by the Parliament. We can see why Jefferson's *Summary View,* often cited as a document directed against Parliament, has so many counts (seven) against the executive itself—he was drawing up a suggested Peti-

---

* Numbers in brackets mean the grievance in the Declaration is *part* of the clause or clauses referred to in the other document.

tion, not a Bill of Rights plus basic constitutional (i.e., legislative) grievances.

2) The second part of the list is introduced by a change of rubric. To this point, each count began "He has . . ." Now nine counts are included in a long paragraph beginning, "He has combined with others . . ." The "others" is Parliament, of course. The executive power has abetted legislative derangement of the constitution. The overall number of charges varies from commentator to commentator depending on their treatment of this paragraph. Some count it all as one charge; others as ten (the nine separate charges and the introductory charge of abetting); some as nine. I list it as count 13 with subdivisions A through I—and correlate it with count 9 of Jefferson's Virginia draft for the constitution, with its subdivisions A through F.

This part of the list has parallels in the three documents already correlated, and with two more—the grievances following the 1774 Bill of Rights (*Respect,* 55–56) and Jefferson's own Declaration of the Causes and Necessity for Taking Up Arms (*Papers,* 1:200). I refer to these in the following lineup as B (for Bill) and C (for Causes):

13	(9)	Abetting Parliament	
A	(A)	Quartering troops	P[14], B5
B		Military trials	P[14]
C	(B)	Trade bans	SV126–7, P[14]
D	(C)	Taxation	SV125–6, P11 [12], B1, C1
E	(D)	Jury trial	P11 [12], B2, C3
F	(E)	Venue change	SV128 P13, B2, C4
G		Quebec Act	P[14], B4, C6
H		Dissolving charters	P[14], B3, C5
I	(F)	Dissolving assemblies	

The list of parliamentary usurpations was at the heart of the first actions for redress. Here it is incorporated within a general claim that the King failed to redress those grievances when they were brought to his attention. If the congressional petitions failed, it was because the *King* did not respond, though the grievances were, all along, directed against Parliament's acts. Parliament was never the petitioners' addressee. The Continental Congress differed in this from the Stamp Act Congress which, a decade earlier, petitioned *both* the King and Parliament.

3) The third part of the list is the only one that does not draw on earlier documents, for two reasons. It deals with things more recent than the events of 1774, or even of 1775. Also, more narrowly, it recognizes the state of war that had to be minimized while the Congress was engaged in a process of loyal petition. That is: Counts 14 through 18 of the Declaration make up a list of *war atrocities*, whose only parallel is in the list Jefferson had just drawn up for the Virginia constitution's preamble.

14 (16) Negative aggression
15 Positive aggression
16 (14) Use of mercenaries
17 Use of prisoners
18 (13) Use of Indians

4) The fourth and final section is summary and corresponds to count 18 of the first petition: the King has not redressed any of the grievances voiced to him. Here, of course, the Congress does not merely suspend trade awaiting redress, as it had in 1774. It announces the end of the petitioning process because of its repeated failures.

19 Refusal to redress   P18

Only when we have grasped the overall logic and shape of Jefferson's list are we in a position to estimate the real force of his clause on slavery. Congress omitted just two counts from Jefferson's list, and they both come from the third section of that list, the war-atrocities part. Count 18 accused the King of inciting "merciless" Indians to wage war on the colonists. The next charge reads, in Jefferson's draft:

He has incited treasonable insurrections of our fellow-citizens, with the allurements of forfeiture & confiscation of property.

The Virginians accepted this count (11 on their list) in the preamble to their constitution, though they deleted one earlier charge (number 3 in the Declaration).

The next (and only other) deletion from Jefferson's list for the Congress follows directly on this charge of inciting loyalists to turn against their fellows. This omission deals with slaves, and opens with the two sentences already quoted; but the item's place on the list shows Jefferson is here discussing *war atrocities,* and we do not get the real point of his accusation till we reach its conclusion:

And that this assemblage of horrors might want no fact of distinguishing die, he is now exciting those very people to rise in arms among us, and to purchase that liberty of which he has deprived them, by murdering the people on whom he also obtruded them: thus paying off former crimes committed against the *Liberties* of one people, with crimes which he urges them to commit against the *lives* of another.

This atrocity is a third example of the theme Jefferson has pursued in the last two counts—the provocation of continental inhabitants to fight against the Revolution. Count 18 looked to the raising of Indian raids; the first omitted charge looked to loyalist subversion; and the second omission looked to slave rebellions. The King's crime is his use of blacks as he has been using Indians and loyalists. That is: The real onus of the charge is that the King has been *freeing* slaves to fight against their American owners—a reference to Governor Dunmore's call, in 1775, for Virginia slaves to attack their masters. The irony of charging the King with manumission as a crime led Jefferson to write his tortuous preamble to this charge. He was trying to erect a shaky moral platform from which to denounce the novel "atrocity" of freeing slaves.

Jefferson no doubt resented, as all Virginians did, Lord Dunmore's invitation to chaos. Significantly, the Virginia convention adopted his indictment of the King on this charge. But it is also significant that Jefferson put the charge more bluntly for his fellow Virginians, who knew what he was talking about:

[The King has perverted government] by prompting our Negroes to rise in arms among us, those very negroes whom, by an inhuman use of his negative, he hath refused us permission to exclude by Law (*Papers,* 1:378—cf. 338, 357).

There is no preliminary rhetoric against enslavement here. Jefferson speaks frankly of "our Negroes," and only adds that the King had vetoed Virginia's attempts to put a restrictive tariff on the import of further slaves.

The Congress had good reason to think Jefferson's longer, morally convoluted charge would just open it to ridicule. It posed the same problem that the first omitted item had—the accusation that the King is committing the crime of asking loyalists to be loyal. Yet in striking Jefferson's words, the Congress found a way to *retain* the most defensible part of both charges. It inserted the essence of them both in Count 18. Before "[he has] endeavored to bring on the inhabitants of our frontiers the merciless Indian savages," Congress inserted "[he has] excited domestic insurrection amongst us, & has . . ." That was meant to cover both loyalists and slaves, without going into the self-defeating rhetoric about forfeitures and enslavement. This kept Jefferson's two charges, while making them less vulnerable.

Just how vulnerable they were is made apparent by John Lind's swoop down on this small phrase. He refuses to consider that appeals to loyalists could be called "insurrection," and concentrates on the implied charge of freeing slaves:

But how did his Majesty's governors excite domestic insurrections? Did they set father against son, or son against father, or brother against brother? No—they offered freedom to the slaves of these assertors of liberty. Were it not true that the charge was fully justified by the necessity to which the rebellious proceedings of the complainants had reduced the governor, yet with what face can they urge this as a proof of tyranny? Is it for them to say that it is tyranny to bid a slave be free? To bid him take courage, to rise and assist in reducing his tyrants to a due obedience to law? To hold out as a motive to him that the load which crushed his limbs shall be lightened, that the whip which harrowed his back shall be broken, that he shall be raised to the rank of a freeman and a citizen? It is their boast that they have taken up arms in support of these their own self-evident truths—that all men are created equal, that all men are endowed with the unalienable rights of life, liberty, and the pursuit of happiness. Is it for them to complain of the offer of freedom held out to these wretched beings; of the offer of reinstating them in that equality which, in this very paper, is declared to be the gift of God to all; in those unalienable rights with which, in this very paper, God is declared to have endowed all mankind? (*Answer*, 107).

Lind answers Jefferson's clause without ever having seen it. No matter what the King's motive, is not freedom a boon—accidental freedom, no less than principled manumission? Lind supplies a rhetoric as heated as Jefferson's, and better grounded. If he did this to the deft little phrase of Congress, imagine what polemical use he could have made of Jefferson's rationalizing turns and twists.

The placement and phrasing of Jefferson's attack on Lord Dunmore's proclamation show that this paragraph should not be used to indicate Jefferson's own attitude toward slavery. He was responding to a particular war measure that posed immediate hazard to the Revolution as well as to Virginia's establishment. To give genuine fears a moral coloring, he twisted language and logic in an unfortunate way. Indeed, the juggling of arguments to express the feeling of grievance on this point is like the tortured expression of anti-Catholicism in the strange legal attack on the Quebec Act. (It should be noticed that both Hutchinson and Lind also scored effectively in their discussion of Count 13-G, the Quebec Act, asking what right America had to object to the free exercise of the Catholic religion in a different country.)

Here, then, are the final two reasons for doubting that Jefferson resented changes in his document only, or even principally, because this clause was omitted. In the first place, it was *not* omitted—its real point was inserted in Count 18 of the official document. Did he regret, then, the excision of his preliminary rhetoric? It is hard to think that could offend him much, since *he omitted that rhetoric himself* in presenting this count to the Virginia convention.

The slave paragraph deleted from the Declaration has b   read by modern commentators through a haze of false assumptions   ., the assumption that Congress omitted the grievance (when it included it under an earlier heading), or that Jefferson was attacking the institution of slavery itself (rather than the King's part in first enslavement); the assumption that the basis for the charge was Virginian opposition to further enslavement (rather than control of slave imports); the assumption that Jefferson attacked the King's vetoes for keeping men enslaved (rather than maintaining the traffic where it would devalue slaves). But the main misreading comes from a refusal to look at the paragraph's conclusion and real point—the accusation that the King's real crime is his attempt to *free* Virginia's slaves. *That* was the war atrocity at issue in this part of Jefferson's list.

Jefferson's real intent, in this charge, is better read from the clause he submitted to the Virginia convention. It contains the basic elements of the Declaration paragraph, without preliminary rhetoric or moral decoration—that the King vetoed tariffs on the

slave trade, and that his agent proclaimed freedom for slave re-
cruits in the ongoing war. Yet for every hundred or so historians
who quote Jefferson's charge in the Declaration, only two or three
cite the Virginia text.

"... the circumstances of our emigration ..."

In this doctrine however I had never been able to get anyone to agree with me but Mr. Wythe.
—Jefferson, of his *Summary View*

Jefferson, it has been noted, went to Philadelphia in 1775 as a substitute for Peyton Randolph. Governor Dunmore had been forced, in Virginia, to reconvene the Burgesses he dissolved the year before. He was under instruction to place before the House Lord North's conciliatory proposal; the British hoped, by putting concessions before each separate legislature, to split the colonies. Randolph was called back to Williamsburg to keep the House firm and aligned with Congress. Jefferson, instead of going straight to Philadelphia, joined Randolph in Williamsburg to help draft the reply to Lord North—another mark of Randolph's patronage. This was Jefferson's first state paper, and he delayed his departure for Congress until he could take a copy with him. Randolph had no doubt informed him of the Congress's need for spirited reply from the provinces to keep up the will to resist parliamentary overtures. Also, Virginia had taken a certain pride in being the first to report a nonimportation resolution to Philadelphia—a record it would maintain by bringing in the demand for independence in 1776. In his *Autobiography*, Jefferson remembered (erroneously) that Randolph felt Virginia's would be the first response to Lord North's proposal. Actually, Pennsylvania had replied three weeks before Randolph left Philadelphia. But this did not much lessen the importance of getting a strong statement back to Congress. So Jefferson, his draft completed and approved in committee, set out for Philadelphia before the final House vote on a slightly changed form of the document (Boyd, in *Papers,* 1:174).

Then he typically dawdled, even on this urgent mission, stopping to buy books and an expensive horse (fifty pounds for a stallion sired by the famous Janus). There was a perverse instinct in him for leaning farthest off from action, the more pressing its need seemed to others. For ten days he traveled, adjusting himself, adding fancier harness and gear to his phaeton, before delivering the desired reply into the hands of Benjamin Harrison.

Jefferson came, of course, speaking the language of the first Congress—how else, when he had been coached by the admired president of that body? His reply, which he could present as certain of passage in Virginia, was based on the rights of petition: it said that relaxation in the mode of taxing the colonies was not a sufficient settlement, since "the other grievancies of which ourselves and sister Colonies separately and by our representatives in General Congress have so often complained, are still to continue without redress" (*Papers,* 1:172).

The Congress was always looking for fresh returns from the provinces—new instructions, new delegates, new reports and papers. This would obviously be true of responses to the conciliatory proposal. Refusal to take this bait would be an important test of the colonial will to resist. Jefferson's draft was bound to be read, quoted, and discussed by other delegates, and when Congress drew up its own answer, Jefferson was not only on the committee for drafting it, but wrote the draft which the whole Congress adopted (with emendations).

It is often said that Jefferson was known as an author when he arrived in Philadelphia because his rejected instruction to Virginia's first delegation had been printed as *A Summary View of the Rights of British America.* It is true that some delegates, at least, knew Jefferson as the author of this anonymous pamphlet, and spoke well of it (*Papers,* 1:676, n. 16). But there was much in the draft to trouble a Congress that, so far, preferred the nice legal distinctions of John Dickinson to the rhetoric of orators. Jefferson's reply to Lord North, on the other hand, was not only more sober, more weighty because of its object and the backing of the House of Burgesses; it entered directly into the business before Congress. The *Summary View* naturally wins more attention today, as a reve-

lation of Jefferson's mind in its first ambitious work of theory—just
as the Declaration's preamble interests us more than its list of
grievances. But this does not reflect the priorities of the delegates in
Philadelphia, who were trying to make a sound legal case for constitutional revolution.

Julian Boyd (*Papers*, 1:676) thinks John Adams was referring to
the *Summary View* when he wrote: "Mr. Jefferson had the reputation of a masterly pen; he had been chosen a delegate in Virginia in
consequence of a very handsome public paper which he had written
for the House of Burgesses, which had given him the character of a
fine writer" (JA, *Papers*, 3:335–36). But that pamphlet was *not* a
public paper, and it did not get even the limited reception it first
aimed at. It was not written for the House of Burgesses (dissolved
at the time of its composition). Nor is there any evidence that the
paper led to his choice as a delegate. On the contrary, after the first
delegation rejected his draft instruction, the second was formed
without him. His acceptance as a substitute is more likely to have
come from his work in implementing the nonimportation scheme
than from a pamphlet. The pre-eminence of Randolph and Harrison in the delegations shows that parliamentary art was the desired skill. The reply to Lord North *was* a public paper, and *was*
drafted for the reconvened House of Burgesses, and would naturally
have been connected in Adams's mind with the appearance of the
new delegate who bore this composition hot from the debates in
Williamsburg.

Jefferson, in later life, felt that his proposals of the mid-seventies
ran far ahead of those acceptable to a timorous majority of delegates to Philadelphia, or even to the Virginians met in committees
and conventions. This may have been true at a philosophical level.
But in day-to-day tactical terms, the differences were less pronounced at the outset than participants would later remember.
Julian Boyd has demonstrated that John Dickinson did not (as
Jefferson alleged) soften Jefferson's draft Declaration of the Causes
and Necessity for Taking Up Arms. (*Papers*, 1:187–92). Nor did the
Virginia House throw cold water on his reply to Lord North (ibid.,
174).

Despite such later accounts, colored by intervening clashes with
the principals, Jefferson had achieved a working accord with the
delegates' efforts by the time he reached Philadelphia. In the *Sum-*

mary View, he denied that England had any right to regulate American trade (ibid., 123), though the first Congress had consented to "bona fide" exactions in its Bill of Rights (*Respect,* 54). By the time he drafted his reply to Lord North, he was able to cast his objection in terms that not only passed the House of Burgesses but were voted through the Congress itself. He argued that exclusive right to America's trade gave England commercial advantages amounting to an indirect tax. Yet England was now asking for a direct revenue to support "proportionately" America's place in the Empire. Jefferson said that either the indirect tax should be counted as a part (or whole) of the colonies' contribution to the Empire, or a direct payment should free Americans to trade anywhere they liked (compare *Papers,* 1:172 and *Respect,* 121). This was not a new argument. Adams would use it on his Massachusetts audience shortly afterward (*Novanglus,* 46), and it had been broached before. But its presence in Jefferson's Virginia draft, like its acceptance in the congressional document, proves that Jefferson could modify his denial of any rights over trade regulation and that Congress was now mounting an indirect attack on those rights.

All six of Jefferson's arguments against Lord North's proposal were reproduced in the ten counts given for its rejection by the Congress; but Jefferson's second argument in the Virginia paper— that Lord North was changing the *mode* of taxation while still claiming the *right*—was expanded into four separate counts in the congressional document.* Benjamin Franklin, who served on the committee with Jefferson, helped in the expansion of these points (*Papers,* 1:230, n. 2), as he would co-operate with Jefferson on the Declaration's text. When we remember how many proposed grievances were rejected in the first Congress, and think of the intransigent stand taken by Jefferson in his *Summary View,* it is striking that his answer to Lord North could be adopted with so few changes. Jefferson had entered into the consensus worked out by the first two Congresses as they shaped their petitions. That is one way he expressed the delegates' "common sense of the subject"— not by voicing a "Lockean" orthodoxy in the preamble, but by

* Listing the counts of his Virginia draft in Roman numerals, and those of his congressional document in Arabic: I became 9; II was parceled out in 1, 2, 3, 5; IV became 6 (with parts of the argument also in 10); V became 8 (with parts in 7); and VI became 4.

making a hard list of specifics that would pass the objections of
men with great experience at testing such claims.

But Jefferson was still Jefferson, even when forced to accommodate political realities. And the *Summary View* does give us evidence of the way Jefferson's mind worked when he was addressing
a subject on his own, without regard for consensus. It is his most
ambitious political statement from the period preceding the Declaration; yet many have found it somewhat embarrassing. From a
man who later disdained rhetorical effusion, it seems a bit per-
fervid. This cannot be blamed on youth—Jefferson was thirty-one
when he wrote it, a mature age among colonials. We can hardly
argue that he "grew up" in the two years separating the *Summary
View* from the Declaration.

Some modern uneasiness with the document is caused by historical accident. The most-quoted sentence of the *Summary View* is
the advice directed to King George: "The whole art of government
consists in the art of being honest" (*Papers,* 1:134). That sounds a
bit simple-minded, like Ruskin's childhood sermon, "Little children,
be good." But honesty had a partisan meaning in eighteenth-century political dispute. It was the catch term of the "country party"
in its criticism of court practices (cf. *Papers,* 1:173 on the elder
Pitt's government). So John Adams, while admitting that whigs
were just as fallible as tories (*Novanglus,* 75), argued that tories
worked on policies that were structurally at odds with honest government (ibid., 73, 79, 97). Those with a nice feel for eighteenth-
century English should guess that Jefferson was saying something
more than he is made to say in platitudinous modern quotations
from his pamphlet. One word gives the thing away—"the *art* of
being honest." He is talking about an *acquired* strategy of government, not a mere natural response. We misread his phrase exactly
as we have Dr. Johnson's "Patriotism is the last refuge of scoun-
drels." Patriotism, too, was a party slogan of opposition, with a concrete body of doctrine behind it (as in Bolingbroke's description of
The Patriot King).

The concluding section of the *Summary View* deliberately imitates the tone of "Junius" and other pamphleteers of the "country
party" in England. In his Letter 35 (1769), for instance, Junius has
"an honest man" conduct a hypothetical conversation with the
King:

Do justice to yourself. Banish from your mind those unworthy opinions with which some interested persons have labored to possess you. . . . Withdraw your confidence equally from all parties, from ministers, favorites, and relations, and let there be one moment in your life in which you have consulted your own understanding.

Compare Jefferson's exhortation:

Let not the name of George the third be a blot in the page of history. You are surrounded by British counsellors, but remember that they are parties [to the dispute]. . . . It behoves you therefore to think and to act for yourself and your people. The great principles of right and wrong are legible to every reader; to pursue them requires not the aid of many counsellors . . . Only aim to do your duty . . . (*Papers,* 1:134).

Other faults in Jefferson's paper can be excused by a lack of trustworthy information—as when he misrepresented the tea incident in Boston. But these peripheral things are not what embarrass in the document. It is the central argument that men have found so hard to take seriously. Even Dumas Malone, noting the paper's lack of historical precision, says that it "borders on recklessness" (1:182). One way Jeffersonians have coped with their unease was to treat the paper as prophetic, i.e., it did not describe a political reality, but (accidentally or otherwise) predicted the shape of a later British Empire as the "commonwealth of nations" (ibid., 183). It is astonishing how much mileage this assertion has got in discussions of the *Summary View.* Yet it has no real basis. Jefferson was describing an assemblage of nations, each with its own legislature, but sharing a common executive. (with full executive authority, including the veto and powers of arrest). The twentieth-century commonwealth referred to by Jeffersonians was a union of states, each with its *own* executive, in a league whose mere *symbol* was the King (or Queen).

Nor is it true, as some claim, that Jefferson invented the idea of several independent legislatures sharing one king. It was implicit in American practice, and express in American arguments, well before 1774. Edmund Morgan has established (*WMQ,* 1948) that it was the most common American view of the Empire as early as 1765. At the very time when Jefferson's pamphlet was first circulating in Virginia, the idea was familiar enough for Daniel Leonard to scoff at it, speaking of a supposed "King of Massachusetts, King of Rhode

Island, King of Connecticut, &c, &c." And John Adams answered with a straight face that this would, indeed, be the appropriate form of address for George III (*Novanglus*, 115). Americans had for a long time thought of their council and lower house, in each colony, as a sister parliament to the Houses of Lords and Commons. Two provinces (Georgia and South Carolina) even called their lower house the Commons. Adams traced the independence of these various parliaments back through the Stamp Act controversy (*Novanglus*, 20, 48–49, 65).

Discussion of Jefferson's "commonwealth model" just distracts from the heart of the *Summary View* argument. Jefferson himself stuck by that argument, though he made no converts to it beyond George Wythe. Even his own source had not gone with him all the long way he chose to pursue his basic principle. That source was Richard Bland's Stamp Act pamphlet, *An Inquiry into the Rights of the British Colonies* (1766). Jefferson described the mixture of inspiration and frustration he drew from that work in the imagery of a Virginia horseman with a balky mount:

He wrote the first pamphlet on the nature of the connection with Great Britain which had any pretension to accuracy of view on that subject, but it was a singular one. He would set out on sound principles, pursue them logically till he found them leading to the precipice which he had to leap, start back alarmed, then resume his ground, go over it in another direction, be led again by the correctness of his reasoning to the same place, and again back about, and try other processes to reconcile right and wrong, but finally left his reader and himself bewildered between the steady index of the compass in their hand, and the phantasm to which it seemed to point (Ford, 9:474).

Bland wrote to answer the charge that Americans were "virtually" represented in Parliament and could therefore be taxed. After all, many places in England itself had no direct representatives. Bland contended that this argument was confusing "virtual representation" with "tacit consent" to the social contract. (This latter concept he took, not from Locke, where he could have found it, but from Wollaston's *Religion of Nature Delineated*, printed in 1724.) Any man tacitly consents to the social contract of the place where he lives if he "refuses to exercise his natural right of quitting the country" (10). But that is precisely the right Americans *had* exercised: "becoming private adventurers, [they] established themselves, without any expense to the nation, in this uncultivated and almost uninhabited country" (13). Expatriation is an implicit rejection of the contract: "when men exercise this right, and withdraw themselves from their country, they recover their natural freedom and independence. The jurisdiction and sovereignty of the state they have quitted ceases" (13).

That was Bland's hard ride toward the jump that so inspired Jefferson, who opens his own instruction to the 1774 delegation with the observation that Americans "possessed a right, which nature has given to all men, of departing from the country in which chance, not choice, has placed them, of going in quest of new habitations, and of there establishing new societies, under such laws and regulations as to them shall seem most likely to promote public happiness" (*Papers*, 1:121). This is closely modeled on Bland: "their engagements to the society, and their submission to the public authority of the state, do not oblige them to continue in it longer than they find it will conduce to their happiness, which they have a natural right to promote" (10).

But if expatriation is itself a rejection of the basic social bond, the colonizing expeditions had already declared their independence long ago. Why, then, bother with things like petitions to the King? Here, in Jefferson's eyes, is where Bland balked. Bland described the withdrawal of consent as merely conditional, as arranged beforehand: Americans were "men who came over voluntarily, at their own expense, and under charters from the Crown, obtained for that purpose" (15). How can men be withdrawing from sovereignty when they arrange for the sovereign's *permission* and when they carry off *instructions* they mean to follow? Bland wrote: "They must have a right, by *compact with the sovereign* of the nation, to remove into a new country, and to form a civil establishment *upon the terms of the compact* . . ." (15, italics added). Bland was trying to have it both ways, in Jefferson's view—to keep Americans subject to the King in the very act of withdrawing from his realm.

No such half-measures suited Jefferson. If a break occurred, it was total. If any union succeeded that break, it would have to be a new one formed *after* the break, on terms set by the independent new country: "Settlements *having been thus effected* in the wilds of America, the emigrants thought proper to *adopt* that system of

laws under which they had hitherto lived in the mother country . . ." (*Papers,* 1:122, italics added—cf. Jefferson's first statement
of this theory in the Albemarle Resolutions, *Papers,* 1:117). Jefferson
seizes on a historical parallel suggested in Bland (7) but not used
to polemical advantage: since common law was derived (by whig
myth) from Saxon settlements in the English "wilds," it was as il-
logical for England to assert jurisdiction over Americans as for Germans on the Continent to claim "motherland" rights of obedience
from England (*Papers,* 1:122).

Jefferson felt that Bland balked at the logical consequences of his
own theory. But, in pursuit of logic, Jefferson had to defy history
and the law. John Quincy Adams put it succinctly in 1831: "The argument of Mr. Jefferson that the emigration of the first colonists
from Great Britain which came to America was an expatriation, dissolving their allegiance and constituting them independent sovereignties, was doubtful in theory and unfounded in fact. The
original colonists came out with charters from the King, with the
rights and duties of British subjects. They were entitled to the protection of the British King, and owed him allegiance" (*Memoirs,*
8:279).

All those Jeffersonians who have talked nervously about something else—e.g., "commonwealth" ideas—are tacitly admitting the
force of this objection to Jefferson's basic argument in the *Summary
View.* And no wonder. Jefferson relied on no precedents, history,
statutes, or even arguments to support his thesis. It is simply *stated,*
as a self-evident truth. This was a position taken abruptly, but not
lightly. Jefferson repeated his assertion in the most important contexts and never abandoned his special theory of American independence.

It is revealing to contrast Jefferson's approach with that of John
Adams in his "Novanglus" papers, written a year and a half after
the *Summary View.* Adams, as I noted earlier, agreed with Jefferson that the King should be treated as the link between several independent legislatures (but, unlike Jefferson, Adams refused to
grant the term Empire any legal status, 106–7). Adams did not
found his conception of union under a common king on the right of
expatriation. He seems to flirt with that theory in his seventh paper
(102), but only to contrast his view of Greek and Roman colonies
with that of "Massachusettensis." Greece and Rome, according to

Adams, either a) sent out colonizers to found independent cities or b) took under their protection cities already established. British subjects on the American continent were neither colonizers of the natives (ruling Indians in the name of the King) nor a colonized people taken over by a "foreign" governor from England. They were, in effect, *colonizers of themselves*—an entity which had no clear precedent in international law or imperial theory (121). Adams anticipates modern scholarship when he admits the American condition was neither simply opposed to the British constitution nor expressly based on it. It represented, for England, "a defect in her government, which ought to be supplied by some just and reasonable means" (108). Adams meant to work out such means, using what *already* existed in the British system to fashion an *extension* of it adapted to new uses. By contrast with a benign imperialist like Pownall, who claimed that the governing machine was complete in its dependence on London and had only to be maintained in working order (see pp. 44, 47 above), Adams argued that both sides were in fact inventing new parts, but that the ministry was botching its job:

She [England] has found out that the great machine will not go any longer without a new wheel. She will make this herself. We think she is making it of such materials and workmanship as will tear the whole machine to pieces. We are willing, if she can convince us of the necessity of such a wheel, to assist with artists and materials in making it, so that it may answer the end. But she says, we shall have no share in it; and if we will not let her patch it up as she pleases, her Massachusettensis and other advocates tell us, she will tear it to pieces herself, by cutting our throats (108).

Americans, he claimed, had already improvised things better fitted to the original design of the system, with the result that "we enjoy the British constitution in greater purity and perfection than they do in England" (117).

In his next (eighth) paper, Adams takes a new point of departure —not expatriation, but peregrination—to explain how subjects may be bound to a ruler in widely differing ways. British law, by the statute *ne exeat regno*, impowered the King to forbid a subject's departure from his geographical sphere of authority (121). Those who left peaceably were therefore presumed to do so with permission, in the King's good grace and with continuing loyalty to him. Yet the

King is unable to exercise his authority over them while they travel in foreign lands, e.g., he cannot enforce English law in French domains. The subject's allegiance survives without his concomitant protection (122) and therefore with altered responsibilities—an English subject does not have to observe English law while traveling in France; yet failure to do this does not mean rebellion against the English King.

But what happens when a loyal subject reaches the American realms of Indian kings like Philip or Massachusetts? (124). Adams denies that the colonizers came as His Majesty's troops to annex subjects by conquest (125), though Jefferson had advanced the dangerous claim that Americans held the continent by right of conquest (*Papers,* 1:122). International law of the time would have made the conquests part of the sovereign's domains. Adams recalls the purchases of land and the treaties enacted with Indian kings— acts in which the Americans exercised sovereignty with the King's blessing, establishing a new kind of realm with new kinds of ties to his person. To prepare for this novel claim, he notes that the King, under feudal law and its remains in the British constitution, held the allegiance of different corporations under many different kinds of charter.

In the ninth paper, Adams distinguishes three kinds of dependence on the King. There is loyalty to his person, to his crown (i.e., to his family line, to the crown as hereditary), and to his crown and realm (the King-in-Parliament). Citing legal cases with great ingenuity, Adams proves such distinctions existed in the time of Coke. It would be no argument against his view to say things had changed since then. Adams, after all, admits a novelty of justification for colonial states but argues it is based on ancient models. Yet America's settlement took place when feudal divisions in the King's holdings still applied. The ninth paper gives the theoretical basis for arguments Adams had adumbrated earlier:

Some of the colonies, most of them indeed, were settled before the kingdom of Great Britain was brought into existence. The union of England and Scotland was made and established by act of parliament in the reign of Queen Anne, and it was this union and statute which erected the kingdom of Great Britain. The colonies were settled long before, in the reigns of the Jameses and Charleses. What authority over them had Scotland? Scotland, England, and the colonies were all under one king before that; the two crowns of England and Scotland united on the head of James I, and continued united on that of Charles I, when our first charter was granted. Our charter, being granted by him who was king of both nations to our ancestors, most of whom were born after the union of the two crowns, and consequently, as adjudged in Calvin's case, free natural subjects of Scotland, as well as of England—had not the king as good a right to have governed the colonies by his Scottish as by his English parliament, and to have granted our charters under the seal of Scotland as well as that of England? (123).

By which of his parliaments was the King to rule America?

But will any man soberly contend that America was ever annexed to the realm? To what realm? When New England was settled, there was a realm of England, a realm of Scotland, and a realm of Ireland. To which of these three realms was New England annexed? To the realm of England, it will be said. But by what law? No territory could be annexed to the realm of England but by an act of parliament. Acts of parliament have been passed to annex Wales &c. &c. to the realm; but none ever passed to annex America. But if New England was annexed to the realm of England, how came she annexed to the realm of, or kingdom of, Great Britain? The two realms of England and Scotland were, by the act of union, incorporated into one kingdom, by the name of Great Britain; but there is not one word about America in that act (123).

In his last three papers, Adams shows how various realms had been annexed to the crown without being subjected to the King in Parliament. Even areas within the main English realm had been held by separate charters, e.g., the counties palatine of Chester and Durham. Particular duties and exemptions were established with the King, bypassing parliamentary legislation.

The "Novanglus" papers afford us one of the best exercises in political theory and legal analysis from the whole of the revolutionary period. They seem heavily influenced by Thomas Pownall's great book of the 1760s, *The Administration of the Colonies*. ("Novanglus" calls Pownall "a friend to liberty and to our constitution," 21.) But Pownall's book has the same relationship to Adams's work that Bland's pamphlet had to Jefferson's. The earlier man did not go far enough to suit his more ardent follower. Pownall wanted to keep the colonies dependent on London in all their trade relations, while protecting American rights through representation in Parliament. Adams wrote that such representation

would not in fact give Americans equal protection (20, 116–18).
But Pownall *had* pointed the way for Adams, by basing his discussion on the altered conditions of allegiance during peregrination or emigration (50–55, 118–20), by treating the status of the colonies as undefined in the British constitution (45–46, 59), by distinguishing the various objects of allegiance in "the crown" (61, 65, 120, 138), by using the counties palatine (56, 60, 138, 147) and other provinces annexed to the realm (145–46, 166–67) as models for the analysis of America.

Adams, if he ever read the *Summary View*, would have found it even more objectionable than Paine's *Common Sense*. He was too good a Massachusetts man to dismiss the charters agreed on before emigration as Jefferson did. Pownall had shown him how to argue from the charter itself to a new kind of allegiance (see *Administration*, 118–20). On the other hand, Jefferson was clearly not converted from his own view by any rumor of the Adams position. Later in the year when Adams's papers appeared, Jefferson repeated his argument that withdrawal was secession from allegiance, in his draft Declaration of the Causes and Necessity for Taking Up Arms. He says Americans, on this continent, "arranged themselves by charters of compact under one common king" (*Papers*, 1:193). John Dickinson altered this statement of American initiative in adopting a king to read: "Societies or governments, vested with perfect legislatures, were formed under charters from the crown . . ." This eliminated the lacuna during which Americans had full independence before adopting a royal executive. It also suggested derivation of the charter from the King rather than initiation of it by the people.

Jefferson included the essential notes of his theory in his Virginia draft of a reply to Lord North. That was one of only two substantive points dropped in the text adopted by Congress (the other was a reflection on Lord Chatham's proposal for dealing with the colonies—see *Papers*, 1:173).

Jefferson was undiscouraged by these previous two failures to get official backing for his theory of American independence. He included it in his last and best-known paper written for the Congress. The Declaration of Independence, as adopted, reads:

Nor have we been wanting in attentions to our British brethren. We have warned them from time to time of attempts by their legislature to extend an unwarrantable jurisdiction over us. We have reminded them of the circumstances of our emigration and settlement here.

Jefferson, in his draft, had denied Parliament any "jurisdiction" at all. The Congress softened this with "an unwarrantable jurisdiction." Besides, Jefferson had continued the reference to emigration with this clause: "no one of which [circumstances] could warrant so strange a pretension [i.e., to jurisdiction]." This was excised. So was the following assertion that "we had *adopted* one common king" (*Papers,* 1:318, italics added). Once again, the distinctive Jeffersonian theory of expatriation as secession had been rejected.

This whole passage, coming at the climax of Jefferson's draft, was heavily cut by the Congress. Many assume, with John Quincy Adams (*Memoirs,* 8:282), that the passage was a rhetorical flourish tacked onto the legal argument. This is not only out of character for Jefferson; the connection between this passage and all of Jefferson's earlier papers of major import shows that he, at least, thought the point needed making. He tried repeatedly to make it, but was thwarted in every effort except the pamphlet called *A Summary View,* and even that has been given skimpy and rather embarrassed treatment by later readers. If the expatriation theory of independence was wild and groundless, Jefferson showed extraordinary attachment to it—something worth study in itself. If it was not entirely groundless, what assumptions made it so dear to Jefferson? These are matters we must address when we approach his original draft on its own terms. They are mentioned here only to show that —while Jefferson was expressing a common American mind on the concrete grievances that filled the practical debates at Philadelphia —there was something uncommon going on in his own mind, something that did not reach public expression in any of his documents as these were passed by Congress.

Congress deleted Jefferson's slavery clause, but retained its central point. His emigration theory it simply excised, along with over three hundred words of accompanying material. We do not know its motive for this action, but we can say that this omission rid the Declaration of its one theoretical novelty. As it stands, the official document is a restatement of whig theory vindicated in the 1688 Revolution. The heart of that theory—the right to alter or abolish governments that subvert the constitution's ends—was not contested, even by the Declaration's fiercest British critics (see

Robert Ginsberg, *Studies on Voltaire*, 152:885). The real points of early controversy were not questions of theory but questions of fact. Were the grievances legitimate? If they were, then the Revolution was justified. At the theoretical level, there is nothing in Jefferson's Declaration (as Congress passed it) that was not expressed or implied in Dickinson's Bill of Rights. In fact, the Declaration only became by later accident what the English Bill of Rights was to the Revolution of 1688. In some ways, it would make better sense to treat the 1774 Bill of Rights as the basic charter of our Revolution. As we shall see, the Congress did not realize the import of the document it cleared for printing on July 4, 1776.

The first of many accidents that helped promote the Declaration was that it concluded with a charter form deriving from the first Association's pledge. Our later cult of "the signers" as individuals has obscured the fact that the "we" who "mutually pledge our lives, our fortunes & our sacred honour" are the "united states" of the document's title. Though individuals signed as members of the clustered delegations, only states voted, one vote per state. This compact-form gives the Declaration a greater solemnity than the Bill of Rights possessed, while taking up a greater responsibility than the first pact, the Association, looked toward.

The Declaration became our revolutionary charter in part because it expressed such "antient principles" (as Jefferson put it when referring to the Glorious Revolution—*Papers*, 1:131). After the congressional excisions were made, the document seemed to stand much closer, say, to the "Novanglus" papers than to *A Summary View*. Congress had spoken for "the united states" in terms of the most comprehensive and unifying doctrine available to it.

But Jefferson had written things Congress did not wish to voice. And when we read Jefferson's own text in its integrity—as he took pains we should be able to do—even some of the things retained by Congress take on more special (and sometimes different) meanings than any that could validly be derived from the congressional document standing on its own. It is time to turn from the revolutionary charter of the Congress to the revolutionary theory Thomas Jefferson expressed in his own draft.

PART TWO

A SCIENTIFIC
PAPER

SEVEN

". . . necessary . . ."

Newton . . . in his garden watching
The apple falling towards England, became aware
Between himself and her of an eternal tie.
            —W. H. Auden

The Declaration's opening is Newtonian. It lays down the law: "When in the course of human events it becomes necessary . . ." Jerome Vercryusse has said that these few words put us firmly in the age of the scientific revolution. In the flow of things there is perceivable necessity, a fixity within flux.

Words like "course" and "events" had a slightly different force in Jefferson's day. Each was more active, closer to its familiar Latin source—course (*cursus*) a run or rush, its verb still in common use; event (*e-ventus*) an out-come, what results.

A woman's menstrual flux was her "course." So was a hunter's pursuit. Addison wrote in *Cato* (i, 3):

> Alas! thou knows't not Caesar's active soul,
> With what a dreadful *course* he rushes on
> From war to war.

Medical experiments had to run their graded course. The rotation scheme of Jefferson's crops from farm to farm was called "the regular course of my husbandry" (*Farm Book*, 310, 311; *Garden Book*, 196). He described his *Notes on the State of Virginia* as a first effort at "calculating the course and motion of this member of our federal system" (LB, 14:221). Diderot, stressing the total reality of the world presented in Richardson's novels, says: "*Il me montre* le cours géneral des choses *qui m'environnent*" (*Éloge de Richardson, Pleiade*, 1061). He gives us the "*phénomènes moraux*" on which we can make human experiment ("expérience"). Hume put it this way: "There is a general course of nature in human actions, as well as in the operations of the sun and the climate" (*Treatise*, Selby-Bigge ed., 402).

In the Virginia *Notes* (85), Jefferson distinguished conjectures "certain in event" from those merely possible or probable in their outcome. Francis Hutcheson's system described the "event" of any passion as its desired outcome (2:16–17); and he judged actions "good or evil by the events" (1:266). In Addison's *Cato*, Marcia says:

> But to the Gods permit th'event of things.

But the word with full Newtonian *pondus* in Jefferson's opening phrase is "necessary." It was the proudest boast of the world opened by Newton's *Principia* that men could discern necessity at work, invariable, in the flow of apparent chance. Jefferson had a reverent attitude toward the work that made this claim possible; and he was not one to use the crowning boast lightly. If we are to read his Declaration with the requisite seriousness, we must gauge the high ambition of its opening. He is not saying that the separation of Americans from the English motherland is defensible, merely; preferable; or even desirable. He says it is *necessary*. Out of a sequence of observed results, a pattern emerges, and is stated as a law. The revolution of the colonies, like the revolving of heaven's bodies, is a process open to scientific observation and description. Jefferson has come to describe it.

John Adams, remarking the difficulty with which the resolution of independence was passed, said it was like getting thirteen clocks to strike at the same instant. In other letters from the Philadelphia Congress, men like Jefferson and Richard Henry Lee spoke of the way events were "ripening" or "maturing." Plantation owners knew the importance of timing things exactly so that their work force and its needed resources would be ready to cut, transport, and store tobacco. At Philadelphia they observed the pace of events in this spirit. There was a sense of some great process at work, glimpsed in fragments of observable motion. Wollcott of Connecticut wrote to his wife, "Everything is leading to the lasting independency of these colonies" (Burnett, 711). Adams said "Every post and every day rolls in upon us independence like a torrent" (ibid., 66). Richard Henry Lee applied Shakespeare's words to the development:

"There is a tide in the affairs of men" (*Letters*, 79). But the mechanical image was the most effective one. John Adams, struck by his cousin's organizing genius, boasted of his own passage through Samuel's back alleys of maneuver: "When I consider the great events which are passed, and those greater which are rapidly advancing, and that I may have been instrumental in touching some springs and turning some small wheels which have had and will have such effects, I feel an awe upon my mind which is not easily described." He was allowed to adjust the very clockworks of history.

It is hard for us, who live after romanticism's assault on the industrial revolution, to remember how liberating was the vision of a human *machinery* in the eighteenth century. Newton's ordering of the inanimate universe led men to seek an equivalent pattern in *human* activity. They initiated the long effort at inventing a science of man. Some called this a political mathematics (Condillac) or geometry (Beccaria) or calculus (Condorcet) or algebra (Hutcheson). A favorite model of the period (as it had been for the early Greek philosophers) was the empirical science of medicine. In time it would cease to be a mere model for the science of man and become *itself* the science of man. Antoine Le Camus would write *La médecine de l'esprit* (1753) and J. L. Moreau de La Sarthe would construct a *Médecine morale* (1797). This approach took its origin from Locke's theory of sensation, a theory treated in the *Encyclopédie* under the heading of Medicine. Locke had subjected the mind to the body in a way that seemed to make physiology the necessary basis for all philosophy. And he encouraged the comparison of thought to chemical action when he described the "inner sense" as *compounding* simple ideas into complex ones. In the course of the century following his, the figure of the *médecin-philosophe* would become so familiar that certain people thought *only* a physician could become a good philosopher. When the Marquis de Chastellux undertook his philosophy of public happiness in 1770, he presented it as a form of moral medicine, with all the exactitude of medical science (i, 70–71).

But even those who took medicine as their starting point often stressed the mechanical side of that art. Anatomy was a favorite study of men like Vicq d'Azyr, as it had been for the seventeenth-century physician, William Petty. Edmund Burke and Edward Gib-

bon attended the popular lectures on anatomy delivered by Dr.
William Hunter; and William Shippen brought this gentlemanly exercise to Philadelphia. Thinkers were fascinated with the muscle-
pulleys and bone-levers of the human machine. This growing interest can be traced in quotes like the following:

1) John Wilkins, in his *Mathematical Magic* (1648), included a
chapter (i, 5) on the lever-mechanics of human motion: "We do
not go, or sit, or rise, without the use of this mechanical geometry."

2) Dr. Arbuthnot, in *The Usefulness of Mathematical Learning*
(1700), wrote: "It is true, we cannot reason so clearly of the internal motions of an animal body as of the external, wanting sufficient
data and decisive experiments; but what relates to the latter (as the
articulation, structure, insertion, and *vires* of the muscles) is as subject to strict mathematical disquisition as anything whatsoever; and
even in the theory of diseases and their cures, those who talk me-
chanically talk most intelligibly."

3) Francis Hutcheson stressed, in 1725, the pulley-apparatus of
the body: "And how amazing is the unity of mechanism when we
shall find that almost infinite diversity of [animal] motions—all their
actions in walking, running, flying, swimming, all their serious efforts
for self-preservation, all their freakish contortions when they are gay
and sportful in all their various limbs—performed by one simple
contrivance of a contracting muscle, applied with inconceivable
diversities to answer all these ends. Various engines might have obtained the same ends; but then there had been less uniformity, and
the beauty of our animal systems, and of particular animals, had
been much less when this surprising unity of mechanism had been
removed from them" (1:22).

4) By the time Ephraim Chambers compiled his Cyclopaedia
(1741), the basis for the Encyclopédie, he felt that "Mechanical
Reasoning" deserved a separate entry because of its medical application: "This manner of thinking and arguing, Dr. Quincy insists, is
the result of rightly studying the powers of a human mind, and the
ways by which it is only fitted to get acquaintance with material
beings. For considering an animal body as a composition out of the
same matter from which all other bodies are formed, and to have
all those properties which concern a physician's regard only by virtue of its peculiar make and constructure, it naturally leads a person to consider the several parts, according to their figures, contex-
ture, and use; either as wheels, pullies, wedges, levers, screws,

cords, canals, cisterns, strainers, or the like; and throughout the whole of such inquiries, to keep the mind close in view of the figures, magnitudes, and mechanical powers of every part or movement; just in the same manner as is need in inquiring into the motions and properties of any other machine. For which purpose it is frequently found helpful to design, or picture out in diagrams, whatsoever is under consideration, as it is customary in common geometrical demonstrations."

5) In 1770, Chastellux called anatomy (*"cette science utile et terrible"*) the revelation of "the numberless quantities of machinery needed to drive our life's most trifling outworks" (2:86).

It was the human structure that set man apart from other animals; and much of the eighteenth-century aesthetic was devoted to celebration of the human body's perfection—i.e., efficiency—as animal form. Even Locke's theory of sensation was treated as a problem in mechanics—the irritation of excitable material that keeps the man-machine moving, bombarded from place to place like a billiard ball (in Locke's comparison). Poetry, too, had to admire the exquisite machinery of the senses. Henry Brooke was just one of the many poets who read their Locke with the help of Newton:

> When objects on the exterior membrane press,
> The alarm runs inmost thro' each dark recess,
> Impulsive strikes the corresponding springs,
> And moves the accord of sympathetic strings . . .
> (*Universal Beauty*, iv, 41–44)

Here as elsewhere, Locke was a secondary deity to that "prime mover" of all Enlightenment thought, Sir Isaac Newton. When the 1771 Encyclopaedia Britannica (a product of the Scottish Enlightenment) took up the definition of mechanics, it included under that head all the laws of matter considered as moveable. The article—which ran to twenty-three pages, with five plates including fifty-three figures—comprehended electricity as well as gravity, astronomy as well as dynamics. To the growing school of materialists on the Continent, it would comprehend everything—sensation as well as electricity, and thought as well as sensation. The eighteenth century sought a grand unifying science, what Antoine Lasalle called *"une loi universelle appliquée aux sciences, arts et métiers"*

in his 1789 work *La balance naturelle.** And what better model
could it have than the dense equations of Newton's *Principia,* so
complex in result yet simple in concept? What stunned men about
Newton's work was his combination of separate observations within
theoretical unity, all his complex simplicities. As James Thomson
put it, in the most famous of many poetic tributes to Newton:

> O wisdom truly perfect! thus to call
> From a few causes such a scheme of things.
> *(To the Memory,* 69–70)

All mechanics acquired, for a while, the charm of complexity controlled. The spirit of the time touches even Dr. Johnson when he
comes to define Mechanism in his Dictionary: "Construction of
parts dependent on each other in any complicated fabric." Any fabric. Even the universe. Even society. Even man.

"A Mechanic." That was the signature David Rittenhouse put to
his first technical remarks submitted to a newspaper. But he did not
do this with any false modesty. He was using a proud title, one that
had moved a long way off from Shakespeare's "base mechanicals."
The change was well on its way by the time the Royal Society was
set up (1662). Of the eight original committees of the Society, the
mechanical was far the most popular, with sixty-nine members, as
opposed to thirty-five on the trades committee and thirty-two on
the agricultural. In 1660 Thomas Powell had written *Humane Industry* to prove that the mechanical arts are a product of "humane
wit." Soon prizes were offered, chairs established, and exemptions
given to dissenting teachers, all to encourage the mechanical arts.
The love of "curious" workmanship—of intricacy combined with exactitude—is reflected in the frequent, praising use of that adjective:
a *curious* machine, a *curious* mechanic. As Sir William Petty put it,
"Curious dissections cannot be made without variety of proper in-

---

* The very title of this book confirms Sir George Clark's suggestion that "balance," used in phrases like balance of power, balance of nations, etc., had moved
off from its accountant's sense in "balance of trade" to a recognizably mechanical sense. See, as well, Chastellux (2:72) on the means of achieving international *"équilibre"* (2:72)—*"disposer les forces."* Jefferson in his first printed
work, described King George as "holding the balance of a great, if a well poised
Empire" (*Papers,* 1:135).

struments" (Pref., *Political Anatomy*). In this context, the word is equivalent to the modern use of "scientific."[*]

In the Enlightenment, the mechanic became the very model of utilitarian ingenuity. Plate after plate in the supplementary volumes of the Encyclopédie gives us, in lovingly etched detail, each ratchet and spring of the most complex machines. One is watching the birth, in august surroundings, of *Popular Mechanics,* at a time when the very popularity was a challenge to the old guilds' "mysteries." Diderot boasted that he wrote articles on such machines only after working them, or even disassembling and reassembling them (or models of them). His enemies tried to cloud that boast. They accused him of *not* being a mechanic.[†]

Some modern biographers of Franklin and Jefferson have described as peculiarly American their subjects' love of "tinkering." What truth there is in that claim comes from the fact that the United States is so characteristic a product of the Enlightenment. The mechanical taste was an expression of the time. The gadgets at Monticello, which seem to impress visitors more than the building itself, are almost all copied from European models. Franklin, first trained to service a printing press, moved up the scale of physical problems by a *gradus* familiar to Europeans. Men recognized his genius precisely because he moved faster and farther by his native skill than most of his Enlightenment peers of the workshop. When

---

[*] The force of the word for Jefferson appears in a passage like this: "It is a common opinion that the climates of the several States, of our Union, have undergone a sensible change since the dates of their first settlements; that the degrees both of cold and heat are moderated. The same opinion prevails as to Europe; and facts gleaned from history give reason to believe that, since the time of Augustus Caesar, the climate of Italy, for example, has changed regularly, at the rate of $1°$ of Fahrenheit's thermometer for every century. May we not hope that the methods invented in later times for measuring with accuracy the degrees of heat and cold, and the observations which have been and will be made and preserved, will at length ascertain this curious fact in physical history?" (*Garden Book,* 622).

[†] The *philosophes* did criticize one kind of "mechanicism," that of the Cartesian vortices and the "medicine" based on Descartes's dualism (e.g., Boerhaave's). The Encyclopedists led the assault, in the article on "Méchaniciens" and d'Alembert's *Discours préliminaire* (vii, xxv–xxvi), and in Diderot's disapproval of La Mettrie's *l'homme machine.* But d'Alembert went out of his way to praise the *true* mechanics, based on Newtonian empiricism not Cartesian deductions (vi, xiii). This is part of his distinction between *"le véritable esprit systématique"* and *"l'esprit de système"* (vi). Cf. Hutcheson, 1:58; Moravia, 133–79.

Voltaire and Franklin embraced at the Academy of Sciences, it was the meeting of Art and Science—of two practical men; one dusty, as it were, from the labors of the theater, one sooty from the forge that made his stoves. Even Jefferson, who never used a plow, would take extreme pride in his one truly original invention, the formulae for a moldboard's "curve of least resistance"; and, like Thomas Reid, he used "a ploughman" as his test of the moral sense that is equal in all men. The love of machinery was such that Defoe could make Robinson Crusoe, in the *Further Adventures,* describe his dead wife this way: "She was, in a few words, the stay of all my affairs, the centre of all my enterprises, the engine that by her prudence reduced me to that happy compass I was in."

It is not surprising, then, that the American for whom Jefferson showed the most persistent and thorough admiration was America's supreme mechanic, David Rittenhouse. In the *Notes on Virginia* (64), in order to prove that America can nurture genius, he produced three names—Washington, Franklin, and Rittenhouse. And he reserved the highest praise for the last of these:

We have supposed Mr. Rittenhouse second to no astronomer living: that in genius he must be the first, because he is self-taught. As an artist he has exhibited as great a proof of mechanical genius as the world has ever produced. He has not indeed made a world; but he has by imitation approached nearer its Maker than any man who has lived from the creation to this day.

Jefferson did not feel he had to identify with any further description the world-famous "orrery," or working model of the universe constructed by Rittenhouse. Jefferson's admiration for that machine was almost religious. He wrote to Rittenhouse in 1778: "The amazing mechanical representation of the solar system which you conceived and executed, has never been surpassed by any but the work of which it is a copy" (*Papers,* ii, 203). He wanted Rittenhouse to build another orrery for the college of William and Mary; but he insisted that it be given its proper name, "a ryttenhouse." The *planetarium Americanum* should not be named after an earlier (lesser) machine made for the Earl of Orrery.

Jefferson's praise of Rittenhouse was an extension of the conventions surrounding the cult of Newton, who was often compared to his own Maker as a governor of the universe by thought. The convention did not signal any lack of sincerity. Jefferson saw in the self-taught Rittenhouse a proof that Nature can speak directly to her student, without priestly or professorial intermediary. Critical as Jefferson was of his own college at Williamsburg, he opposed the policy of the Lees and Randolphs, who sent their sons back to England to study arts and the law. He felt that Newton was best deciphered in the wilderness, where Rittenhouse repeated his experiments and put them to new uses. It was the attitude of Defoe's *Crusoe:* "So I went to work; and here I must needs observe that as reason is the substance and original of the mathematics, so by stating and squaring everything by reason, and by making the most rational judgment of things, every man may be in time master of every mechanic art" ("I Build My Fortress").

It was on his farm at Norriton, just outside Philadelphia, that Rittenhouse began work on what *he* called "the orrery," in 1767. He did not want to imitate the comparatively crude models he knew about from Europe. He had been led to the sun and planets by way of the moon as it showed up on his clocks. The linking of human measure, in clock and calendar, to the measured universe was accomplished by the better clockmakers of the eighteenth century, who showed phases of the moon and days of the month on their clockfaces. Rittenhouse went far beyond this. In a famous clock made in 1767, now at the Drexel Institute of Technology, he created an astronomical face-design that included six dials—one registering "the equation of time," or the varying ratio of local to sidereal time. There was a lunarium and a planetarium. This latter showed the rough relationships of the planets as they moved. The clockworks included a music box that could play ten different tunes on the hour-chime—truly a music of the spheres. After making such a clock, Rittenhouse conceived the idea of building a machine that would present the exact relationships of the planets, tangible proof of a beautiful simplicity in the universe's mechanics.

No period in history thought so regularly of the clock as a little universe in itself. For one thing, it was needed to measure astronomical motion. For this purpose Christian Huygens built the first pendulum-clock. One reason Rittenhouse was summoned to observe the transit of Venus in 1769 was that he could build "an astronomical clock," with dead-beat escapement to give the pendulum an exact second-oscillation. A clock was the moving measure of a moving universe, both the imitator and the norm of heaven's machinery. When John Adams spoke of thirteen clocks made so precisely they would strike in perfect unison, he meant they would all be geared exactly to the motion of their astonomical Model. The clock was a symbol of man's ability to correspond with nature. When Jefferson wrote to Rittenhouse in 1778, he urged him to give up politics for astronomy in order to *live* the mechanical laws he *studied*: "Cooperating with nature in our ordinary economy, we should dispose of and employ the geniusses of men according to their several order and degrees" (*Papers*, ii, 203).

The appeal of this vision was so great that we can misread eighteenth-century texts if we do not rightly estimate that appeal. While reading with some students Adam Smith's *Theory of Moral Sentiments* (1759), I found they were supplying a musical image behind Smith's descriptions of "sympathy." It is true that we meet many passages like these, where musical meter and vibration could be suggested to us:

The spectator, therefore, must find it more difficult to sympathize entirely, and keep perfect time with his sorrow, than thoroughly to enter into his joy . . . (i, 3, i)

He, therefore, appears to deserve reward, who, to some person or persons, is the natural object of a gratitude which every human heart is disposed to beat time to . . . (ii, 1, ii)

Our heart, as it adopts and beats time to his grief, so is it likewise animated with that spirit by which he endeavours to drive away or destroy the cause of it (ii, 1, ii).*

In some other authors of the time, we could safely assume that the sympathy of vibrating strings was being described ("*les fibres*" in Diderot's *Rêve*). But Smith never spells out the musical image in his treatise; on the contrary, he often develops a *mechanical* model

---

* Hume had used virtually the same language in his *Enquiry Concerning the Principles of Morals* (1751): "Reduce a person to solitude and he loses all enjoyment, except either of the sensual or speculative kind; and that because the movements of his heart are not forwarded by correspondent movements in his fellow creatures. . . . In general, it is certain that wherever we go, whatever we reflect on or converse about, everything still presents us with the view of human happiness or misery and excites in our breast a sympathetic movement of pleasure or uneasiness. . . . The perusal of a history seems a calm entertainment, but would be no entertainment at all did not our hearts beat with correspondent movements to those which are described by the historian" (iv, 2).

for this kind of language. Contrasting the virtuous man with the vicious, he writes:

> The first turn of mind has at least all the beauty which can belong to the most perfect machine that was ever invented for promoting the most agreeable purpose; and the second, all the deformity of the most awkward and clumsy contrivance (iv, ii).

And when he describes useful social ordinances, he says:

> They make part of the great system of government, and the wheels of the political machine seem to move with more harmony and ease by means of them . . . If you would implant public virtue in the breast of him who seems heedless of the interest of his country, it will often be to no purpose to tell him what superior advantages the subjects of a well-governed state enjoy; that they are better lodged, that they are better clothed, that they are better fed. These considerations will commonly make no great impression. You will be more likely to persuade, if you describe the great system of public police which procures these advantages—if you explain the connections and dependencies of its several parts, their mutual subordination to one another, and their general subserviency to the happiness of the society; if you show how this system might be introduced into his own country, what it is that hinders it from taking place there at present, how those obstructions might be removed, and all the several wheels of the machine of government be made to move with more harmony and smoothness, without grating upon one another, or mutually retarding one another's motions. It is scarce possible that a man should listen to a discourse of this kind, and not feel himself animated to some degree of public spirit. He will, at least for the moment, feel some desire to remove those obstructions, and to put into motion so beautiful and so orderly a machine (iv, i).

Smith thought sheer admiration of mechanical beauty would inspire a greater public spirit than any dry calculation of utility, so great was his trust in the age's delight at a well-made machine. Compare Hutcheson 1:41: "We may only here observe the pleasure which anyone shall receive from seeing any design well executed by curious mechanism, even when his own advantage is no way concerned."

The Rittenhouse orrery was a machine perfectly geared to that delight. It displayed, on a beautiful field, the motion of earth round the sun and of earth's moon around its properly tilted axis. The other planets moved in corrected relationship, and all were worked from one great spring (the mark of a superior machine according to Hutcheson, 1:61-62). The device, exquisitely crafted, was used by Rittenhouse and others to lecture on the Newtonian system, and it drew upon itself the same response that poets had been giving to its original:

> Nature, bright effluence of the One Supreme!
> O how connected is thy wondrous frame!
> Thy grand machine, thro' many a wanton maze,
> Steered where it winds, and straight'ning where it strays,
> There most direct where seeming most inflex'd,
> Most regular when seeming most perplex'd,
> As tho' perfection on disorder hung,
> And perfect order from incaution sprung.
> Still endless as thy beauteous scenes arise,
> Still endless multiplies our deep surprise.
>   (Brooke, *Universal Beauty*, ii, 261-70)

Philadelphia and Princeton competed for the "astronomical machine" on which Rittenhouse had lavished years of his skill, and Princeton won—its president, Dr. Witherspoon, bid 300 pounds for the wonder, though his whole budget for the college's "philosophical apparatus" had been fixed at 250 pounds. William Smith, the president of Philadelphia College, was so upset that Rittenhouse had let the orrery escape his native province that he persuaded him to build another one for Philadelphia and to keep the first one on hand for lecture purposes until the second one was built. When the first one finally arrived in Princeton, it was used in advertisements to attract students to the college. Enshrined in Nassau Hall, it became the object of scientific pilgrimages, even for visitors from abroad (like the Marquis de Chastellux). When the British took Nassau Hall, an "atrocity story" was circulated, alleging that they smashed the orrery. The same tale was repeated after Philadelphia's seizure. But the orrery survived; and though few people at Princeton knew, the last time I asked them, where it is kept (in Peyton Hall), it was beautifully restored in 1953 after being lost for half a century. The second orrery is on display in the University of Pennsylvania's library. The orrery became one of America's proudest boasts and was displayed on the first state seal of Pennsylvania. Only one man outranked Rittenhouse in scientific repute—and when Franklin died, there was only one successor possible as president of the Philosophical Society. Charles Willson Peale painted Rittenhouse in the same gown he had used to portray Franklin, and William Smith wrote what was in effect a coronation ode. Speaking of Franklin, he effuses:

> What though he yields to Jove's imperious nod?
> With Rittenhouse he left his magic rod
> (Hindle, *Rittenhouse*, 311).

Jefferson loved not only the Rittenhouse machine, but the whole mechanical vision of the universe it opened up for him. This was confirmed when Jefferson went to Rittenhouse with his great scheme for establishing the weights and measures for America. In our *novus ordo seclorum*, Jefferson did not want to borrow the standards of Europe, any more than he wanted "a ryttenhouse" to be known as an orrery. America, born in the age of science, should be able to achieve an unparalleled precision in her way of doing business. Jefferson wanted all that and something more: He was determined to measure things by a machine. Motion was the most regular thing in the universe; so *only* motion should be allowed to dictate what measures would apply in the New World.

The basic unit—from which Jefferson would derive everything else, even the nation's coinage—was one of length. Jefferson mounted a series of arguments against any stationary measure. There is no natural object both common and uniform enough to serve as the unit of length. Ye ,y artificial object made to serve . .t purpose is inconvenient. s material will expand and contract with temperature and moisture. To assure absolute uniformity, only one bar can be used as the norm—so that resort to it becomes difficult. If it should be lost, the whole basis of the system disappears. Rittenhouse, consulted by Jefferson, did not find these arguments convincing:

> I am not quite satisfied with the reasons given (page 1) for having recourse to motion for a standard of measure. The true reason seems to be, not because all matter is variable in its dimensions, for that is a difficulty we have to contend with after recourse is had to the motion of pendulums, but because a standard rod of any given length may be irrecoverably lost, and because no such rod has been preserved for us from ancient times, nor can we undertake to transmit them to posterity with sufficient authenticity, or to different countries for general use (*Papers*, xvi, 545).

But modern times, as more settled and civilized, seemed to minimize the danger of losing the rod; and Rittenhouse devoted the rest of his criticisms to the fact that Jefferson's scheme would introduce more variation and uncertainty than the expansion and contraction of any stationary physical object.

Jefferson's plan was to use Newton's argument that any pendulum of the same length, suspended at the same latitude (and therefore responding to the same forces of gravity), will complete its swing in the same amount of time. Or, to reverse things, that any pendulum completing its "oscillation" at the same time in the same latitude must have a single length. Jefferson's problem seemed solved. Establish the pendulum conditions for one latitude, and anyone could arrive at the same length, around the whole earth's circuit, by repeating the conditions as described in basic formulae. Then, by allowing for the differing forces of gravity at different latitudes, one could arrive at comparable formulae for them. The measure of length would be transferable as a mathematical proposition; and it could be established anywhere in the world by setting up the pendular machine. Jefferson meant to divide the measure arrived at to set up a decimal system. The resulting system of length would be used to measure containers for a constant unit of weight (water), and coins would be weighed by that standard according to their precious metals. Every unit employed in America would thus be derived from the motion of the universe, as conveyed to the motion of the earth, and then to the motion of the pendulum. Man's mechanics would echo heaven's. Even the decimal system responds to nature. It was an Enlightenment commonplace that counting by tens was based on the number of man's fingers (cf. Condillac, *Langue des Calculs,* first chapter). Buffon concluded: "This way of numbering is natural to man; it probably has been and will be in continual use because it is formed on a physical and invariable relationship that will last as long as the human species does and because it is not confined to any one time or set of artificial presuppositions" (N. H. Suppl. 4:713–14). The decimal system is as free of the arbitrary and temporal as Jefferson's pendulum length. Besides, as Wilkins and others argued, the hand is the supreme triumph of mechanics in man's body.

Jefferson's was a noble concept; but it ran into insuperable obstacles from the outset. For one thing, the string-and-bob pendulum used by Newton in his experiments produced a cycloid pattern of oscillation, bending the unit of length. Besides, the bobs would all have to be of uniform weight and shape, returning Jefferson to a dependence on one arbitrary physical object as the measure of everything else. Beyond that, the center of oscillation would be in the center of the bob, so one must *estimate* the terminus of the suspending string.

In answer to this problem, Jefferson adopted the proposal of Robert Leslie that a bobless rod, stiff enough to be unbending, should replace the string-and-bob. But that led to difficulties, too. As Rittenhouse wrote to Jefferson:

> Perhaps so great a preference is not due to the vibrating rod of an uniform diameter. That preference seems to be founded on an opinion that the radius of oscillation is precisely ⅔ of the length of the rod. But this is not true unless the thickness of the rod be infinitely little with respect to its length. In all other cases a correction is necessary (ibid., 546).

The requisite precision seemed less attainable the more Jefferson sought it. Rittenhouse had blow after blow to deliver to the plan: Jefferson assumed that all parts of earth along the same latitude were equidistant from the center and that earth's rotation was unvarying. Neither assumption would stand the test for absolute precision Jefferson was aiming at. Rittenhouse pointed out that English and French computations with apparently identical pendulums had not reached perfect uniformity: "All this I mention to show the uncertainty we are in respecting the figure of the Earth, and consequently the length of pendulums in different latitudes" (ibid., 596):

> That the motion of the earth about its axis is sufficiently uniform for every human purpose I have very little doubt. But there are good reasons for supposing that it is not perfectly equable. The unequal attractions of the sun and moon are sufficient to produce a sort of libratory motion in the earth's axis, and when this motion is increasing the rotatory motion is probably decreasing, and the contrary. There are other causes which may perhaps sensibly diminish the earth's motion on its axis in a long course of time. Would it not therefore be best to avoid asserting that it is uniform and invariable, without any restriction? (ibid., 546)

Jefferson had addressed his proposals to the man who knew as much about pendulums as anyone alive at that period. Rittenhouse was embarrassed that, in charting the 1769 transit of Venus, he had not been given time to correct his astronomical clock, built for the purpose, to counter expansion and contraction in the pendulum rod (Hindle, p. 50). He also tried to suggest some of the problems Jefferson would face in terms of air-density resisting the pendulum —as well as variations in the stuff of the pendulum itself, beginning with the suspension mechanism's friction:

On the fifth article, "the practical difficulty resulting from the effect of the machinery and moving power," you have left a blank as if intending to say more. This is a subject which I have fully considered for several years past, and have written something on it which I intend to print. I have therein demonstrated that the force of the moving power may, at pleasure, be so applied to the pendulum as to make it vibrate either quicker or slower, in equal arches, than it would do in a vacuum, at perfect liberty. And consequently that it may be so applied that it shall not change the times of vibration at all. The errors arising from unequal arches of vibration I have likewise proposed to remove with geometrical accuracy, without using the cycloid, and there is now going a time piece in our university so constructed (ibid., 595).

Rittenhouse thought accuracy in the use of the pendulum, if that had to be used, lay in the direction of a double pendulum, one correcting the other, not in the "vibrating rod." But at least he knew that every element in the physical makeup of a pendulum introduced the problems Jefferson objected to in a stationary material measure.

Visitors to Monticello admire its large clock above the carriage-entrance door, its escapement driven by cannon balls that descend along the wall and into the basement. Jefferson himself would have had the grace, if he entertained Rittenhouse, to apologize for what was a clumsy mimicking of the clockmaker's real achievements in the eighteenth century. But he did not have the heart to abandon his grand scheme for gauging American life by the measure of the universe itself. Rittenhouse knew—what his admirer could not bring himself to believe—that the orrery itself was only a rough indicator of what the heavens really do. Jefferson claimed too much for his own invention of a measuring machine, just as he claimed too much for his hero's astronomical machine. Rittenhouse corrected Jefferson's mathematics, supported his proposal in public, but tried gently to undermine the Secretary of State's confidence in his basic concept.

To no avail. It was a case of Jefferson's finding his own personal Plato great, but greater his platonic Truth. He incorporated each of Rittenhouse's suggestions that could be accepted without scrapping the whole scheme—and then argued, ever after, for his plan. It was an episode quite typical, as we shall see. Jefferson, so critical of concepts in the metaphysical mode, had an artist's love for the aesthetics of Newtonian mechanics. He grew fond of his own measuring apparatus, just as he had of "the ryttenhouse." And not even Rittenhouse could come between lover and loved in this instance. Jefferson was publicly mocked for his proposal, as well as privately corrected. Noah Webster wrote an unfair squib on Jefferson as a confidence man promising a solution to all life's problems if only we took the bobs off our pendulums (*Papers*, xviii, 481–82). But Jefferson could not be laughed away from his proposal, any more than he could be argued out of it.

He hoped, always, to get directly at Nature and at Nature's Laws. That is evident in passage after passage of his work. When, for instance, he denied that maritime fossils discovered in mountainous parts of Virginia could have been deposited there by waters reaching that height, he was working from his disbelief in a biblical Deluge. But he tried to make his case from the nature of things as well:

The atmosphere, and all its contents, whether of water, air, or other matters, gravitate to the earth; that is to say, they have weight. Experience tells us, that the weight of all these together never exceeds that of a column of mercury of 31 inches height, which is equal to one of rainwater of 35 feet high. If the whole contents of the atmosphere then were water, instead of what they are, it would cover the globe but 35 feet deep; but as these waters, as they fell, would run into the seas, the superficial measure of which is to that of the dry parts of the globe as two to one, the seas would be raised only 52½ feet above their present level, and of course would overflow the lands to that height only. In Virginia this would be a very small proportion even of the champaign country, the banks of our tide-waters being frequently, if not generally, of a greater height. Deluges beyond this extent then, as for instance, to the North mountain or to Kentucky, seem out of the laws of nature (*Notes*, 31).

To get the full impact of that passage we must remember that "experience," in the second sentence, means "experiment." Tests have established the bounds of possibility, and a simple application of mathematics solves our problem. Jefferson decided that the "seashells" were really an odd rock formation.

But Rittenhouse performed simple chemical tests on the objects and found they *were* sea shells (*Papers,* viii, 566). Jefferson politely said he would reconsider his opinion, without accepting the direct evidence of Rittenhouse that the shells were shells (ibid., ix, 216). And he kept looking for evidence that the shells were a rocky growth (ibid., xi, 460–61). He preferred a "mechanical" answer to his problem, one based on hydraulics and meteorology, to a direct chemical experiment. He wanted the largest possible "laws of nature" to declare what could or could not be.

Even when Jefferson erred, he erred in the pursuit of accuracy, certainty, necessity. He detested metaphysics; yet his own bias for the mathematics of motion had something of the mystical about it, a mysticism of the specific—he was never vague or "idealistic" in his treatment of natural laws. Those laws state, for him, how things happen and why they could not happen any other way. If that is *not* what he means to describe in the Declaration of Independence, then he has—by his own standards—seriously misled us in his opening phrase. He knew how large the claim was when he spoke of the separation of one people from another as "necessary."

EIGHT

"... *course of human events* ..."

> The public happiness is indeed, as to external appearance, a very uncertain object; nor is it often in our power to remedy it by changing the course of events.
> —Francis Hutcheson (1728)

The year 1769 brought to a climax much of the Enlightenment's scientific effort. It was the century's last chance to observe a transit of Venus across the sun's face. By a proper sighting and timing of that event, astronomers might formulate the solar parallax, a momentous step forward in astronomy. To quote Harry Woolf: "The importance of this measurement can hardly be exaggerated. Expressed as the mean radius of the earth's orbit, it becomes the standard measure of the universe, a kind of celestial meter stick of no less importance than its terrestrial counterpart. . . . It is quite likely that no other particular scientific problem of the eighteenth century brought so many interests to a single focus as the concern for solar distance." This one sum fixed, the rest of the solar system—whose distances were merely relative in Newton's formulae—could be rendered absolute. And after 1769, another transit would not occur for over a century.

The transits of Venus come in pairs—there had been one in 1761. Since the transit was not visible from Europe, France and England sent out perilous expeditions, in the midst of the Seven Years War, to observe the transit. One of these missions brought British astronomers Charles Mason and Jeremiah Dixon to that part of the globe where they would chart their famous line dividing Maryland from Pennsylvania. But unforeseen problems made the 1761 sightings imprecise. That year's work was taken as a test run for the age's second (and last) chance in 1769.

America was anxious to demonstrate, against some philosophes' doubt, that its culture was fully a part of the Enlightenment. Harvard had sent an expedition to Newfoundland to observe the 1761 transit. But 1769 presented a much greater opportunity to the American colonies. The moment of ingress on the sun's face—the only one needed for charting by the Delisle method—would be visible along the whole East coast. Despite this, even so patriotic a Philadelphian as Benjamin Franklin advised the Royal Society in England to rely on Massachusetts Province for any American sightings. He had been absent from the colony while the fame of Rittenhouse grew. Also, with Franklin absent, a bitter fight had developed for political control of the Philosophical Society he had founded. John Ewing, the Society's secretary, raised one hundred pounds from the Pennsylvania assembly to purchase a reflecting telescope with micrometer to time the transit. But William Smith, the devious Provost of the College of Philadelphia, had an even more potent weapon on his side: David Rittenhouse. Smith wrote to the colony's proprietor, Thomas Penn, for a second telescope, to be set up at Rittenhouse's Norriton farm.

For months, the scientific competition took on the air of modern football rivalries. Ewing commandeered all the philosophical apparatus in Philadelphia, on the grounds that Rittenhouse the great inventor could create his own precision instruments. So, in fact, Rittenhouse constructed:

1) An equal altitude instrument, for establishing (by a series of sightings) the exact local noon.

2) A transit telescope for checking local noon by direct sightings of the sun along a fixed meridian.

3) An astronomical clock, with second vibrations, its pendulum with a dead-beat escapement to correct for errors caused by anchor escapements—he included compensating devices to prevent deviations brought about while winding.

4) A telescope made with lenses ordered by Harvard for observing the transit. (The ship bringing the lenses docked in Philadelphia, and Smith decided it was too late to get the lenses to Cambridge in time for a telescope to be constructed; so he borrowed them for use in Norriton.)

5) Another telescope to supplement that sent by Penn.

6) An observatory, whose exact location was established by a series of star-sightings.

Rittenhouse, who had chronic health problems, worked feverishly to get all his instruments ready for the June 3 transit. Bad weather threatened, as clouds settled in on the first of June. Rittenhouse went into a deep depression—it looked as if all his months of day-and-night labor would be wasted. But his spirits cleared with the skies on June 3. Neighbors and sightseers clustered at the Norriton farm and were warned to keep silence lest they upset the independent sightings, hand signals, and time recordings of three teams stationed at separate telescopes. Stretched on the muddy ground, a friend pillowing his head, Rittenhouse held his sickly body tense with concentration under the telescope he had made with Harvard's lenses. (The instrument is displayed in the American Philosophical Society's building.) The first evidence of Venus's approach was a trembling out toward it of the sun's rim, fuzzing the moment of contact, then viscously engulfing the small dot. Rittenhouse, intent on the precise time of contact, saw this dissolution of his certitudes, desperately signaled contact on a guess, and went into a swoon of six or seven minutes' duration, a scientific ecstasy of fear. His friend, Benjamin Rush, described the moment with reverent awe, a Bernini recapturing St. Theresa's bliss and agony: "It excited, in the instant of one of the contacts of the planet with the sun, an emotion of delight so exquisite and powerful, as to induce fainting" (Hindle, p. 55). The god of the Enlightenment would not let his servants come too near the throne.

This moment of exalted collapse did not invalidate the Rittenhouse mission. For one thing, William Smith had rather pompously commandeered the best telescope, that sent by Thomas Penn, inside the observatory; and he estimated the instant of contact with its help. But, more important, the crucial instant was still to come, the internal contact, when the outer edge of Venus parted from the sun's outer edge in its course across the sun's face. Rittenhouse was fully conscious again for this, and was thwarted only as all observers had to be, by the effect of Venus's atmosphere. As the planet moved inward on the sun's face, it briefly trailed a black "thread" with it, "denting" the sun's rim, leaving an excruciating margin of error. Still, from the three sightings at Norriton, Rittenhouse was able to produce a report that won the praise of Britain's astonomer royal. (Smith privately smuggled the report of Rittenhouse's work off to Benjamin Franklin in England, while blocking in the Society a move to send both this and Ewing's report to the Royal Society.) The publication of Rittenhouse's observations before, during, and after the transit assured his European reputation, putting his name beside Franklin's when Jefferson felt the need to boast of American genius. And despite his general modesty, Rittenhouse made his own quiet boast visible on the face of one of his clocks in the Smithsonian: It shows the track of Venus making contact with the sun.

Though Rittenhouse knew how elusive Nature remained when one tried to pin it down to the fraction of a second, the aesthetics of science and the mystique of measured motion led most philosophes to think total accuracy was already achieved in astronomy and could be achieved in the study of man. They tried to apply the same techniques of measurement to conjunctions even fuzzier than that of Venus with the sun. As Diderot put it, voicing the hope of *philosophie:* "We draw no conclusions. They are drawn by nature. We simply describe linked phenomena—the linkage is either necessary or contingent, and the phenomena are discovered by experiment" (*Rêve,* Pléiade, p. 883). The observation of regular processes in nature should reveal the will of nature. Thus one way to study man was in terms of his continuity and discontinuity with other animals. The periodicity of animal sex was, for this reason, a matter of wide interest to the philosophes.

Edmund Burke wrote, in his 1757 *Philosophical Enquiry into the Origin of our Ideas of the Sublime and Beautiful:*

The difference between men and brutes, in this point, seems to be remarkable. Men are at all times pretty equally disposed to the pleasures of love, because they are to be guided by reason in the time and manner of indulging them. Had any great pain arisen from the want of this satisfaction, reason, I am afraid, would find great difficulties in the performance of its office. But brutes, who obey laws in the execution of which their own reason has but little share, have their stated seasons; at such times it is not improbable that the sensation from the want is very troublesome, because the end must be then answered, or be missed in many, perhaps forever; as the inclination returns only with its season (i, 1, ix).

Compare Hume's essay on *Polygamy and Divorces:*

"Among the inferior creatures, nature herself, being the supreme legislator, prescribes all the laws which regulate their marriages . . . But nature, having endowed man with reason, has not so exactly regulated every article of his marriage, but has left him to adjust them by his own prudence according to his particular circumstances and situation."

Burke was distinguishing the "soft" urge toward beauty (e.g., toward the preservation of the human species) from the "hard" impellings toward sublimity (e.g., toward individual self-preservation). Sex is put at the more leisurely disposal of reason since man's hunger for it is not as imperious and discomfiting as that for food.

Different lessons would be learned by different observers; but it was clear, to those who differed on everything else, that the "phases" of nature would reveal nature's laws. That was accepted even by those who came to destroy the concept of "natural law" in the classical or scholastic sense. Chastellux, introducing his work on public happiness (1770), used the periodicity of sex in other animals to distinguish his study of nature, empirical and "mechanical," from the static natural law preached by divines. He points out, to start with, that male and female animals are not different, in their social functions, except at the mating season. But male and female humans differ all the time, since they react "artificially" to the challenge of existence, using mechanical aids: "The less complex the structure of things, the more similar their operations" (1, v). One important theme of the Enlightenment is that modern society is *bien organisée*—and that this makes it more *natural* than earlier societies. After all, the correlated work of expeditions sent out to observe the transit of Venus shows that man can achieve his accord with nature only by the most sophisticated techniques. The simplicity of the scientific effort comes from its end—merely to observe and measure nature. Complexity comes from the imitation of nature's own multiplicity—in specific observations, in division of labor, in development of specialties, in cultivation of expertise. As Adam Smith might put it, the invisible hand of providence works best when a busy mind parcels out all the separate operations in making a pin. One travels toward unity through complexity. A "curious" machinery of effort is the best—even the simplest—imitation of the laws of nature. This attitude explains how eighteenth-century thinkers could combine their doctrine of stable species with a concept of progress: You build better machines if the parts do not keep melting into something else.

Since man is the organizer of nature, he escapes the fixity of those things he organizes. Chastellux attacks any "state of nature" for man that is made a frozen ideal—Rousseau's original bliss along with St. Augustine's original sin: "If one is to consider as natural all that is contained in the order of nature, all that happens as a result of its powers and laws, then there is a state of nature for cities as well as the country, for mechanics as well as farmers, for social man as well as isolated man" (1, xii).

Chastellux argues, then, from natural economy that monogamous union is not the sole—nor, for many people, the best—organization of the human sexes: "Because animals' time for mating, gestation, and delivery are all the same for each individual in the same species, their situation is always identical, and the general order of things cannot be interrupted except momentarily by the conjunction of their needs. But with humans, since desire and the means for satisfying it are always present, the union of couples will be disturbed every time one partner is not ready to respond to the other's solicitings" (1, viii). Pietro Verri, as we shall see, treated happiness in general as a problem in calculus—how to equate all unavoidable desires with all available capacities. Chastellux does the same here, and lets mere numbers dictate the solution: Given the persistence of the sexual urge, and no limited schedule for its satisfaction, the variability of response from any *one* person is compensated for by the presence of *many* potential respondents.*

---

* This is only one of the Enlightenment's efforts to prove scientifically that amorous constancy offends nature (Mauzi, 392–93, 428–29, 443–44; Helvétius, *De l'homme*, Sect. 8, n. 3). As in so many other areas, William Petty anticipate this development. He noted: "A man doth differ from all other animals in use of the female, and generation. By using the same without design or desire of generation, and when generation is needless or impossible" (Lansdowne, *Papers*, 1:156). Trying to maximize population, Petty found the will of nature in various combinations of polygyny and polyandry; and he tried to establish formulae for the cheapest, most convenient arrangements:

A (the Master) hath—n, o, p, q wive-servants; all to cost £140 per annum.
Coitors B, C, D, E, F have—M for their mistress and W for common.
The 12 spend £320 per annum.
M, n, o, p, q, W all between 16 and 46 [woman's bearing age].
A, B, C, D, E, F all above 20 and under 60 years old [man's responsible years].
M to expend 40 + 125 + 15 = £180 per annum.
B, C, D, E, F to spend 25 on W 25 (ibid., 2.54).
But John Graunt, the other founder of "political arithmetic," argued statistically that the balanced male-female offspring of monogamous *marriages* proves *they* are the manifest will of nature (*Observations Upon the Mortality Bills*, 1662, ch. 8).

The colonial planter or farmer had an elaborate calculus to work out between his overseas market, his domestic resources, and the demands of sky, land, seeds, and labor: "I believe," wrote Jefferson in 1792, "in general it may be advisable to cultivate several species of food, as wheat, rye, Indian corn, potatoes, peas &c. in order that if the season occasions some of them to fail entirely, we may find a resource in the others" (*Farm*, 310). In a colony whose main crop exhausted the soil so quickly, and where manure was not plentiful, work had to be carefully planned long in advance—timber cleared for future fields, old fields sown with a restorative like clover, slave quarters shifted, routes to water cleared and leveled for transport, a crop-rotation scheme planned and recorded in detail. The image for this kind of organization was—not surprisingly—mechanical. William Byrd II wrote, in 1726, "I must take care to keep all my people to their duty, to set all the springs in motion and make every one draw his equal share to carry the machine forward."

Here as elsewhere, the basis for a properly constructed mechanism was prior observation. One had to adjust one's effort to the observed features of climate, soil, and crop behavior. When Jefferson sent an original scheme of rotation to his son-in-law, the latter spotted at once a flaw in its time-meshings: "If I understand your system, one of the fields destined for wheat will be ploughed the first time, between harvest and seed-time, and will be sown immediately after. Would this not be inconvenient, as that season is rendered the busiest in the year by our apprehension of the weevil?" (*Garden*, 201). Jefferson had to cede the point: "One difficulty you suggest is a very great one indeed, that I shall have too much ploughing in the fall, considering how busy a season our apprehensions of the weevil make that" (ibid., 202).

The allotment of forces resembled that of a general anticipating multiple assaults: "I am at a loss what standing force will be sufficient for such a rotation. Taking gangs of half men & half women, as with us, I guess we must allow a hand for every 5. acres constant of each feild, say 12. hands if the feilds are of 60. acres each" (ibid., 200). Failure to have one's resources in place at the proper time could throw the whole scheme off: "I had great expectation from a green dressing with Buck wheat, as a preparatory fallow for a crop of wheat; but it has not answered my expectation yet. I ascribe this however, more to mismanagement in the times of seeding and ploughing in, than to any defect in the system. The first ought to be so ordered, in point of time, as to meet a convenient season for ploughing it in while the plant is in its most succulent state; but this has never been done on my farms, & consequently has drawn as much *from,* as it has given *to* the earth" (*Farm,* 313–14).

Jefferson tried to work out the answers to such problems mathematically, seeking inflexible "laws of combination" (*Garden,* 194) in the flux of times. He tried to pin down all the interdependent phenomena of the seasons as precisely as Rittenhouse charted the skies. Year after year Jefferson recorded the first appearance of each species of bird, the year's first frog or butterfly, the time of every flower's opening. Even in the White House he observed the first appearance of thirty-seven different kinds of vegetable in Washington's market and charted variations over an eight-year period (Randall, 1:44). He would govern his life by the transit of radishes. One seven-year chart he drew up from such "sightings" gave the outer limits, over the period, for these phenomena:

The Red Maple comes into
  blossom
The Almond
The Peach
The Cherry
The Tick appears
The house Martin
Asparagus comes first to table
The Shad arrives
The Lilac blossoms
The Red bud
The whip-poor-will is heard
The Dogwood blossoms
The wood Robin is heard

The Locust blooms
The Fringe tree blooms
The red clover first blossoms
The garden pea first at table
Strawberries first ripe
Fire flies appear
Cherries first ripe
Artichokes first at table
Wheat harvest begins
Cucumbers first at table
Indian corn first at table
Peaches first ripe
The Sawyer first heard (ibid.,
  627–28)

When traveling, he kept to this habit of recording first sightings, according to the laws of his georgic astronomy. Thomson, in his poem on Newton, called that scientist "all eye." The phrase is better applied to Jefferson. He lacked the uniquely creative imagination of Newton; but he observed a discipline of constant observation that went beyond what one might suppose the normal human boundaries. (In Europe he liked to travel alone, lest conversation distract him from any features of the passing scene.) When Dabney Carr—the closest friend of his youth, who had become his brother-in-law—died young, Jefferson had him buried at a sentimental spot the two had chosen when boys; yet he did not neglect to observe the labor force expended on this task: "2. hands grubbed the Grave yard 8o.f.sq. $= \frac{1}{4}$ of an acre in 3½ hours so that one would have done it in 7. hours, and would grub an acre in 49. hours $= 4$. days" (ibid., 40).

Fawn Brodie tries to derive profound psychological insights from the fact that, five days after his wife's death, Jefferson wrote down a taxidermist's method he had come across for mounting a bird. She does not mention the estimation of labor hours at the grave of Carr or the barter arrangement he made for the sermon at his sister's funeral.* This kind of observation and accounting was a constant discipline with him. The only record he left of the day when the Declaration of Independence passed was an entry on the purchase of a thermometer and seven pairs of women's gloves, the amount he gave to charity, and four readings of the temperature (Randall, 1:179).

* Typical of Fawn Brodie's method is the proof she offers that Jefferson was already in love with the quadroon slave Sally Hemings in France during 1788 (where the fifteen-year-old slave had just arrived, attending his daughter). This is established by the "singular" fact that Jefferson used the word "mulatto" eight times in twenty-five pages describing his tour through Holland in that year. But in all eight places he refers to the color of soil, where the term was a technical and indispensable one. Jefferson always noted, in his European travels of that time, the condition of the soil considered under four categories: *color, consistency* (mold, rotten rock, loam, clay, gravel, sand), *quality* (rich, good, middling, poor, barren), and the *crops* sown. The color notation is the most frequent and consistent in his journal. It covers this spectrum: black, dark, dark brown, reddish brown, red, mulatto, gray, white. The repetition of the word mulatto eight times means no more than the repetition of red seven times in the same pages, or gray three times—unless Jefferson is deliberately falsifying his observations in order to respond to Sally's image. The word mulatto described a precise shade (yellowish-brown). He had used it for this shade during his tour of Southern France, before Sally ever came on the scene. Ah, says Brodie, but *then* he only used the word once, because he was not thinking of Sally. Actually, he used it twice—she cites *Papers*, 11:415 and misses 11:429. And the obvious explanation of the differing figures is that the soil of Southern France was different from that of Holland—a fact borne out by the varying use of all the other color terms. On the Holland tour, he used the word red only seven times in seven weeks; but in France he used it thirty-eight times in nine weeks. Does that mean he was entertaining incestuous anticipations of the arrival of his red-haired daughter? No, it means the soil was redder in France (*and* less mulatto) than in Holland.

Jefferson's attitude toward observation was dutiful. The observed phenomena would not repeat themselves in exactly the same way, and a notation missed could rarely be supplied afterward. He lamented the necessary lacunae in his meteorological charts caused by absence from Monticello. He would not fail to record everything he could when he *was* present—would Rittenhouse forget about the transit of Venus because of a death in the family? Nor was it enough to observe disjunct things. They must be compared over long periods, and from various places, to discern interrelationships —to define, behind all change, the Laws of change: "Having been stationary at home since 1809, with opportunity and leisure to keep a meteorological diary, with a good degree of exactness, this had been done; and, extracting from it a term of seven years complete, to wit from January 1, 1810, to December 31, 1816, I proceed to analyze it in the various ways, and to deduce the general results, which are of principal effect in the estimate of climate. The observations, three thousand nine hundred and five, in the whole, were taken before sunrise of everyday; and again between three and four o'clock P.M." (ibid., 622). Among the results he drew from his compendious charts were these:

During the same seven years there fell six hundred and twenty two rains, which gives eighty nine rains every year, or one for every four days; and the average of the water falling in the year being 47½ inches, gives fifty three cents of an inch for each rain, or ninety three cents for a week. Were this to fall regularly, or nearly so, through the summer season, it would render our agriculture most prosperous, as experience has sometimes proved (ibid., 625).

The course of the wind having been one of the circumstances regularly observed, I have thought it better, from the observations of the seven years, to deduce an average for a single year and for every month of the year. This table accordingly exhibits the number of days in the year, and in every month of it, during which each particular wind, according to these observations, may be expected to prevail. It will be for physicians to observe the coincidences of the diseases of each season, with the particular winds then prevalent, the quantities of heat and rain, &c. (ibid., 626).

In this separate table I state the relation which each particular wind appeared to have with rain or snow: for example, of every five north winds, one was either accompanied with rain or snow, or followed by it before the next observation, and four were dry. Of every four north-easters, one was wet and three, dry. The table consequently shows the degree in which any particular wind enters as an element into the generation of rain, in combination with the temperature of the air, state of clouds, &c. (ibid., 627).

On an examination of 15 springs in the body of the hill of Monticello, the water of the coolest was 54½, the outer air being then at 75° (ibid., 628).

As always, the justification for science lay in its usefulness: "These degrees *fix the laws* of the animal and vegetable races which may exist with us" (ibid., 622, italics added). Nature sets limits which man must know, in order to overcome those limits by man's artifice—*"soumettre la nature,"* as Chastellux put it (2:85), *"par les forces de la nature même."* Jefferson was forever trying to increase his leverage upon nature, find new ways to get more work done with less expenditure. Here, for instance, he works out the comparative efficiency of wheelbarrows with one and with two wheels:

Julius Shard fills the two-wheeled barrow in 3. minutes and carries it 30. yds. in 1½ minutes more. Now this is four loads of the common barrow with one wheel. So that suppose the 4. loads put in the same time viz 3. minutes, 4. trips will take 4 × 1½ minutes = 6' which added to 3' filling is = 9' to fill and carry the same earth which was filled & carried in the two-wheeled barrow in 4½'. From a trial I made with the same two-wheeled barrow I found that a man would dig & carry to the distance of 50. yds 5. cubical yds of earth in a day of 12. hours length. Ford's Phill did it; not overlooked, and having to mount his loaded barrow up a bank 2.f. high & tolerably steep (ibid., 34).

Jefferson shared Sir William Petty's famous desire "to make a par [equation] between hands and lands." He drew up elaborate work tables (e.g., *Farm*, 230–34). Eighth among the things he listed as needing study by agricultural societies was this: "Calendars of works, showing how a given number of laborers and a draught of animals are to be employed every day in the year so as to perform within themselves, and in their due time, according to the usual course of seasons, all the operations of a farm of given size. This being essential to the proportioning the labor to the size of the farm" (i.e., proportioning hands to lands—*Garden*, 641).

He worked out, for British agriculturist Arthur Young, the ratios

of black compared to white labor and the return on American acreage compared to English (Ford, 6:81–87). He offered his figures
diffidently, but "as an essay of the mode of calculating the profits"
and of establishing "the principles of calculation." He promised,
after further collection of data, to "make the calculation on rigorous principles" (ibid., 82–83). He noted that the American hands-
lands ratio is the inverse of Europe's—a point made eleven years
earlier in the Notes on Virginia: "In Europe the object is to make
the most of their land, labour being abundant; here it is to make
the most of our labour, land being abundant" (85). But time will
bring the two, at a certain rate, into direct proportion: "When land
is cheap, & rich, & labour dear, the same labour, spread in a slighter
culture over 100. acres, will produce more profit than if concentrated by the highest degree of cultivation on a small portion of the
lands. When the virgin fertility of the soil becomes exhausted, it becomes better to cultivate less & well. The only difficulty is to know
at what point of deterioration in the land, the culture should be increased, and in what degree" (Ford, 6:85).

The hands-to-lands formula depends on a whole series of other ratios—of newer to older tools, of livestock to acres, of grazing to
growing sections, and so on. "If sheep, instead of cattle should be
made the principal object, what number of sheep are equivalent to a
given number of cattle old & young, for making manure? Th: J. is
desirous of substituting sheep for cattle to as great an extent as a
true calculation of interest will admit" (Garden, 196).

Jefferson was better at accurate and constant observation of the
phenomena than at formulating a program to mesh with them. He
wanted to construct an orderly farm-machine, one that would
achieve the exactitude and regularity he attributed to his pendu-
lum-measure:

In all successions of crops, the feilds must be supposed equal, each
feild to go through the same succession, and each year's crop to be the
same. On these data the laws of combination pronounce that the number
of feilds & number of years constituting a compleat rotation, must be always equal. If you cultivate three equal feilds only, your rotation will be
of 3. years, 5. feilds 5 years and I suppose 8 feilds of 60. acres each, & of
course an 8. years rotation, in the following succession . . . (ibid., 192).

He sought the permanent in the ephemeral: "I am asking the observations of 2. or 3. other friends in like manner and on receiving

the whole, shall proceed to *fix my rotation permanently,* and put it into the hands of my manager" (ibid., 196—italics added). The scheme was too rigid, as his son-in-law tried to suggest, writing that Jefferson must at least supplement "the great system" with more flexible and informal use of small fields. Different crops will not, after all, submit to an identical regimen: "From the diversity of constitution in plants, some are injured while others are benefited in the same stage of growth, by great heats or colds, by excessive moisture or droughts" (ibid., 200). Where the plan depends on total regularity in all the parts, one irregularity wrecks the whole. Jefferson had to admit that: "Clover, when I can dress lots well, succeeds with me to my full expectation; but not on the fields in rotation; although I have been at much cost in seeding them. This has greatly disconcerted the system of rotation on which I had decided" (*Farm,* 313). This was not like the plan for weights and measures—never adopted, and therefore entertainable in theory till Jefferson's death. He actually *tried* the farm formulae, and soon had to abandon them.

But if Jefferson had bad luck charting the transit of crops around his various farms, he felt more confident about a grander project still: He meant to establish the boundaries of contractual and political legitimacy from the very transit of man through life. Working from Buffon's mortality tables, he argued that the average man would live thirty-four years after reaching his legal majority at twenty-one. If such a man is not to impose his will on later generations (a notion always repugnant to Jefferson, who fought the entailing of lands and slaves), then he should confine his commitment to others within that period.

But then Jefferson introduced a further statistical refinement. The man of twenty-one who will live thirty-four more years is contracting with other men whose lives are "in a constant course of decay and removal" (*Papers,* 15:394). So Jefferson tries to discover where and when, in this flux of lives, a whole generation may be said to have gone off the stage of legal responsibility and a new one arrived. Back to the mortality tables:

Take, for instance, the table of M. de Buffon wherein he states 23,994 deaths, and the ages at which they happened. Suppose a society in which 23,994 persons are born every year, and live to the ages stated in this table. The conditions of that society will be as follows. 1st. It will consist constantly of 617,703. persons of all ages. 2ly. Of those living at any one instant of time, one half will be dead in 24. years 8. months. 3rdly. 10,675 will arrive every year at the age of 21. years complete. 4ly. It will constantly have 348,417 persons of all ages above 21. years. 5ly. And the half of those of 21. years and upwards living at any one instant of time will be dead in 18. years 8. months, or say 19. years as the nearest integral number. Then 19. years is the term beyond which neither the representatives of a nation, nor even the whole nation itself assembled, can validly extend a debt (ibid.).

It is easy to see why this mathematical operation appealed to Jefferson. Once again, careful observation of nature leads man from the facts to a law, from the phenomena of change to fixed pattern: Since living men should not be bound by the will of the dead, no contract's term should be extended for more than nineteen (or, in the rounded number, twenty) years. This is the numerical path Jefferson trod to some of his most famous and revered statements— e.g., that "the earth belongs in usufruct to the living" (ibid., 392). He concluded that "Every constitution then, and every law, naturally expires at the end of 19 years. If it be enforced longer, it is an act of force, and not of right" (ibid., 396). It was an opinion he never reversed, and one that underlies other famous comments— that there should be a revolution every twenty years; that his own election in 1800, roughly twenty years after the Articles gave the colonies a single government, was a second revolution; and that America by the 1820s needed a new revolution.

Admirers of Jefferson tend to praise the "moral ideal" they find expressed in such slogans. But they are embarrassed by the mathematical argument that led Jefferson to such precise numerical conclusions. They will accept as slogans what they edge off from as axioms. And no wonder. Although Jefferson pretends to adjust (down from a thirty-four-year term to a nineteen-year one) for the arrival and departure of individuals in the flow of time, his fixed term is as much at odds with the realities of human change as his farm program was with the hazards of weather and seeds. One can see this by trying to imagine what his scheme would be like if put into practice.

If I enter into a contract with two other men who happen to be partners by a prior agreement—one that has already run half of its course—then *their* contractual tie, on which *ours* depends, will lapse halfway through the new agreement. Besides, a twenty-one-year-old who enters into a contract with a fifty-year-old would circumvent the aim of the decree that dictates a maximum term of nineteen years for the contract—since the old man will have bound his estate when he dies (as the odds were then) five years later, leaving fourteen years of the contract still to run. Thus, in the mass of the population, there would still be a constant binding of living individuals to the will of the dead, especially since property tends to accumulate toward the end of a man's active life, rather than at the beginning—a tendency that would actually be increased by Jefferson's laws against inherited estates. If the average contracting age of the major property holders were to be forty-five (a low estimate if anything), then contracts for the mass of property would still bind the living to the dead for over half of their term. If you and I had set up a contract when we were both twenty-one, then we could not admit partners to the arrangement later on without depriving them of the long-term advantages or us of the long-term duties agreed upon. With the prescribed termination date approaching, a contract would lose its value to one or the other side. Why join what must so soon be dissolved? If, however, at the dissolution of a contract, the living signators were simply to renew its provisions (at their older ages) for another nineteen years, the intent of Jefferson's decree would be not only evaded but undermined by its own provisions.

I have begun, as Jefferson did, with the private contract and have only hinted at the thousand difficulties coming at once to the mind —difficulties such that merely to imagine the system is to grant it too much. This is one of those cases where even to argue with a position is to compliment it—one grants it a hypothetical prior existence in order to criticize its "consequences," when the real impossibility is for the thing to get into a position to have any consequences. The difficulty of imagining such a system at work becomes far more pronounced when we move up the scale from private contracts to national constitutions. All those reaching their majority later than the last redrafting time would have a dwindling term of government in which to form their first political experience —some of them being governed for a year, some for two, and so on, before the whole thing must be reformulated. Jefferson foresaw a rapid growth of American population; so the number of those having so brief a first experience of government would constantly be increasing. Those of a more advanced age would, by contrast, be forced late in life to adopt brand-new social arrangements whose long-term benefit they could not expect to share; to which, correspondingly, their commitment would be slight. If, as with property, power accumulates during a man's active years, this older class would oppose the procrustean deadline interrupting their prime of achievement—and they would foreseeably have the means, along with the will, to circumvent or overthrow the decree imposing the deadline. As Madison observed in his response to Jefferson's proposal, the plan would make every government an "interregnum" (ibid., 16:148), separating the interests of old and young, creating "faction" and destroying men's mutual stake in society. Actually, Madison's objections had been formulated earlier. Even before Jefferson came up with the plan, Hume had foreseen and dismissed it. That "skeptic" was more truly empirical than Jefferson:

> Did one generation of men go off the stage at once, and another succeed, as is the case with silk-worms and butterflies, the new race, if they had sense enough to choose their government, which surely is never the case with men, might voluntarily, and by general consent, establish their own form of civil polity, without any regard to the laws or precedents which prevailed among their ancestors. But as human society is in perpetual flux, one man every hour going out of the world, another coming into it, it is necessary, in order to preserve stability in government, that the new brood should conform themselves to the established constitution, and nearly follow the path which their fathers, treading in the footsteps of theirs, had marked out to them (Essay, "Of the Original Contract").

Modern liberals, while glossing over the arithmetical basis of Jefferson's famous letter to Madison, like to quote lines from it for pulse-quickening purposes. This is understandable: The fallacy adopted and spelled out so meticulously by Jefferson is the same one that hides behind modern sloganizing about a new deal or fair deal, about an equal start (or, where society has rigged the odds, a compensatory head start). The metaphor implies that the ongoing game or race can be stopped, to be started over fresh—the cards dealt again, the starting gun refired, as Jefferson's contracts were all to be redrafted. But individuals are, at each second, entering and leaving the "game" or "race" of life. Fire the starting gun now, and those who drift up immediately after must run from way back or

not at all. So: start over? Then you must keep doing that in an endless sequence of "starts." The staggered individuals' infinite starting
(and finishing) lines cannot be systematized by the game metaphor, which hides all the problems of Jefferson's contract scheme in
vague imagery. Both are efforts to make consequent (*first* line up
and *then* start running) what is irreducibly concomitant; to arrive
at discrimination (a winner) by repeated efforts at nondiscrimina-
tion; to make equality mean the same thing as competition. The
logical confusion arises from an attempt to preserve opposed values
in a simple scheme—to make commitments mean the same thing as
freedom from commitments. (I can contract, making a mark on the
world; but I must leave my son free to start all over, on an unmarked world). The scheme tries to imagine the continuous flow of
human society cut up into enclosed game-sequences, detachable
from what precedes and follows.

Aside from the logical and practical flaws in Jefferson's plan, does
it really offer an inspiring moral ideal, as its defenders claim? Is it
either generous or just to deny any obligation to one's forebears?
Madison pointed up the problem—if one generation, in passing on
land to the next, leaves it tamed and cultivated, then the next generation is not beholden to nature alone, but to those who gave them
nature "improved." The urge to benefit one's posterity is a noble
one, to be recognized and encouraged: One generation fights for a
liberty only its descendants will enjoy in peace. By making each
generation live only for itself, Jefferson would not only inhibit the
entailing of one's posterity, but the enhancing of its life. He would
teach men not only to live quit of any claim from the dead, but quit
of the unborns' claims as well—since only the living should enjoy
earth's usufructs.

For that matter, why does Jefferson limit the living generation to
enjoyment of earth's usufructs? If earth *belongs* to the living, why
should one generation not acquire the means for its own enjoyment
by aliening the land itself—sell it off and leave none of it to native
posterity? Or use up the land by shortsighted management, returning quick profits? After all, if improvements of the land do not bind
descendants, there can be no corresponding claim against those
who exhaust the land in their lifetime.

Presumably Jefferson would answer that the earth is nature's constant gift to all men, while particular claims are only to the land's

use. Still, even abuse is a use of the earth, not its total destruction. All that the sale of a whole nation's land to some other prince affects is the shifting of national contracts, which *should* be short and fluctuating by Jefferson's own rationale. If nature, not one's forebears, grants the living unencumbered title to the earth, then let nature take care of its own. The distinction between owning and using the earth tends to disappear when all contracts of ownership are reduced to the brief tenure of Jefferson's plan.

The artificiality of this scheme derives from the attempt to find some *numerical* point in time when one generation can be dismissed as finished and a new one greeted as fully arrived. For actual people, their own children *are* the living, in fact and in desire, and possession is shared with them in all the overlapping mutuality of men at every age with their fellow men of every age. The attempt to destroy these complexities is not a worthy ideal. Jefferson's proposal is not merely—like the pendulum or farm proposals—impossible to put into effect; it is, by real human standards, immoral—what Madison meant when he gave the obligation of generations to each other a foundation *in the nature of things:*

> There seems then to be a foundation in the nature of things, in the relation which one generation bears to another, for the *descent* of obligations from one to another. Equity requires it. Mutual good is promoted by it. All that is indispensable in adjusting the account between the dead and the living is to see that the debits against the latter do not exceed the advances made by the former. Few of the incumbrances entailed on nations would bear a liquidation even on this principle (ibid., 148).

Of course Jefferson thought his plan moral because it clearly enunciated, for him, the will of Nature as that was measured by Number. The mathematical details embarrass his modern admirers, but they were his own proudest boast. He remained true to the scheme because he felt it was true to nature, as measured in *what happens.* Even when he failed as a practical scientist, it was by adhering to the vision of science afforded him. He erred by sheer thirst for inerrancy.

He shared with many great minds of his period an aesthetics of science. As a result of some romantics' opposition to practical industry, we are tempted to think of art and science as tending of necessity toward quarrel—of the aesthete at odds with the robot. But the

Augustan period saw art and science as necessary and profitable allies. The beauty of the universe was refracted through them both, in analogous ways. The accurate vocabulary of Johnson, the well-oiled meters of Cowley, voiced nature's order much as Rittenhouse's clocks did. Pope labored to achieve the tick-tock regularity Keats rebukes him for. An aesthetic vision drew Pope; yet the Keatsian does not find a different *kind* of art in Pope so much as a failure to be an artist at all.

Perhaps I risk misunderstanding when I say that Jefferson was a great artist. I do not mean merely that he built what is perhaps the most beautiful building in America, one of the nation's supreme artifacts; but that he lived with an *aesthetic* grasp upon the ideals offered by the science of his day. He not only drew the plans for Monticello and kept its labyrinthine farm records, without feeling any tug of contradiction between the two kinds of activity. For him they were *not* two different kinds of activity: Each traced the plan of Nature with accuracy. Jefferson felt that the mathematical ratios of Palladio were as much a part of nature's order as the relation of a man's head to his torso or the relation of Venus to the sun.

The Augustan poet felt called not only to celebrate Newton's achievement but to repeat it in his own terms. A shrewd observer like Adam Smith perceived how much of this artist's instinct went into the purely mechanical and scientific work of his time. Men strove to make even pocket watches accurate beyond the norm of *convenience* or practical *use*, out of aesthetic regard for the curious machines that keep time with the universe:

A watch . . . that falls behind above two minutes in a day, is despised by one curious in watches. He sells it perhaps for a couple of guineas, and purchases another at fifty, which will not lose above a minute in a fortnight. The sole use of watches, however, is to tell us what o'clock it is, and to hinder us from breaking any engagement, or suffering any other inconveniency by our ignorance in that particular point. But the person so nice with regard to this machine will not always be found either more scrupulously punctual than other men, or more anxiously concerned upon any other account to know precisely what time of day it is. What interests him is not so much the attainment of this piece of knowledge, as the perfection of the machine which serves to attain it (*Moral Sentiments*, iv, 1).

Smith, realizing the usefulness of this taste, joined his century's debate over "*le luxe*" on the side of men like Voltaire. Admittedly, the superfluous "conveniences" do not give men the practical satisfaction they seem to promise. Indeed, the whole "machinery" of conveniences can reach a point of redundancy, one *demanding* constant care rather than *taking* care of men:

Power and riches appear then to be, what they are, enormous and operose machines contrived to produce a few trifling conveniencies to the body, consisting of springs the most nice and delicate, which must be kept in order with the most anxious attention, and which, in spite of all our care, are ready every moment to burst into pieces, and to crush in their ruins their unfortunate possessor. They are immense fabrics which it requires the labour of a life to raise, which threaten every moment to overwhelm the person that dwells in them, and which, while they stand, though they may save him from some smaller inconveniencies, can protect him from none of the severer inclemencies of the season. They keep off the summer shower, not the winter storm, but leave him always as much, and sometimes more, exposed than before to anxiety, to fear, and to sorrow; to diseases, to danger, and to death (ibid.).

But the contemplation of such ingenious mechanical effort is pleasing, and beguiles us into doing the world's work:

If we consider the real satisfaction which all these things are capable of affording, by itself and separated from the beauty of that arrangement which is fitted to promote it, it will always appear in the highest degree contemptible and trifling. But we rarely view it in this abstract and philosophical light. We naturally confound it in our imagination with the order, the regular and harmonious movement of the system, the machine or economy by means of which it is produced. The pleasures of wealth and greatness, when considered in this complex view, strike the imagination as something grand, and beautiful and noble, of which the attainment is well worth all the toil and anxiety which we are so pat to bestow upon it. And it is well that nature imposes upon us in this manner. It is this deception which rouses and keeps in continual motion the industry of mankind.

(This is the very paragraph where—a few sentences further on— Smith uses the term "invisible hand.")

Whatever one thinks of the lesson Smith drew from his observations, there can be no doubt that he observed what was there—an aesthetics of accuracy in his period—and that Jefferson is an outstanding example of this phenomenon at work. Some of Jefferson's modern biographers think they discern an indirect criticism in his description of his tutor, James Maury, as "an accurate classical scholar." Post-Romantics want enthusiasm from their teachers; but we know what the Augustans thought of enthusiasm. Jefferson wanted an accurate scholar, just as he wanted an accurate building.

Visitors to Monticello often wonder at its practical accessories. But Jefferson labored a month to save a minute. His home was impractical from the start—by reason of its very site (on a mountain), by the height given the first version of the building (later disguised in a way that left useless spaces in and around its dome), by the perpetual "course" of its dismantling and reassembly. To make the house more convenient, he made his daughter and her children live for years in a chaos of artistic second thoughts, sometimes sheltered only by canvas as the roof rose, fell, and assumed new shapes in his mind. He had a *vision* of convenience that, like many an artist's vision, tortured him to endless efforts at perfection. Adam Smith might have been describing Monticello when he wrote: "To obtain this conveniency he voluntarily puts himself to more trouble than all he could have suffered from the want of it. . . . What he wanted therefore, it seems, was not so much this conveniency, as that arrangement of things which promotes it" (ibid.).

Something like that last distinction must often be made in considering Jefferson's visions. Yet much later commentary makes such a distinction difficult. Time after time, when men feel themselves at odds with Jefferson's views, they try to accommodate them to ours by removing the "outdated" science presupposed in the original text. Yet the vision arose precisely from the particulars of that science, and can be grasped only in those terms. Jefferson was convinced—what is probably true, if in unintentional ways—that he was most creative when he was most slavish to the laws of nature, *cui servire regnare.*

NINE

". . . let facts be submitted . . ."

When he was born he gave an algebraic
Cry; at one glance measured the cubic content
Of that ivory cone his mother's breast
And multiplied his appetite by five.
So he matured by a progression, gained
Experience by correlation, expanded
Into a marriage by contraction, and by
Certain physical dynamics
Formulated me. And on he went
Still deeper into the calculating twilight
Under the twinkling of five-pointed figures
Till Truth became for him the sum of sums
And Death the long division.
—Christopher Fry

Though later admirers of Jefferson want to disencumber his nine-teen-year-contract scheme of its embarrassingly concrete mathematics, Franz Bühler has demonstrated that the plan arose in just those circles where Number ruled supreme (cf. *Verfassungsrevision und Generationenproblem*, Freiburg, 1949). The closest parallel to the Jefferson proposal is not to be found in Thomas Paine or Richard Gem (as Adrienne Koch and Julian Boyd, respectively, suggest) but in the Marquis de Condorcet. Condorcet was part of that Parisian circle of *idéologues* that was busy drafting and revising constitutions and elaborating a theory that demanded frequent redraftings. Bühler cites (32) Condorcet's *"Sur la nécessité de faire ratifier la constitution par les citoyens,"* and the 1793 Declaration of Rights: *"Un peuple a toujours le droit de revoir, de reformer, et de reviser sa Constitution. Une génération ne peut assujettir à ses lois des généra-tions futures."*

Condorcet's work was the culmination of a whole century's effort to reduce the problems of life to mathematical form. Condorcet called his grand scheme a *"mathématique sociale."* Even some idéologues—like Thurot and La Harpe—thought Condorcet carried his reliance on numbers too far (Moravia, 735–38). La Harpe mocked him for trying to cure men's troubles in quarto volumes abristle with algebra, judging matters of life and liberty "by tenths, by twentieths, by fractioned proofs weighed against one another, reduced to equations, sums, and products" (*Lycée*, 17:7).

But if Condorcet was the culminating representative of this mathematical tendency, he was also its most expert spokesman. Earlier efforts had been cruder, had claimed even more while doing far less. To chart man's life by a moral geometry, using algebra and the calculus, was the philosopher's stone to men of the Enlightenment, men who dreamed of Newtonizing all reality. One expression of this was the "political arithmetic" that earned an entry in the major encyclopedias of the time (Chambers, Diderot, Demeunier). These articles traced their subject back to work done by the Royal Society in its early days, and especially to Sir William Petty, charter member of the Society (and of "the Invisible College" that preceded it).

Petty, the inspired crank of Aubrey's pages, took the new science of his day and applied it in dozens of unlikely areas, forecasting many a development of the next century. He invented the term "political arithmetic," which was later restricted to economic statistics and demography. But Petty himself gave it a far wider definition and application. There was practically nothing he would not undertake to translate into "numbers, weight, and measure." He had run off to sea as a boy, cadged an education from Jesuits in France, and become amanuensis to Thomas Hobbes. His mathematical ability was apparently innate, but he studied medicine as his profession and became very famous for reviving a hanged woman.* By the age of twenty-seven he had become professor of

---

* "And while she was hanging, divers friends of hers and standers by, some hung with their whole weight upon her, others gave her great strokes on the breasts; and moreover a soldier did the same several times with the butt end of his musquet. When she was cut down and put into the coffin (which was sent for her by those to whom her body was consigned to be dissected) and brought to the place where the said dissection was to be made, and the coffin opened, she rattled in the throat; whereupon a lusty fellow standing by stamped upon her breast and stomach several times with his feet" (Petty's account, *Papers*, 2:157–58).

anatomy at Oxford, where he could teach that subject as a branch
of natural mechanics: "[Man's] most mysterious and complicated
enginry is nothing to the compounded and decompounded mysteries
in the fabric of man. All their static and hydrostatic, their hydraulic
and trochaulic, thermoptic and scenoptic, their recoustics and
music, their pneumatics and ballistics and all other their mechanics
whatsoever, are no more compared to the fabric of an animal than
putting two sticks across is to a loom, a clock, or a ship under sail—
the latter whereof, supposing [i.e., granting] her men to be animal
spirits, comes nearest to an animal of anything I know" (Petty, *Papers*, 2:172). Petty also became professor of music at Gresham college, the birthplace of the Royal Society. His inventions extended
into many areas—like Jefferson he fiddled with that troublesome and
temperamental "convenience," the polygraph. His plan for a dou-
ble-hulled boat, put to elaborate tests, was sequestered from public
view by the Royal Society's president, lest England's enemies profit
from it—so early was scientific material "classified."

It was as the physician to Cromwell's army in Ireland that Petty
began his most sustained effort. Since Cromwell meant to distribute
parcels of Irish land as a reward for his soldiers, Petty drew up the
official map of that land and undertook a detailed survey of County
Down, employing a little scientific army of his own for the job. The
scheme, at first, was to give each man forty acres—much like the
fifty acres used to lure adventurers to Virginia in the parliamentary
Articles of 1651 (*Notes*, 114) or the fifty acres Jefferson wanted to
give to each free male in Virginia. But the forty acres in Ireland
had to be good land, and its worth was a function not only of the
soil's fertility but of access to water, to the sea, to high roads, to
mills, etc. Petty conceived the idea of a calculus that would allow
for a single scale of measurement for each estate's entire value. It
was the beginning of a lifetime's labor to reduce all natural phenomena to numerical equations. When, for instance, the government wished to raise taxes in Ireland for defense purposes, Petty
objected in hard numbers:

You know my virtue and vanity lies in prating of numbers, weight and
measure; not sticking to talk even of the proportions of kingdoms and
states. Now upon this head I have sometimes said that England is ten
times richer and Scotland a third poorer than Ireland; that Ireland doth
now pay £240,000 per annum; that the charge of collecting the same is

viis et modis per annum £ 60,000 more, so as the poor people of Ireland do pay £ 300,000 per annum to somebody. Now if England paid ten times as much, and Scotland two thirds of the same, the whole would be three millions and a half; which sum (said I) would set forth and maintain the ablest fleet that ever was known, and about 80,000 horse and foot besides. . . . This discourse did not tend toward the intended raising and increasing of the revenue here [in Ireland], and was said to have been more properly held forth in the Parliament of England, which therefore I now tell you; and this is the reason why I fear ill success in my business. But I assure you, Cousin, that I had rather live upon herb pottage all the days of my life (as I did with advantage all the time of my sickness) than not to study truth and those symmetries whereby the world stands and which are the causes why *Res nolunt male administrari*. But oh that I had the discretion not to value truth nor scorn lying! (Lansdowne, *Corr.*, 51–52).

Petty was constantly telling statesmen what they could or could not do in the areas of taxation, military preparation, and economic planning—things the laws of nature, spelled out in his equations, made it impossible to do or to avoid. The reaction often saddened him: "The world do fear and therefore hate that things should be tried by number, weight, and measure" (ibid., 97).

Yet only number could truly report the facts, not going beyond them: "The method I take to do this, is not yet very usual; for instead of using only comparative and superlative words, and intellectual arguments, I have taken the course (as a specimen of the political arithmetic I have long aimed at) to express myself in terms of number, weight, and measure; to use only arguments of sense [i.e., of sensible experience] and to consider only such causes as have visible foundations in nature; leaving those that depend upon the mutable minds, opinions, appetites, and passions of particular men to the consideration of others" (Pref., *Political Arithmetic*). The aim of his labors was not pure truth arrived at for its own sake, but the happiness of men: "God send me the use of things and notions whose foundations are sense and the superstructures mathematical reasoning; for want of which props so many governments do reel and stagger, and crush the honest subjects that live under them" (*Papers*, 1:111). His practical work was devoted to the improvement of agriculture, the development of demographic and meteorological statistics.

Like Jefferson, Petty formed his geometric concepts from the art of surveying—his own boasts about the scientific achievement of his Irish map resemble the pride expressed by Jefferson in his father's great map of Virginia. Petty felt he could establish the *total* value of various segments of Irish land—and saw no reason why he should not do the same for countries, governments, and civilizations. His aim was all-embracing: "To make a par between lands and hands, between labor and art, between work and authority, between office and favour with the prince" (ibid., 1:196). One can see in the contrasts chosen—between work done, for instance, and authority wielded; or between office filled and favor won—why Petty's schemes would embarrass politicians. They opposed real worth to trappings of office. Petty could only estimate values by *averaging* the work done in a kingdom, and he clearly felt that reality should approximate this distribution. Petty questioned the worth of priests and expensive ritual and wondered what return society gets for its investment in certain professions, including his own: "The number of people dying where the faculty of medicine is numerous and where the same is otherwise shows the value and effect of that art. The same may be said of professors of the law" (ibid., 1:195).

In weighing kingdom against kingdom, Petty found France more populous than England, but its men less valuable for trade, war, or work. This was partly because of England's situation—its ports and rivers, its higher ratio of seamen to farmers; and partly because of a better balance of production to consumption (making the English "superlucrators"); and partly because of special factors—e.g., the high number of unproductive priests in France. So he concluded that ten million Englishmen were worth twelve to thirteen million Frenchmen (*Political Arithmetic*, ch. 4), a confident bit of nationalism that brings to mind U. S. Secretary of Defense Clark Clifford's boast in the 1960s that an American fighting in Vietnam would be the equal of fifteen Asian soldiers. Naturally, Diderot reported Petty's computation only to reject it.

In *Verbum Sapienti*, Petty figured the productive value of the English laborer at sixty-nine pounds. But he also planned to compute the *decline* in worth as a man moves from his prime toward death, a forecast of the actuarial tables Buffon would make and Jefferson rely on. In a manuscript titled *Of Lands and Hands*, Petty sketched a proposal for the universal valuation of a realm, one that would establish numerically the degree of national vice and learning, health and religion. The project takes on, as one reads it, the feel of a litany. "By the number" becomes almost an incantation:

By the number of people and provision of cattle and corn, to frame a sumptuary law in case of famine; as also rules for exportation in case of plenty . . .

By the number of ships yearly cast away and of seamen drowned, to compute freight and insurance . . .

By the perimeter of the island and what part thereof is fit for landing, to compute what force is necessary against invasion . . .

By the number of souls, and church rules, and quality of land, to know the just number of priests and churchmen.

By the number of decrees, verdicts and judgments in all courts, to know the number of judges and lawyers necessary. And by the number of writs and bills to know who is vexatious.

By the number of people, the quality of inebriating liquors spent, the number of unmarried persons of between fifteen and fifty years old, the number of corporal sufferings and persons imprisoned for crimes, to know the measure of vice and sin in the nation.

By the number of twenty sorts of books, sold yearly in the nation, to know the genius of the people (*Papers*, 1:196–97).

Most of Petty's grander schemes were stillborn, in his lifetime, for lack of solid data to build on. But many of the programs were taken up again during the eighteenth century as men acquired, or thought they had, accurate statistics. There were large attempts to measure all kinds of things "by the number." The Marquis de Chastellux tried to discover an arithmetical measure for the happiness of various epochs in human history. Since superstition clouds man's happiness, one could arrive at one standard of public felicity by counting the number of a country's priests (*De la félicité*, 1:17–18). Diderot, in the "Sarassins" article for his Encyclopédie, refined the technique. He would measure the progress of enlightenment by counting the number of communion wafers consumed annually in a large city parish—a pronounced falling off in the numbers would provide a "*règle très-sur pour calculer* . . . *le déclin de la superstition nationale*." D'Alembert stated the same law inversely, saying the way to end the Inquisition was to increase the number of mathematicians in the affected countries, since superstition must yield to any considerable exposure to mathematics (1812 *Oeuvres*, 1:571).

We find here the background of thought that could make Jefferson propose as his measure of national virtue the number of farmers, and of national corruption the number of city-dwellers: "Generally speaking, the proportion which the aggregate of the other classes of citizens bears in any state to that of its husbandmen, is the proportion of its unsound to its healthy parts, and is a good barometer whereby to measure its degree of corruption. . . . The mobs of great cities add just so much to the support of pure government, as sores do to the strength of the human body. It is the manners and spirit of a people which preserve a republic in vigour. A degeneracy in these is a canker which soon eats to the heart of its laws and constitution" (*Notes*, 165). He is merely restating one of Chastellux's laws for measuring happiness (*De la félicité*, 1:60–61). Chastellux had even compared "the mobs of great cities" to the swarm of germs revealed by a microscope, tracing a political disease to the cities as part of his "moral medicine."

Madame de Staël hoped to create an exact science of happiness on the basis of statistics for murder, divorce, and other extreme products of human passion, region by region. Exact measurement of the passions would make it possible to arrange precise counterbalances in the law, leading to the "*équilibre*" of an ideal constitution (Intro., *De l'influence des passions sur le bonheur des individus et des nations*).

Political science by the numbers was the goal of Turgot and Condorcet. Chastellux had already tried to set up a mathematical formula for tyranny. He approached the task with the jauntiness of the philosophes: "Here too one can use the calculus—it is a problem reducible to algebraic terms and then stated easily in numerical ratios" (*De la félicité*, 1:14). First one must count the number of hours in the day, and days in the year, during which men can (on the average) work without major inconvenience. Then one must establish the number of hours in the day, and days in the year, during which men *must* work for reasonably comfortable subsistence. Subtracting the second figure from the first gives one the number of spare (*disponibles*) workdays. If the state service and taxation do not exceed the value of the spare days, then its exactions are not tyrannous. If they do, then mere numbers brand the despot (1:9–14). Like Petty, whose work he knew (1:20), Chastellux based all his estimates on a labor theory of value. His formula for spare days repeats Petty's scheme for calculating the spare manpower that can be devoted to military service (*Papers*, 1:194). A modern economist, a student of Petty, rephrased part of the Chastellux thesis this way: "Plenty is the excess of free energy over the collective calorie debt of human effort applied to securing the needs which all human beings share" (Lancelot Hogben, *Political Arithmetic*, 1938, p. 42). Chastellux goes on to argue the paradox that such "plenty," seen as national capital, tends to reduce the chances for national happiness, since it tempts rulers to projects that imperil the subjects' happiness (1:17–19).

In one important area, Petty did not go far enough for eighteenth-century taste. He forswore the use of numbers to calculate the odds in games of chance: Dismissing vain opinion, he described himself as "unable to speak satisfactorily upon those [i.e., such] grounds (if they may be called grounds) as to foretell the cast of a die [or] to play well at tennis, billiards, or bowls (without long practice) by virtue of the most elaborate conceptions that ever have been written *de projectilibus et missilibus*, or of the angles of incidence and reflection" (Pref., *Political Arithmetic*). Yet his own work rested on probability theory—his statistics were meant to establish the degree of likelihood for the event of death or disease in specific ages and places. Thus, in his *Discourse of Duplicate Proportions* he wrote (84): "Roots of every number of men's ages under 16 (whose root is 4) compared with the said number of 4, doth show the proportion of the likelihood of such men reaching 70 years of age. As for example, it is 4 times more likely that one of 16 years old should live to 70 than a new-born babe."

Pascal, who studied gambling odds, used that study to formulate his famous wager (*pari*) on the existence of God—what Ian Hacking has called "the first well-understood contribution to decision theory." Much of the seventeenth-century's moral controversy had centered around probability. In judging moral cases of conscience (casuistry) for the confessional, exceptions to general law were admitted if one solidly probable authority could be cited for the exception (probabilism)—this was the Jesuit position. Less permissive theologians demanded proof that no *other* authority could be cited as giving a *more* probable view of the matter (equiprobabilism). The strictest attitude, popularly identified with Pascal's Jansenists, demanded that one follow only the *most* probable authority applicable to the issue (probabiliorism). The Port Royal *Logic* supplied norms for judging the probability of conflicting testimony (cf. Hacking, 73–78). In 1740 the Chambers Cyclopaedia still devoted much of its "Probability" entries to this dispute.

The tests for probability of testimony were applied to the Christian gospel by Newton's friend, John Craig, who measured their loss of credibility over time and came to the comforting conclusion that this would not reach the zero point until A.D. 3150. (The title of Craig's 1699 book typifies the search for a Newtonian theology: *Theologiae Christianae Principia Mathematica.*) The rules for probability of *testimony* were spelled out in Cesare Beccaria's great book of penal reform, *Dei Delitti e delle Pene* (1763). He offers "a general theory very useful for calculating the certitude of an [alleged] fact" (63). Three situations are to be distinguished "by the number":

1) When the evidence of witnesses depends on nothing but internal consistency, the greater the number of arguments advanced, the less the probability of the whole.

2) When many witnesses offer only a single proof, the probability remains the same no matter how many witnesses adduce that proof.

3) When each bit of testimony offered appeals to different evidence, probability increases with each additional witness. Enough of these imperfect proofs can, by addition, become the virtual equal of one perfect proof, establishing "moral certitude" of guilt or innocence (63–65—Jefferson copied out this whole passage in his *Commonplace Book*, 301–2).

Beccaria also uses *"il calculo delle probabilità,"* part of his *"aritmetica politica"* (44), to establish the unlikelihood of procuring truthful evidence from torture (70), the superior likelihood of testimony regarding *actions* over that relating *words* (62), and the greater likelihood of false testimony in the more atrocious crimes (61). Condorcet went beyond the probability of testimony to measure the likelihood that a composite jury can reach the truth. This effort, the basis of Condorcet's extended theorizing on electoral systems, was long dismissed as misguided on the basis of Todhunter's well-known criticisms; but Duncan Black has offered a strong defense of Condorcet's arguments on pages 57–59, 159–80 of *The Theory of Committees and Elections* (1963).

The improbability of regular results from chance occurrences was often used by Royal Society lecturers to establish the existence of God. John Graunt argued to God's superintendance of the universe from his mortality tables, concluding that the steady proportion of male to female births could only be maintained by constant correction from divine providence. Dr. Arbuthnot made this argument in a way that was often imitated, and that led to theoretical controversy with Nicolas Bernoulli, Abraham de Moivre, and 'sGravesande (Todhunter, 130–31, 196–99). There were many attempts to reduce the argument from design (as used, say, in Butler's *Analogy*) to precise mathematical form. Francis Hutcheson (1:51) in 1725 calculated the odds on the world's taking its present shape without a supreme Designer at infinity to the fifth power. Diderot warned theologians against relying on this argument (*Pensées philosophiques*, No. 21) and later grew skeptical about the use of mathematics for the study of society. But in 1761 he clashed with his fellow encyclopedist, D'Alembert over the possibility of basing social policy on probability statistics. D'Alembert disagreed with Daniel Bernoulli's defense of inoculation from the comparative statistics of those contracting small pox *after* inoculation and those contracting it *without* inoculation. D'Alembert said the statistics left out the time factor and the quality of life to be preserved: those who contracted the pox as a result of inoculation died soon, in their youth or at their prime. Even if they would later contract the disease, the higher *odds* of contraction had to be placed against the later *time* of contraction (cf. Todhunter, 224–28, 270–71, 277–83). Diderot entered the controversy on Bernoulli's side; and though D'Alembert had written most of the Encyclopédie articles on mathematics and chance (e.g., "*Avantage*," "*Bassette*," "*Carreau*," "*Dé*," "*Loterie*," "*Pari*"), Diderot assigned himself the important article on "*Probabilité*" in the 1765 volume. There he distinguished various kinds of probability and hoped they would all be reduced in time to a precise calculus for ruling human action.

Since lotteries and annuities played such a large part in eighteenth-century economics, statistics of the kind Petty sought were often used to analyze games of chance. To study the profitability of *tontines*, Deparcieux wrote his *Essai sur la probabilité de la durée de la vie humaine* (1736). By 1777, the great Buffon was basing all the physical sciences on mathematical probability ("Essai d'arithmétique morale," *Supplément*, 4:46–148). We do not know why the sun rises every day, so we cannot claim to know that it must rise. But the odds for its doing so are very high—Buffon figured them at twice-the-number-of-times-the-sun-has-risen to one (47–58). All odds above ten thousand to one he considered equivalent to certainties. His was a world of scientific relativism which nonetheless allowed for precise measurement and for "moral certitude" arising from such measurement: "All forms of our knowledge are based on ratios and comparisons."

Measuring became a kind of mania for many Enlightenment figures. In America, Petty's work was well known and admired. (Benjamin Franklin spoke especially well of it.) Jefferson's main library had four genuine works by Petty in it, and a spurious one (Sowerby, 3:120, 198, 237–78; 4:233). His enthusiasm for Petty began early, well before he wrote the Declaration. In 1769 he was ordering Petty's *Survey of Ireland* (*Papers*, 1:34), and two years later he recommended the *Political Arithmetic* for Robert Skipwith's basic library (ibid., 1:79). It is easy to understand Jefferson's interest. If he was not quite the man described by Christopher Fry's Jeanette Jordemain, his first preserved writing delivers him to us with an almost "algebraic cry." Asking his guardian's permission to leave the Shadwell estate for William and Mary College, he gives a precise measurement of the time this move will save: "In the first place as long as I stay at the Mountains the Loss of one fourth of my Time is inevitable, by Company's coming here and detaining me from school" (ibid., 1:3). There is an economic corrolary to this first computation: "And likewise my Absence will in a great Measure put a Stop to so much Company, and by that Means lessen the Expences of the Estate in House-Keeping." It is not surprising to hear, after this, that he wants to go to Williamsburg to "learn something of the Mathematics." In time he would become so famous for his arithmetical preoccupations that he could mock himself mildly to Abigail Adams: "I have ten and one-half grandchildren and two and three-fourths great-grandchildren, and these fractions will ere long become units." Jefferson liked to correlate numbers in his ample record books, e.g., calculating health conditions by the conjunction of winds, temperature, barometric readings, and diseases (to get what Petty called a Scale of Salubrity). Thus did he use numbers from mortality tables—those matrices of probability theory—to establish the limits of contractual legitimacy.

His greatest invention, the moldboard for a plow, was the solution to a geometric problem he set himself: "The offices of the mould-board are to receive the sod after the share has cut under it, to raise it gradually and reverse it. The fore end of it then should be horizontal to enter under the sod, and the hind end perpendicular to throw it over, the intermediate surface changing gradually from the horizontal to the perpendicular" (*Papers*, 13:27). He used Emerson's *Fluxions* (i.e., calculus) to study the wedge principle when moving an obstacle in a single direction (*Farm*, 51–52). But he knew he had to go beyond the "twisted plane" concept of a wedge: "It's first office is to receive the sod horizontally from the wing, to raise it to a proper height for being turned over, & to make, in it's progress, the least resistance possible; & consequently to require a minimum in the moving power. Were this it's only office, the wedge would offer itself as the most eligible form in practice. But the sod is to be turned over also. To do this, the one edge of it is not to be raised at all: for to raise this would be a waste of labour. The other edge is to be raised till it passes the perpendicular, that it may fall over with its own weight. And that this may be done so as to give also the least resistance, it must be made to rise gradually from the moment the sod is received. The mouldboard then in this second office, operates as a transverse, or rising wedge, the point of which sliding back horizontally on the ground, the other end continues rising till it passes the perpendicular" (*Garden*, 649–50). He pitted two wedges against each other in working out the formula whose claim, like that of the pendulum-length, was to be transferable by a set of ratios on paper. ("One fault of all other mouldboards is that, being copied by the eye, no two will be alike.") William Strickland wrote Jefferson that his moldboard was "formed from the trueest and most mechanical principle of any I had seen" (*Farm*, 52). His solution resembled John Hudde's use of mathematics to determine the most efficient slope of Holland's dykes.

Like his European counterparts, Jefferson was willing to be guided by numbers in ways that may strike us as fanciful. His use of statistics to solve a moral problem is exemplified by his reaction to Shays's Rebellion. Instead of discussing the particular merit or fault of this rebellion, he justifies it on a frequency scale: "The late rebellion in Massachusets has given more alarm than I think it should have done. Calculate that one rebellion in 13 states in the course of 11 years, is but one for each state in a century and a half. No country should be so long without one. Nor will any degree of power in the hands of government prevent insurrections. France with all it's despotism, and two or three hundred thousand men always in arms has had three insurrections in the three years I have been here in every one of which greater numbers were engaged than in Massachusets and a great deal more blood was spilt. In Turkey, which Montesquieu supposes more despotic, insurrections are the events of every day. In England, where the hand of power is lighter than here, but heavier than with us they happen every half dozen years" (*Papers*, 12:442).

Petty had proposed that a nation's genius be measured by the number of books made and sold in it. Jefferson proposed, rather, to measure it by the men of recognized merit produced nationally. When the Abbé Raynal said that America had not brought forth one man of genius, Jefferson cited three such: Washington, Franklin, Rittenhouse. Then he used the mathematics of probability to prove the American continent could not be inimical to genius:

For comparing it with those countries, where genius is most cultivated, where are the most excellent models for art, and scaffoldings for the attainment of science, as France and England for instance, we calculate thus. The United States contain three millions of inhabitants; France twenty millions; and the British islands ten. We produce a Washington, a Franklin, a Rittenhouse. France then should have half a dozen in each of these lines; and the British islands and Great-Britain half that number, equally eminent. It may be true, that France has: we are but just becoming acquainted with her, and our acquaintance so far gives us high ideas of the genius of her inhabitants. It would be injuring too many of them to name particularly a Voltaire, a Buffon, the constellation of Encyclopedists, the Abbé Raynal himself, &c. &c. We therefore have reason to believe she can produce her full quota of genius. The present war having so long cut off all communication with Great-Britain, we are not able to make a fair estimate of the state of science in that country. The spirit in which she wages war is the only sample before our eyes, and that does not seem the legitimate offspring either of science or of civilization (*Notes*, 65).

Jefferson turns the tables, even in this bit of scientific propaganda meant to recruit French support—he finds that America is the measure of other countries; that France "perhaps" measures up, and England probably does not. All by the numbers. Give him three of anything, and he can work out the most amazing sums.

Jefferson also solved the problem of the Indian tribes' antiquity by studying numbers. First, he considers numbers themselves the part of language most common to different tongues and dialects: "When a tribe has gone farther than it's neighbors in inventing a system of enumeration, the obvious utility of this will occasion it to be immediately adopted by the surrounding tribes with only such modifications of the sounds as may accommodate them to the habitual pronunciation of their own language" (*Notes*, 102). Yet even the numbers of the various Indian tribes in America showed a wide enough divergence to indicate long and fundamental development, proving these peoples more ancient than the Asian tribes:

Arranging them under the radical ones to which they may be palpably traced, and doing the same by those of the red men in Asia, there will be found probably twenty in America for one in Asia, of those radical languages, so called because, if they were ever the same, they have lost all resemblance to one another. A separation into dialects may be the work of a few ages only, but for two dialects to recede from one another till they have lost all vestiges of their common origin, must require an immense course of time; perhaps not less than many people give to the age of the earth. A greater number of those radical changes of language having taken place among the red men of America, proves them of greater antiquity than those of Asia (ibid.)

Like Petty, Jefferson tries to make a par between hands and lands in the political realm:

Thus the [Virginia] county of Warwick, with only one hundred fighting men, has an equal representation with the county of Loudon, which has 1746. So that every man in Warwick has as much influence in the government as 17 men in London. But lest it should be thought that an equal interspersion of small among large counties, through the whole state, may prevent any danger of injury to particular parts of it, we will divide it into districts, and shew the proportions of land, of fighting men, and of representation in each. . . . An inspection of this table will supply the place of commentaries on it. It will appear at once that nineteen thousand men, living below the falls of the rivers, possess half the senate, and want four members only of possessing a majority of the house of delegates; a want more than supplied by the vicinity of their

situation to the seat of government, and of course the greater degree of
convenience and punctuality with which their members may and will attend in the legislature. These nineteen thousand, therefore, living in one
part of the country, give law to upwards of thirty thousand, living in another, and appoint all their chief officers executive and judiciary (*Notes,*
118–19).

Jefferson established the commercial value of laboring men in the
Petty manner:

The labour of a negro Mr. [Arthur] Young reckons cent. per cent. dearer
than the labour of England.—To the hirer of a negro man his hire will cost
£9. and his subsistence, cloathing & tools £6. Making £15, sterl. or at
the most it may sometimes be £18.—To the owner of a negro his labour
costs as follows. Suppose a negro man of 25. years of age costs £75.
sterling: he has an equal chance to live 30. years according to Buffon's
table; so that you will lose your principal in 30 years. Then say,

	£	
Int. of £75. annually	3.	15
One thirtieth annually of the principal	2.	10
Subsistence, clothes, &c., annually	6.	
	12.	5

There must be some addition to this to make the labour equal to that of
a white man, as I believe the negro does not perform quite as much work,
nor with as much intelligence.—But Mr. Young reckons a laboringman in
England £8. & his board £16. making £24.

Petty, who tried to balance lots of forty acres so that they had
equal value, also wanted to change the parish system of England,
imposing a régime of equal curacies tending an equal number of
souls. This resembles Jefferson's quest for perfect regularity among
his farms, or his plan for equally balanced tiers of states to be
carved out of the Western territories of America. His collaborator
in this last effort, David Howell, described the plan for mechanical
equilibrium: "It is proposed to divide the country into fourteen
new states, in the following manner. There are to be three tiers of
states: one on the Atlantic, one on the Mississippi, and a middle
tier. The middle tier is to be the smallest, and to form a balance
betwixt the two more powerful ones" (*Papers,* 6:592). Jefferson
even wanted to give out systematizing names, ahead of time, to the
states thus neatly drawn up in his study—names like Metropotamia

and Polypotamia for the river-bounded and river-filled states (ibid., 6:604-5).

It is often remarked that Jefferson advocated universal education. But the characteristic touch in his proposal was the use of a mathematical progression of students through a sieve of equal units. He wanted the State of Virginia to "lay off every county into small districts of five or six miles square, called hundreds" (*Notes*, 146). Each "hundred" was to offer every child a three-year course of publicly supported education in reading, writing, and arithmetic. From each hundred the one best student still needing public support was to advance to a grammar school (one for every five hundreds) to learn Greek, Latin, geography, and higher mathematics. After one or two years in grammar school, the "best genius" in each class was to be granted a further education of six years "and the residue dismissed." The crop of children has now been reduced to "twenty of the best geniusses raked from the rubbish annually." At the end of six years, *this* class was to be halved *again*, only its *top* part going on to college. The system, he claimed, had the merit of "turning out ten annually of superior genius" and another ten, of the second rank, who would not go to college but receive a good education nonetheless. Meanwhile, the "rubbish" would at least have been introduced to reading and writing.

Such a plan would, in operation, be even more chaotic than Jefferson's revolving-farm scheme or the nineteen-year cycle for contracts. Tremendous competitive pressure is exerted on children from the outset, with only one pupil allowed to advance from the local "hundred." Even if that one could be rapidly identified and promoted with equity, the results would be essentially unfair. One "hundred" might have several students better than any in neighboring locales; yet only one from this superior cluster could advance. In such a situation, the task of choosing the *absolute* best would become especially difficult and odious. Jefferson no doubt wanted equal representation of all the hundreds for as long as he could maintain it while encouraging competition; but this would be purchased by the loss of some of the "best geniusses" back to the rubbish—in a system geared to promote only the best. The norms of excellence and equality would be pitted against each other in a way bound to cause resentment and a sense of injury.

Jefferson let the beauty of a mathematically regular scheme blind him to the recalcitrant human realities being schematized. But once again we find him as far removed as possible from vagueness or ambiguity in his social thought. He preferred to do things "by the numbers" because of the precision and definition given to anything under numerical control. He even thought of happiness, the pursuit of which is sometimes called the vaguest thing in the Declaration, as susceptible of numbered measurement and distribution.

"... effect their safety & happiness ..."

O mortel, puisses-tu *mesurer* désormais
L'héroïsme des rois au bonheur des sujets!
—Helvétius

Francis Hutcheson launched the Scottish Enlightenment with his 1725 *Inquiry into the Original of our Ideas of Beauty and Virtue.* The book's success brought him back to his own University of Glasgow as the Professor of Moral Philosophy. He began the practise of lecturing in English instead of Latin, and his influence radiated through all of mid-eighteenth-century ethical thought, either directly or through Hume. His first book is a sturdy piece of prose, as well as a strict logical exercise—it set the standard for expository writing that Hume and Adam Smith, Thomas Reid and Adam Ferguson would maintain.

But there was one aspect of the book which became the butt of jokes, even among those who admired the general argument of Hutcheson. This was his attempt to measure morality by algebraic formulae. These had, by his second edition in 1726, become fairly elaborate. Thus, where B = Benevolence, A = Ability, S = Self-love, and I = Interest, we get these equations: "M = (B + S) × A = BA + SA; and therefore BA = M − SA = M − I, and B = $\frac{M-I}{A}$. In the latter case, M = (B − S) × A = BA − SA; therefore BA = M + SA = M + I, and B = $\frac{M+I}{A}$" (1:293).

Richard Griffith, in *The Koran* (often misattributed to Laurence Sterne), justifiably complained: "Hutcheson, in his philosophic treatise on beauty, harmony, and order, pluses and minuses you to

heaven or hell by algebraic equations—so that none but an expert
mathematician can ever be able to settle his accounts with St. Peter
—and perhaps St. Matthew, who had been an officer in the customs,
must be called in to audit them" (#70 of "Memorabilia"). And
Griffith probably had Hutcheson in mind when he wrote that "Algebra is the metaphysics of arithmetic" (#77 of the "Callimachies").

We shall consider, later, the theoretical basis for Hutcheson's
formulae. Here it is important to notice what emerges from them,
almost as an afterthought, to become one of the most powerful concepts of the Enlightenment. The equations were set up to measure
in quasi-Newtonian fashion the "moment" (motive force) of B, Benevolence; and since Benevolence is defined as the desire to promote happiness in others, the moment of virtue gives us the amount
of happiness spread around in society. The concept of distributable
quanta of happiness is born of the numbering urge:

> In comparing the moral qualities of actions, in order to regulate our
> election among various actions proposed, or to find which of them has
> the greatest moral excellency, we are led by our moral sense of virtue
> thus to judge: that in equal degrees of happiness expected to proceed
> from the action, the virtue is in proportion to the number of persons to
> whom the happiness shall extend (and here the dignity or moral impor-
> tance of persons may compensate numbers); and in equal numbers, the
> virtue is as the quantity of the happiness or natural good; or that virtue
> is in a compound ratio of the quantity of good and number of enjoyers.
> And, in the same manner, the moral evil or vice is as the degree of
> misery and number of sufferers. So that, that action is best—[here comes
> the momentous formula]—which accomplishes the greatest happiness for
> the greatest numbers . . . (1:163–64).

Hutcheson's formula became a touchstone for enlightened thought.
It spread through philosophe circles by way of its 1749 French
translation and entered the Encyclopédie by way of Jaucourt's article, "Gouvernement": "Le meilleur des gouvernements est celui
qui fait le plus grand nombre d'heureux." Cesare Beccaria had used
the formula earlier (1763), in what was to be one of its most
influential appearances: "la massima felicità divisa nel maggior nu-
mero" (30). By the 1760s it had become the focus of much French
thought. In Mercier de La Rivière (1767), government's role is "as-
surer le plus grand bonheur possible à la plus grande population
possible." In Chastellux (1772): "Le plus grand bonheur du plus

grand nombre d'individus" (2:54). In Helvétius (1773): *"le plus grand plaisir et le plus grand bonheur du plus grand nombre des citoyens."* Robert Shackleton has traced the movement of the phrase through the century (*Studies on Voltaire,* Vol. 90). He misses the use in Helvétius (*De l'homme,* i, 10) but demonstrates that Bentham inherited the phrase by way of an English translation of Beccaria.

The extraordinary power of this concept in its time arose from the fact that it meant something very specific—the twofold mensurability of happiness, in terms of *quantity* within the individual and of the *sum* of individuals. Happiness was not only a constant preoccupation of the eighteenth century; it was one inextricably linked with the effort to create a science of man based on numerical gauges for all his activity. Seen in this light, happiness was not just a new subject but a dangerous one. This was not only, as d'Alembert put it, a case where superstition shrinks from the calculus. Happiness had been the preserve of theology; now secularizers were taking it over. The editor of the *Encyclopédie méthodique* felt that, despite articles on *"Bonheur"* and *"Félicité"* in Diderot's volumes, a new article should deal with the political concept of *"Félicité publique."* He commissioned the author of the treatise on that subject, the Marquis de Chastellux. to compose the article, but when it was submitted, the censors forbade its publication. It pitted, by implication, public happiness against celestial bliss. There was a note of possible heresy in the way men had begun to talk of happiness.

Hutcheson, a Presbyterian divine, could get away with more than his counterparts in lands where the Inquisition was still active. The escalation of earthly claims can be traced in three books on the subject published under the priests' watchful eyes in Italy. In 1749, Ludovico Muratori, the Jesuit archivist and librarian to the Prince of Modena, published *Della Felicità Pubblica.* It was, in form, an example of the old treatise *De Principe* or *De Regimine,* the education of a ruler. But the book took a radical approach to its topic. It no longer stressed above all the need for a prince to protect the faith and morals of his subjects—that was the realm of private happiness, in this world and the next. Muratori recognized that the ability of the prince to make his subjects virtuous was limited in any case. But he *can* secure the peace and tranquillity that are conditions of public happiness (6)—can, for instance, make sure the tax collectors only *sheer* the flock and do not *skin* it (7). In keeping with this conception of the ruler's job, Muratori feels the prince needs mathematicians around him as well as theologians (144–45). He asks that the ruler encourage scientific farming on the new model (178) and address himself to the eighteenth-century awareness of *"le luxe"* as a problem of state (316).

Enlightened as this treatise was—and coming from a pioneer in the study of historical documents—it did not go far enough for Pietro Verri (cf. Sola di Felice, *Felicità e morale*, 1970, 19–24). Verri, the leading figure in the Milan group of economists, posed the problem of happiness in terms of a calculation: one must equate abilities to desires, where desire tends always to outrun the ability to satisfy it. Put this way, the problem of happiness admits of three solutions: to decrease one's desires, the answer of ascetics; or to increase one's abilities, the answer of the Machiavellians; or to do both, in an equilibrating operation which becomes the answer of the enlightened. One must discern what desires need cutting back (e.g., that for mere wealth as such) and what ones need stimulating as a help to the increase of one's abilities (e.g., the desire for knowledge).

Verri's book, *Meditazioni sulla Felicità* (1763), ends with a glorification of the eighteenth century as the happiest period in man's history. That was the point religious authority found repugnant to orthodoxy. For Verri went farther than the "moderns" of the seventeenth-century dispute between ancients and moderns. He does not say that men have built better upon the ancient plan with the help of Christian religion, but that recent years, with their *dilution* of Christian authority, were an improvement on the ages of superstition.

Another book, appearing a year later, took the step that led to condemnation and frenzied religious attack. This was Cesare Beccaria's *Dei Delitti e delle Pene*, one of the principal texts of the Enlightenment, and a special favorite of Jefferson, who copied long passages from it in his *Commonplace Book* and used it as his principal modern authority for revising the laws of Virginia. This short work dazzled Europe. It was translated, reprinted, read everywhere, condemned by Rome, canonized by Voltaire. Some later readers have wondered what all the stir was about, and Beccaria has been left largely to the historians of penology. But it is clear that the Enlightenment, while hailing the book's practical suggestions for penal reform, thought of it as a standard for all enlightened thinking. In fact, the penal suggestions were the very things Voltaire and Diderot did not entirely agree with—neither, for instance, could go along with Beccaria's argument that *all* capital punishment should be abolished. Europeans were moved, it seems, by the very thing that chills some later readers, by the mathematical procedure of the book, its attempt to measure all human reactions in terms of pleasure and pain. Beccaria tried to reach a balance between punishment's *certainty, intensity, duration,* and the length of its *expectation.* This looked like a cramped and desiccating approach to men of the nineteenth century, who had read the romantic outbursts against penal savagery by Alessandro Manzoni, the great novelist who was also Beccaria's grandson.

Beccaria demystified the awesome power to punish by treating it as a form of payment to the state, whose amount must be adjusted by practical considerations. He even gave to social-contract doctrine an economist's reading. Men leave the state of nature by giving over a part (*porzione*) of their liberties for use by the state: "The sum of all these small pieces of liberty sacrificed for each one's own benefit makes up the sovereign power of the state, and a ruler is the legitimate custodian and dispenser of it" (32). Kings are reduced to the level of a bank dick. Crime is man's attempt to rob the bank (*togliere dal deposito*) of his own original part of surrendered power, and of some belonging to his neighbors. The penalty should be an exaction just enough in excess of expected advantage to deter or reform the would-be crook. So Beccaria speaks of crimes as compounding their interest (44) and needing just the right surplus of repayment. This resembles Petty's treatment of penalties in chapter Ten of his *Treatise of Taxes,* where he asks that penalties be repayments to the national wealth.

Arguing against capital punishment, Beccaria relies on the bank-model: "This vain excess of punishment which has not ever improved men leads me to question whether the death penalty can be truly useful or just in a well-organized government. By what right do men arrogate to themselves the power to kill their fellows? Clearly not the right from which sovereign power and laws are derived. They are simply the sum of least small pieces (*minime porzioni*) of each man's personal freedom; they represent the general will, which is simply an accumulation of the particular acts of will. But who has ever wished to give other men the right to kill him? How can the least sacrifice of each man's freedom equal the sacrifice of that greatest of all goods, life?" (103). We might object to Beccaria's argument here. He himself says that when the state acts, it acts by right of the *entirety* of powers ceded to it. These accumulated powers must always overbalance the individual's contribution, or the state could never punish men at all, even in noncapital ways. But Beccaria is saying that the deposit was always, of necessity, partial, never total. The aim of the contract is to preserve the greater part of a man's freedom; so deprivation of *all* goods—which *only* occurs in capital punishment—is outside the contract's ambit. It is not dealing in the relevant currency of *porzioni*.

He saved a weapon for use here from the armory of his clerical critics. In the effort to reduce penalties, he suggested that suicide not be punished at all, though it should be retained as a criminal category. This puzzled Voltaire, who wanted to expunge this so-called crime from the books entirely. Why retain a criminal offense for which there is no penal response? Beccaria has done it to show that the authorities themselves admit man has no right to give his life away, yet that is what he did in the original compact, according to the defenders of capital punishment. They would make everyone join society by committing virtual suicide. This was truly fighting the Jesuits with their own weapons.

The rigor with which Beccaria pursues his quantified version of freedoms given, banked, drawn on, stolen, recovered, shows up in every section of his work. The social contract was based on a mutual agreement to levy from any citizen the least possible amount of his freedom. Since the state punishes a man only inasmuch as he is a citizen, it proclaims his contracting status precisely by holding him to account. But since the contract was based on the principle of least-necessary levying, any time the state punishes a citizen *beyond* the minimum necessary to good order, it undermines itself; it breaks the contract; it commits a new crime on top of the old one.

Put another way, the duty of least-levying on a citizen's freedom is a duty of maintaining the maximum freedom and happiness among all contractors. So Beccaria applies the Hutchesonian measure to his whole project, saying the true student of the law should be able to "give the multiplicity of human acts a single center, and consider them in this single light: the greatest happiness distributed among the greatest number" (30). If penalties are measurable in terms of man's "*sensibilità*," then pleasures should be too. In fact, by gauging the things that need protection from criminals, Beccaria suggested the positive side of his own science of penalties. He writes, for instance: "Societies have, like the human body, prescribed limits; if they excede these, the body's internal order is disrupted. The size of a state should be in inverse ratio to the affections of those who make it up" (98—cf. Montesquieu, xviii, 8). The sense of cohesion must be stronger as social density is lessened. Beccaria, like most philosophes, thought a greater population made for easier life under the law.

Beccaria gave a logic and large scheme to the measurement of pains meted out for crimes. He was systematizing the conclusion to be drawn from Enlightenment beliefs: a) that all human action is caused by what Beccaria called the *sensibile motivi* of pleasure and pain; b) that pain is more intense and sustainable than pleasure; but c) that delicate pleasures can make up in refined prolongability for the grosser impact of pain. These beliefs will be considered in Part Four below. Beccaria made his contribution by applying them in detail to the solution of a social problem.

The idea of measuring comparable units of pain and pleasure over certain lengths of time dates back at least to 1724, when William Wollaston published his influential *Religion of Nature Delineated.* That book's long treatment of happiness set up as a norm "true" happiness any sum of pleasures that exceeds the sum of pains:

Pleasure compared with pain may either be equal, or more, or less; also, pleasures may be compared with other pleasures, and pains with pains. Because all the moments of the pleasure must bear some respect or be in some ratio to all the moments of pain; as also all the degrees of one to all the degrees of the other; and so must those of one pleasure, or one pain, be to those of another. And if the degrees of intenseness be multiplied by the moments of duration, there must still be some ratio of the one product to the other. . . . When pleasures and pains are equal, they mutually destroy each other; when the one exceeds, the excess gives the true quantity of pleasure or pain. For nine degrees of pleasure, less by nine degrees of pain, are equal to nothing; but nine degrees of one, less by three degrees of the other, give six of the former net and true. As therefore there may be true pleasure and pain, so there may be some pleasures which, compared with what attends or follows them, not only may vanish into nothing but may even degenerate into pain, and ought to be reckoned as pains; and, vice versa, some pains thus may be enumerated and annumerated to pleasures. For the true quantity of pleasure differs not from that quantity of true pleasure; or it is so much of that kind of pleasure which is true (clear of all discounts and future payments); nor can the true quantity of pain not be the same with that quantity of true or mere pain. Then, the man who enjoys three degrees of such pleasure as will bring upon him nine degrees of pain, when three degrees of pain are set off to balance and sink the three of pleasure, can have remaining to him only six degrees of pain; and into these therefore is his pleasure finally resolved. And so the three degrees of pain, which anyone endures to obtain nine of pleasure end in six of the latter. By the same manner of computing, some pleasures will be found to be the loss of pleasure, compared with greater; and some pains the alleviation of pain because, by undergoing them, greater are avoided (35–36).

Setting up this kind of pleasure/pain calculus was a common enough exercise for Sterne to mock it in *Tristram Shandy* (5, iii): "A blessing which tied up my father's tongue, and a misfortune which set it loose with a good grace, were pretty equal: sometimes, indeed, the misfortune was the better of the two; for instance, where the pleasure of the harangue was as *ten*, and the pain of the misfortune but as *five*—my father gained half in half, and consequently was as well again off as if it never had befallen him."

Wollaston, it will be seen from his language ("clear of all discounts and future payments"), used an *economic* model like Beccaria's. He directly applies the concept of measured sensibility to penalties, asking judges to lessen punishment where the sensibility is greater (34). And, like Beccaria, he constructs the moral judgment as a syllogism (20 ff.—cf. Beccaria on the *"sillogismo perfetto"* of moral judgment, 28). Hume, following Hutcheson, directed his "is-ought" critique against Wollaston.

The Religion of Nature Delineated kept its measurement of pains and pleasures on the level of theory—it did not show men how to "trade off" pains and pleasures in the practical realm of the legislator and the judge. This was first accomplished by Beccaria. Men guessed at once that Beccaria's little book would be, as it turned out, the most effective study in the history of all penal reform—

achievement enough, in itself, but also suggestive of other projects, since it had vindicated a whole method while solving one specific problem.

It has been widely thought, in the past, that Beccaria got the "greatest happiness" principle from Helvétius. It is true that Helvétius formulated it just as Hutcheson had, in De l'homme; but that appeared nine years after Beccaria's book. The concept is suggested, but not exactly given, in De l'esprit of 1758—("l'intérêt public, c'est-à-dire celui de la plus grand nombre," ii, 23; "actions utiles au plus grand nombre," ii, 24). It is also true that the Verri circle was concerned with Helvétius and Maupertuis; but often critically. Yet we know that Beccaria was an enthusiastic reader of Hume; and the Verri circle's principal concern was with political economy, for which Scotland was the world center even before Adam Smith's long-awaited Wealth of Nations came out in 1776. The Verri group, like most illuministi at mid-century, admired the English-speaking world and modeled its journal Il Caffè, on The Spectator. Pietro Verri had used variants on the Hutcheson phrase in issues of the Caffè preceding the appearance of Beccaria's book, and had put happiness at the center of his own political thinking with the publication of the Meditazioni (later expanded and reprinted as the Discorso sulla felicità). Shackleton (loc. cit., p. 1471) finds traces of Hutcheson's influence on Verri.

Beccaria's view of the social contract is admittedly closer to that of Helvétius (based on "amour de soi") than to Hutcheson's or Hume's. And the use of penalties as educational tools resembles the Helvétius approach to government as a conditioner of men's interests. But Beccaria could admire Hume while keeping the moral syllogism Hume attacked in Wollaston. And the precise measurement of pleasure and pain was a theme more advanced among the English-speaking philosophes than in France (cf. Burke's use of such norms in his 1757 Enquiry). Beccaria was rigorous in the application of principles within his framework, but he was eclectic in fashioning the framework.

Beccaria felt that human action could be measured so precisely that a punishment one degree too intense became something totally different in kind, not a punishment but a crime. Again and again he leads us to see that his book on "crimes and punishments" is really about punishments as crimes. He is punishing the punishers by a code not more lenient than theirs, but stricter—so rigorous that it lays down laws for both sides, criminals and punishers, impartially regulating cops as well as robbers. He reduced the criminals to averages and general rules, undercutting all exemptions for aristocrats or clergy. He saw everyone as ruled by impersonal number.

Voltaire, as I say, became an ardent champion of Beccaria's book and system. A young nobleman who had tried to catch Voltaire's eye, in that very decade when Jefferson was studying his Beccaria at Williamsburg, decided to apply the method of *Dei delitti* to a measurement of happiness instead of pain. He was so successful that his two-volume work, *De la félicité publique*, led to his admission into the French Academy; it was as one of the forty "Immortals" that he came to test his mortality in the American struggle for the rights of man.

There is not much original research in Chastellux's book. It is based heavily on Boulanger's *Despotisme orientale* (1755), on arguments of the "moderns" against Greek and Roman claims, on Voltaire's *Essai sur les moeurs* (1756), and on Hume's essay "On The Populousness of Ancient Nations" (1742). But Chastellux brought all his sources together under the rubric of a science of measurable happiness. All of history was to be searched for the *"indices du bonheur"* (2:98).

His task, as his subtitle indicates, was to determine *"le sort des hommes dans les différentes époques de l'histoire."* This was a new effort, he claimed, since previous history had been written about the triumphs or defeats of rulers and great men. Chastellux would use those histories only indirectly, reasoning from them as economic indicators to the lot of ordinary people (1:9–10, 111–12). Jefferson, too, felt any culture must be judged by its effects on the mass of men. Advising Thomas Lee Shippen in 1788, he told him to take particular note, in his travels through Europe, of agriculture, gardens, mechanical arts, for their usefulness to life at home. Politics should be studied only with relation to their effect: "Examine their influence on the happiness of the people: take every possible occasion of entering into the hovels of the labourers, and especially at the moments of their repast, see what they eat, how they are cloathed, whether they are obliged to labour too hard; whether the government or their landlord takes from them an unjust proportion of their labour; on what footing stands the property they call their own, their personal liberty &c." (*Papers*, 13:269). He thought even a Frenchman like the Marquis de Lafayette needed to be introduced to the real state of his own country: "You must ferret the people out of their hovels, as I have done, look into their kettle, eat their bread, loll on their beds under pretence of resting yourself, but in fact to find out if they are soft" (*Papers*, 11:285).

Chastellux, within his generally chronological framework, stressed the obstacles to happiness in the first volume of his work and the positive indexes of it in the second. The greatest cause of unhappiness is slavery. If the majority of the population is enslaved (as Chastellux thought was the case in classical Greece), then unhappiness obviously prevails—far more so than simple comparison of the numbers of slave and free men would indicate when "thirty thousand men hold sixty thousand men in a condition one hundred times more pitiable than that of work animals" (1:47). Indeed, the existence of slavery is the strongest argument against Chastellux's own thesis that modern times are the happiest. While deploring the remains of slavery, he offers five arguments to show that this evil is finally abating:

1) Slaves are maintained only in Europe's colonies, not in the motherland.

2) They are taken only from the most "savage and brutal" continent of Africa, where fellow Africans first captured and sold them.

3) Their physical differences from their masters weakens the claims of sentiment between fellow beings.

4) The practice of slavery is criticized now, not universally defended as it was in antiquity.

5) The last and strongest argument is, again, from the numbers. "For the more than hundred million Christians alive today one cannot number even one million slaves, while for one million Greeks there were more than three million of these unfortunates" (1:49).

The position of Chastellux is exactly that of Jefferson, who was a critic of slavery looking toward its extinction, while noting that the physical differences and weaker claims of sentiment ameliorated the evil (see chapter Twenty-two below).

The next most pervasive evil of antiquity is, in the scheme of Chastellux, religious—superstition, as in Egypt (1:18); asceticism, as in Sparta (which he calls "one big cloister," 1:26); and diversion of the national wealth into temples and ceremony (1:46). He even distinguishes between various kinds of religious expenditure: "One can almost always gauge a people by its ritual: When that is simple and modest, the people are active and industrious; when it is solemn and exaggerated, the people are puffed up and silly; when it is gloomy and stiff, the people are fierce, bellicose, and opinionated" (1:46). Jefferson, of course, identified Europe with superstition because of the Catholic church. He thought that Christianity had been perverted by ascetical and unnatural Greek ideas (cf. Cappon, 2:383–85, 433). His composition of Virginia's "Bill For Establishing Religious Freedom" was one of the three achievements he wished placed on his monument.

The third great obstacle to happiness, in Chastellux's view, is war. This depopulates a land (2:116), subjects the common folk to the vanity of rulers (1:xiv–xv), and encourages a harsh temper (1:44, 98). The eloquence of Chastellux on this point is very striking, since he was a soldier himself. One reason Jefferson feared "entangling alliances" with Europe was their tendency to bring the new country into a state of war.

When Chastellux turns to the positive indices of happiness in the second volume, he is able to reduce them all to two: agriculture and population. Farming is the ideal state for man. It is the golden mean placed between wandering like nomads and being packed into corrupt cities. In order to advance agriculture, men must tame and enrich the land, use climate to advantage, and perfect wild nature by applied science (2:98–112). Chastellux was thus on the side of Montesquieu (xviii, 7) against Rousseau on the subject of civilization's blessings, though he could inveigh against cities with a fervor resembling Rousseau's.

Jefferson's physiocratic enthusiasm is well known. He called farming the noblest occupation and thought it combined profitable knowledges in the most perfect way. His 1803 letter to David Williams gives his mature view of agriculture's importance:

The same artificial means which have been used to produce a competition in learning, may be equally successful in restoring agriculture to its primary dignity in the eyes of men. It is a science of the very first order. It counts among its handmaids the most respectable sciences, such as Chemistry, Natural Philosophy, Mechanics, Mathematics generally, Natural History, Botany. In every College and University, a professorship of agriculture, and the class of its students, might be honored as the first.

Young men closing their academical education with this, as the crown of all other sciences, fascinated with its solid charms, and at a time when they are to choose an occupation, instead of crowding the other classes would return to the farms of their fathers, their own, or those of others, and replenish and invigorate a calling, now languishing under contempt and oppression. The charitable schools, instead of storing their pupils with a lore which the present state of society does not call for, converted into schools of agriculture, might restore them to that branch qualified to ·enrich and honor themselves, and to increase the productions of the nation instead of consuming them (LB, 10:429–30).

The second index of happiness in any culture is, for Chastellux, density of population. The eighteenth century worried as much about underpopulation as Malthus would teach the nineteenth to worry about overpopulation. William Petty had been so convinced of the need for high population that he recommended moving all the natives of Ireland to England. Only when the home population reached a clear surplus should Ireland be resettled, if at all. He opposed all colonial settlements as a drain on population—and Franklin, followed by Chastellux (2:114), answered that fear by arguing that people multiply faster in the colonies, giving the earth a net gain in men to work it.

Chastellux, like Petty, thought people were any nation's true capital and wealth (2:137). It was essential to his argument that the eighteenth century, as the *happiest* epoch, should have the largest population known to history. In the seventeenth century's battle of the ancients and the moderns, the ancients claimed that the earth was degenerating, its climate becoming less congenial, its fields depleting, and men declining in energy. Chastellux had already opposed this view in his section on agriculture, finding earth more fertile than in the past, the arts of working it more advanced. He devotes an even longer section of his book to proving that population was on the rise as never before (2:112–48). His main arguments are taken from Hume's essay on ancient population—but Hume had argued simply that modern times were not *less* populous than ancient ones. Chastellux, paying Hume a compliment for "his gift of deciding others by his very doubts" (2:112), goes farther than that. As usual, he tries to work from numbers: the variety, proximity, and number of wild beasts referred to in antiquity shows that humans had not been populous enough to dislodge such animals from

their environs (2:127). Chastellux also believed in the need for
large numbers of people to make an efficient division of labor. Antiquity had to make every man a soldier, politician, businessman, etc.
—which limits the economic progress any such society can make
(1:43–44).

Jefferson had a special reason for opposing the degeneracy
theory of modern times. Some philosophes, including the great
Buffon, had rejected that theory as it applied to the whole of mo-
dernity; but they accommodated some of the evidence offered for
the theory by granting that certain portions of the globe—like
Africa, the islands of the South Atlantic, and America—were in a
state of necessary decline. The climate was too moist and hot to
nurture vigorous life; men and animals were small and reproduced
only with difficulty. Much of Jefferson's *Notes on the State of Virginia* is devoted to a refutation of those charges. America's native
Indians are said to reproduce themselves well and to be physically
and mentally full grown. Any slighter reproduction rate is explica-
ble on the grounds that Indian women's hard "male" work makes
them slightly less suited to child-bearing (61). In another part of
the *Notes,* Jefferson had made an injudicious reference to the "in-
fecundity" of the Indians' women (281). He deleted this, lest
Buffon have a weapon against America, and spoke more vaguely of
"obstacles opposed to it [generation]" (96). The antiquity and
number of flourishing Indian tribes, the ease of Indian self-government, are among Jefferson's favorite themes in the book—along with
description of the large and manifold animal life supported by the
continent.

On the question of population, Jefferson finds his colony doing so
well that he recommends against encouraging large-scale immigration to increase the working force. His argument has three stages.
The first sets the positive rate of increase among Virginians and the
date at which the optimum desirable population might be achieved.
He concludes, from the evidence available, that Virginians over the
last 118 years had doubled themselves every twenty-seven-and-a-
half years (as opposed to Franklin's claim in his essay on population, that Americans doubled every twenty years). Jefferson saw his
state "filling up" within a century:

Should this rate of increase continue, we shall have between six and
seven millions of inhabitants within 95 years. If we suppose our country

to be bounded, at some future day, by the meridian of the mouth of the Great Kanhaway, (within which it has been before conjectured, are 64,491 square miles) there will then be 100 inhabitants for every square mile, which is nearly the state of population in the British islands (83).

In the second stage of his argument, Jefferson describes with the help of multiplication charts the way a "competent" population could be reached by adding to the native stock:

Now let us suppose (for example only) that, in this state, we could double our numbers in one year by the importation of foreigners; and this is a greater accession than the most sanguine advocate for emigration has a right to expect. Then I say, beginning with a double stock, we shall attain any given degree of population only 27 years and 3 months sooner than if we proceed on our single stock. If we propose four million and a half as a competent population for this state, we should be 54½ years attaining it, could we at once double our numbers; and 81¾ years, if we rely on natural propagation, as may be seen by the following table.

In his argument's third stage, Jefferson asks if the quicker rate of increase to be secured from immigrants is balanced by other factors that make a quarter century or so gain in reaching "competency" worth the acceptance of foreigners. The test is the contribution made to human happiness. Admittedly, Chastellux had made population in itself an index of happiness, and Jefferson's own argument implies that this is the case if mere population is considered apart from other matters. But America offers a special problem, in that its Republican ethos is at odds with monarchical ways. "It is for the happiness of those united in society to harmonize as much as possible in matters which they must of necessity transact together." Jefferson doubts that large numbers of immigrants can be absorbed into such amity, since it takes long experience of self-rule to reach the state of "temperate liberty" achieved in America. "Is it not safer to wait with patience 27 years and three months longer, for the attainment of any degree of population desired, or expected? May not our government be more homogeneous, more peaceable, more durable?"

Finally, Jefferson explains the impact of even a small number of immigrants on America by setting up a ratio with France's population. (It is the same kind of equation he worked out for comparing the *amount* of genius it would take in Europe to balance America's acknowledged product). "Suppose 20 millions of republican Americans thrown all of a sudden into France, what would be the condition of that kingdom? If it would be more turbulent, less happy, less strong, we may believe that the addition of half a million of foreigners to our present numbers would produce a similar effect here." Notice how, in that quote, the amount of *happiness* is forecast *on the basis of numbers.* Jefferson's treatment of this problem is a model of the scientific method used by philosophes like Chastellux to study and increase human happiness. It proceeds from a detailed statement of the facts, on which are based alternate numerical projections. Only then, when Jefferson has set the limits of numerical gain to be made, can he weigh that against other factors. Even in the last, most "subjective" stage of the argument, he appeals to the hard evidence of numbers.

When Jefferson spoke of pursuing happiness, he had nothing vague or private in mind. He meant a public happiness which is measurable; which is, indeed, the test and justification of any government. But to understand why he considered the pursuit of that happiness an unalienable right, we must look to another aspect of Enlightenment thought—to the science of morality.

PART THREE

A MORAL PAPER

ELEVEN

"... *attentions to our British brethren* ..."

It was my great good fortune, and what probably fixed
the destinies of my life, that Dr. William Small of
Scotland was then Professor of Mathematics, a man
profound in the most useful branches of science, with a
happy talent of communication, correct and gentlemanly manners, and an enlarged and liberal mind. He,
most happily for me, became soon attached to me, and
made me his daily companion when not engaged in the
school; and from his conversation I got my first views of
the expansion of science, and of the system of things in
which we are placed.

—Jefferson, *Autobiography*

One of the great blows to American scholarship took place on February 1, 1770, when a modest upland plantation burned to the
ground. At the time, it was an entirely personal tragedy. The young
master of Shadwell, Thomas Jefferson, was absent, and his mother
was with him, so no lives were lost. But time would reveal what the
world had lost: It had lost a world. Except for a few papers he
carried with him—his account book, mainly, and two books of his
private "florilegia"—this compulsive writer and record keeper lost
everything he had composed to the age of twenty-seven, along with
the library he had been assembling with great care and cost for over
a decade.

The loss is easily put in concrete terms. Though the great Boyd
edition of Jefferson's papers promises to stretch out to the crack of
doom, only twenty-five pages of the first volume are devoted to his
writings before the fire occurred—letters saved by their recipients

(mainly John Page), one advertisement in the newspapers, one draft of a public paper.

That accident goes far toward explaining one of the odd things about Jeffersonian scholarship. Despite the fact that the Declaration of Independence is Jefferson's most influential composition, studies of his intellectual world tend to pick him up after 1776, when he wrote it. Daniel Boorstin, for instance, tries to reconstruct the "lost world" of Jefferson's thought around the Philadelphia activities of the American Philosophical Society, which Jefferson did not even join until 1780, and where he was not active for another decade—not, that is, until his Philadelphia years as Secretary of State and Vice President, the years when he turned fifty.

Other scholars pick Jefferson up, intellectually, when he reaches Paris (1784), in his forties. Gilbert Chinard (*Jefferson et les Idéologues*, 1925) and Adrienne Koch (*The Philosophy of Thomas Jefferson*, 1943) "place" him among the idéologues he knew and admired during and after his Paris sojourn. Useful as such studies may be for other purposes, they obviously tell us little about the formation of Jefferson during his prolonged stay in Williamsburg, when he laid the foundations of his vast reading and acquired his first views of the world.

The loss of Jefferson's earlier papers and books helps explain another oddity of Jeffersonian scholarship. That scholarship, so far as it touches on the intellectual sources of the Declaration, has stood virtually still for over half a century—ever since the publication of Carl Becker's little book on the subject. The foremost students of Jefferson have said, with surprising unanimity, that Becker's is the last word on this subject. Julian Boyd bowed to him at virtually every turn of his book on the evolution of the text:

> Mr. Becker's work contains a masterly analysis of the natural rights philosophy and of the American view of the nature of the British constitution. . . . I wish to acknowledge an indebtedness which all readers of this book must feel and which in my case is very great.

Malone relied as much on Becker's analysis (1:222–23), and William Peden spoke for his Jeffersonian mentors when he said: "Of all Jefferson's writings excepting the works published for the first time in this century, such as the Jefferson Bible and Chinard's editions of the Commonplace books, the Declaration of Independence alone has received what could properly be called authoritative and more or less final treatment. I have never heard anyone suggest that much of importance could be added to Carl Becker's book on the subject" (*Some Aspects of Jeffersonian Bibliography*, 1941).

What has made Becker's book so conclusive that even half a century later students of Jefferson found nothing important to add to it? It is true that Merrill Peterson could express misgivings about Becker's own relativism (*The Jefferson Image*, 308); but he had to concede, nonetheless, that Becker remained "the outstanding interpreter of the Declaration's philosophy" and his book was "a small masterpiece" (305). The secret of this universal acclaim lies in the inability of any later student to challenge Becker's basic thesis—that Jefferson found in *John Locke* "the ideas which he put into the Declaration."

You see how convenient this is. If we assume that there was a Lockean orthodoxy in the air, coloring all men's thoughts about politics in the middle of the eighteenth century, we do not have to worry much about the loss of Jefferson's own first lucubrations on the state, whatever philosophical jottings went up in flames when Shadwell burned. This assumption has, therefore, held its ground even though the public philosophy foisted, thus, on Jefferson conflicts with the private morality attributed to him by those who find his "lost world" in the moral-sense views of Philadelphians or the sociology of idéologues. Some people have noted this inconcinnity (e.g., Cecelia Kenyon and Morton White); but they explain it by saying that Jefferson later changed his mind—from the individualism of the (Lockean) Declaration to wider communitarian values and morality. All such constructions rest on the certainty that Jefferson's first thoughts on politics *had* to be Lockean. But did they? There is, among modern Locke scholars, a heretical tendency to doubt that eighteenth-century politics had an orthodoxy derived from their man.

Locke's *Essay Concerning the True Original, Extent, and End of Civil Government*, known as the *Second Treatise*, written in the seventeenth century, was one of the canonical books of nineteenth-century liberalism. This has led us, looking back through the period of John Mill and David Ricardo, to forget how equivocal was the work's status in the eighteenth century. For the generally educated man or woman of today, Locke has become pre-eminently the man of the *Second Treatise* and only incidentally the author of the *Essay on Understanding*. In the eighteenth century, exactly the opposite was true. The *Essay*, by shaping the Enlightenment, had reshaped the world. The *Two Treatises*, appearing anonymously, had taken eighty years to make their mark in the English-speaking world, and never had much impact on the continent of Europe. Even when the *Second Treatise* became a standard work, it was at first revered because of its connection with the author of the *Essay*. Locke had original things to say in the *Second Treatise*, but they were not grasped or emphasized. His glorious name was just added to the list of authors in the whig tradition.

The work which best traces the spread of the *Second Treatise*'s influence and editions is John Dunn's seminal essay of 1969, "The Politics of Locke in England and America in the Eighteenth Century" (in J. W. Yolton's *John Locke: Problems and Prospectives*). Dunn notes that Locke was even less known and studied in America than in England during the first half of the eighteenth century. Here too, the "great Mr. Locke" was Locke of the *Essay*. The impact of that work on Jonathan Edwards and Benjamin Franklin is well known. There is no similar epiphany traceable to the day when an American picked up the *Second Treatise*. The book was not much quoted until the eve of the Revolution, when men brought out all available spokesmen for the "whig" attack on absolutism. As Dunn puts it:

There is no evidence that the *Two Treatises* figured in the set curriculum of any American college before the Revolution. . . . It never held the unimpeachable eminence of the works of Grotius or Pufendorf. . . . The book was of no great popularity before 1750, and the tradition of political behavior within which the colonists conceived their relationship with England was already highly articulated by this date. . . . It was only one among a large group of other works which expounded the Whig theory of the Revolution, and its prominence within this group is not noticeable until well after the general outline of the interpretation had become consolidated.

The *great* Mr. Locke was the one who figured in that major trinity of the Enlightenment—Bacon, Newton, and Locke. It was a lesser figure who rounded out the lower triad of "Commonwealthmen" (as Caroline Robbins has called them)—Sidney, Harrington, and Locke.

Support for Dunn's argument can be gleaned from the survey of colonial and Early American libraries by David Lundberg and Henry F. May (*American Quarterly*, 1976). Copies of the 1714 edition of Locke's works can be found, at some point before 1776, in 23 per cent of the known colonial libraries; but the distribution of interest in the different volumes of those works is measured by the fact that separate volumes of the *Treatise(s)* show up in only 15 per cent of the libraries, while separate copies of the *Essay* were in 41 per cent. Even in the politicized period from 1776 to 1790, when Dunn finds more interest in Locke's politics, appearance of the *Treatise* only went up to 24 per cent (well behind, e.g., Montesquieu's *Spirit of the Laws* at 48 per cent), while the *Essay* climbed to 62 per cent. After 1790, the *Essay* continues popular while the *Treatise* dwindles drastically to 4 per cent in the period 1790–1800, 2 per cent (one copy!) in the period to 1813. This is hardly the "omnipresent" political Locke of our national myth.

Locke was, for men of Jefferson's period, the Newton of the mind —the man who revealed the workings of knowledge, the proper mode of education, and the reasonableness of belief. The most vivid and traceable influence Locke had on Jefferson was in the area of religious tolerance (*Papers*, 1:544–51). Elsewhere, when Jefferson refers to Locke, it is to his role in the major Enlightenment trinity, where the contribution was epistemological. He sought both busts and paintings of Bacon, Newton, and Locke—and drew an oval design to contain all three (*Papers*, 14:467–68, 525, 561).

When Jefferson refers to Locke's politics, he links him, not with Bacon and Newton, but invariably with Sidney. The two were catalogued together in his own library (Sowerby, 3:12) and cited together in the list for a basic library (*Papers*, 1:79), for law readings (Ford, 9:480), and for the University of Virginia's curriculum. They lead the list of works on the rights of man, "for want of a single work" (Ford, 9:71). These recommendations fully accord with Dunn's argument that Locke was seen as a typical antiabsolutist of the whig tradition, without very specific reference to his originality. Locke was the Newton of the mind, not of the state.

Nowhere is the casual nature of Jefferson's references to Locke more evident than in the one place where he expressly links Locke

with the Declaration. Repudiating the charge that he had plagia-
rized Locke, Jefferson wrote of his document: "All its authority
rests then on the harmonizing sentiments of the day, whether expressed in conversation, in letters, printed essays, or in the elemen-
tary books of public right, as Aristotle, Cicero, Locke, Sidney, etc.,
&c." (Ford, 10:343). Four things are interesting in this 1825 passage: 1) The only time Jefferson links Locke's name with the Declaration, he is minimizing a connection first brought up by another. 2)
He makes the customary pairing of Locke with Sidney as types of
the whig ancestry claimed for the Revolution. 3) He is deliberately
citing works of general regard, rather than a set of specific
influences on him. 4) The latter point is confirmed by the inclusion
of Aristotle, not one of Jefferson's favorite authors. He had a low
regard for Greek metaphysicians in general (Cappon, 433) and for
Aristotle's politics specifically:

I think little edification can be obtained from their writings on the
subject of government . . . [which] relieves our regret if the political
writings of Aristotle or of any other ancient have been lost (LB, 16:15).

Dunn notes that Locke was not considered a very practical guide
by the very colonists who quoted him vaguely on matters of principle. Dr. Benjamin Rush, for instance, wrote in his *Observations on
the Government of Pennsylvania:* "Mr. Locke is an oracle as to the
principles, Harrington and Montesquieu are the oracles as to the
forms of government." That rubric would also cover what is perhaps the highest praise ever given to Locke's *Treatise* by Jefferson:
"Locke's little book on Government is perfect as far as it goes. Descending from theory to practice, there is no better book than the
Federalist" (*Papers,* 16:449).

There is little in such references, scattered through his large body
of writings, to justify the picture of Jefferson as a close student of
Locke's politics. Yet Herbert Friedenwald spoke for many others,
down to our day, when he claimed that the Declaration "repeated
the concepts, often even the very phraseology and arguments, of his
master John Locke. . . . A reading of Locke's *Second Treatise* will
show how thoroughly every sentence and expression in it were
graven on Jefferson's mind" (*Declaration,* 201). There are two
verbal echoes of the *Treatise* in the Declaration—in the passage that

says a "long train of abuses" (#225) can provoke revolution even in a people "disposed to suffer" (#230). This is good Blackstone doctrine, shared by all whigs and voiced in earlier documents of the Congress (*Respect* 85, 128)—nothing distinctively Lockean.* The Declaration was written early in Jefferson's public career, not long after the deep course of political study traceable in his *Commonplace Book* and the so-called *Literary Bible.* In those books Jefferson copied out by hand long extracts from the standard authors (e.g., Montesquieu) and from private favorites (e.g., Bolingbroke). Yet there is not a single passage, in either book, copied out of Locke's *Treatise*—a book Jefferson never directly quoted.

There is one citation of the *Treatise* (not a quotation from it) in the *Commonplace Book.* But it is probably derived at second hand. It occurs in Jefferson's survey of governments and their forms, a survey derived from multiple sources. When Jefferson assembles the evidence for grounding the authority of kings in election, he appends a reference to the eleventh chapter of the *Treatise* on legislative supremacy—which is not the same matter at all. Apparently some reference in his reading made him think this citation apropos. Although the *Commonplace Book* has later additions and expansions, Jefferson never explained or corrected this reference.

The survey of governments in the *Commonplace Book* follows on the long extracts devoted to laws of property, a matter of consuming interest to Jefferson as well as Locke. It is hard to imagine that Jefferson could find no pertinent passages to quote or cite if he had his Locke at hand while working on this problem. Most of his later ideas on private property (107-20), entail (137-49) and inheritance (149-68) are traceable to the passages quoted here from Lord Kames and Sir John Dalrymple. Locke is never adduced; and if Locke is not relevant here, how can he be counted the major influence—or even *a* major influence—on Jefferson's political thinking?

The nature of the omission is best appreciated by noting that the very chapter of Locke cited once by Jefferson begins, "The great end of men's entering into society being the enjoyment of their properties . . ." and goes on to argue that taxation is never legiti-

---

* Becker makes an attempt to trace another verbal echo, at second hand through James Wilson. I deal with that in chapter Eighteen. Chinard found more parallels in Montesquieu than in Locke (*Commonplace Book*, 258-61).

mate "without the consent of the people." If Jefferson had been reading Locke at this point, he would have had many appropriate passages to cite, instead of the one inappropriate reference he made.

There is no indication Jefferson read the *Second Treatise* carefully or with profit. Indeed, there is no conclusive proof he read it at all (though I assume he did at some point). There would be nothing dishonest about his general recommendation of the *Treatise*, made to others while he lacked any close acquaintance with the text—any more than in his crediting Aristotle (of all people) with formation of the background for his Declaration. Jefferson clearly had read, and admired, and learned from Locke's works on understanding, on education, on religious tolerance; and, like most of his contemporaries, he was willing to defer to the man's authority in politics without owing any specific debt to the *Treatise*.

We cannot look, for evidence that Jefferson read the *Treatise*, to his own copy of it, for no such copy exists. We know he ordered and received a copy of the *Treatise* late in 1769 (*Papers*, 1:33–34), but that volume perished almost immediately in the Shadwell fire. Jefferson listed the *Second Treatise* in his catalogue of books sold to the Library of Congress in 1815, but it does not show up in the list of books received (Sowerby, 3:12). He could not have withheld the book, since Congress did not allow that (Peden, University of Virginia diss. 1942, p. 154), and it seems unlikely it would have been lost in the short time between his compilation of the catalogue and completion of the sale. In any event he did not replace the book, as he did so many others. The 1829 list of his final library shows he had not owned the book since 1815—and perhaps he had not owned it since the fire of 1770.

A possible explanation for the missing *Treatise* of the sale comes from the way Locke was regularly linked with Filmer, whom he refuted. Jefferson lists the *Treatise* right after two separately mentioned works of Filmer—but those Filmer works are bound together, in a neat leather book Sowerby thinks was purchased as part of Richard Bland's library in 1776. The first book included is a 1696 collection of Filmer's political tracts, whose table of contents lists as its sixth and final tract the *Patriarcha*. But that tract has been shorn away from the 1696 volume, and an earlier version of the *Patriarcha* (from 1690) is bound in its place. The book, which I have handled, seems to fall into three parts, since it opens easily to the Y binding signature, which begins the fifth tract, *The Power of Kings*. A quick glance may have led Jefferson to think *this* was *Patriarcha: Or the Natural Power of Kings*, and that the thing bound in after it was not *Patriarcha*, but "Locke's little book" written (as he thought) to answer Filmer. That would explain his belief that he sold the book to Congress. But even if this guess (and it is no more) be rejected, the evidence of Jefferson's physical connection with the book remains slight.

Of course, there is no proving a negative here (that Jefferson *could* not have been influenced by Locke)—which is not my aim, anyway. All I assert is that we have no reason to keep assuming that a Lockean orthodoxy explains the early formation of Jefferson's political thought. That short cut is no longer self-evidently valid. We must do the harder and slower work of trying to reassemble from fragments the world almost entirely lost in the Shadwell fire.

There *are* fragments to work on—the early parts of Jefferson's "florilegia," with their long extracts from Bolingbroke and Kames and Beccaria. And there is an important basic library list drawn up by Jefferson for a friend (Robert Skipwith) in 1771—that is, in just the period when he was replacing his own lost library. His list indicates the core of the library Jefferson had first owned or aspired to own; and he told his friend that Monticello already held a more extensive collection than the 147 titles on the list. (That list is more extensive than the count of titles might indicate, since some of the single titles are things like "Milton's works" or "Dryden's plays"— *Papers*, 1:78.)

There are several interesting things about this list. One is the heavy component of novels and light literature, defended in the body of the letter in terms of a "moral sense" aesthetics—a trademark of such Scottish Enlightenment thinkers as Lord Kames. Kames, who figures so largely in the *Commonplace Book*, is represented in three different categories on the 1771 list—Law, Religion, and Criticism on the Fine Arts. He is only one of several Scots included—e.g., Adam Smith, Thomas Reid, David Hume (for both his essays and his history).

There should be nothing surprising in this concentration on Scottish thinkers. By the middle of the eighteenth century, Scotland's five universities had far outdistanced somnolent Oxford and

Cambridge in the study of science, philosophy, and law. Edinburgh was replacing Leiden as the center of medical experiment and training. Glasgow had been renovated by the reforms of Francis Hutcheson. The two universities in Aberdeen were straining to catch up to the lead of Edinburgh and Glasgow. These schools had all thrown off the yoke of Dutch Calvinist professors just in time to adopt the new scientific outlook based on Newton and Locke. In the forties and fifties of the century, Scotland had a constellation of original thinkers not to be equaled anywhere in Europe—not only Hume and Smith, Kames and Hutcheson, but Adam Ferguson, Thomas Reid, and the young Dugald Stewart. Even before the publication of the *Wealth of Nations,* Scotland was known as the world's leader in the new field of "political economy." Scottish students were well trained in astronomy, mathematics, and the "mechanical" sciences. James Watt, the brilliant instrument-maker, found in Glasgow open-minded professors (Joseph Black and John Robison) who put him on the path toward perfecting the steam engine. The leadership that had been taken fifty years earlier by the Royal Society in London, and which would pass to France when the Encyclopédie began appearing, was held by Scotland in just those years when Jefferson was laying his own intellectual foundation, under the guidance of a typical product of the Scottish efflorescence, William Small. By 1781, when Jefferson was composing his *Notes on the State of Virginia,* he could say that Great Britain's empire was "fast descending" because "her philosophy has crossed the channel, her freedom the Atlantic" (65). The philosophy he speaks of was that of the great Scottish thinkers of the mid-century. For him Scotland was a country "possessing science in as high a degree as any place in the world" (*Papers,* 9:59–60).

America in general had gone to school to the Scots in its last colonial period. At Princeton, Dr. Witherspoon was teaching his Presbyterian students (including his future son-in-law Samuel Stanhope Smith), and even an odd Anglican outsider like James Madison, from the ethics texts of Francis Hutcheson. At the College of Philadelphia, that tempestuous Scot William Smith aimed his curriculum toward the culminating study of the same philosopher, and Francis Alison drilled five future signers of the Declaration of Independence in Hutcheson's texts (cf. D. F. Norton, *Studies on Voltaire,* vol. 154, 1976). Even at the established church's King's College in New York, the moral philosophy of Hutcheson, a dissenting minister, took up the final two years of study. (See Anna Haddow's *Political Science in American Colleges*, 11–12, 14 and Douglas Sloan's *The Scottish Enlightenment and the American College Ideal*, 76, 122–25). Benjamin Franklin's scientific ties with Scotland were very close, as were those of men like Ezra Stiles (Sloan, 1–2, 86–88).

What was true of America in general had particular import for Virginia, where a Scot educated at Marischal College in Aberdeen had founded the College of William and Mary in the seventeenth century. A wave of Scottish Presbyterian emigrants, washed up toward and past the Piedmont of Jefferson's home, was cresting during Jefferson's youth. Lord Bute had made the Scots prominent in colonial administration—nowhere more so than in Virginia, which had a Scottish governor (Robert Dinwiddie) already in the 1750s. There was a regular exchange of people and goods between Scotland and Virginia, since Glasgow was the principal port for receiving the colony's tobacco (cf. J. A. Price, *WMQ*, 1954). Jefferson himself had a regular agent for purchasing books and other things in Glasgow—Alexander McCaul, a Scot who had spent time on business in Virginia (*Papers*, 1:97, 51–52, 92–93). A wave of young teachers and ministers was shaking up the colony, to the distress of conservatives like Edmund Pendleton. Their support helped break the hold of the religious establishment, paving the way for Jefferson's statute of religious toleration. (Jefferson's own principal teacher at William and Mary, William Small, tried to have the oath of allegiance set aside as a requirement for the presidency of that college.)

Even the Anglican parson who first taught Jefferson his letters (Greek, Latin, and French) was a Scot, William Douglas of Glencairn, who had been trained at Glasgow (just before Hutcheson's arrival) and Edinburgh (in "physics" as well as Hebrew). Douglas, who directed Jefferson's studies for four years, had left Scotland in the 1730s—too early to experience the heady ferment just making itself evident at his two colleges. But William Small, a far more talented man, came along at just the right time. Born in 1734, the brother of a brilliant mathematician, Small attended Marischal College during the early fifties. His classmate there was James Macpherson, the fabricator of Jefferson's favorite poet, "Ossian." Small

studied medicine with John Gregory, the center of a "philosophical" circle in Aberdeen (where he sometimes lectured at
King's College). Gregory was the author of an influential work on
the animal basis of human education, and his *Father's Legacy*
would later be part of Jefferson's library.

Small came to Virginia in 1758, to teach mathematics at the College of William and Mary. Two years later, when Small was
twenty-six, Jefferson (ten years his junior) took up residence at the
College. Luckily for both men, the demoralized and half-soused
faculty chose this moment to fall apart, and young Small became
professor of practically everything during Jefferson's years as an un-
dergraduate. In teaching ethical philosophy, Small used the vernacular lecture-course method with which Hutcheson had revitalized
teaching in Scotland twenty-five years earlier. Men like Hutcheson
and Adam Smith used the ethics course to expound their central
philosophical tenets, connecting them with the sciences through
mathematics and with "rhetoric" through a philosophy of beauty.
Behind it all lay "the moral sense," expounded as an epistemological tool. This seems to be what Small attempted in what
Jefferson calls his "regular [i.e., connected] lectures on Ethics,
Rhetoric, and Belles Lettres" (Ford, 1:3).

Small, despite great personal charm, ran into enmity at Williamsburg, prompted in part by the popularity of his teaching methods.
It came as a relief to everyone but his students when he returned to
England for a rest in 1764—his health was never good. He negotiated his return from afar, wondering if the oath of allegiance could
be set aside to make him president of the college. In 1767 he undertook to select the "philosophical apparatus" (i.e., laboratory equipment) for the college; his well-chosen instruments became the
possession of Rev. James Madison, with whom Jefferson would conduct his meteorological experiments through the years.

Before Small left Williamsburg, he had included Jefferson in a
friendship with the two older men in Williamsburg who were most
alive to the intellectual forces of their time—Governor Francis Fauquier, a member of the Royal Society who had been connected
with that center of scientific interest, the Royal Mint; and the self-
educated classicist and lawyer, George Wythe, who (as we have
seen) alone stood by Jefferson's "moral sense" defense of the Revolution as based on the right of expatriation.

Back in Scotland, Small picked up his physician's degree at Marischal College (based on his earlier studies there with Dr. Gregory) and went to London. There he was processed through that great intellectual control center, Benjamin Franklin, who circuited him off to Matthew Boulton in Birmingham. Boulton was a principal Maecenas of the early industrial revolution; and Small, with his genius for friendship, became the great dispenser of amity at the Soho estate Boulton called his "*hôtel de l'amitié.*" Around Boulton and Small and Erasmus Darwin gathered a band of jesting experimenters who became known as the Lunar Society, the butt of Blake's satire, *An Island in the Moon.* The Lunar Society came, in time, to include James Watt and Joseph Priestley and Josiah Wedgwood.

Though Small was a physician optimistic on principle, he was cursed with bad health and fits of depression. When the hypochondriac James Watt stopped off in Birmingham on his way back from London to Glasgow, the two Scots of similar temper became instant friends, of frequent correspondence. Small was Watt's intermediary when Watt sought new backing (from Boulton) for his steam "fire engine." The two men bantered and badgered each other into intermittent cheerfulness, joking about death and sex while trading notes on their inventions.

For Small was a creative "mechanic" in the *médecin-philosophe* tradition of his time. He took out patents on new kinds of clocks— one hydraulically driven, one without hands. It is easy to see why Jefferson, with his hero worship for Rittenhouse, admired his own teacher, who could design a "clock with one wheel of nine inches diameter which is to tell hours, minutes, and seconds, and strike, and repeat, and be made for thirty shillings" (Dickinson and Jenkins, *James Watt and the Steam Engine,* 31–35). Small and Watt debated the concept of a "spiral oar" nearly half a century before the screw propellor was made to work. Small would be famous in the history of science if he had lived a few years longer: his name was scheduled to join Watt's and Boulton's in the firm producing steam engines. But the poor health Small tried to drug and jest away from Watt felled Small himself at the early age of forty-one. The year was 1775, and his former student in America had just sent him three dozen bottles of Madeira—grateful, despite the war already begun with Great Britain and its "Scotch mercenaries," to the man who had opened up for him "the system of things in which we are placed."

Jefferson spent the four most intellectually exciting and influential years of his life studying that entire "system of things" under Small's guidance. Then he stayed on in Williamsburg for three more years, reading and trading ideas with the two friends to whom Small had introduced him. (Jefferson's best young friend at Williamsburg, John Page of nearby Rosewell, was also an admiring student of Small. When Jefferson and Page studied their astronomy in the lofty lantern-cupolas of Rosewell, they were continuing work first done under Small's instruction.)

The ideas expressed by Jefferson in 1776 were first introduced to him, and examined by him, in the prior decade of intense reading and discussion that formed his mind. These same ideas went into his major philosophical work, the *Notes on the State of Virginia*, composed five years after the Declaration, when Jefferson had still made only a few short journeys outside of Virginia. Those ideas were not derived, primarily, from Philadelphia or Paris, but from Aberdeen and Edinburgh and Glasgow. We have enough evidence of his reading, and of his conclusions from that reading, to establish that the real lost world of Thomas Jefferson was the world of William Small, the invigorating realm of the Scottish Enlightenment at its zenith.

TWELVE

". . . self-evident . . ."

> Moral truths, therefore, may be divided into two
> classes, to wit: such as are self-evident to every man
> whose understanding and moral faculty are ripe, and
> such as are deduced by reasoning from those that are
> self-evident. . . . I apprehend that in every kind of
> duty we owe to God or man the case is similar: that is,
> that the obligation of the most general rules of duty is
> self-evident; that the application of those rules to par-
> ticular actions is often no less evident. . . .
>
> —Thomas Reid

Though we may properly doubt the impact of Locke's *Second
Treatise* on Jefferson, it is harder to challenge the importance of his
Essay on Understanding. And since self-evident truths make up one
important category in Locke's analysis, it might seem that any question about Jefferson's use of that term would be solved simply by
opening our Locke to the chapter "Of Maxims." But many students
have followed that course; and they went away more confused than
enlightened on the meaning Jefferson gave to the adjective "self-
evident."

For Locke, the self-evident truth was a proposition whose subject
and predicate have a relation of uncontestable identity: "The mind
cannot but assent to such a proposition as infallibly true, as soon
as it understands the terms" (Fraser edition, 2:277). All such
"maxims" or axioms would be reducible to the identity principle—
i.e., "the same is the same" and "the same is not different" (27)—except that Locke says they are *not* reducible beyond themselves.
They are concrete instances of identity, too immediately percep-
tible to be reduced to anything else, or to lead to anything else.
Locke insists on the *barren* infallibility of such maxims, to prevent
their serving as the basis for deductions (278–80).

Thus Jefferson cannot be using "self-evident" in the technical Lockean sense. Such "truths" as the fact that "all men are created equal" do not have an incontestably identical subject and predicate. If that kind of proposition is true at all, it has what Locke called the truth of demonstration—i.e., what can be arrived at by argument from certain evidence. But the very presence of argument proves the matter is not self-evident. Locke's "maxims" admit no argument —indeed, they admit no challenge, no doubt to be *resolved* by argument. Besides, Jefferson clearly hopes his "self-evident truths" will lead to further truths, to a whole political system. That is why he says the named truths are "among these" connected truths unspecified in his brief statement; and he has listed only "certain" of the rights that self-evidently belong to men. Nothing could be further from Locke's discrete and intransitive maxims.

Locke talks, at times, more loosely of truths derived "from the evidence of the thing itself" (435) and not from authority or a priori certitudes. Jefferson thought all truths should be derived that way; unlike Locke, he left no room for divine revelation. But we cannot equate the empirical method with self-evidence, or all true propositions would have to be self-evidently true; and there would be no reason to single out the few self-evident truths of the Declaration.

So even in the area of epistemology, where Jefferson granted Locke his exalted status in the trinity of thinkers with Bacon and Newton, he did not follow him in a close and literal way. Some therefore assume Jefferson's use of "self-evident" is loose and exaggerated, or merely rhetorical. (No one will in fact question these things in this audience.) But we should not too quickly assume, against the general tenor of his thought, that Jefferson was being vague and rhetorical in this important statement.

There is no reason to assume that the only well-defined use of self-evident in the eighteenth century was Locke's. In fact, the term is central to the work of another philosopher, Thomas Reid—and it is significant that Reid's *Inquiry Into the Human Mind* is the only other book on epistemology contained, along with Locke's *Conduct of the Mind*, in the 1771 list of basic books Jefferson sent to Robert Skipwith (*Papers*, 1:79). Reid was lecturing at King's College in Aberdeen while Small studied at Marischal College in the same city. (Reid had received his own schooling at Marischal.) In the 1750s, Reid was the center of an active group of intellectuals, and

Small was bound to have met him through his medical preceptor, John Gregory, also a lecturer at King's.

Reid's important text might well have been on Jefferson's list of select books even without this connection; but the gossip of Aberdeen, relayed to him by his principal witness to intellectual life abroad, must have made him greet the book with special interest when it was published in 1764 (the year Small returned to Aberdeen). In the same way, Jefferson felt a personal connection with Small's classmate, James Macpherson—enough to embolden him to write Macpherson's brother in Edinburgh, asking for copies of original Ossian manuscripts (*Papers*, 1:96, 100–2). Jefferson had met that brother, Charles, in Virginia; and James Macpherson himself had visited America in 1764–66, on business for the central colonial administration—further signs of the massive Scottish presence in America.

Locke defined self-evident truths only to confine them, to prevent others from building a deductive philosophy upon them. Reid, while equally insistent on inductive method, extended the sphere of self-evident truths and made them the basis for his whole philosophy. He is *the* exponent of self-evidence in the English-speaking world of the eighteenth century (as Claude Buffier had been their exponent on the Continent). Reid opened up the principal intramural debate of the Scottish Enlightenment when he challenged Hume's epistemological skepticism. With marvelous satiric energy, he took on not only Hume but Locke himself.

According to Reid, Locke had built his view of sensation on a sunken image, a half-confessed metaphor. Not only was the mind a *tabula rasa* for Locke; it was a kind of waxen stuff able to take images from the "imprint" of outside realities. Ideas were images minted in men by sensible impressions (*Inquiry*, Duggan ed., 269). Hume, by emphasizing that men know only these images of things, and not the things themselves, suggested that all man's intellectual traffic is with the coinages of reality, not with reality.

Reid denied that ideas had to be, or even could be, image-repetitions of outside reality. He worked from a sunken metaphor of his own—the one that makes us speak of mental "grasp" or apprehension.* The mind is prehensile of reality. We do not say the hand

---

* So important was "grip" to Reid's way of thinking that he argued "real" geometry was established by touch, not vision (cf. Norman Daniels, *Thomas Reid's Inquiry*, 1974).

must be (or become) an apple in order to pick up an apple. But Reid says Humeans indulge in a parallel kind of learned idiocy— like talking about the hand only grabbing the hand when it holds anything, or the hand only being able to grab the handlike properties of the apple, or of being able to hold an apple only with another apple (which must, in turn, be held by another apple and so on in an infinite regression). All these fictive operations are paralleled in Hume's discussion of the mind as only knowing itself or its own alterations (ibid., 206, 244–45).

Reid argued that the basic knowing operation was as simple and inexplicable as the basic bodily actions. We do not ask whether we can breathe; we just breathe. In the same way "simple perception . . . is the same in the philosopher and in the clown [i.e., rustic]" (ibid., 211). Reid, with the common man, knows that he perceives a tree when he looks at it, and not merely an image of that tree: "I know, moreover, that this belief is not the effect of argumentation and reasoning; it is the immediate effect of my constitution" (207). Reid believed that Locke and Hume had retreated from the humble empiricism of Bacon and Newton by reintroducing the metaphysical machinery of a scholastic system (16). The Newtonian method was to observe what happens, record it accurately, and discern nature's laws behind the regularities discovered—exactly the way Newton traced the principles of gravity (208). But Hume tried to go back of this observing process, to describe a wholly *unob*served (and therefore scientifically unsound) knowledge-prior-to-knowledge.

Reid's main impact on American education, which was profound and long-lived, grew out of the *Essays* he wrote, toward the end of his life, in the 1780s. But three of his principal themes are sounded repeatedly in the 1764 *Inquiry* that came along at Jefferson's formative time of life and earned inclusion in his select list of 1771. These are Reid's egalitarian epistemology, his humble empiricism, and his communitarian morality.

Reid's egalitarian epistemology: Reid constantly asserts that the basic perceptions of the common man are equal in validity to those of philosophers (i.e., scientists). In fact, sometimes the "clown" is wiser than the philosopher, because his grasp of reality has not been dimmed or perverted by theoretical presuppositions: "It is genius, and not the want of it, that adulterates philosophy, and fills it with error and false theory. . . . Invention supplies materials where they are wanting" (ibid., 9—cf. 31–32, *Essays*, 2:700–2). In the *Inquiry*, Reid argues principally for the existential grasp of simple perception. But he sketches a wider area, more properly called that of common sense, which he must fill in later when he writes the *Essays* (269). Common sense is the exercise of what he calls "the inductive principle" upon simple perceptions (213, 245–47). He talks of knowledge as having three main parts—root, trunk, and branches (212–14). 1) The root is simple perception, common to men, children, brutes, and even lunatics. This is the realm of experience; it has no basis in anything prior to itself. 2) Next comes the sphere of common sense, of rational experiment, with immediate conclusions drawn from these experiments. All rational adults share in this exercise of common sense, which is not infallible like simple perception—but is not, either, so wayward or arbitrary as most "scientific" conjecture. Common sense deals with self-evident propositions (e.g., man should help, not hurt, himself and others) and the immediate consequences of those propositions (which are certain though not infallible). 3) Last come the sciences, the realm of argument and reflection, of remote and less-certain consequences drawn from self-evident propositions. This last kind of knowledge is the highest, yet the most vulnerable, achievement of the human mind. These "branches" are sound only when still connected with the "roots" of existential perception and the "trunk" of common sense.

These three realms produce, as characteristic separate products, 1) the perfect savage (with certain advantages of an uncorrupted instinct), 2) the good citizen (with moral responsibility), and 3) the philosopher (25). Reid talks of the "skillful artisan" to whom "reason and reflection must superadd this tutory" if we are to have "a Bacon or a Newton," in exactly the way Jefferson spoke of "the mechanic" whom science can lift on the shoulders of "a Locke or Bacon, or a Newton" (Ford, 15:211).

Reid always held that the philosopher and the clown were on an even footing with regard to the most important kinds of knowledge. And this is one of Jefferson's most celebrated assertions: "State a moral case to a ploughman and a professor. The former will decide it as well and often better than the latter, because he has not been led astray by artificial rules" (*Papers*, 6:258). Jefferson wrote that in 1789, after he had met and admired Dugald Stewart, Reid's student

and friend, who would become Reid's biographer; and after Reid
had published more versions of his characteristic dictum:

> In a matter of common sense, every man is no less a competent judge
> than a mathematician is in a mathematical demonstration. . . . The first
> principles of all sciences are the dictates of common sense, and lie open
> to all men (*Essays*, 2:611–12).

> The most uninstructed peasant has as distinct a conception, and as
> firm a belief, of the immediate objects of the senses as the greatest phi-
> losopher (ibid., 287).

Reid's humble empiricism: We have already seen how Reid attacked the "additions" that genius tries to make to nature. He constantly emphasized that man must take a humble stance before the
phenomena of nature: "If we would know the works of God, we
must consult themselves with attention and humility, without daring to add anything of ours to what they declare. . . . Whatever
we add of our own is apocryphal and of no authority" (*Inquiry*, 4;
Essays, 2:699–700). One of his favorite examples of the need for
receptivity before nature, rather than a proud and dictatorial air, is
his emphasis on the limits to be observed in medical speculation:
"Nature hath her way of rearing men, as she hath of curing their
diseases. The art of medicine is to follow nature, to imitate and to
assist her in the cure of diseases; and the art of education is to follow nature, and to assist and to imitate her, in her way of rearing
men" (ibid., 250). In the same way, men should humbly submit to
nature in their own thought processes, recognizing that simple perception is grounded in "the constitution of our nature" and not in
anything we can invent or correct (212, 245–46). Reid's attitude toward nature is constantly expressed in terms of what might be
called the "God bungleth not" rule. When Humeans tell him reason
can question the accuracy of sense perception, he answers:

> Why, sir, should I believe the faculty of reason more than that of per-
> ception; they came both out of the same shop, and were made by the
> same artist; and if he puts one piece of false ware into my hands, what
> should hinder him from putting another? (*Inquiry*, 207–cf. 238–39,
> 243–44; *Essays*, 1:138–39, 2:726)

Jefferson's attitude toward "the laws of Nature and of Nature's
God" was exactly that of Reid. We can see this from his contention

that "a physician should be a watchful but quiet spectator of the operations of nature," not claiming that his own special theory can "let him into all nature's secrets at short hand" (LB, 13:224; Cf. Reid, *Essays*, 2:701). The ingenious are too "fond, by a kind of anticipation, to discover her [Nature's] secrets. Instead of a slow and gradual ascent in the scale of natural causes, by a just and copious induction, they would shorten the work." Daniel Boorstin connects this attitude with Jefferson's admiration for Dr. Benjamin Rush, but it was clearly formed before these men became friends in the 1790s; and Rush's own attitude was formed by his studies in Scotland (Sloan, 186 ff.).

Jefferson also grounded his humble receptivity to nature in the reflection that God bungleth not. He told Peter Carr, in the famous "ploughman and professor" letter:

He who made us would have been a pitiful bungler, if he had made the rules of our moral conduct a matter of science. For one man of science, there are thousands who are not. What would have become of them? Man was destined for society. His morality, therefore, was to be formed to this object (*Papers*, 12:15).

He wrote others in the same vein:

It would have been inconsistent in creation to have formed man for the social state, and not to have provided virtue and wisdom enough to manage the concerns of the society (Cappon, 388).

The Creator would indeed have been a bungling artist, had he intended man for a social animal, without planting in him social dispositions (LB, 14:142).

Morals were too essential to the happiness of man to be risked on the incertain combinations of the head. She [Nature] laid their foundation therefore in sentiment, not in science. That she gave to all, as necessary to all: this to a few only, as sufficing with a few (*Papers*, 10:450).

"The knowledge that is necessary to all must be attained by all. . . . It may therefore be expected, from the analogy of nature, that such a knowledge of morals as is necessary to all men should be had by means more suited to the abilities of all men than demonstrative reasoning" (Reid, *Essays*, 2:726-27).

Reid's communitarian morality: All thinkers of the Enlightenment were opposed to the eremitical ideals of Christianity (a favorite theme of Voltaire); but few were as thoroughgoing in their attack on "solitude" as Thomas Reid. He held that community is a necessary guide and corrective for all thought: "When a man suffers himself to be reasoned out of the principles of common sense by metaphysical arguments, we may call this metaphysical lunacy—which differs from the other species of the distemper in this, that it is not continued, but intermittent. It is apt to seize the patient in solitary and speculative moments; but when he enters into society, common sense recovers her authority" (*Inquiry*, 268–69—cf. 35–36; *Essays*, 1:158–59, 161). Reid even thought the nature and structure of language proved that all thinking is really a thinking-*with*. Intellection is of itself communication: "The Author of our being intended us to be social beings, and has for that end given us social intellectual powers as well as social affections . . . Why have speculative men labored so anxiously to analyze our solitary operations, and given so little attention to the social?" (*Essays*, 2:72–73)

Reid did not take "common" sense to mean *ordinary* or "garden variety." He saw it as a *communal* sense, the shared wisdom of the community. Its propositions "serve to direct us in the common affairs of life, where our reasoning faculty would leave us in the dark. They are part of our constitution, and all the discoveries of our reason are grounded upon them. They make up what is called the common sense of mankind; and what is manifestly contrary to any of those first principles is what we call absurd" (*Inquiry*, 268).

The tenets of common sense constitute our joint recognition of the situation we share as rational beings: "The more obvious conclusions drawn from our perceptions by reason make what we can call common understanding, by which men conduct themselves in the common affairs of life, and by which they are distinguished from idiots" (ibid., 213). The idiot, or the solipsist, stands outside the common language of mankind, apart from the principles of common sense "we are under a necessity to take for granted in the common concerns of life" (ibid., 32). Otherwise we could not judge each other under law, assume rationality and obligation in one another, contract on terms we presume to be universally understandable and binding.

Common sense is thus a body of truths vouched for by the suffrage of mankind, a *vox populi* that Reid took for the voice of God:

It is this degree [of knowledge] that entitles them [men] to the denomination of reasonable creatures. It is this degree of reason, and this only, that makes a man capable of managing his own affairs, and answerable for his conduct toward others. . . . The same degree of understanding which makes a man capable of acting with common prudence in the conduct of life makes him capable of discovering what is true and what is false in matters that are self-evident and which he distinctly apprehends (*Essays*, 2:567, 559).

Jefferson's comments on "bungling not" prove he thought the divine artisan displays his handiwork in the social inclinations of human beings, who are "destined for society," designed to function in community. Whenever he talks of God's design as manifested in men's natures, it is to stress their fittedness for life with each other. This is true even in his earliest writings. In the 1771 letter to Robert Skipwith, he defends novels as stimulating our interest in others, our "moral feelings" of sympathy and helpfulness: "We are therefore wisely framed [not by a bungling artisan] to be as warmly interested for a fictitious as for a real personage" (*Papers*, 1:77). In his famous letter of 1786 to Maria Cosway, Jefferson connected the "generous spasm" of the heart with "a benevolent arrangement of things" (*Papers*, 10:450). The Heart argues that the world has been "wonderfully contrived" for human happiness (447).

In that letter—to be treated at greater length in chapter Twenty—the Head makes an argument for solitude and "safe" isolation: "The most effectual means of being secure against pain is to retire within ourselves and to suffice for our own happiness. Those, which depend on ourselves, are the only pleasures a wise man will count on: for nothing is ours which another may deprive us of. . . . Leave the bustle and tumult of society to those who have not talents to occupy themselves without them" (449). As one might expect, after reading Thomas Reid's attack on the intellect at odds with man's communal nature, Jefferson gives the victory to the Heart, which delivers a crushing rejoinder to eremitical vices: "Let the gloomy Monk, sequestered from the world, seek unsocial pleasure in the bottom of his cell! Let the sublimated philosopher grasp visionary happiness while pursuing phantoms dressed in the garb of truth! Their supreme wisdom is supreme folly. . . ." (250) Reid, defending man's heart against his head, wrote: "Without society and the intercourse of kind affection, man is a gloomy, melancholy, and joyless being" (*Essays*, 1:161). Against the background of his thought, the charge Jefferson's Heart makes against his Head does not seem as exaggerated as many have considered it: "In short, my friend, as far as my recollection serves me, I do not know that I ever did a good thing on your suggestion, or a dirty one without it" (451).

Not only are men designed for life in community; Jefferson expects them to achieve a communal wisdom in their life together: "I have great confidence in the common sense of mankind in general" (Ford, 7:455). Since Jefferson came to know Reid's *Inquiry* sometime between its appearance in 1764 and the drawing up of his Skipwith list in 1771, and since his knowledge of Reid grew through the admiring friendship with his student, Dugald Stewart, we might expect "common sense" to have a special and technical force in Jefferson's writings—and that is borne out in his most famous use of the term.

Jefferson's aim in writing the Declaration, he told Henry Lee in 1825, was "to place before mankind the common sense of the subject" (Ford, 10:343). Jefferson can hardly mean that he was saying banal things. Yet the way some people cite or understand this remark is enough to make people wonder why Jefferson listed his composition of the Declaration among the three achievements he wished to be remembered for. What is so memorable about saying what everybody else is saying?

This objection would not arise if we reflected on the dignity Reid gave to common sense as the faculty for grasping self-evident truths. If Jefferson used "self-evident" in Reid's sense while writing the Declaration, we should be prepared to entertain the possibility that he used "common sense" in a technical way when describing that document. Thus Jefferson's statement is not modest or self-deprecating in its purpose. Reid distinguished between 1) the grasp of self-evident truths experienced by all well-disposed men once the truths are set distinctly before them, and 2) the problem of setting the truths out in terms thus distinct. It is the difference, he said, between knowing there is a county named York and being able to trace its boundaries precisely (*Essays*, 2:560). Only the philosopher may be able to state the self-evident in properly distinct terms; yet, as we have seen, the philosopher can deceive himself and others with a misguided ingenuity. Thus there is a labor to be performed in grasping even the self-evident. Man can assent only to what he "distinctly apprehends" (ibid., 559), when he "takes due pains to be rightly informed" (724).

Thus Jefferson was not performing a superfluous labor when he set the common sense of the subject before what he calls, in his letter, "the tribunal of the world" for its suffrage. We can see, if we continue the quotation, that he approaches the matter in Reid's way and that his statement comes closer to a boast than to self-deprecation: "to place before mankind the common sense of the subject *in terms so plain and firm as to command their assent*" (emphasis added). We should notice, also, that it is "the common sense *of the subject*" that Jefferson places before mankind—the self-evident truths with regard to this one particular subject (first identified as the Americans' rights). This is quite a different matter from saying he supplied the world with the "lowest common denominator," or vague common talk, on the subject of natural rights.

There is one more condition Reid finds necessary to the apprehension of self-evident truths by common sense. The mind approaching the proposition must have "candour" (*Essays*, 2:693, 724). The candid or "white" mind must be open to evidence, a true *tabula rasa* in that respect, not scribbled over with prior theorizing or prejudices (ibid., 703, 708). That is why Jefferson first offered his self-evident truths to "a candid world" in the Declaration.

Thus Jefferson was given, in Reid's work, a concept of self-evident truths that accords well with his general training, his known reading and recommendations, and the language he used both in and of the Declaration. But recognizing this source for his thought on self-evident moral truths will not solve all the problems connected with that term. For one thing, Jefferson's enumerated truths are both more specific than the kind normally offered by Reid himself to exemplify his theory, and more confusing than Jefferson's own claim to perfect clarity would seem to justify. There are many people who have not found the terms "so plain as to command their assent." Is that because of a failure in "candour" on their part, or because of a failure in clarity on Jefferson's part? Or has Jefferson set things out in a distinct way that men now find indistinct because of the passage of time and changes in the language? To deal with these problems, we must pass from Thomas Reid to an even more important and influential Scottish thinker, Francis Hutcheson.

"... *endowed by their Creator* ..."

> We have, always, the strongest disposition to sympa-
> thize with the benevolent affections. They appear in
> every respect agreeable to us. . . . These affections,
> that harmony, this commerce, are felt not only by the
> tender and the delicate, but by the rudest vulgar of
> mankind, to be of more importance to happiness than
> all the little services which could be expected to flow
> from them.
>
> —Adam Smith (1759)

When Thomas Reid attacked the epistemology of Hume's *Treatise
on Human Nature,* he took a term—common sense—from that loose
and genial collection of essays, Lord Shaftesbury's *Characteristics,*
and gave it a more rigorous philosophical meaning. Almost a generation earlier, Francis Hutcheson had attacked the moral pessimism
of Bernard Mandeville's *Fable of the Bees* by taking another term
from Shaftesbury and giving it a technical meaning: the moral
sense.

When Locke argued that the mind had only the ideas received
from external evidence, he based his theory on the mechanics of
sensible stimulation. Man was seen, after Locke, as determined by
the impact of pleasure and pain upon his senses. Reid saw this as a
challenge to the certainty of knowledge. Hutcheson saw it as a
threat to the very possibility of virtue. If man has to respond in
necessary and predictable ways, to seek pleasure and avoid pain,
how can he ever act for nonhedonistic or altruistic motives? Hobbes
and Mandeville said, in effect, that he cannot. What looks like generous or benevolent action is actually just a shrewder form of
selfishness. Society itself can be based on selfishness—forming the
social contract on a trade-off of fewer pleasures for more stable
ones.

Defenders of the old morality of reason—men like Wollaston and Butler—tried to beat off Locke's challenge with Neo-Platonic or rationalist or conscience-school arguments. But Hutcheson was more successful precisely because he accepted the basic sensational determination of Locke, yet found a way to preserve the virtue of benevolence. His first work, *An Inquiry into the Original of Our Ideas of Beauty and Virtue* (1725), established a meaning for "moral sense" that dominated the whole Scottish Enlightenment, spread quickly to America, and found pupils like Burlamaqui and Jaucourt on the Continent. When Jeremy Bentham began to publish his ethical theories toward the end of the eighteenth century, he complained that moral-sense theory reigned unchallenged throughout Europe.

The huge success of Hutcheson's theory indicates how acute was the problem he had come to solve. People were willing to accept a complex and rather roundabout solution to difficulties that pressed so hard upon them. Hutcheson came up with a *mechanics* of virtue, since he forswore all the old solutions to the problem of unselfish action. He would not allow God to act directly on the conscience or to motivate man through his reason; he agreed with the Enlightenment view that only a bungling artisan would confess the breakdown of his own natural order by intruding upon it with miracles or private revelations (1:63–64). He not only rejected Wollaston's view that a moral syllogism can motivate man; he made the first distinction between "is" and "ought" propositions that Hume picked up and developed fourteen years later (1:247–48). For Hutcheson, reason was not a principle of action. "Speculation" was just what its etymology suggested to men who learned their philosophy in Latin—a mirror (*speculum*) in which things were reproduced, measured, compared. It must be still and receptive, simply registering reality. Shake the mirror, muddy the pond, and reason's basically "reflective" function is destroyed. With all the former paths closed to him, Hutcheson had to come up with an entirely original approach to the problem of motivating man toward other than animal gratifications.

His starting point was aesthetics. The *Inquiry* of 1725 (which led to his appointment to the chair of moral philosophy at Glasgow) linked the ideas of beauty and virtue. In the first part of the book, Hutcheson argued that one of the *pleasures* motivating man is his delight in order and harmony. This delight is as real as any pleasure of the senses, yet it is not limited to them. There is a gratification of a higher appetite as well, to which Hutcheson gives the name "internal sense" (previously used by Locke for the combinative activity of the mind as it receives sensations). This is a separate faculty, Hutcheson argues, neither simple reason nor (simply) external gratification—something with its separate needs. It is an appetite, not a mere judgment of reason; yet it is not predatory. We do not consume beauty like food—what we have is not denied to others. On the contrary, since the delight is in evidences of a cosmic order, we like to see it extended to others throughout the whole universe. In responding to this order, we align ourselves with it, reenact it, as it were, in our own lives. This explains the civilizing effect of the arts, the formation of graceful and delicate habits (1:89 ff.). Having been put into motion toward beauty as a spectator of it, one becomes an agent of that beauty, its disseminator.

After he established one internal sense, which acts like the external senses without being one of them, Hutcheson found another separate faculty, gratified by the sight of benevolence. This is very similar to the first "internal sense," without being exactly the same. The two seem to interact when we unselfishly take joy in cheering the hero of a play, or booing the villain; yet the same delight in benevolent acts can be separated from aesthetic gratification—and this delight leads to acts of virtue instead of the development of aesthetic gracefulness. The pleasure or displicence with which we look on acts of benevolence or malevolence is disinterested—we feel it even if the generous acts do not benefit us or the vicious ones threaten us. It is true that the gratification is *our* gratification. In that sense, but not the normal one, we react "selfishly," for our own pleasure. But that is just the point: Hutcheson's problem was to get the self into motion *for* itself, while performing acts that are not predatorily selfish. The "internal" sense was gratified with beauty in a way that did not seek to deny it to others—quite the opposite, it made one repeat and spread the beauty, giving it to others in order to possess it oneself.

In the same way, one must be put into action as a benefactor to satisfy one's own needs, not those of another. It is not enough to sympathize with the needs of the person being benefited by a generous act. That is *his* need and cannot motivate the benefactor. No, the need satisfied when the moral sense acts is a delight in the deed itself. That is why virtue begins with a *spectator*'s joy in the action of a prior *benefactor*. The delight aroused is then prolonged—much as aesthetic delight was—by re-enacting what aroused it in the first place. One keeps the pleasure by giving it. Thus there are, at a minimum, *four* people involved in any act of Hutchesonian benevolence —a man (A) sees B being kind to C and prolongs the pleasure caused at that sight by being kind, himself, to D. This act will, of course, stimulate pleasure in other onlookers, E, F, and so on. Virtue spreads by a billiard-ball sequence dear to post-Lockean students of social mechanics.

Adam Smith, when he wrote his *Theory of Moral Sentiments* (1759), actually made the operation of moral faculties more complex. He added a fifth "person" to the minimal social group necessary to keep benevolence in action. This simply spelled out the implications in Hutcheson's own scheme. After all, the source of action was the reception of a *spectator*'s joy from the original deed. In performing the resultant benefaction, the spectator needs to keep watching *himself* to prolong the original satisfaction. This aspect of the agent Smith calls "the man within the breast," the hypothetical "disinterested spectator" motivating our virtuous acts by watching them.

Modern students of philosophy often study Hutcheson's system without knowing it. David Hume took all the essential parts of his moral philosophy directly from Hutcheson, making no attempt to disguise his indebtedness. The existence of a separate moral faculty, looking to gratification rather than verification, allows Hume to treat morals without reference to his epistemological doubts. The only connection is a repeated *denial* that reason can have anything to do with moral motivation—an assertion that shocks modern moralists when they first encounter it. They do not realize that it was a view formulated by the pious (though enlightened) Presbyterian divine, Francis Hutcheson.

Hume's *Enquiry Concerning the Principles of Morals* (1751), which he called his finest book, spelled out his indebtedness to Hutcheson even more clearly than the *Treatise of Human Nature* (1740) had. In the *Enquiry* his definition of virtue is modeled directly on Hutcheson's. Hume argues:

It [his moral system] defines virtue to be whatever mental action or quality gives to a spectator the pleasing sentiment of approbation; and vice the contrary (Appendix I).

That just tightens up Hutcheson's 1725 definition:

The word moral goodness denotes an idea of some quality, apprehended in actions, which procures approbation and love toward the actor from those who receive no advantage by the action. Moral evil denotes an idea of a contrary quality (1:101).

In the *Treatise,* Hume had put the same concept this way:

The approbation of moral qualities most certainly is not derived from reason, or any comparison of ideas; but proceeds entirely from a moral taste, and from certain sentiments of pleasure or disgust which arise upon the contemplation and view of particular qualities or characters (Selby-Bigge ed., 581).

The two essential notes in both men's moral thought are 1) the disinterested spectator's contemplation of a moral act (or immoral one) and 2) concentration on the benefactor (or malefactor) and not on the beneficiary or the wronged person. Many other thinkers (and most of the Scots) would use the term "moral sense" in ways that derived from Hutcheson and approximated his views. But no one grasped and adhered to his essential points more faithfully than Hume. In fact Hume developed lines of thought in Hutcheson with such fidelity to his starting point (e.g., the relation of reasoning as concerned with *means* and moral sense with *ends*) that Hutcheson incorporated these formulae into his later writings. (The two men, like most of the Scottish thinkers, were friendly with each other, even in areas where they disagreed: Hume sent his first writings to Hutcheson for criticism before publication.)

Hume felt that Hutcheson's explanation of morality was so self-evident that he actually dropped his cool and doubting mode. He rebukes an imaginary challenger more in the tones of his legendary opponent Dr. Johnson than in those of Davy Hume, "le bon David":

All this is metaphysical, you cry. That is enough; there needs nothing more to give a strong presumption of falsehood. Yes, replied I, here are metaphysics, surely; but they are all on your side, who advance an abstruse hypothesis which can never be made intelligible nor quadrate with

any particular instance or illustration. The hypothesis which we embrace
is plain. It maintains that morality is determined by sentiment. It defines
virtue to be whatever mental action or quality gives to a spectator the
pleasing sentiment of approbation; and vice the contrary. We then proceed to examine a plain matter of fact—to wit, what actions have this
influence; we consider all the circumstances in which these actions agree,
and thence endeavor to extract some general observations with regard to
these sentiments. If you call this metaphysics and find anything abstruse
here, you need only conclude that your turn of mind is not suited to the
moral sciences (Appendix I).

Henry Home (pronounce Hume), Lord Kames, was an older
cousin of David Hume (who changed his name's spelling to match
pronunciation), and he drew from both Hume's *Treatise* and Hutcheson's *Inquiry* in his own *Essays on the Principles of Morality
and Natural Religion* (1751). But he felt he had to correct both of
them. Hutcheson erred, he thought, in making *love* of others the
basis of morality, rather than minimal *duty* toward others (55–57).
Kames returned to a more conventional ethics by grounding morality in justice, not benevolence. Hume, on the other hand, had
dealt more fully with justice; but made it result from artificial
human conventions, not from the structure of nature (103–8).
   In his effort to rescue the old concept of morality as right reason,
yet to incorporate Hutcheson's reliance on Locke's sensationalism,
Kames resorted to a juggling act—he shifted Hutcheson's term
(*moral sense*) over to Bishop Butler's concept of *conscience;* and
used *Hutcheson's* concept (stripped of its name) as one component
in a long list of "active principles." Kames exemplified what Reid
thought would be the fatal result of Hutcheson's approach—the multiplication of separate faculties to explain every isolable form of
human action. Kames, starting with aesthetics as Hutcheson had,
listed four rational ways of enjoying the beautiful (44–47)—sensible
delight, delight in the vision of usefulness, delight in beneficial
usefulness, and delight in the intention to be useful. (This last is
"Butlerian conscience.") Then, to account for man's activity *subsequent* to the delight in moral benefits, he lists (123–26) four
moral appetites (corresponding to Hutcheson's two inner senses)—
self-love, fidelity, gratitude, and benevolence (this latter is Hutcheson's moral sense.)
   We have seen something of Jefferson's debt to Thomas Reid in

the matter of common sense and self-evident truths. Reid had substituted his common sense for Hutcheson's moral sense. Like Kames, he felt that morality should still be guided by reason, lest Hume's morality leave room for the skepticism of Hume's epistemology. But Reid's common sense is not based on argumentative or reflective reason. He called it instinctual, a kind of "prescience" (*Inquiry*, 245–49). It was almost a preknowing; at least a prereasoning. Reid refused to accept Hume's and Hutcheson's claim that mere knowledge cannot set man in motion, since Reid's mental activity was prehensile, a motion to "grasp" reality, not the passive reception and mirroring of facts.

Moral sense became in Adam Smith moral sympathy, overseen by the "man within," which Smith himself equated with conscience (*Moral Sentiments*, 1, iii). But he did not mean, like Kames, to say that conscience was a reasoning power, for elsewhere Smith expressly endorses Hutcheson's rejection of reason as the basis of morality:

> Dr. Hutcheson had the merit of being the first who distinguished, with any degree of precision, in what respect all moral distinctions may be said to arise from reason, and in what respect they are founded upon immediate sense and feeling. In his illustrations upon the moral sense, he has explained this so fully, and in my opinion so unanswerably, that if any controversy is still kept up about this subject I can impute it to nothing but either to inattention to what that gentleman has written, or to a superstitious attachment to certain forms of expression (ibid., 7, iii, 2).

Like Hume, Smith thought anyone who could not accept Hutcheson's view must have a "turn of mind . . . not suited to the moral sciences."

Jefferson was familiar with every one of the men so far discussed in this chapter, and familiar with them well before he wrote the Declaration of Independence. Their world of shared discourse and sharp disagreements constituted the arena for his early training. All students of Jefferson's philosophy have known that he believed in the moral sense as a separate faculty, but they have underestimated the importance of that fact. They do not see how central the moral sense was to the whole British-American philosophical endeavor by the middle of the eighteenth century—central to politics and "political economy" as well as to epistemology and aesthetics. And they have vaguely talked of the moral "school" without noting important internal differences. Jefferson knew what these points of disagreement were, and he "took sides" in his own reflections on the matter. There have, as well, been particular obstacles in various authors to a just evaluation of Jefferson's debt to moral-sense thinkers. Adrienne Koch considered moral-sense philosophy "anti-intellectual" and tried to play down Jefferson's subscription to it as "a minor intellectual enthusiasm" of his youth, a passing "flirtation" that faded when Jefferson met his real philosophical mentors, the idéologues (*Philosophy of Thomas Jefferson,* 44–45). But some of Jefferson's most complete statements of the moral-sense case come well after his exposure to the idéologues. Indeed, at the height of his propagandizing for the French thinkers, and especially for his friend Destutt de Tracy, he deplored Tracy's mistaken denial that the moral sense is the basis of politics and morality (Cappon, 2:492).

Daniel Boorstin concentrated so narrowly on Jefferson's intellectual relationship with the Philadelphia circle of thinkers that his book on Jefferson's intellectual milieu never even mentions Hume or Hutcheson or Kames. Never, for that matter, mentions William Small. Nor is it true, as Boorstin argues, that Jefferson was "the human magnet who drew them [the Philadelphia circle] together." The Philosophical Society was first dominated by Benjamin Franklin, then by William Smith and John Ewing, and then by Rittenhouse. So far as friendly leadership and daily intercourse are concerned, Boorstin describes the lost world of Benjamin Rush. Jefferson was president of the Society while serving as Vice-President and President of the United States—i.e., when he could give the Society only limited amounts of his time, though his political offices shed luster on its activities.

Gilbert Chinard, too, neglects to mention Hume or Hutcheson, Kames or Adam Smith in his book on Jefferson's thought (*Apostle of Americanism*). He thinks Jefferson's thinking reached full flower among the Idéologues (which, even if true, would have nothing to do with the Declaration of Independence, written before he met those thinkers). His early formation Chinard restricts to the impact of English deism—Shaftesbury and Bolingbroke, leaning on Locke.

In order to correct these typical readings of Jefferson's intellectual background, it is necessary to emphasize his exposure to the moral-sense thinkers. What is often said about Locke's politics was literally true of Hutcheson's ethics—it was "in the air," making up an intellectual "atmosphere," a kind of tacit orthodoxy. Hutcheson was *the* author on the central topic of philosophy as it was taught at Philadelphia and Princeton and New York. What was true elsewhere was doubly true of William and Mary in Dr. Small's time there. Small taught Hutcheson's own discipline (moral philosophy) by Hutcheson's own method (the connected vernacular lecture series, not tutoring on Latin texts). In the library Jefferson sold to Congress, he owned not only Hutcheson's original *Inquiry*, but the 1744 *Synopsis Metaphysicae* and the 1747 *Short Introduction to Moral Philosophy* (the principal text used in American colleges). More important than this, however, is that Jefferson repurchased the *Inquiry* and the *Short Introduction* for the personal library assembled after the sale of his great collection to Congress (1829 Catalogue, items 460, 461). Hutcheson was not only "in the air." Unlike Locke's *Treatise*, Hutcheson's moral works were regularly in Jefferson's hand. When "moral sense" without further specification was used in the later eighteenth century, it was Hutcheson's concept that was referred to. But we do not have to assume for Hutcheson, as men have for Locke, some vague "infection" of Jefferson's thinking from a general diffusion of his doctrine. Jefferson knew it from its source.

Lord Kames was an intellectual hero of the young Jefferson. He is quoted and recommended often in the early writings. Millicent Sowerby argues that Jefferson's copy of Kames's *Essays on the Principles of Morals and Natural Religion* was one of the books that escaped the Shadwell fire, since it has marginal notations in a very young hand (including a Hutchesonian attack on slavery). Jefferson had ten books by Kames in his major library, and he owned one of these (*The Principles of Equity*) in three different editions. But Kames, who is superficial compared to Hutcheson and Hume, did seem to fade from Jefferson's mind with time. He bought no copies of his work in the private collection made during his last eleven years of life.

Jefferson developed a bitter hostility to Hume—one that ranks with his souring attitudes toward Blackstone and Montesquieu—because of the biting things said about Commonwealth Whigs in the *History of England*. (Hume called Paul de Rapin, Jefferson's favorite "modern" historian, the author of "compositions the most despi-

cable, both for style and matter.") The hostility on this point has
made some doubt that Jefferson learned from or respected Hume's
ethical writings. But the *Essays*, which are full of Hume's moral-
sense teaching on justice, benevolence, property, and rights, were
favorites of Jefferson early and late. They show up on the 1771 list
of basic books, and Jefferson repurchased them for his own use late
in life (1829 Catalogue, item 485). He recommended them to others
and copied a passage from one of them into his copy of Blackwell's
Homer (cf. Lucia White, *Journal of the History of Ideas*, 1976).

Adam Smith's *Theory of Moral Sentiments* was on the 1771 list of
recommendations, in the category of criticism that took up a surprising amount of Jefferson's thinking and reading in early years.
(Hutcheson had set the fashion, by moving toward his moral-sense
theory by way of the "inner sense" of beauty.) As was noticed in the
last chapter, Reid's *Inquiry* was the only epistemology text on the
1771 list except for Locke's *Conduct of the Mind*.

Jefferson's discussions of moral sense begin with a passage copied, in his teens, into Lord Kames's *Principles of Morality;* and
they continue through his life—in the 1771 letter to Robert Skipwith, the 1781 *Notes on the State of Virginia*, and (e.g.) letters to
Maria Cosway (1786), Peter Carr (1787), Thomas Law (1814),
and John Adams (1816). The Peter Carr letter proves that, though
Jefferson used Reid's characteristic "philosopher and clown" comparison, he distinguished Hutcheson's moral sense from Reid's common sense. Jefferson's moral sense, like Hutcheson's and Hume's, is
submitted in some measure to reason (for information about *means*
to ends chosen by the moral faculty) but is not itself an act of
reason, as in Reid:

Man was destined for society. His morality, therefore, was to be
formed to this object. He was endowed with a sense of right and wrong,
merely relative to this. This sense is as much a part of his nature as the
sense of hearing, seeing, feeling; it is the true foundation of morality, and
not the to kalon, truth, etc., as fanciful writers have imagined. The moral
sense, or conscience, is as much a part of man as his leg or arm. It is
given to all human beings in a stronger or weaker degree, as force of
members is given them in a greater or less degree. It may be
strengthened by exercise, as may any particular limb of the body. This
sense is submitted, indeed, in some degree, to the guidance of reason;

but it is a small stock which is required for this; even a less one than what we call common sense. State a moral case to a ploughman and a professor. The former will decide it as well and often better than the latter because he has not been led astray by artificial rules (*Papers*, 12:15).

Jefferson calls the moral sense "conscience," but Adam Smith proves that the term could be loosely used without reference to the moral *reason* of Bishop Butler. Jefferson goes on immediately to say that "truth, etc." cannot be the foundation of morals. In saying this, he departs from his own early hero, Lord Kames.

Nor is this the only disagreement Jefferson has with Kames. Kames had attacked Hutcheson for saying that benevolence, the love of others, was the basic constituent of morality. He thought this left too little room for legitimate self-love and for the minimal demands of justice, as opposed to the maximum demands of love; he accused Shaftesbury and Hutcheson of taking too high a view of mankind, just as Hobbes and Machiavelli took too low a view (*Principles*, 120–21). Kames said that conscience (*his* moral sense) adjudicates between the appetitive drives of self-love and love for others (ibid., 55–57, 76–81, 123–26). Hutcheson had defined the "moment" of virtue as an overbalancing of I (for self-interest) by B (for benevolence). Hume followed Hutcheson in this as in most moral matters. Where self-love does not actually thwart benevolence (and thus become immorality), it is an indifferent matter to the moral questioner: "Avarice, ambition, vanity, and all passions vulgarly though improperly comprised under the denomination of self-love [he would prefer Hutcheson's term, Interest] are here excluded from our theory concerning the origin of morals, not because they are too weak, but because they have not a proper direction for that purpose" (*Inquiry, Morals*, 9, i—cf. Hutcheson, 1:160; Burlamaqui, 1, v, 7; Ferguson, *Civil Society*, 22–25). This is Jefferson's doctrine precisely:

Self-interest, or rather self-love, or egoism, has been more plausibly substituted as the basis of morality. But I consider our relation with others as constituting the boundaries of morality. With ourselves we stand on the ground of identity, not of relation, which last, requiring two subjects, excludes self-love confined to a single one. To ourselves, in strict language, we can own no duties, obligation requiring also two parties. Self-love, therefore, is no part of morality (LB, 14:140).

Nothing could be a flatter rejection of Kames's major criticism of Hutcheson. The same rejection occurs in Jefferson's defense of moral sense against Destutt de Tracy, where "doing good to others" is the whole scope of morality, in which man takes the pleasure proper to the moral sense:

I gather from his other works that he adopts the principle of Hobbes, that justice is founded in contract solely, and does not result from the construction of man. I believe, on the contrary, that it is instinct, and innate, that the moral sense is as much a part of our constitution as that of feeling, seeing, or hearing; as a wise creator must have seen to be necessary in an animal destined to live in society: that every human mind feels pleasure in doing good to another. . . . The essence of virtue is in doing good to others (Cappon, 2:492).

In the letter to Law, Jefferson talks of the way "good acts give us pleasure" (LB, 14:141), both when we see them and when we (consequently) perform them—the Hutchesonian explanation of benevolence as a gratifiable appetite providentially built into man's "constitution" or "frame" (these very words become trademarks of the moral-sense school).

Excerpts of the sort I have been quoting were not lightly framed or offered by Jefferson. The one addressed to John Adams takes exception with an admired friend's system at the very time when he was promoting that system. The letter to Law is a little compendium of the moral thinking current in Jefferson's time. Before advocating the moral sense theory, he rejects with incisive brief arguments the five leading challengers to that system: right reason, conscience, aesthetic taste (Hutcheson's "inner sense" as opposed to his moral sense), and self-interest in the terms of Helvétius. (This last argument involves rejection of another favorite thinker's tenets so far as they touch moral theory.) In the 1787 letter, Jefferson makes a distinction between common sense and moral sense in terms of reason's role; he shows familiarity with the basic lines of division within the moral-sense theorists of the Scottish Enlightenment.

We must conclude, therefore, that Jefferson held to moral-sense doctrine in its classic form, as first expounded by Hutcheson and adhered to by Hume, Burlamaqui, and Adam Smith (among others). We shall see in the next chapter that he explained perversions of the moral sense in the same way that they did. This does not mean that he did not learn from and use Thomas Reid's theory of common sense. Even Hutcheson's moral appetite had to presuppose a first (nonreasoning) discernment of the thing to be desired. Hutcheson himself thus had a kind of implicit common-sense theory of self-evidently desirable things; but Jefferson would not follow Reid in substituting that power for the moral appetite itself. He draws from both men, with Hutcheson in charge.

In the same way, he learned from Lord Kames in matters of law, politics, and literary criticism. But he does not allow a sense of justice to replace benevolence as the criterion of morality. Jefferson's thought touches at some places all the leading thinkers of the Scottish Enlightenment; but the most entire correspondence is with Hutcheson. Jefferson, like Hume, speaks with the voice of Hutcheson on moral matters. Submit a passage like the following to a Jeffersonian and he will call to mind dozens of similar phrases in Jefferson; indeed, if he has not read those passages recently, he could easily mistake this passage for the very words of Jefferson:

Human nature was not left quite indifferent in the affair of virtue, to form to itself observations concerning the advantage or disadvantage of actions, accordingly to regulate its conduct. The weakness of our reason, and the avocations arising from the infirmity and necessities of our nature are so great that very few of mankind could have formed those long deductions of reason which may show some actions to be in the whole advantageous to the agent (and their contraries pernicious). The Author of Nature has much better furnished us for a virtuous conduct than our moralists seem to imagine, by almost as quick and powerful instructions as we have for the preservation of our bodies. He has made virtue a lovely form to excite our pursuit of it; and has given us strong affections to be springs of each virtuous action (1, vi–vii).

Those words come from the opening pages of Hutcheson's famous *Inquiry,* which first proposed the theory of moral sense. They would echo through many other writings of the eighteenth-century moralists, not least in the works of Thomas Jefferson:

It is really curious that on a question so fundamental, such a variety of opinions should have prevailed among men, and those, too, of the most exemplary virtue and first order of understanding. It shows how necessary was the care of the Creator in making the moral principle so much a part of our constitution as that no errors of reasoning or of speculation might lead us astray from its observance in practice. These good acts give us pleasure, but how happens it that they give us pleasure? Because nature hath implanted in our breasts a love of others, a sense of duty to them, a moral instinct, in short, which prompts us irresistibly to feel and to succor their distresses (LB, 14:139, 141).

FOURTEEN

"... *created equal* ..."

> Every history of the creation, and every traditionary ac-
> count, whether from the lettered or unlettered world,
> however they may vary in their opinion or belief of cer-
> tain particulars all agree in establishing one point, the
> unity of man; by which I mean, that men are all of one
> degree, and consequently that all men are born equal,
> and with equal natural right, in the same manner as if
> posterity had been continued by creation instead of
> generation, the latter being only the mode by which the
> former is carried forward; and consequently every child
> born into the world must be considered as deriving its
> existence from God. The world is as new to him as it
> was to the first man that existed, and his natural right
> in it is of the same kind.
>
> —Paine, *Rights of Man*

Jefferson believed in the perceptions of Reid's common sense and
the appetites of Hume's moral sense. Those beliefs do not, at first,
seem to explain his belief in the Declaration's "self-evident truths."
But they give us the material for that understanding.

Take the truth that bothers people most: that all men are created
equal. Many have, over the years, claimed this was not only not
self-evident but not true. Or, if true, only minimally or mystically so
—equal "before the law" or equal "in God's eyes." Certainly Jefferson could not be saying that men are equal in talent, in fact, in social reality. But we should not let him off the hook even before discussion begins. The only two references to equality in Jefferson's
pre-Declaration writings are to equality of ability and equality of
property. In his draft instruction for the Virginia delegation to
1774's Continental Congress (*A Summary View*), Jefferson wrote:
"Can any one reason be assigned why 160,000 electors in the island

of Great Britain should give law to four millions in the states of America, every individual of whom is equal to every individual of them in virtue, in understanding, and in bodily strength?" (*Papers*, 1:126). That is a very literal reading of equality, at least as between the island British and the continental British.

The only other reference to equality is a paraphrase from his reading of Montesquieu: "In a democracy, equality and frugality should be promoted by the laws, as they nurse the amor patriae. To do this, a census is advisable, discriminating the people according to their possessions; after which, particular laws may equalise them in some degree by laying burthens on the richer classes, and encouraging the poorer ones" (*Commonplace Book*, 259). The plantation owner may look like an unconvincing socialist; but Jefferson thought Montesquieu's plan worth copying into his book of favorite quotes.

I argued in the second part of this book that Jefferson's scientific approach to things often looks like a very *literal* approach in our terms—e.g., his belief that one generation should not "entail" the next led him to search for a date certain when the obligation must cease. And he often cast the most unlikely things in mathematical terms. It is at least possible, then, that he took "equal" in a similarly literal, indeed mathematical, way. This would fit the "averaging" tendencies encouraged by one of Jefferson's seventeenth-century heroes, William Petty. For purposes of planning and analysis, Petty's formulae had to assume that all men and women do the same work in the same circumstances and should therefore consume the same amount of the national wealth.

But there was an even more powerful force making the leaders of Enlightenment thought assume a literal equality of men. The tendency of Locke's sensationalism was to make men's perceptions determined entirely by their object. The mind begins as a blank receiver of things, which things shape and form it. All the receiving apparatus was presumed to work in essentially the same way, prior to conditioning. So Lockeans spoke regularly of the "automatic" and "infallible" process of sensation. This doctrine would be carried very far. Helvétius argued (*De l'esprit*, 3, i) that men's faculties are the same in nature, with nurture explaining all subsequent differences; so that education became the center of his social thought, and he aimed at the equal happiness of people who have all been equally conditioned (*De l'homme*, 8, i:9, ix). Jefferson copied long extracts from *De l'homme* in later sections of his *Commonplace Book* (328–34), with special emphasis on the soul as a property of the body, acting as automatically through the senses as magnetism is exerted by certain metals (329–30).

Carried far enough, the view of man as determined by his conditioning would become, in men like Diderot and Hume, a complete determinism, canceling free will. Even Hutcheson admitted that any science of man must be based on the element of necessity in his acts (1, v–vi). This thought became the basis of Hume's sociology, history, and politics:

> Mankind are so much the same in all times and places that history informs us of nothing new or strange in this particular. . . . Were there no uniformity in human actions, and were every experiment which we could form of this kind irregular and anomalous, it were impossible to collect any general observations concerning mankind, and no experience, however accurately digested by reflection, would ever serve to any purpose. . . . Are the manners of men different in different ages and countries? We learn thence the great force of custom and education, which mold the human mind from its infancy. . . . (*Enquiry, Understanding*, 8, i).

The ideal of a science of man is what led Jefferson to think there was a necessity in the course of human events.

Even that author often cited by men who praise competition as a principle of human differentiation was more struck by man's uniformity than by his differences. Adam Smith wrote in his *Wealth of Nations:*

> The difference of natural talents in different men is, in reality, much less than we are aware of; and the very different genius which appears to distinguish men of different professions, when grown up to maturity, is not upon many occasions so much the cause as the effect of the division of labor. The difference between the most dissimilar characters, between a philosopher and a common street porter, for example, seems to arise not so much from nature as from habit, custom, and education (1, ii).

This view of the matter was widely shared by the Scottish thinkers. Hume wrote in his essay "Of the Original Contract":

> When we consider how nearly equal all men are in their bodily force, and even in their mental powers and faculties, till cultivated by education, we must necessarily allow that nothing but their own consent could

at first associate them together and subject them to any authority . . . [a truth seen] plainly in the nature of man, and in the equality, or something approaching equality, which we find in all the individuals of that species (cf. *Enquiry, Morals,* 3, i; and Hutcheson, 4:144).

In "the chain of being," that favorite Enlightenment concept, each link must be distinguished from that immediately above it and immediately below; and it must therefore have identity with itself. Man must differ from beasts and angels, but not from himself—man is uniformly man in all times and places, in each exemplification of his species. The great biological classification system of Buffon, which Jefferson studied and used, depended on the stability of the species—none could undergo fundamental alteration, including extinction: Any species that ever existed still exists—as Jefferson argued when saying the American mammoth must still be roaming somewhere (*Notes,* 43 ff.).

The Lockeans knew that any sense can be damaged. A man can be born color-blind, just as he can be born without an eye. But these are freakish departures from the norm. Nature, the undamaged norm, is presumed to be uniform. The undamaged sensible equipment, given the same conditioning, would operate the same way. (Hume, Diderot, Helvétius, and others were intrigued with the sensing procedures of blind men: A necessary reliance on the other senses allowed observers to study the human apparatus, as one studies a machine by taking parts out.) Jefferson himself put it this way: "Some men are born without the organs of sight, or of hearing, or without hands. Yet it would be wrong to say that man is born without these faculties; and sight, and hearing and hands may with truth enter into the general definition of man. The want or imperfection of the moral sense in some men, like the want or imperfection of the senses of sight and hearing in others, is no proof that it is a general characteristic of the species" (LB, 14:142).

Kames argued that the senses are not so often deceived as one might think, and only then because their sphere is limited (*Principles of Morality,* 153). But the limits are far fewer on *internal* senses than external. If men in general agree on what is meant by "red," they are in even greater and more certain accord on what is "right." On that, as Thomas Reid said, the philosopher and the clown are at one. And Hutcheson's moral sense is an even simpler faculty than Reid's instinctual prescience. Hutcheson regularly uses the analogy of external senses, but adds: "The uniformity is much greater in our moral faculty than in our palates" (5:89). Jefferson, as we have seen, called the moral faculty "irresistible" (Ford, 141). Hutcheson called it "uniform in its influence" (5:85), and Hume "the same in all" (*Enquiry, Morals,* 9, i). And for both men the moral sense was man's highest faculty, what Jefferson described as "the brightest gem with which the human character is studded" (LB, 14:141). To say that men are equal in their exercise of this faculty is to define them as *essentially* equal, for the moral sense is what makes man accountable to himself and others, self-governing and consenting to social obligation. This separate faculty, equal in all, makes differences in other capacities comparatively minor, unable to reach the rights of self-regulation.

Neither Hutcheson nor Jefferson will let apparent differences overthrow their basic insight on equality. The natural faculty may be stunted by mistreatment of it: "By education we may contract groundless prejudices, or opinions about the qualities perceivable by any of our senses," says Hutcheson (5:85). The solution is to remove the inhibiting conditions and restore the moral sense's autonomy. As I mentioned earlier, Hutcheson profited from Hume's discussion of this matter, which granted that reason can mislead moral choice, even though moral sense is in control. "Sentiment" chooses the end, but reason must judge the means to those ends that are not immediate but remote. This is the only scope for that utilitarianism that many people wrongly identify as the basis of Hume's morality. "Usefulness is agreeable and engages our approbation. This is a matter of fact confirmed by daily observation. But useful for what? For somebody's interest surely. Whose interest then? Not our own only, for our approbation frequently extends further. It must therefore be the interest of those who are served by the character or action approved of" (*Enquiry, Morals,* 5, i). The good of others is the end of moral actions—i.e., of benevolence, of the moral sense.

By the time he wrote his *System of Moral Philosophy* (1755) Hutcheson regularly distinguished the role of moral sense and of reason in Hume's terms of ends and means:

We may indeed often imagine, without ground, that actions have good effects upon the public, or that they flowed from good affections, or that they are required by the Deity and acceptable to him; and then under these appearances we approve them. It is our reason which presents a false notion or species to the moral faculty. The fault or error is in the opinion or understanding, and not in the moral sense: what it approves is truly good, though the action may have no such quality. We sometimes choose and like, in point of interest, what is in event detrimental to ourselves—no man concludes that we are not uniform in self-love or liking or our own interest. Nor do like mistakes about the moral qualities of actions prove either that we have no moral sense or that it is not uniformly constituted (5:91).

Locke said man automatically and infallibly pursues pleasure. Hutcheson adds that he pursues the good of others by an urge equally necessary, though reason may err in choosing means to that end:

Now almost all our diversities in moral sentiments, and opposite approbations and condemnations, arise from opposite conclusions of reason about the effects of actions upon the public or the affections from which they flowed. The moral sense seems ever to approve and condemn uniformly the same immediate objects, the same affections and dispositions, though we reason very differently about the actions which evidence certain dispositions or their contraries (5:93).

Jefferson agreed with Hutcheson on this; he said different judgments on means to the end of happiness may be valid when the circumstances differ:

Some have argued against the existence of a moral sense, by saying that if nature had given us such a sense, impelling us to virtuous actions, and warning us against those which are vicious, then nature would also have designated, by some particular ear-marks, the two sets of actions which are, in themselves, the one virtuous and the other vicious. Whereas, we find, in fact, that the same actions are deemed virtuous in one country and vicious in another. The answer is that nature has constituted utility to man the standard and test of virtue. Men living in different countries, under different circumstances, different habits and regimens, may have different utilities; the same act, therefore, may be useful, and consequently virtuous, in one country which is injurious and vicious in another differently circumstanced (LB, 14:143).

The non-existence of justice is not to be inferred from the fact that the same act is deemed virtuous and right in one society which is held vicious and wrong in another; because as the circumstances and opinions of different societies vary, so the acts which may do them right and wrong must vary also. For virtue does not consist in the act we do, but in the end it is to effect. If it is to effect the happiness of him to which it is directed, it is virtuous, while in a society under different circumstances and opinions the same act might produce pain, and would be vicious. The essence of virtue is in doing good to others (Cappon, 2:492).

Since the moral sense was considered man's highest faculty, the basis of his moral accountability, and the bond with other men, it had to be the basis for man's politics and political right. Some authors have noticed that Jefferson took his division of rights into alienable and unalienable from Hutcheson, who had made the distinction popular and important (cf. Burlamaqui, *Naturel,* 1, iv, 1); but they have not appreciated that these rights were based on the moral sense, *not* based on a theory of moral reason. The Scottish approach has been largely neglected, except for some notice of Hume's account of the state's origin, differing so dramatically from that of Locke.

The Lockean view of natural right could dominate political thinking in the nineteenth and twentieth century, because the very concept of right is comparatively recent in political theory; it did not have a long classical tradition of discussion and internal debate to expand the term's possibilities. A human right is now most often thought of as a power the individual retains over-against the state. But its earlier use was as a power exercised in the name of the state. "Right" was right order, the *rectum* or *directum* (*droit*—cf. Burlamaqui, *Naturel,* 1, v, 1). It was the power of dominion or position, as in Spencer's mention of "the Souldans right" (= territory) at *Faerie Queene,* 8, xxvi, or Swift's recognition of the Lilliputian treasurer's "right of post" (= power of office) at *Gulliver's Travels,* 1, vi.

Insofar as a sovereign had right or rule over something, it was properly his (*proprium*), an *alienum* to others. To transfer, he must "alien" it—and the juridical literature first used "alienable" about this power to surrender territory or peoples while retaining rule over the *proprium.* Fiefs and domains were defined in terms of their alienability from the prince or crown. The same legal language was used for any title-transfer over an estate or property (see Chambers Cyclopaedia, s.v. "alienation"). Whatever subsidiary holdings might be disposed of, the sovereign could never alien the realm's very substance. (Sovereignty, after all, implied that nothing can be "supremer" than supremacy, so supremacy cannot yield its essence to another.) Even Rousseau, while drastically changing the definition of sovereignty, maintained the rule that sovereignty was unalienable (*Contrat*, 2, i). The right to alien property was a legal question Jefferson studied in Sir John Dalrymple, taking notes and copying extracts (*Commonplace Book*, 142–47).

Jefferson, in his attack on Virginia's laws of entail, argued that private property should be easily alienable. But he, too, held that the sovereign nation could not alien territory held in pledge for its citizens. This principle made him attack a national debt entailed on later generations. He gave this view sharpest statement in the dispute over the extent of Georgia's territory. Writing as Secretary of State, Jefferson advised President Washington against yielding to Spanish claims: "For as to territory, we have neither the right, nor the disposition to alienate an inch of what belongs to our Union" (Ford, 5:444). Hamilton, making notes on this draft, wondered how this principle might affect later actions by the government and counseled milder wording: "Is it true that the U.S. have no right to *alienate an inch* of the territory in question, except in the case of necessity intimated in another place? Or will it be useful to avow the denial of such a right? It is apprehended that the doctrine which restricts the alienation of territory to cases of *extreme necessity*, is applicable rather to peopled territory, than to waste & uninhabited districts. Positions restraining the right of the U. States to accommodate to exigencies which may arise, ought ever to be advanced with great caution?" (ibid.).

Jefferson, in his reply, adapted to republican sovereignty the rules that had, for ages, been applied to kings who tried to alien their subjects or domains: "The power to alienate the *unpeopled* territories of any state, is not among the enumerated powers, given by the constitution to the general government, & if we may go out of that Instrument & *accommodate to exigencies which may arise* by alienating the *unpeopled* territory of a state, we may accommodate ourselves a little more by alienating that which is *peopled*, & still a little more by selling the *people* themselves" (ibid.).

So much for the unalienable rights of sovereignty. How could such a concept apply to the individual? In classical and mediaeval thought, the "rights" of the individual were not a topic of conventional discourse; there, the citizen did not rule but was ruled. Of course every man had certain things owed to him by divine and human law—his *dikē* or *jus*. But these were not pregovernmental "rights" in the modern sense. They could not be. A man received political status by initiation into a tribe or people, by vows to a liege lord or suzerain. These ties gave each member privileges *of the body*.

The idea of an original "rule" over oneself, partly surrendered to another power (aliened), arose as a corollary to fully articulated social-contract theory in the seventeenth century. Only then was one's own government thought of as other-than (over-against) one's proper self and interests. The question then became: What powers *can* one renounce as an individual, and what ones are (like a king's sovereignty) unsurrenderable? The individual was now the master of his own multiple "realm," parts of which he could dispose of—"property" in the external sense (often called "propriety" in the eighteenth century), as opposed to a man's "property" over his own thought and body.

It is easy to see, against this background of dividable realms or estates, why natural right was thought of so readily as a kind of property. Hobbes, Locke, and Rousseau, despite their various differences, all assume an original "sovereignty" over oneself. But this approach made no sense to the Scottish school of politics and economics. These writers did not, and could not, begin (like Locke) with an idea of right as rule over oneself. Ruler and ruled must be different in order to create a mutuality of obligation. As we have seen, Jefferson rejected the idea of contract *with oneself* as nonsense: "To ourselves, in strict language, we can owe no duties, obligation requiring also two parties. Self-love, therefore, is no part of morality" (LB, 14:140). No such contract could be the basis of political morality, of right or obligation.

The moral sense was directed to others—it was the principle of sociability, of benevolence, not selfishness. No politics built upon the moral sense could make self-interest the foundation of the social contract. That is why Hume contrasted his approach to the state with "Hobbes and Locke, who maintained the selfish system of morals" (*Enquiry, Morals,* App. 3). Critics of the moral-sense politics thought it too optimistic about human nature.

For Hume and Hutcheson, right had to be a power extended *over others,* or over some aspect of their lives. Right was the exercise of moral sense in some way that affected the lives of others for general good. The basic notion of right was, for Hutcheson, the power "to direct our own actions either for public or innocent private good before we have submitted them to the direction of others" (1:257). Burlamaqui argued that one can never alien one's power to act morally, since that would give one's master the ability to deny response to humane duty (*Principes du droit naturel*, i, 7, viii). One's ability to affect the welfare of others cannot be given over to others.

Hutcheson's full definition of right ran this way: "Whenever it appears to us that a faculty of doing, demanding, or possessing anything, universally allowed in certain circumstances, would in the whole tend to the general good, we say that any person in such circumstances has a right to do, possess, or demand that thing. And according as this tendency to the public good is greater or less, the right in question is greater or less" (1:256). This definition escapes what the moral-sense school felt was the absurdity of a rule over oneself. Right arises in, and because of, society; it is a power over others so long as benevolence or innocence are directing the powers. The test is public good.

Hutcheson then divides rights into perfect and imperfect. The perfect, as essential to the public good, can be defended even with private force. The first example he gives is the right to life. The basis of the societal bond is benevolence, and no society can undermine its own fundamental value. Yet security in the possession of life is not only the basis for all goods one can bestow on others; it is, more important, the necessary precondition for *doing* good—no man can be benevolent unless he is first alive. Burlamaqui's argument against slavery as making virtue impossible is, a fortiori, an argument against depriving any man of his life. Even the slave can have a kind of maimed virtue; but the dead man has none at all. Hutcheson defines a right to life without imagining a prepolitical "sovereignty" or absolute right of property over oneself (1:256–57, 5:293); so he reshapes the prohibition against suicide in terms of life as a precondition of benevolence (6:105–6).

He asserts the right of liberty on similar grounds: "As nature has implanted in each man a desire of his own happiness and many tender affections toward others in some nearer relations of life, and granted to each one some understanding and active powers, with a natural right to exercise them for the purpose of these natural affections, it is plain each one has a natural right to exert his powers, according to his own judgment and inclination, for these purposes, in all such industry, labor, or amusements as are not hurtful to others in their persons or goods, while no more public interests necessarily require his labors or require that his actions should be under the direction of others. This right we call natural liberty" (5:294). Himself a Presbyterian minister, Hutcheson was for absolute freedom of conscience and of public religious exercise (1:261–62, 3:124, 6:295–96).

Life and liberty are the principal rights in Hutcheson's scheme of things. They are also the principal duties. He does not, like those who treat rights as a form of property, think duties *arise* correlative to rights in some negotiating give-and-take that sets up a social contract. Men have a duty to stay alive and to stay free in their thoughts and actions. Duty is simply one's right considered from another aspect.

Hutcheson also embraced a right to property, but it was subordinate to life and liberty, not the foundation and model of all rights. Before we consider the evidence that Jefferson understood rights in Hutcheson's sense, not Locke's, and the consequences for his view of property, we must face the difficulty that intrudes the minute we see how seriously Jefferson took his proposition that all men are created equal. What about blacks? Did he hold that they were equal to whites? And if so, how could he hold them in bondage? Just when we find that Jefferson thought men quite literally equal, we have to remember that he specified quite literal *inequalities* between blacks and whites.

FIFTEEN

"... all men ..."

> How have you weathered this rigorous season, my dear
> friend? Surely it was never so cold before. To me who
> am an animal of a warm climate, a mere Oran-ootan, it
> has been a severe trial.
>
> —Jefferson (*Papers*, 14:446)

There is no minimizing Jefferson's views on Negro limits. He catalogued what he saw as multiple inferiorities in the first and only
book he ever published (*Notes*, 138–43). The black's weak points
are listed with a ruthless scrutiny meant to impress the philosophes
of France. Blacks lack intelligence, beauty, most skills except music.
Perhaps the most damaging item within Jefferson's own scheme of
things is the claim that they are weak in Hutcheson's "inner sense"
of aesthetic delight at finer things. Jefferson approaches the whole
Negro phenomenon with the air of a Buffon studying some rare in-
sect, though his vocabulary comes closer to Dr. Johnson's:

> They secrete less by the kidneys, and more by the glands of the skin,
> which gives them a very strong and disagreeable odour. This greater de-
> gree of transpiration renders them more tolerant of heat, and less so of
> cold, than the whites. Perhaps too a difference of structure in the pulmo-
> nary apparatus, which a late ingenious experimentalist has discovered to
> be the principal regulator of animal heat, may have disabled them from
> extricating, in the act of inspiration, so much of that fluid from the outer
> air, or obliged them in expiration to part with more of it (139).

> Whether the black of the negro resides in the reticular membrane be-
> tween the skin and scarf skin, or in the scarf skin itself; whether it pro-
> ceeds from the colour of the blood, the colour of the bile, or from that of
> some other secretion, the difference is fixed in nature. . . . (138).

Nor did Jefferson think these differences were caused by education
or conditioning—i.e., by slavery itself—since white slaves under the

Romans did not exhibit the same disabilities. When Jefferson denies that their condition can explain blacks' limits, the modern student is apt to remark that Jefferson's own conditioning is at work here, making him inconsistent in theory because he was guilty in practice. The slaveowner speaks, not the scientist.

But David Hume neither preached nor practiced slavery, and his attempts at a scientific conclusion on this matter are similar to Jefferson's:

> I am apt to suspect the Negroes to be naturally inferior to the whites. There scarcely ever was a civilized nation of that complexion, nor even any individual eminent either in action or speculation. No ingenious manufactures among them, no arts, no sciences. On the other hand, the most rude and barbarous of the whites, such as the ancient Germans, the present Tartars, have still something eminent about them, in their valor, form of government, or some other particular. Such a uniform and constant difference could not happen, in so many countries and ages, if nature had not made an original distinction between these breeds of men. Not to mention our colonies, there are Negro slaves dispersed all over Europe, of whom none ever discovered any symptoms of ingenuity; though low people, without education, will start up amongst us, and distinguish themselves in every profession. In Jamaica, indeed, they talk of one Negro as a man of arts and learning; but it is likely he is admired for slender accomplishments, like a parrot who speaks a few words plainly ("Of National Characters," 1748).

A modern reader may find Jefferson's views most shocking when he claims that black men admit white superiority through "their own preference of them [white women], as uniform as is the preference of the oran-ootan for the black women over those of his own species" (138). Here is confusion of species indeed, with orangutans lusting after black women as black men lust after white women. The crazed sexuality that haunts so much of black-white relations in our history seems to derange with a leer Jefferson's pose of scientific observation. Even our best student of racial attitudes in American history, Winthrop Jordan, refers to this "gratuitous intrusion of the man-like ape," and says that Jefferson wrote this passage with a "geyser of libidinal energy" (*White Over Black*, 458–59).

But Jordan himself documents the fascination orangutans exercised over philosophes. (And see Robert Workler, *Studies on Vol-*

taire, vol. 155.) The tailless chimpanzee posed the most immediate challenge to the taxonomists' separation of animal species. The eighteenth century lived in a seizure of cataloguing impulses (to which Jefferson was especially susceptible), and the orangutan seemed hard to place in the known systems. The great systemizer of the time, the Comte de Buffon, was puzzled for a while by this effort to place the orangutan (Jordan, 230), and one of the things that puzzled him most was the credible report of mating between women and orangutans. (The intercourse was always between male chimp and female human—not only because males were presumed to have the fiercer sexual drive, but because women were less able to beat off an assailant by sheer strength.) These widespread tales were not more astonishing than many travelers' reports that gained acceptance during and after the age of exploration.

Evidence of cross-breeding had a more than prurient interest for an age experimenting with hybridization, after the example of Linnaeus. The possibility of fertility in the product of an ape-woman mating not only threatened the division of species; it led to speculation that some known creatures (the orangutan and the Hottentot were the favorite candidates) were themselves the product of such unions. Diderot tells the story of Cardinal Polignac addressing the famous orangutan (observed by Jefferson) in the Paris Zoo: "But speak and I baptize you" (*Rêve de d'Alembert,* Pléiade, 941). That passage in Diderot is interesting because it shows that the more daring philosophes were willing to challenge the Church's ban on "bestiality" (sex with animals): Diderot defends what has come to be called polymorphous sexuality (935–42) as the logical consequence of his view that sensation should "accord" one to all the vibrating fibers of the universe.

By telling the story of Cardinal Polignac, Diderot recalls debates on the advisability of baptizing the various kinds of "natives" found by explorers in distant places—Hottentots, pygmies, Negroes, Indians, etc. The question was not only, Are these men, but Are they descendants of Adam? Perhaps there were other races of men outside the Fall of Adam, and needing no redemption. God could have made several Edens; and even if these Edens, too, gave evidence of a fall, they were not in the economy of redemption by Christ if they had not fallen in the first Adam.

At the point where Hottentot seemed to dwindle into orangutan, where (if anywhere) could a distinction be drawn? A typical answer is that of Sir Richard Blackmore in The Lay Monastery (1714), cited by Arthur Lovejoy as an example of the Enlightenment's approach to the orangutan:

The ape, or the monkey that bears the greatest similitude to man, is the next order of animals below him. Nor is the disagreement between the basest individuals of our species and the ape or monkey so great but that, were the latter endowed with the faculty of speech ["But speak, and I baptize you"], they might perhaps as justly claim the rank and dignity of the human race as the savage Hottentot or stupid native of Nova Zembla. . . . The most perfect of this order of beings, the orang-outang as he is called by the natives of Angola—that is, the Wild Man, or Man of the Woods—has the honor of bearing the greatest resemblance to human nature. Though all that species have some agreement with us in our features, many instances being found of men with monkey faces, yet this has the greatest likeness, not only in his countenance, but in the structure of his body, his ability to walk upright, as well as on all fours, his organs of speech, his ready apprehension, and his gentle and tender passions, which are not found in any of the ape kind, and in various other respects (The Great Chain of Being, 234–35).

The similarities between animals—including the human animal—were topics of "philosophie" because the common basis of sensation had taken on new importance in the wake of Locke. For men like Helvétius, to whom "juger est sentir" (De l'esprit, 1, i), the animal basis of human action—and even human thought—had brought men very close to beasts in the chain of being. This was a line of research that fascinated Jefferson all his life and made him follow the theories of Pierre-Jean-Georges Cabanis and the research of Pierre Flourens with enthusiastic approval (Cappon, 562, 564, 605–6). Hume devoted a chapter of his Enquiry Concerning Human Understanding to "The Reason of Animals," concluding: "Though the instinct be different, yet still it is an instinct which teaches a man to avoid the fire, as much as that which teaches a bird, with such exactness, the art of incubation and the whole economy and order of its nursery."

Diderot went farther in approximating man to a bird:

First [in the egg] there is a wavering speck, a lengthening and darkening thread, fleshing itself out, beak, wing-tips, eyes, claws becoming visible. A yellowish substance arranges itself into intestines. It is animate. The animal moves, thrashes, peeps—I can hear it through the shell! It becomes furry; it looks about. The heaviness of its wavering head throws the beak repeatedly against the inner prison-wall—see it broken through! It emerges, walks, flies, is sensitive to irritants, skits off, comes near; it moans, suffers, loves, yearns, plays. It has all your affections. All you can do, it does (*Rêve de d'Alembert,* Pléiade, 881).

One reason Diderot admired Greuze so much was their shared "sentimentality," which was actually sensationalism in the post-Locke sense. Greuze fits out the "natural" family with dogs and cats and birds that guard and play with the children, teaching adults a proper responsiveness to instinct. Greuze not only paints propaganda for the encyclopedist cause of breast-feeding; he has dogs menace the nurse who tries to take off the child, and he includes dogs nursing their young in pictures of family affection. In his "Portrait of Comtesse Molline," one pup of the newborn litter even nuzzles the breast of the girl holding it. The continuity of the animal spectrum is repeatedly emphasized. If the mediaeval world had its symbolic "bestiaries," so did the Enlightenment—and both were constructed for moral instruction.

Jefferson's use of the orangutan in his extensive effort to "place" the Negro is not, therefore "gratuitous." We may think it unfortunate; but it was also inevitable. Not to note this well-known "fact" would have been considered remiss in a discussion of Negro faculties and their closest analogues. That is why an ardent opponent of slavery like Dr. Rush felt obliged, even while defending the equality of black and white human beings, to admit that black women had been raped by orangutans (*American Philosophical Society Transactions,* 4:291). Dr. Charles White, a physician who had seen the results of vegetable cross-breeding, remained skeptical that the orangutan matings with women (which he assumed had occurred) could produce offspring (*An Account of the Regular Gradation of Man,* 1799, 11–12). Jordan lists (236–37) others who took the union of women with orangutans as an adequately reported fact and then discussed the scientific consequences of this phenomenon. The boldness of investigation that men celebrate in the Enlightenment, the openness to all new things, led to the kind of conjecture Jordan calls "gratuitous" in Jefferson. It should be remembered that Jefferson was addressing the French philosophes in his book. Though written in answer to a request by Barbé-Marbois, it was aimed especially at Buffon, to challenge his theories about America's climate and wild life. When Jefferson talked of matings with orangutans, he was addressing a man who had already admitted that "fact" into his great *Histoire Naturelle*.

Enlightenment schemes of education turned to animal example for the discovery of nature's method in training the young. Thomas Reid urged this (*Enquiry*, 249-50) as a corollary of his teaching that doctors should imitate nature's healing process. Perhaps the most thorough discussion of this commonplace among Scottish philosophes was written by William Small's teacher, Dr. John Gregory. His *Comparative View of the State and Faculties of Man with Those of the Animal World*, published in 1765 in two volumes, provided a remarkably "permissive" guide to child-rearing; it was the Dr. Spock handbook of its day. Parents were urged not to force knowledge on children too early or by punishment (1:98 ff.). Sociability should be strengthened by loving care; the mother should fondle and breast-feed her child, preferably for a year: "When a mother does not nurse her own infant, she does open violence to nature" (1:44). It was vital to Gregory's thesis that men should resemble other animals in his faculties and upbringing. As he put it: "One species often runs into another so imperceptibly that it is difficult to say where the one begins and the other ends. This is particularly the case with the lowest of one species and the highest of that immediately below it" (1:11).

Still, there *is* a basis for the distinction between other animals and man; and Gregory proves he is a good member of the Scottish school when he tells us what that is: "Above all, they [men] are distinguished [from other animals] by the moral sense, and the happiness flowing from religion and from the various intercourses of social life" (1:16). The piety and sociability that end that list are simply different aspects of the moral sense. Man is distinguished from the beasts by his highest faculty—which, for the Scottish moral-sense philosopher, is not reason but benevolence, not the head but the heart.

This is, of course, Jefferson's position on the blacks:

Whether further observation will or will not verify the conjecture that nature has been less bountiful to them in the endowments of the head, I believe that in those of the heart she will be found to have done them justice. That disposition to theft with which they have been branded, must be ascribed to their situation, and not to any depravity of the moral sense . . . we find among them numerous instances of the most rigid integrity, and as many as among their better instructed masters, of benevolence, gratitude, and unshaken fidelity (*Notes*, 142–43)*ι*

It is easy for a modern reader to think Jefferson has thrown an unimportant sop to the blacks with his praise for the "heart." After all, our culture takes reason and intellect to be the highest of man's faculties. Jefferson's Scottish mentors did not. To appreciate the real force of this passage, we must look at the technical meaning it had for Jefferson. This can be seen in three of its themes, put unmistakably in this brief statement of moral-sense doctrine.

First, the distinction of heart from head. This was a common enough distinction; but the reason it became so common in the eighteenth century was the weight several philosophical camps gave to it. And no camp took the matter more seriously than the Scottish moral-sense philosophers. For them, the heart was often another word for moral sense (as was benevolence, humanity, or sociability). In discussing the concept of natural rights, Hutcheson wrote: "The sense of everyone's heart, and the common natural principles, show that each one has these perfect rights; nor without maintaining them can there be any social life" (4:143—cf. 2:315). Adam Smith, making the normal Humean distinction between moral sense as the faculty that chooses *ends* and intellect as the one that chooses *means*, says that the highest human ideal is to unite these powers, benevolence with prudence: "It is the best head joined to the best heart. It is the most perfect wisdom combined with the most perfect virtue. It constitutes very nearly the character of the Academical or Peripatetic sage" (*Moral Sentiments*, 6, i). Perfection of the head is necessary to make the sage; but the faculty of the heart is the same in all men and makes them men.

Hume said that the head discerns fact and the heart discerns right, so that all *moral* blame must be directed at the heart: "The approbation or blame which then ensues cannot be the work of the judgment but of the heart; and it is not a speculative proposition or affirmation, but an active feeling or sentiment" (*Enquiry, Morals*, App. 1). Later, when discussing terms for separating "intellectual and moral endowments," he says: "The distinction between the heart and the head may also be adopted" (ibid., App. 4—cf. *Treatise*, 586, 603). We shall find, in a later chapter, that Jefferson's famous "head and heart" letter to Maria Cosway has been misread by eminent Jeffersonians because they failed to see how necessary, in the Scottish scheme, is the heart's superiority to the head, as the ground of right and dignity. The moral sense is not only man's *highest* faculty, but the one that is *equal* in all men.

A second proof that Jefferson is speaking in the strict terminology of Hutcheson comes from the list of virtues he recognizes in the Negro: "integrity . . . benevolence, gratitude, and unshaken fidelity" (*Notes*, 143). Hutcheson treated benevolence as the moral sense par excellence. It best illustrated the nonselfish aspect of that faculty. But benevolence can take other forms less obviously disinterested. These manifestations of the moral sense were less useful to the philosopher in establishing the nature of virtue. Gratitude, for instance, could be mistaken as a form of long-range selfishness, a *quid pro quo* for favors received. In the same way, honor could be taken for pride, or fidelity for caution. Only after he had established the mechanics of the moral sense as *benevolent* could he show that benevolence takes these other forms as well (1:197).

Gratitude was second in importance only to benevolence pure and simple. It figured largely in his original analysis, the 1725 *Inquiry* (1:50, 197–99), and it remained second in rank of all the moral virtues for him. Other theorists of the moral sense gave it similar rank (Smith, *Moral Sentiments*, 2, ii, 1; 3, iii, 6; Hume, *Treatise*, 603; *Enquiry, Morals*, 5, ii, App. 2). Even those Scottish thinkers who differed from Hutcheson on the exact meaning and rank of benevolence treated gratitude as one of the principal moral phenomena to be explained by moral science (Kames, *Principles*, 90; Reid, *Essays*, 1:149).

At first Hutcheson ranked honor third after benevolence and gratitude (1:200–3). It was the public virtue confirming sociability. But "fidelity" assumes that role in his later work, since faithfulness to contracts underlies all social transactions. "Fidelity" had the large sense of truth to commitments for Hutcheson—to marriage vows, friendship pledges, and national allegiance (4:177–79, 6:34–52). Hume understood it the same way (*Treatise*, 603, *Enquiry, Morals*, 6, i), as did Kames (*Principles*, 89). Jefferson's regard for it appears in the Declaration's protestation of "a faith yet unsullied."

Thus when Jefferson says that blacks are equal to whites in "benevolence, gratitude, and unshaken fidelity," he is listing the cardinal virtues of moral-sense theory, the central manifestations of man's highest faculty. What does he mean, however, by a fourth heading of his own, "the most rigid integrity"? Integrity was usually contrasted, in his day, with the kinds of political corruption Americans attributed to the British in their pamphlets on the Revolution. That does not seem appropriate when describing slaves. Once again, the explanation is to be found in the theorists of moral sense. Hutcheson used integrity as a synonym for his political virtue of fidelity: "By violating our faith we may quite defeat the desires of such as trusted to our integrity" (4:178). It belongs to that cluster of virtues variously described as "veracity, sincerity, fidelity," and contrasted with "falsehood, dissimulation, and deceit" (4:177). Hume, in the same way, spoke of "honesty, fidelity, truth" (*Enquiry, Morals*, 6, i). Thus Jefferson is recognizing in slaves, so often accused of compulsive lying, a basis for trust that lies behind all social compacts based on the moral sense.

The one criticism Jefferson deals with, raised against the assumption of equal moral sense in black slaves, is our third and in some ways most striking proof that he was talking about a literal equality of men. Jefferson refers to the slaves' well-known thieving ways. He was not exaggerating. It is actually a tribute to their skills that the slaves were successful in carrying out what Gerald Mullin describes as the masked rebellion of underground trade. The slaves at times controlled the chicken market so entirely that plantation owners had to buy their own chickens from their slaves. George Washington lamented that the slaves got two glasses of wine for every one served in the house; and he ordered all dogs shot at Mount Vernon because they served as sentinels for night raids on plantation stores (Mullin, *Flight and Rebellion*, 60–62). Plantation owners were understandably angered at these successes; but Jefferson will not let such acts stand as accusations of inequality. His answer not only acquits blacks of inferiority in this sense; it declares that blacks are not *bound* to any social arrangement, since they have been denied reciprocity:

That disposition to theft with which they have been branded must be ascribed to their situation, and not to any depravity of the moral sense. The man, in whose favour no laws of property exist, probably feels himself less bound to respect those made in favour of others. When arguing for ourselves, we lay it down as a fundamental, that laws, to be just, must give a reciprocation of right [cf. Jefferson's denial that one can form a pact with oneself]: that, without this, they are mere arbitrary rules of conduct, founded in force, and not in conscience: and it is a problem which I give to the master to solve, whether the religious precepts against the violation of property were not framed for him as well as his slave? And whether the slave may not as justifiably take a little from one, who has taken all from him, as he may slay one who would slay him. . . . Notwithstanding these considerations which must weaken their respect for the laws of property, we find among them numerous instances of the most rigid integrity . . . (*Notes*, 142–43—cf. *Papers*, 14:492).

Without the duty to live by fidelity to compact, blacks still manifest that virtue. This is very strong language for a Virginia plantation owner. In denying any duty to the social bond, he has asserted the right of rebellion. However timorous his own actions, he cannot justly be accused—as he so often is—of denying the same rights of revolution to blacks that he had proclaimed for whites.

Winthrop Jordan calls Jefferson inconsistent for using an environmental defense of blacks' thefts while denying that palliative to the blacks' intellectual gifts. But Jefferson's system did not commit him to equality of "mind and body" (as he put it to Chastellux, *Papers*, 8:186). He thought some men physically inferior (e.g., pygmies) and some superior (e.g., Indians). Like the majority of philosophes he thought some men superior mentally—the Bacons and Lockes and Newtons—and some stunted, by original deprivation or evil circumstances (as whole cultures had been blighted by superstition and "priestcraft"). But these are minor differences by comparison with the faculty that gives man his unique dignity, that grounds his rights, that makes him self-governing. Equality of moral sense was not otherworldly, like equality of the soul in Christian thought. It was, Jefferson thought, a scientifically observable fact of our present life. Not even slavery and the evil nurture that promoted theft could hide the basic integrity and equality of blacks themselves.

When Jordan says that Jefferson taught later generations that "the Negro was to be judged on a thoroughly distinct matter—his intellectual capacity" (455), he fails to take with full seriousness just what Jefferson meant by the moral sense. Jordan, accusing

Jefferson of emotional disturbance in his scientific inquiry, is carried away by emotion himself when he makes an accusation like this:

Here at last, proclaimed in language at once passionate and clinical, was the Negro's true rank in nature's scale—exactly midway between ("as uniformly as") the white man and the most man-like ape. This connection with the ape was forged by Jefferson [sic] in his passage on the superior beauty of white women (490).

Most naturalists of Jefferson's day believed that orangutans had raped black women; but most of them also believed in the equality of men. They were not carried away by emotion at the report, as Jordan allows himself to be. Jefferson was not original in his belief in the one or the other. But he did depart from some of those naturalists in a programmatic insistence on the equality of the moral sense, which was a liberating doctrine. Hutcheson, in his introduction to morals, built his concept of political freedom and equality entirely on the basis of *equal* moral faculty in all men:

In this respect all men are originally equal, that these natural rights equally belong to all, at least as soon as they come to the mature use of reason; and they are equally confirmed to all by the law of nature. . . . Nature makes none masters, none slaves (4:143–44).

Jefferson believed in a literal equality more far-reaching than most educated people recognize today. For him, accidental differences of body or mind were dwarfed by an all-important equality in the governing faculty of man. There is no inconsistency in his theory, whatever one may think of its validity. For him it was valid, and everything he wrote about blacks in his extended analysis for the *Notes* is derived from its principles. Admittedly, to call Jefferson consistent in theory may make him seem even more cruelly inconsistent in practice: How could he remain a slaveholder after adopting such an egalitarian philosophy as Hutcheson's? The answer to that question, insofar as it has an answer, must wait for a later chapter (Twenty-two). It is enough for now to see that his political beliefs grew directly from the philosophy of moral sense, which had egalitarianism as an essential ingredient; and that his statements on black disabilities are not inconsistent with that egalitarian philosophy.

SIXTEEN

"... *inalienable rights* ..."

> All human power or authority must consist in a right
> transferred to any person or council to dispose of the
> alienable rights of others . . . Consequently, there can
> be no government so absolute as to have even an exter-
> nal right to do or command everything. For whenever
> any invasion is made upon unalienable rights, there
> must arise either a perfect or external right to resist-
> ance. . . . Unalienable rights are essential limitations
> in all governments.
>
> —Francis Hutcheson (1:302–3)

Those who think Jefferson's Declaration is Lockean have been
justifiably puzzled by the omission of property from the brief list of
"inalienable rights" in that document. Property in the broad sense—
one's *proprium* or realm—was the basis for all other rights in Locke.
The canonical list of rights had become, by Jefferson's time, "life,
liberty, and property"—the rights claimed by the Continental
Congress when it first assembled in 1774 (*Respect*, 53—cf. 12, 63).
This is often called a "Lockean" triad, though Locke usually distinguished property in his broad sense (which would include life and
liberty) from exchangeable real goods by calling the latter "estate"
or "fortune." Thus in chapter Eleven of the *Second Treatise* (the
only one Jefferson ever referred to, and that misleadingly), Locke
says men form the social contract "to preserve their lives, liberties,
and fortunes" (par. 137). He speaks of "life, liberty, and estate" at
paragraphs 17 and 123. In other listings, the third component is
"goods" (par. 6) or "possessions" (par. 57).

But Jefferson does not include property under any of these titles
within his brief list of "inalienable rights." If he meant to signal dependence on Locke in his Declaration, he chose an odd way of

doing it when he omitted the central concept of Locke in its most expected place. This puzzles the Lockean interpreters. Howard Mumford Jones wrote: "As for the unalienable right to pursue happiness, no one, so far as I know, has ever understood why Jefferson substituted the phrase for John Locke's comprehensible trilogy [sic], life, liberty, and property, except that Jefferson may have had in the back of his mind an imperfect recollection of a passage which George Mason wrote into the Virginia Declaration of Rights of June 1776 . . ." (*Declaration of Independence*, American Antiquarian Society, 1976).

But the omission in the Declaration was not an isolated act. Jefferson suggested that Lafayette remove "*propriété*" from his draft Declaration of Human Rights for France. Jefferson bracketed two phrases in that 1788 text: "Every man is born with inalienable rights; such are [the right of property,] the care of [his honor and] his life, the entire disposal of his person and industry, as well as his faculties, the pursuit of his own good, and resistance against oppression" (*Papers*, 15:230—see Chinard, *Letters of Lafayette and Jefferson*, 138, with photostat, for the end of the first bracket).

What are we to make of these two omissions? Were they deliberate, meant to be *taken* as deliberate? Few people, if any, have been bold enough to entertain the suspicion that Jefferson could be not only non-Lockean but anti-Lockean in his Declaration. Scholars argue that these omissions were either casual or inexplicable—meaningless in either case. They can cite evidence of Jefferson's respect for property from the very documents in question. In the Declaration of Independence, Jefferson concludes, for Congress, with a pledge of "our lives, our *fortunes*, and our sacred honor." And in Lafayette's draft, while striking *propriété*, Jefferson allowed *la disposition entière . . . de son industrie* to stand. Furthermore, if we go outside the two documents, we find other texts asserting the right of property: In the Declaration of the Causes and Necessity for Taking Up Arms, written the year before the Declaration, Jefferson said Americans came to this continent for "the acquisition & free possession of property" (*Papers*, 1:193).

Yet quotations of this sort are a bit beside the point. No one can doubt that Jefferson—like all whigs of his time (and all tories too)—recognized a right to private property. The problem is more circumscribed: Did he recognize it as *the* fundamental right, in

Locke's sense; and if so, why did he exclude it from the list of basic rights given in the Declaration? Put more precisely: Did he recognize it as an unalienable right?

For the answer to this question, we should turn to the principal delineator of unalienable rights in Jefferson's intellectual milieu—to Francis Hutcheson. We shall find that calling property "unalienable" was confusing in the Hutchesonian scheme of things, a scheme whose broad outlines were followed by David Hume, Adam Smith, and Jean-Jacques Burlamaqui. Hutcheson held that property, depending on agreement (compact) for its definition (its delimitation, or division), *follows* on society rather than precedes it. Thus he places it among the "adventitious" rights, not the "natural" ones (4:147, 5:309):

> Our rights are either alienable or unalienable. The former are known by these two characters jointly, that the translation of them to others can be made effectually, and that some interest of society, or [of] individuals consistently with it, may frequently require such translations. Thus our right to our goods and labors is naturally alienable (5:261).

Of course, Hutcheson recognized man's right to the fruits of his labors (1:257, 262–63). But he put this in terms of a paradoxically unalienable right to alienate one's property (1:264–65). The explanation of this paradox lies in Hutcheson's starting point. For him, the right of *exchange* is the basic one, not the right of retention. He sees the clearest need for title to goods arising out of men's social interdependence, on the necessary division of labor and exchange of its product:

> The common interest of all constantly requires an intercourse of offices and the joint labors of many. . . . When mankind grows numerous, all necessaries and conveniences will be much better supplied to all when each one chooses an art to himself, by practice acquires dexterity in it, and thus provides himself great plenty of such goods as that art produces, to be exchanged in commerce for the goods produced in like manner by other artisans, than if each one by turns practised every necessary art, without ever acquiring dexterity in them . . . There must therefore be a continual course of contracts among men, both for the transferring of property or real rights and the constituting claims to certain services, and to certain quantities or values, to be paid in consideration of these services—which are personal rights (4:163–64—cf. 5:288–89).

Hume, too, grounds the right of property in man's need for social intercourse, symbolized in the division of labor:

'Tis by society alone he is able to supply his defects, and raise himself up to an equality with his fellow creatures, and even acquire a superiority above them. By society all his infirmities are compensated; and though in that situation his wants multiply every moment upon him, yet his abilities are still more augmented, and leave him in every respect more satisfied and happy than 'tis possible for him, in his savage and solitary condition, ever to become. . . . By the partition of employments our ability increases, and by mutual succor we are less exposed to fortune and accidents (*Treatise*, 485–cf. *Enquiry, Morals*, App. 3, and Burlamaqui, *Naturel*, 1, iv, 3–9).

Adam Smith has been misinterpreted by those who base his economics on market *competition*. He began with the need for a division of labor—i.e., for *co-operation*, for prior agreement to do complementary things and share gain from the resulting product. He argued that man has a "propensity to truck, barter, and exchange one thing for another," which is "the necessary consequence of the faculty of reason and speech" (*Wealth*, 1, ii). The first published use of Smith's "invisible hand" concept occurred in his *Theory of Moral Sentiments* (4, i), where he talked of providential *harmonies* within society. Smith praises competition between merchants as a form of *co-operation* with producers and buyers: It keeps a small faction from thwarting the designs of the community at large (*Wealth*, 3, v). Smith was conscripted to individualist uses by nineteenth-century liberalism; but he began as a good communitarian of the Scots school.

Hutcheson had set the tone for Scottish economic thinking, as for so much else:

The labors of each man cannot furnish him with all necessities, though it may furnish him with a needless plenty of one sort—hence the right of commerce and alienating our goods; and also the rights from contracts and promises, either to the goods acquired by others or to their labors (1:265).

Without thus insuring to each one the fruits of his own labors, with full power to dispose of what is beyond his own consumption to such as are dearest to him, there can be no agreeable life, no universal diligence and industry. But by such insurance labors become pleasant and honorable, friendships are cultivated, and an intercourse of kind offices among the good (4:150–51).

Hutcheson, like Locke, attacks Filmer (e.g., at 4:285). But Hutcheson attacks the idea that God has dominion over the world as his property (1:273, 3:214, 4:209), where Locke *used* the idea of God's property to assert each man's derived property in himself (*Second Treatise,* par. 6). This is one of many points of conflict between the two men. Locke took the use of currency to be a form of tacit consent to the social contract, an acceptance of artificial limits upon one's "original" autonomy. Hutcheson, by contrast, took money as a positive exercise of the most basic human instinct, expressing sociability (4:209–13, 6:53–63).

There is in Hutcheson's discussion a continual stress on "frequent translations of property" (6:1), as well as on wide distribution of the goods produced by society's division of labor (6:247–48). A good example of his approach to property is the denial of an absolute right to one's inventions if they would contribute to more basic rights of increased production and intercourse of services:

A like right we may justly assert to mankind as a system, and to every society of men, even before civil government, to compel any person who has fallen upon any fortunate invention, of great necessity or use for the preservation of life or for a great increase of human happiness, to divulge it upon reasonable terms (6:109). As a man cannot hoard useful ideas, he cannot destroy his own property if it is still useful to the community (4:246–47).

Jefferson's attitude toward property was always closer to Hutcheson's than to Locke's. He placed exaggerated emphasis on his effort to free Virginia of laws that made inherited property unalienable. His pride on this point came rather from the principle involved than from any practical innovations he inspired (Malone, 1:251–57). Jefferson, like Hutcheson, looked to a constant transferral of property as the healthy "circulation" of society. (That is one reason he contrived his scheme for limiting contracts to nineteen years.) He felt freedom was impossible in Europe, so long as the land was frozen in feudal molds of entail. This explains his extraordinary hostility to Norman law as having canceled the "allodial" method of holding land under the Anglo-Saxons. Jefferson sponsored the easy availability of land, wanting grants of it for settlers, free white males, and deported ex-slaves. Nothing could be more Jeffersonian than this passage from Hutcheson's best-studied work: "Lands must be dispersed among great multitudes, and preserved (thus dispersed) by agrarian laws, to make a stable democracy" (4:295).

The only time Jefferson upheld the *un*alienability of land was in the name of the "sovereign" during the dispute over Georgia's extent. This was a corollary of his wish to keep land available for individual tenure. He wanted a territory of great extent for the American experiment with liberty—land without entailment to foreign laws or tradition, where fluidity of contract would make all men partakers of the public good. As early as 1790 he was urging President Washington to take American land from French and Spanish tenure (*Papers*, 17:86, 111–16, 121–23, 127–29). In 1792 he took the same position in the Georgia matter and on navigation rights for the whole Mississippi. Despite charges of inconsistency, there was a long-standing concern that justified Jefferson's quick action on the Louisiana Purchase, thirteen years after his first counsel to President Washington on the need for American possession of the continent.

The harmony between Jefferson's and Hutcheson's views on property is illustrated by their attitude toward rights over inventions. Jefferson opposed long-standing patents, and suggested to Madison that his contract limit of nineteen years might get its first trial in patent and copyright law (*Papers*, 15:397). In his letter on the subject to Isaac McPherson (1813), Jefferson even claimed "it is a moot question whether the origin of any kind of property is derived from nature at all" (LB, 13:333). He meant "nature" as Hutcheson did, before any "adventitious" arrangements; for he goes on to say: "Stable ownership is the gift of social laws" (ibid.). Since property's real end is the interchange of goods and services, a patent law meant to inhibit that interchange strikes at the very basis of ownership.

If nature has made any one thing less susceptible than all others of exclusive property, it is the action of the thinking power called an idea, which an individual may exclusively possess as long as he keeps it to himself; but the moment it is divulged, it forces itself into the possession of every one, and the receiver cannot dispossess himself of it. Its peculiar character, too, is that no one possesses the less, because every other possesses the whole of it. He who receives an idea from me, receives instruction himself without lessening mine: as he who lights his taper at mine, receives light without darkening me. That ideas should freely spread from one to another over the globe, for the moral and mutual instruction of man, and improvement of his condition, seems to have been peculiarly and benevolently [the Hutchesonian touchstone] designed by nature, when she made them, like fire, expansible over all space, without lessening their density in any point, and like the air in which we breathe, move, and have our physical being, incapable of confinement or exclusive appropriation. Inventions then cannot, in nature, be a subject of property.

Society may give an exclusive right to the profits arising from them, as an encouragement to men to pursue ideas which may produce utility, but this may or may not be done, according to the will and convenience of the society, without claim or complaint from anybody (ibid., 333-34).

This passage recalls not only Hutcheson's direct treatment of patents (6:109), but his discussion of the duty to be truthful in speech (4:195-202, 6:28-43). There should be frequent and honest exchange of *ideas* for the general good. Indeed, Hutcheson puts this chapter early in his section on contracts, since they all involve an honest use of language. Speech is itself a social compact: "This use of signs, too, imports a tacit convention to impart our sentiments to the person we address them to" (6:31).

Disagreement with Locke on the basis of natural rights, including the right of property, was bound to involve disagreement on the nature of the social bond itself. Hutcheson denied that society can be based on the interest of the individual considered as "a separate system from his fellows" (2:67). He relied on the standard Scottish argument, that God bungleth not, to counter the Lockean presuppositions: "The Author of our nature is traduced—as if he had given us the strongest dispositions toward what he had in his laws prohibited, and directed us by the frame of our nature to the meanest and most contemptible pursuits; as if what all good men have represented as the excellence of our nature were a force or constraint put upon it by art or authority" (2:68).

Hutcheson treated contracts—including the social contract—in the work that summed up his whole lecture system in brief compass, his 1747 *Short Introduction to Moral Philosophy* (sometimes called *Morals*), whose subtitle was *The Elements of Ethics and the Law of Nature.* For Hutcheson "faith in commerce" arises directly from the moral sense (4:178). Men are already associated in families, and in the exchange of goods and ideas, before it becomes necessary for them to form civil government. We *begin* in society, which *is* our state of nature: "It is also a foolish abuse of words to call a state of absolute solitude a natural state to mankind, since in this condition neither could any of mankind come into being, or continue in it a few days without a miraculous interposition" (5:283–cf. 5:287–88; Burlamaqui, *Naturel*, 1, iv, 2; and Ferguson, *Civil Society*, 6: "Mankind are to be taken in groups, as they have always subsisted").

Hutcheson admits that civil power is needed to prevent "mischief" by providing men with a binding common arbiter for their disputes. But "there is something in our nature which more immediately recommends civil power to us"–a regard for "eminent virtues and our natural high approbation of them" (4:280). He sees civil government as another form of the division of labor, putting those "manifestly superior in wisdom" in charge of special civil functions, as we parcel out economic chores to men of various skills:

It is therefore very probable that some of the wiser and more sagacious, observing these inconveniences of a state of anarchy, fell upon this as the only remedy, that a large number of men should covenant with each other about entering into a firm society, to be regulated by the counsel of the wise few, in all matters relating to the safety and advantage either of individuals or the whole body. And discerning the many conveniences to ensue upon such a project, have explained it to others, and persuaded them to put it in execution (4:281–82).

It was precisely the most egalitarian of eighteenth-century reformers who hoped to replace hereditary authority with an "aristocracy" of talent and virtue chosen by the people at large–whence James Madison's trust (expressed in *Federalist*, 10) that the new American federation would choose men of "virtuous sentiments" to lead them.

Locke's system of government began with the individual's autonomy. Hutcheson's begins with social drives and interdependence. Hume, too, made government follow on society, as reason must subserve the moral passions. Government is the sphere of reason, which settles the norms of utility in the name of justice. But the test of utility is the end toward which one ordinates various means, and that is already given by man's frame and social constitution (*Enquiry, Morals,* 5, ii). It is the task of civil authority to help men (by force if necessary) adhere to their real (though remote) interest despite more vivid and distracting promises of immediate advantage (*Treatise,* 535–37; *Inquiry, Morals,* 4). Hume, too, says government works by a division of labor, distinguishing men "with superior personal qualities" and encouraging these traits with rewards of civil rank ("On the Origin of Government"). This political system is expressly contrasted with Locke's ("Of the First Principles of Government").

Jefferson's views on property, rights, and the social nature of man fit perfectly the Hutchesonian background; and this explains his refusal to put property among the "inalienable rights" of his Declaration. For him, property is the transferable commerce of those who have pledged moral "fidelity" to each other and have an equal stake in the public good. To commit one's fortunes and sacred honor to the common effort of society is a duty arising from Hutcheson's belief in property as a form of "language" meant to promote human intercourse and solidarity. The preservation of Lafayette's "entire disposal of . . . [man's] industry" also fits the Hutchesonian preference for "fruits of one's labors" over the term property (as inert and separate from the divided labors of concurring citizens). It was over "the fruits of his labors" that Hutcheson claimed man's "full power to dispose [Lafayette's *"disposition entière"*] of what is beyond his own consumption" (4:150). Indeed, Lafayette's use of *"industrie"* fits a constant theme in Hutcheson, that the creation of more property for trade encourages human industry and mutual prosperity: "Men are obliged to observe such a tenor of action as shall most effectually promote industry" (1:203–cf. 6, 109–10).

Jefferson's view of natural rights was in accord with Scottish thinking, and one change he made in his text helped make that clearer. He first wrote "We hold these truths to be sacred and undeniable" (*Papers,* 1:423). The "sacred" was admissible—he kept it in the conclusion, when he spoke of "sacred honor" as involved in the defense of such truths. Hutcheson called natural rights "sacred" (4:304, 315, 318). But "undeniable" was unfortunate—the perverse can deny anything, as Reid emphasized by saying that even "self-evident" truths demand good faith (candor) in the hearer and distinct exposition in the speaker. Jefferson repaired the phrase, weak by Reid's norms, with Reid's own phrase—"self-evident."[*] But the moral propositions he then listed were not the jejune maxims of Reid. They were the large ends of society posited by Hutcheson, Hume, and others as objects of the moral sense's direct gratification.

It is interesting, as well, that Jefferson's draft came out of committee still reading "inherent and inalienable rights." Reid distrusted Hutcheson's moral faculty because it was an *inherent* determination, which he thought resembled the discredited "innate ideas." Perhaps that is why Congress removed the word; but Jefferson wrote it, and let it stand, in his draft for the *Autobiography*.

Hutcheson's view of human rights, as based on the inherent determination of the moral sense, was even more conducive to egalitarianism than Locke's. The Scots, like whigs of all kinds, believed in the right of revolution over unredressed grievances. But they laid special emphasis on the happiness of the people as the basis of any regime's legitimacy—a point that would be stressed by James Wilson, in a passage very important to Jefferson (see chapter Eighteen). While speaking from shared whig premises, Jefferson was especially attuned to the Hutcheson who wrote:

> But as the end of all civil power is acknowledged by all to be the *safety and happiness* of the whole body, any power not naturally conducive to this end is unjust; which the people, who rashly granted it under an error, may justly abolish again when they find it necessary to their safety to do so (4:302—italics added).

Compare Jefferson's Declaration:

> Whenever any form of government becomes destructive of these ends, it is the right of the people to alter or to abolish it, and to institute new government, laying it's foundation on such principles, & organising it's powers in such form, as to them shall seem most likely to effect their *safety and happiness* (italics added).

One can continue the Hutcheson passage:

> Nor is it justifiable in a people to have recourse for any lighter causes to violence and civil wars against their rulers, while the public interests

[*] The change to "self-evident" has, in the past, been attributed to Franklin (Becker, 142). But there is no external evidence for this, and the handwriting argument is inconclusive at best (*Papers*, 1:427–28). "Self-evident" is in the text, "as originally reported," which Jefferson reprints in his *Autobiography* for pointed contrast with the congressional document.

are tolerably secured and consulted. But when it is evident that the public liberty and safety is not tolerably secured, and that more mischiefs, and these of a more lasting kind, are like to arise from the continuance of any plan of civil power than are to be feared from the violent efforts for an alteration of it, then it becomes lawful, nay honorable, to make such efforts and change the plan of government (4:303).

And Jefferson:

Prudence indeed will dictate that governments long established should not be changed for light & transient causes; and accordingly all experience hath shown that mankind are more disposed to suffer while evils are sufferable than to right themselves by abolishing the forms to which they are accustomed.

More Hutcheson:

A good subject ought to bear patiently many injuries done only to himself, rather than take arms against a prince in the main good and useful to the state, provided the danger extends only to himself. But when the common rights of the community are trampled upon, and what at first is attempted against one is made to be made a precedent against all the rest, then as the governor is plainly perfidious [abandoning the key contract-virtue of fidelity] to his trust, he has forfeited all the power committed to him (ibid.).

With Jefferson:

But when a long train of abuses & usurpations, begun at a distinguished period and pursuing invariably the same object, evinces a design to reduce them under absolute despotism it is their right, it is their duty to throw off such government. . . .

Language and doctrine accord with each other in Jefferson; and both mesh with Hutcheson's teaching and phrasing. I do not argue for direct borrowing, since the Hutchesonian language was shared so widely by Scottish thinkers. I do conclude that Jefferson drew his ideas and words from these men, who stood at a conscious and deliberate distance from Locke's political principles.

SEVENTEEN

"... *pursuit* ..."

> All men are by nature equally free and independent, and have certain inherent rights, of which, when they enter into a state of society, they cannot, by any compact, deprive their posterity; namely, the enjoyment of life and liberty, with the means of acquiring and possessing property, and pursuing and obtaining happiness and safety.
>
> —Virginia Declaration of Rights, 1774

Two "sources" have been adduced, with some regularity, for Jefferson's phrase "the pursuit of happiness." The first, written by George Mason, is prefixed to this chapter. The second, by James Wilson, is prefixed to the next chapter. Although this kind of borrowing, if it exists at all, can hardly be called plagiarism, Gilbert Chinard did write of Jefferson: "The only fault that could be found is that he did not more clearly acknowledge his indebtedness to George Mason" (*Thomas Jefferson, The Apostle of Americanism*, 73).

That comment spurred Herbert Lawrence Ganter to write two long articles in the *William and Mary Quarterly* for 1936 to vindicate Jefferson's "integrity." He proves that the phrase "pursuit of happiness" had been widely used in England ever since 1690. If anyone suggests that "pursuit of happiness" was substituted for "property" as an implicit criticism of Locke, Ganter can produce instances of Locke himself writing "pursuit of happiness." If anyone should suppose that the term meant something new or revolutionary, Ganter can find it in the arch-tory himself, Dr. Johnson. He concludes that the phrase was widely and rather vaguely used, and that Jefferson was correct when he called his Declaration a mere voicing of the age's common sense.

Ganter quotes fourteen authors, stretching back eighty-six years before the Declaration was composed. Not all of these, however, use the exact phrase "pursuit of happiness." Pope, for instance, talks simply of happiness as man's end—and inclusion on those grounds alone would swell the sample past all usefulness. Besides, Ganter misses some obvious places in his search (e.g., Ferguson, *Civil Society*, 95). He gives us four passages where Johnson used the phrase; but neglects to look in the Dictionary under "pursuit," where we find a chiastic line of Matthew Prior quoted: "We happiness pursue; we fly from pain."

Besides, of those who actually use the term, few use it vaguely. Ganter overlooked some of the clues that he himself turned up. Locke, first of all, never used the phrase in his political *Treatises*. All the uses cited by Ganter come from one volume, the *Essay on Understanding*, the "live" work of the eighteenth century. Furthermore, they all come from one chapter of that work, and are clustered in a mere ten or so of that chapter's seventy-five paragraphs. And here the formula "pursuit of happiness" is part of a larger thought-cluster that contains the note of constancy. The first use is in paragraph 44: "Happiness, under this view, everyone constantly pursues." Men are "constant in pursuit of happiness." In paragraph 51 we hear of "a constant determination to a pursuit of happiness," and in 52 of "constant pursuit of true and solid happiness." Later in the same paragraph, constant is glossed as unalterable: "an unalterable pursuit of happiness." The elements of determination and necessity are part of this thought-complex: "necessity determines to the pursuit of bliss," showing "the inclination and tendency of their nature to happiness" (53).

Obviously Locke means something very specific by his concentration on these terms, all linked, in this part of his book. What is that meaning? Chapter Twenty-one of the *Essay*'s Second Book is a long and important text. Its title, "Of Power," barely suggests the wide range of things treated. Locke moves from our idea of power to a discussion of causality, necessity, and freedom. He propounds here his view that the will is not free. The will is determined by its object. Given present pleasure, it must move toward it; given pain, it must move away. The senses are infallible judges of immediate pleasure and pain (60), and the will *must* move on perception of the one or the other.

Freedom arises only when some more remote pleasure or pain is

brought partially into view—so that, for instance, immediate pain is
seen as the means to some greater (but more remote) pleasure.
Man can suspend, in some cases, the prosecution of a desire (48)
while he reckons the long-range calculus of pleasures over pains
(51). He can do this because desire is an uneasiness for
unpossessed good—already under that good's attraction, yet not
fully "targeted" on it. Locke uses several images of Newtonian motion in this chapter—billiard balls, the tennis ball hit by a racket.
But the sunken image in his discussion of desire is that of "cosmic
attraction"—and this image emerges in exactly that part of the
chapter devoted to constant-pursuit-of-happiness. Speaking of
minor but immediate gratifications, Locke says: "We shall find that
a very little part of our life is so vacant from these uneasinesses as
to leave us free to the attraction of remoter absent good" (946).
The uneasiness of desire is the first vague pull of the will entering a
gravitational field. Freedom is the capacity to resist the pull of
things with a small "mass" of happiness but great proximity, in
order to be true to the ultimate goal of "real" happiness.

"Pursuit" is here used as response to the gravitational tug of a
determining object. In the push-pull pain-pleasure world Locke describes, the attraction of happiness gives that constant, that *determination* of reality, on the basis of which one can build a science of
human motion. It is the uniform force giving "the inclination and
tendency" to pursue (53). The French Enlightenment used
"*suivre*" and "*suite*" for the response to cosmic attraction—see the
quotes from Delisle de Sales and Baron d'Holbach at Mauzi 408
and 432. Happiness was also an "*attrait*" in the Encyclopédie
(s.v. "*Bonheur*"). A passage (cited by Ganter), from Peter Paxton's
1703 *Civil Polity*, confirms this meaning:

Although the pursuit of happiness is as inseparable from the nature of
man as the tendency toward its own center is to unthinking matter, yet
as the latter can never attain that desired point, so the former can never
enjoy an uninterrupted bliss, a perfect and lasting content.

Since Ganter ignores Johnson's Dictionary entries on "pursuit,"
he does not see that Johnson cites the very part of Locke's *Essay*
(ii, 21) that we are discussing. Not only did Johnson know Locke's
use of the phrase, he took that use as his own model; for he treats
the pursuit of happiness as a constant force, whose effects man can

partially direct or block, in three of the four passages Ganter cites (*Rambler*, 29, *Idler*, 62, and *The False Alarm*). The fourth use is different (*Rasselas*, 36) only because the character speaking denies there *is* any meaningful end to human endeavor.

Johnson shows how Locke's "constant pursuit" can be put to preaching uses. A more startling example of this, entirely missed by Ganter, occurs in one of Jefferson's favorite authors, Laurence Sterne. The first of the collected sermons of Mr. Yorick is an extended meditation on the pursuit of happiness as "the most unbounded of our wishes." The sermon opens with these words: "The great pursuit of man is after happiness; it is the first and strongest desire of his nature." Though the pursuit is a constant, its objects can vary and deceive:

> The epicure, though he easily rectifies so great a mistake [as the miser incurs], yet at the same time he plunges him, if possible, into a greater; for hearing the objects of his *pursuit* to be happiness, and knowing of no other happiness than what is seated immediately in his senses—he sends the inquirer there . . . [till] the philosopher meets him bustling in the full career of this *pursuit*—stops him—tells him, if he is in search of happiness, he is far gone out of his way. . . .
>
> O God! let us not wander for ever without a guide, in this dark region, in endless *pursuit* of our mistaken good. . . . [teach us] that there can be no real happiness without religion and virtue, and the assistance of God's grace and Holy Spirit to direct our lives in the true *pursuit* of it.
>
> Now, if we take a survey of the life of man from the time he is come to reason, to the latest decline of it in old age—we shall find him engaged, and generally hurried on in such a succession of different *pursuits*, and different opinions of things, through the different stages of his life—as will admit of no explication but this, that he finds no rest for the sole of his foot, on any of the plans where he has been led to expect it. . . . Observe what impressions are made upon his senses, by diversions, music, dress and beauty—and how his spirits are upon the wing, flying in *pursuit* of them. . . . In prosecution of this—he [the ambitious builder] drops all painful *pursuits*—withdraws himself from the busy part of the world—realises—pulls down—builds up again. . . . (italics added).*

Though Sterne uses pursuit of happiness, in Locke's sense, to mean a constant determination of human nature, he differs from Locke on

---

* Jefferson not only knew Sterne's *Sermons* in general; he used a phrase from this particular passage (see chapter Twenty.)

the equation of happiness with pleasure: "For though there can be no happiness without pleasure—yet the reverse of the proposition will not hold true." Sterne, the close student of Locke (and, in *Tristram*, the satirist of him) was on guard against the hedonism that Francis Hutcheson tried to strip from the Lockean ethics.

It is in Hutcheson that we find the most technical repetition and refinement of Locke's "pursuit of happiness." Ganter quotes two of many possible passages from Hutcheson, one from the 1725 *Inquiry*, the other from his 1747 *Short Introduction*. But he entirely neglects the 1728 *Essay on the Nature and Conduct of the Passions and Affections*, whose opening pages are directed against the very chapter in Locke that gave "pursuit of happiness" its currency and technical definition. Here Hutcheson concentrates his own uses of the phrase with exceptional density. We read, for instance: "Men are necessarily determined to pursue their own happiness" (2:33) —the Lockean proposition with its notes of necessity and determination. And Hutcheson speaks of the "constant pursuit" of pleasures at 2:132. We learn again that the tug of a lesser happiness can be resisted for a greater one: "It cannot be pronounced concerning any finite good that it shall necessarily engage our pursuit" (2:32). Pursuit is the term used for attraction and determination of the will throughout this treatise. (See pp. 44, 46, 49, 114, 115, 116, 126, 127, 137.)

Hutcheson's main point of contention with Locke is over the latter's definition of desire as "uneasiness" (2:24—cf. Locke's par. 32). How can one talk, as Locke does, of "prosecuting" or fulfilling an uneasiness? No one prolongs or perfects discomfort:

Sensations which are previous to a desire, or not connected with it, may excite desire of any event, apprehended [as] necessary to procure or continue the sensation if it be pleasant, or to remove it if it be uneasy. But the uneasy sensation accompanying and connected with the desire itself cannot be a motive to that desire which it presupposes. The sensation *accompanying* desire is generally uneasy, and consequently our desire is never raised with a view to obtain or continue *it;* nor is the desire raised with a view to remove this uneasy sensation, for the desire is raised previously to it (2:16).

But Hutcheson argues with Locke only to make the latter's teaching on freedom more consistent. Uneasiness is a concomitant to attraction by a good not yet possessed; or—in the case of passion—by

a confused attraction to differing goods, as present versus remote
(28), internal versus external (36), intense versus prolonged (39),
or so on. Here, immediate sensation is at odds with reflective affection, so that the will is puzzled—and the kind of freedom Locke described is given room to operate.

Whatever the merits of Hutcheson's particular objection here, he
uses "pursuit" as Locke does, even when refining Locke's doctrine
on freedom. And this gives us material enough to remove one misapprehension about Jefferson's phrase. Many note the difference between his language and Mason's—that where Mason referred to
"pursuing *and obtaining* happiness," Jefferson mentioned only the
pursuit. This is said to make Jefferson both more realistic and more
idealistic than his "model." He is realistic because he knows man
cannot arrive at perfect happiness, only aspire to it. He is idealistic
because he puts that aspiration among the basic rights.

Both these observations are outside the moral climate, as it were,
of eighteenth-century language. Aside even from its inclusion in the
complex "constant-pursuit-of-happiness" formula, pursuit had a
"harder" meaning than aspiration in that period. It stood very close
to its cognates, prosecute and persecute. Johnson even puts that
meaning first in his Dictionary:

To PURSUE . . . 1. To chase; to follow in hostility.
PURSUIT . . . 1. The act of following with hostile intention.

In Scottish law, prosecutors were called "pursuers," as Jefferson
knew from Lord Kames, whom he quoted on the matter in his
Commonplace Book (109). And even where the aggressive note
was missing, a thoroughness was implied. One followed *through* or
followed *along*. Bacon had written in the *Advancement*: "It is
order, poursuite, sequence, and interchange of application, which is
mighty in nature." Jefferson himself said in 1788, "[I] shall pursue
the course of the Rhine as far as the roads will permit me" (*Papers*,
12:697). The Declaration of Independence itself denounces the
British "abuses & usurpations . . . pursuing invariably the same object" (ibid., 1:315).

Thus Jefferson talks of man as "following after" happiness by
more than vague yearning—indeed, by a uniform necessity of his
nature, something as regular as a magnetic needle's turn to the
North. This is a law that is normative, one man can steer by. James

Thomson made the regular comparison in 1720, in his poem *Upon Happiness* (vv. 10–12):

> An appetite as fixèd as the pole
> That's always eager in pursuit of bliss,
> And always veering till it points to this . . .

Man's pursuit is his natural bent, the magnetic response of his nature. So Sterne's Mr. Yorick can describe his sentimental journey as "a quiet journey of the heart in pursuit of Nature" (Stout ed., 219).

Those who take "pursuit" to suggest an idealistic yearning reduce the Declaration to triviality if not absurdity, making a right of mere velleity. Men may generally wish to be millionaires; but it is politically silly to make that wish a right, on a par with the most basic rights. One might as appropriately say man has a "right" to wish he were a petunia. It is interesting that the first published attack on the Declaration tried to minimize it by treating pursuit as "want" in the double sense of desire and lack. If one "wants" happiness, one does not have it—so the Declaration says it will not take away a not-having! "An Englishman," the anti-American polemicist in the *Scots Magazine,* wrote in the August issue of 1776:

Did ever any mortal alive hear of taking a pursuit of happiness from a man? What they possibly can mean by these words, I own is beyond my comprehension. A man may take from me a horse or a cow, or I may alienate either of them from myself, as I may likewise anything that I have; but how that can be taken from me, or alienated, which I have not, must be left for the solution of some unborn Oedipus.

That passage demonstrates the danger of taking pursuit as mere aspiration. But if one takes it as a law of nature, one can again be accused of stating the obvious, of proclaiming the trivial as the "self-evident." Man is drawn toward happiness, as Newton's apple fell earthward. What practical use is it to state a fact as a law? Quite a bit. Men knew the "facts" about gravity long before Newton wrote. They did not jump off high cliffs, on the hunch that they would not fall—if they jumped, they did it as Sappho does in eighteenth-century paintings. But Newton turned mere facts into law—men could *calculate* effects, with a regularity that made nature comply with human plan, because the human mind had first been submissive enough before the facts to observe repetitive pattern.

Gravity rules, imperious, whether men pay attention or not. But, once men *really* pay attention, they can use the inevitable in new ways, use necessity to escape their own needs. As Locke put it, in his treatment of the will's "pursuit," freedom is based on determination. Adam Ferguson argued that the laws of nature do not take away freedom, either in life or literature:

If we are required to explain how men could be poets or orators before they were aided by the learning of the scholar and the critic, we may inquire in our turn how bodies could fall by their weight before the laws of gravitation were recorded in books. Mind, as well as body, has laws which are exemplified in the course of nature . . . (*Civil Society*, 312).

Jefferson means to state scientific law in the human area—natural *law* as human *right*. He describes what occurs. But knowledge of the law gives man power to alter events ("out-comes"). In that little word "pursuit," as it was actually used from Locke's time to Hutcheson's, we have a shorthand for the linked doctrines of determined will and free act. Man pursues happiness as the stone falls. But the stone can be obstructed in its motion by some accidental prop. A necessity of motion is at work in the stable stone on a hillside, though no consequence is observable. The stone *must* fall, but it *does* not—the illustration is Diderot's (*Rêve de d'Alembert*, Pléiade, 873–74). Only when one recognizes the law of man's nature as his *right* does one remove the obstacles and let him move free, knowing this is consonant with the order of nature.

Within its original rich context, the pursuit of happiness is a phenomenon both obvious and paradoxical. It supplies us with the ground of human right and the goal of human virtue. It is the basic drive of the self, and the only means given for transcending the self. As Hutcheson put it:

The several rights of mankind are therefore first made known by the natural feelings of their hearts, and their natural desires *pursuing* such things as tend to the good of each individual or those dependent on him; and recommending to all certain virtuous offices (4:119).

Men in the eighteenth century felt they could become conscious of their freedom only by discovering how they were bound: When they found what they *must* pursue, they knew they had a *right* to pursue it.

EIGHTEEN

"... of happiness .."

All men are, by nature, equal and free: no one has a
right to any authority over another without his consent:
all lawful government is founded on the consent of
those who are subject to it: such consent was given
with a view to ensure and to increase the happiness of
the governed, above what they could enjoy in an independent and unconnected state of nature. The consequence is, that the happiness of the society is the *first*
law of every government.

—James Wilson, 1774

Things happed well for "happy" as an eighteenth-century word.
That is why we find no systematic effort to divide its labors with
some other word. It was different in France, where *"bonheur"* and
"félicité," without entirely parting company, showed a drift toward different uses. We can see this in successive Encyclopédie entries. The Abbé Pestré wrote the 1751 article on "bonheur" out of
Fontenelle. He contrasts "bonheur" with *"plaisirs,"* as a *state* more
durable than *episodes*. But Voltaire, in the 1756 article on "félicité,"
makes a parallel distinction between disparate "bonheurs" and the
state of "félicité." (Voltaire's whole range of graded meanings
covers this spectrum: *plaisir/événement heureux/bonheur/pros-
périté/félicité/béatitude*).

By the 1780s a new article was commissioned for the expanded
Encyclopédie supplement: *"Félicité publique."* The state of "félicité" was more often used than "bonheur" to describe the complex
of social conditions that made for happiness as a *political* goal.
That is why Robert Mauzi uses the word "bonheur" to organize his
vast study of private happiness in the eighteenth century. Chastellux
had called his work *De la félicité publique,* picking up the discussion of *"felicità pubblica"* by Muratori, Verri, and Beccaria.

Of course, the distinction was never absolute, if only because private and public happiness affect each other. Helvétius rightly called his poem *Bonheur*, since he began with the individual's quest for happiness. But because of his system of self-transcending selfishnesses, he makes man find, by his fourth canto,

Son bonheur personnel dans le bonheur de tous.

By the time of Lafayette's draft Declaration of Rights (1788), a further refinement was added. The phrase normally translated (by Chinard and others) as "pursuit of happiness" is *"la recherche du bien-être."*

The English-speaking people felt no need for such refining or distinctions. "Felicity" was available to them; and sometimes, like "bliss," it approximated man's final state of happiness—as it had in Hamlet's command: "Absent thee from felicity awhile. . . ." But "happy" served most purposes. It was a good native word, whose implications were far-reaching. A thing "haps" or occurs—from this came a whole range of combinations: mayhap, mishap, haply, hapless, haphazard, happenstance. A "happy" thing was fitted to some hap or event—a happy meeting, a happy thought, a happy style. Hap as mere chance did not, at first, have to mean a desirable outcome. It meant whatever occurs—Shakespeare's "hap what hap may." But by a natural tendency mere luck becomes good luck (a "lucky" man) and fortune becomes good fortune (a "fortunate" man). So happy was devoted increasingly to goodhap. The opposite sense had to be specified (as in mishap), and "happy accident" was no longer felt to be tautological (i.e., a happing hap).

Happiness was, therefore, Voltaire's *bonne-heure* (*bonne chance*); but it was also a general tendency to fit all haps, a condition suited to the world, quite "happy" in its use by men who took a pragmatic, mechanical, working view of life. When Hume talks about a "happy theory" (*Enquiry, Morals*, ix, 1), he means one that keeps fitting new material. Earlier he wrote, in the same work: "He is happy whose circumstances suit his temper" (vi, 1). When the British spoke of their "happy constitution," they expressed perfectly the belief in a fortunate arrangement of political power.

We have seen that the problem of measurable pleasure arose in the eighteenth century's efforts at a science of man. This was a project of the whole Continent. Locke made the project possible when he defined happiness as sensible pleasure and graded it from "the utmost pleasure we are capable of" down to "so much ease from all pain, and so much present pleasure, as without which anyone cannot be content" (*Essay*, ii, 21, par. 42—this is the chapter where he launched "the pursuit of happiness" as the supreme determiner of man's actions).

No one did more in the eighteenth century to encourage the measuring of public happiness than did Francis Hutcheson, with his 1725 formula for "the greatest happiness of the greatest number." Happiness had established itself as a term of widest yet most precise meaning. Of course the word pervaded all discussions of politics, ethics, and psychology. It was as important yet shifting in its sense as the more studied term "nature." It could tend toward a psychic invisibility, as the mental air men breathed. Yet more technical senses were always recoverable in the ongoing debate, especially when men made narrow claims upon happiness as the basis of political sovereignty.

The passage from James Wilson, quoted at the beginning of this chapter, was used by Carl Becker to establish the orthodox Lockean nature of Jefferson's Declaration. He calls the Wilson quote "a summary of Locke" (*Declaration*, 108), part of America's common heritage of ideas. But if the idea was so common, why did Wilson give a *particular* source for it, and *only* one? Here is his own footnote to the passage (in his *Considerations on the Nature and Extent of the Legislative Authority of the British Parliament* of 1774): "The right to sovereignty is that of commanding finally—but in order to procure real felicity; for if this is not obtained, sovereignty ceases to be a legitimate authority, 2 Burl., 32, 33." He is quoting in summary Burlamaqui's *Principes du droit politique*, 1, v, 1; 6 (= *Principes du droit naturel*, 1, x, 2). Now Burlamaqui was a disciple of Hutcheson's philosophy of moral sense (*Naturel*, 2, iii, 1) and therefore he differed from Locke on concepts of right (ibid., 1, v, 10) and property (1, iv, 8), of the social contract (1, iv, 9) and the state of nature (2, iv, 11). If Wilson meant to voice a Lockean view of government, as Becker assumed, he clumsily chose the wrong source.

Yet Wilson knew the issues at stake. He was a Scot, born in 1742, educated at St. Andrews, Glasgow, and Edinburgh before coming to America in 1766, where he taught Latin while studying law with

John Dickinson. He came with a letter of recommendation to William Smith's College of Philadelphia, after pursuing Jefferson's leisurely approach to a general education from 1757 to 1765. But he drew his learning directly from Jefferson's remote sources. Wilson knew and held to the moral-sense theory, and was quoting, in Burlamaqui, one of the principal spokesmen for that school during the period when Wilson wrote his pamphlet (1770, four years before publication).

Jefferson copied bits of the Wilson pamphlet into his *Commonplace Book*, but not the words prefixed to this chapter. He wrote out extracts just preceding and just following that quote, but not the quote itself. This puzzled Chinard, who thought with Becker that the Wilson passage was Jefferson's source for the Declaration's preamble. But Jefferson was familiar with Wilson's own source (Burlamaqui), and with Burlamaqui's source (Hutcheson), and with the surrounding literature that phrased and rephrased the idea voiced here by Wilson. There was nothing new to Jefferson in the idea that government exists for the happiness of the governed. What he did find worth copying was the *application* of this norm to Parliament's claims. It was not enough, Wilson was arguing, for sovereignty to reside in King, Lords, and Commons. That sovereignty had to revalidate itself constantly by a regard for the happiness of the governed. Will it insure and increase the happiness of the American colonies to have the parliament of Great Britain possess "a supreme, irresistible, uncontrolled authority over them"? (*Commonplace Book*, 317 = Wilson, McCloskey, ed., 2:723-24).

The important thing to notice about Jefferson's use of Wilson is that he makes happiness a hard political test of any reign's very legitimacy, not a vague yearning of the individual. He could do this because happiness played a very special role in the politics of moral-sense philosophers. They were unanimous on this point, from the very book in which Hutcheson first expounded the moral sense in a technical way. We have seen that Hutcheson derived the concept of natural right from the claims of moral sense. He also traces the notion of obligation from the gratifying of moral appetites, from the happiness necessarily derived by dealing happiness to others:

But if by obligation we understand a motive from self-interest sufficient to determine all those who duly consider it and *pursue* their own advantage wisely, to a certain course of actions, we may have a sense of such obligation by reflecting on this *determination* of our nature to approve virtue, to be pleased and happy when we reflect upon our having done virtuous actions and to be uneasy when we are conscious of having acted otherwise—and also by considering how much superior we esteem the happiness of virtue to any other enjoyment. We may likewise have a sense of this sort of obligation by considering those reasons which prove a *constant course* of benevolent and social actions to be the most probable means of promoting the natural good of every individual (1:250–51, italics added).

Reflection on his own natural drives will inform man that "the surest way to promote his private happiness [is] to do publicly useful actions" (2:208; cf. 4:317–20). Since man finds true happiness only in society, his pursuit of happiness will lead him, if nature is not obstructed (2:208), "to desire the greatest happiness and perfection of the largest system" of those with whom he is associated (5:10). This provides the basis for all social organization, including that of the state: "The general happiness is the supreme end of all political union" (6:226).

Hume also held that the only enlightened *pursuit* of happiness is also a *promotion* of happiness. After admitting that "All men . . . are equally desirous of happiness, but few are successful in the pursuit," he says that is because men are distracted from *real* advantage by the most *immediate* advantage (*Enquiry, Morals*, 6, ii) and concludes by saying there is only one true advantage for man:

Having explained the moral approbation attending merit or virtue, there remains nothing but briefly to consider our interested obligation to it and to inquire whether every man who has any regard to his own happiness and welfare will not best find his account in the practice of every moral duty (ibid., 9, ii).

Thus he defines obligation as gratification of the moral sense, precisely as Hutcheson did:

The sole trouble she [nature] demands is that of just calculation and a steady preference of the greater happiness. . . . Why is it more doubtful that the enlarged virtues of humanity, generosity, beneficence are desirable, with a view of happiness and self-interest, than the limited endowments of ingenuity and politeness? . . . Whatever contradiction may vulgarly be supposed between the selfish and social sentiments or dispositions, they are really no more opposite than selfish and ambitious, selfish and revengeful, selfish and vain. It is requisite that there be an original propensity of some kind, in order to be a basis of self-love, by giving a relish to the objects of the pursuit—and none more fit than benevolence or humanity (ibid.).

Since benevolence is motivated, for Hume as for Hutcheson, by the sight of another's benevolence, and it issues in further acts of benevolence, social virtues spread by a kind of contagion (*Treatise*, 605) or kindling (*Enquiry, Morals*, 9, i, cf. Ferguson, *Civil Society*, 58–59, 67). Men are good only in society, taking and giving the happiness of well-ordinated social creatures:

From the original frame of our temper we . . . feel a desire of another's happiness or good which, by means of that affection, becomes our own good and is afterwards pursued from the combined motives of benevolence and self-enjoyment (ibid., App. 2).

It should be noticed that the pursuit of happiness has all the meaning of a "constant determination" we found in passages considered in the last chapter. It is the pursuit of one's own happiness that is the only efficient motive force for spreading happiness to others, and on this fact of human nature governments must be established, judged, altered, or abolished.

The reciprocity of pursuing and promoting happiness was noticed by Lord Kames: "There is a principle of benevolence in man which prompts him to an equal pursuit of the happiness of all" (*Principles*, 77). Adam Ferguson shared this emphasis on the gratification derived by the benefactor from his bestowal of favors on others:

If, in reality, courage and a heart devoted to the good of mankind are the constituents of human felicity, the kindness which is done infers a happiness in the person from whom it proceeds, not in him on whom it is bestowed; and the greatest good which men possessed of fortitude and generosity can procure to their fellow creatures is a participation of this happy character. If this be the good of the individual, it is likewise that of mankind; and virtue no longer imposes a task by which we are obliged to bestow upon others that good from which we ourselves refrain; but supposes, in the highest degree, as possessed by ourselves, that state of felicity which we are required to promote in the world (*Civil Society*, 99–100).

Ferguson spells out the Hutchesonian reversal whereby the benefactor's original joy is shared with the beneficiary, rather than vice versa—and the real joy is not completely shared until the beneficiary becomes a benefactor in his turn, spreading the "contagion" of social happiness by the social virtues. Ferguson defines this process as the norm of "national felicity," to which he devotes two chapters of his book:

[Men] are really cheated of their happiness in being made to believe that any occupation or pastime is better fitted to amuse themselves than that which at the same time produces some real good to their fellow creatures. . . . If the public good be the principal object with individuals, it is likewise true that the happiness of individuals is the great end of civil society. . . . If the individual owes every degree of consideration to the public, he receives, in paying that very consideration, the greatest happiness of which his nature is capable (ibid., 103–6).

Adam Smith, holding the same views on the individual's moral sense, must reach the same conclusions on public order and legitimate government: "All constitutions of government, however, are valued only in proportion as they tend to promote the happiness of those who live under them" (*Moral Sentiments*, 4, ii). And this promotion of happiness arises, by the work of the invisible hand of providence, when men are freest to pursue their own happiness:

The happiness of mankind, as well as of all other rational creatures, seems to have been the original purpose intended by the Author of Nature when he brought them into existence. No other end seems worthy of that supreme wisdom and benignity which we necessarily ascribe to him; and this opinion, which we are led to by the abstract consideration of his infinite perfections, is still more confirmed by the examination of the works of Nature, which seem all intended to promote happiness and to guard against misery. But, by acting according to the dictates of our moral faculties, we necessarily pursue the most effectual means for promoting the happiness of mankind (ibid., 3, vi).

This was not only the teaching of Shaftesbury's *Characteristics* ("Social pleasures are superior to any other"), but of Voltaire: *Nous vivons en société; il n'y a donc de véritablement bon pour nous que ce qui fait le bien de la société*" (Dictionnaire philosophique, s.v. "*Vertu*").

We found, in Part Two of this book, that public happiness was a secular and scientific term for men of the Enlightenment, a "heretical" displacement of man's hopes from the hereafter to those immediate gratifications that can stimulate Lockean man to action. Jefferson found the perfect framework for making that scientific tool a political norm when he studied and adopted the moral-sense philosophy. His use of the "pursuit of happiness" as the natural right to rank with life and liberty is not a vague or "idealistic" or ill-defined action, but one consistent with everything else he wrote in the Declaration and outside it. Only when we realize this can we bridge the great disjunction that has haunted all Jeffersonian studies of recent years. It has been granted, rather casually, that Jefferson accepted the moral-sense theory of *private* actions. But then, when men moved to the *public* scale of political action, it was assumed even more aggressively that he was a Lockean individualist, basing the social contract on property rights. If the latter were true, he could not be called a moral-sense philosopher in any serious way. But we have seen that it is not true. His social thought was as firmly grounded in the moral sense as was Hutcheson's own.

PART FOUR

A SENTIMENTAL PAPER

NINETEEN

"... of nature and of nature's god ..."

And our own dear Monticello, where has nature spread so rich a mantle under the eye? mountains, forests, rocks, rivers. With what majesty do we there ride above the storms! How sublime to look down into the workhouse of nature, to see her clouds, hills, snow, rain, thunder, all fabricated at our feet!

—Jefferson, in 1786

To understand any text remote from us in time, we must reassemble a world around that text. The preconceptions of the original audience, its tastes, its range of reference, must be recovered, so far as that is possible. We must forget what was learned, or what occurred, in the interval between our time and the text's. We must resurrect beliefs now discarded. Most people remember this when approaching a culture radically different from ours—that of Sophocles, or Dante, or Chaucer. They keep it in mind, but not enough, when reading Shakespeare or Milton. Yet eighteenth-century English is still read as "our" language; and anything written in America is part of the modern world, of our "young" nation's brief history. So we are tempted to read Jefferson as our contemporary.

The dangers of this are perfectly illustrated in Erik Erikson's 1973 Jefferson Lecture, a long address published as *Dimensions of a New Identity*. Looking for the materials of psychohistory in Jefferson's case, Erikson relies especially on Jefferson's single consciously wrought *book*. Precisely because *Notes on the State of Virginia* is a scientific survey, Erikson concludes that personal "asides" came to Jefferson with special urgency, to force themselves in among the dry catalogues and the quibblings with Buffon. Erikson produces, as particularly revealing, Jefferson's description of the Natural

Bridge, which stood on one of Jefferson's own more remote purchases of land:

He admits that this item is "not comprehended under the present
head"; yet, as the "most sublime of Nature's works," it "must not be pretermitted. It is on the ascent of a hill which seems to have been cloven
through its length by some great convulsion. . . . Though the sides of
this bridge are provided in some parts with a parapet of fixed rocks, yet
few men have resolution to walk to them and look over into the abyss.
You involuntarily fall on your hands and feet, creep to the parapet and
peep over it." What follows, certainly, is more detail than the Frenchman bargained for: "Looking down from this height about a minute
gave me a violent headache—if the view from the top be painful and intolerable, that from below is delightful in an equal extreme. It is impossible for the emotions arising from the sublime to be felt beyond what
they are here . . ." Jefferson later noted a certain confusion in his memory; but the point to be made is that in surveying the state of the State
of Virginia, he includes an account of his personal state while doing the
survey—a prime requirement for psychohistory. Note, if you please, for
future reference, the juxtaposition of height and downfall, of sublime
emotions—and the violent pain in the head.

Before looking more closely at Jefferson's description, we should
put ourselves on dutiful alert about eighteenth-century descriptions
"on the scene." They were mandatory on the traveler or diarist.
The Grand Tour, toward which colonial Americans aspired, was
a "sentimental journey" in the technical sense Laurence Sterne
played upon. Men should not only *exercise* their sensibility before
grand or affecting sights, but *display* that sensibility in their record
of the journey.

We know that the Natural Bridge was one of the principal sights
for those who made their grand tour in America. William Car-
michael had viewed it with "romantic enthusiasm," published a
sketch of it in a Philadelphia newspaper, and told the Chevalier de
Chastellux about it when they met in Paris in 1776 (*Papers*,
10:428–29). In 1782 Chastellux, having seen the other marvels of
the New World (like Rittenhouse's orrery), went to the Natural
Bridge by way of Monticello. (Jefferson was always urging people
to go on scientific pilgrimage to the Bridge—*Papers*, 12:601, 13:639,
14:45, 16:129.)

Chastellux may have been swayed, before he saw the Bridge, by

Jefferson's descriptions, though Jefferson had not yet shown him the early draft of his *Notes* (cf. *Papers*, 6:203). But even if Jefferson influenced the reflections of Chastellux, the fact that the latter published his reflections for a French audience proves they were not an entirely personal matter, unique to the Virginian.

Chastellux had difficulty following Jefferson's directions in his quest for the Bridge. But he fell in with an American eager to show off the native spectacle—one who led him, with distracting conversation, up onto the Bridge itself, and then produced the wonder almost by miracle:

I had perceived that there was on each side a considerable deep hollow, but the trees had prevented me from forming any judgment, or paying much attention to it. Approaching the precipice, I saw at first two great masses or chains of rocks, which formed the bottom of a ravine, or rather of an immense abyss; but placing myself, not without precaution, upon the brink of the precipice, I saw that these two buttresses were joined under my foot, forming a vault, of which I could yet form no idea, but of its height. After enjoying this magnificent but tremendous spectacle, which many persons could not bear to look at, I went to the western side, the aspect of which was not less imposing, but more picturesque. This *Thebais*, these ancient pines, these enormous masses of rocks, so much the more astonishing as they appear to possess a wild symmetry and rudely to concur, as it were, in forming a certain design—all this apparatus of rude and shapeless nature, which art attempts in vain—attacks at once the senses and the thoughts, and excites a gloomy and melancholy admiration.

But it is at the foot of these rocks, on the edge of a little stream which flows under this immense arch, that we must judge of its astonishing structure; there we discover its immense spurs, its back-bendings, and those profiles which architecture might have given it. The arch is not complete, the eastern part of it not being as large as the western, because the mountain is more elevated on this than on the opposite side.

It is very extraordinary that at the bottom of the stream there appear no considerable ruins, no trace of any violent laceration, which could have destroyed the kernel of the rock, and have left the upper part alone subsisting; for that is the only hypothesis that can account for such a prodigy. We can have no possible recourse either to a volcano or a deluge, no trace of a sudden conflagration or of a slow and tedious undermining by the water. The rock is of the calcareous kind, and its different strata are horizontal, a circumstance which excludes even the idea of an earthquake or subterraneous cavern. It is not, in short, for a small num-

ber of travelers to give a decided opinion for the public on this phenomenon of nature. It belongs to the learned of both worlds to judge of
it . . .*

The passage is a little model of sensibility joined with science. I
have divided this main part of it into three paragraphs, which enact
a customary "motion" of the mind to, around, and away from the
scene:

A. We are given a shock of encounter, a shudder of awe "which
many persons could not bear to look at." Nature's rudeness stuns,
causes loss of control, assails both thought and the senses. Chastellux strums a wide gamut—classical, biblical, "gothic." The scene
is itself a *Thebais*—rough late epic that gives classicists "romantic"
license. It teeters on an *"abîme immense."* It calls up *"une ténébreuse et mélancholique admiration."*

B. A second view of the Bridge is taken from below, where ex-
citement at the partial glimpse yields to a calmer estimate of regularities—the overall articulation of the Bridge into spurs (literally
contreforts, buttresses), back-bendings (*arrière-voussures,* recessive
vaulting) and the lines (*profils*) that an architect might draw. The
Bridge loses some of its power over the disoriented mind. Ordinat-
ing faculties now measure nature in terms of art.

C. Having moved from nature to art, Chastellux now moves from
art to science. The progression is from transport to connoisseurship
to explanation. Nowhere is his dependence on Jefferson more evident than in his theory of the Bridge's origin. The Portuguese traveler, Don Antonio de Ulloa, accounted for similar marvels in South
America as modern geologists do, supposing a river had tunneled
through the rock. Even Chastellux, once he read Ulloa's analysis
and consulted Buffon back in France, would adopt this explanation.
But Jefferson was loathe to give up a favorite theory; he maintained
in later editions of the *Notes* his view that the formation was
caused by "convulsion"—Chastellux's "laceration" (*déchirement*).
Without the help of Chastellux, writing under Jefferson's influence,
we might think Jeffersonian *convulsion* allowed for earthquake. But
Chastellux expressly rules out *"tremblement."* The two men are obviously thinking of some fault in the rock which caused it to crack

---

* I quote the eighteenth-century translation that appeared anonymously in
1787. J. Hammond Trumbull established in 1869 that George Grieve had made
the version (*Mass. Hist. Soc. Proceedings* 1869–70).

with temperature change so that the core fell away. When Jefferson argued with Ulloa, he referred to the exact fit of fallen and unfallen rock in the parallel Ulloa himself raised—and Chastellux notes that the stratigraphy of the Bridge shows no jumbling produced by earthquake or volcano. All this proves that Jefferson was thinking of convulsion in its root sense, from *convellere,* to tear away. Milton had used it so, describing Samson's action on the pillars. (As a medical term, convulsion meant the cracking of muscles by cramp— a sense we shall come across again, very soon.)

What made Jefferson—and, at first, Chastellux—reject the sounder and more obvious explanation of the Bridge's formation? Jefferson showed a settled bias against any theories that relied on a biblical Deluge—this would later cause slurs against his Christian orthodoxy in the fossil debate. Yet the most famous theory of mountain formation in Jefferson's day was Thomas Burnet's—a theory formulated precisely to explain irregularities of the Natural Bridge sort. Jefferson seems to have reached for any explanation of such oddities *but* the action of water. Thus Chastellux, who is more open than Jefferson about what he wants to exclude, rejects in express terms *"alluvion."* Jefferson's bias is shown just before the Natural Bridge section of the *Notes,* when he excludes the hypothesis that Madison's Cave was formed by an adjacent river.

The scientific agreement of Jefferson and Chastellux, so soon after their discussion, is not surprising. What calls for our attention here is the inclusion of the same range of reactions—fear and awe, aesthetic wonder, then curious inquiry—in Jefferson's scientific text as in the French traveler's journal. Jefferson cannot observe the same arrangement of his material that Chastellux had. He lacks the narrative frame, the guide's trick that makes the grandeur of the Bridge spring into view. He begins, rather than ends, with measurement and explanation; Marbois had asked about cascades and caverns, and this "cavity" in the rock is naturally placed in the catalogue, with the same kind of opening remarks that were devoted to the Falling Spring and Madison's Cave. But then he draws in the fearful and aesthetic reactions. If the order of Chastellux was Nature-Art-Science, A-B-C, then that of Jefferson is C-A-B:

The *Natural bridge,* the most sublime of Nature's works, though not comprehended under the present head, must not be pretermitted. It is on the ascent of a hill, which seems to have been cloven through its length by some great convulsion. The fissure, just at the bridge, is, by some ad-measurements, 270 feet deep, by others only 205. It is about 45 feet wide at the bottom, and 90 feet at the top; this of course determines the length of the bridge, and its height from the water. Its breadth in the middle is about 60 feet, but more at the ends, and the thickness of the mass at the summit of the arch, about 40 feet. A part of this thickness is constituted by a coat of earth, which gives growth to many large trees. The residue, with the hill on both sides, is one solid rock of limestone. The arch approaches the Semi-elliptical form; but the large axis of the ellipsis, which would be the cord of the arch, is many times longer than the transverse.

Though the sides of this bridge are provided in some parts with a par-apet of fixed rocks, yet few men have resolution to walk to them and look over into the abyss. You involuntarily fall on your hands and feet, creep to the parapet and peep over it. Looking down from this height about a minute, gave me a violent head ach.

If the view from the top be painful and intolerable, that from below is delightful in an equal extreme. It is impossible for the emotions arising from the sublime to be felt beyond what they are here: so beautiful an arch, so light, and springing as it were up to heaven, the rapture of the spectator is really indescribable! The fissure continuing narrow, deep, and straight for a considerable distance above and below the bridge, opens a short but very pleasing view of the North mountain on one side, and Blue ridge on the other, at the distance each of them of about five miles.

I have quoted the first edition of the *Notes*, as Erikson did. Later, after a return to the bridge, Jefferson would have to amend the text, since the view contained in the last sentence above is only pos-sible from the top of the bridge, not from below. His memory first deceived him in such a way that he could play off the terror of the height against the soft and pleasing views from below. In this re-spect, as we shall see, he is following a scientific "program" so care-fully that the evidence gets shifted about to fit the hypothesis. When he amended the passage, he managed to retain the contrast he was working for. We must look at that emendation when we come to Burke's volume on the sublime.

First, however, we should glance back at Chastellux, to observe how similar are the two men's texts. Jefferson, indeed, keeps his personal reaction of fear and *awe* (A) comparatively modest. No *Thebais* for him, no *"ténébreuse et mélancholique admiration."* But there is the same precaution in approaching "the abyss," and the same boast that few men can bear this ordeal. Instead of fear and melancholy, Jefferson mentions the headache that so intrigues Professor Erikson. Otherwise, the brief Jefferson passage puts in plainer terms the essentials of the long paragraph in Chastellux. The *aesthetic* section on the sublime (B) refers to the springing vault as an architectural achievement, its lightness moving Jefferson to an extreme of delight contrasted with that of his pain above. We have already considered the resemblance in the two men's *explanation* for this wonder (C).

What accounts for this close similarity of reaction in the French Academician and the Virginia planter? Is it simply their acquaintance, the discussions they engaged in at Monticello? Hardly —for the same kind of mountain description can be found in many eighteenth-century books and diaries. Accurate reporting is joined with panicky admiration. Marjorie Nicholson has traced the development of this reaction to "mountain gloom and mountain glory." She—like others, including Ernest Tuveson—thinks the most important contribution to this aesthetic was made by Thomas Burnet, whose theory of the Deluge has already been referred to.

Burnet, Locke's influential contemporary, helped occasion the Battle of the Books by the publication of his *Theory of Earth* (1684). Burnet, like Jefferson, argued that rain could not have caused Noah's Deluge. But Burnet tried to save the biblical account by an ingenious application of Newton's theory of gravity. The heaviest and hardest parts of earth collected at the center; they were surrounded by a belt of water, as the next-heaviest element. The habitable globe as it came from God's hand was an eggshell crust formed around this water belt. Land was a material *floating* on the water's surface; "scum" formed where it came into contact with precipitations from the air. This gave man an antediluvian world of classical regularity, without the irrational bumps and excrescenses of mountains, our fretted shores and ragged bodies of water.

At the Deluge—man's real fall in Burnet's scheme—the eggshell crust cracked, since it had grown brittle and had shrunk. The fountains of the deep were broken up, water from the belt rushed out, and the crust crumpled in toward earth's core, leaving a wreckage of man's original habitat jammed in around the earth's core. The original water belt, now washed here and there amid the wreckage, formed our oceans and seas. D. C. Allen, in his definitive *Legend of Noah*, could write: "This theory of Burnet's is the most ingenious attempt to explain the mechanics of the Deluge that I have seen." The scheme burst upon physicotheologians as either a great proof of revelation or a great challenge to it. It fathered endless controversy, scientific, religious, and aesthetic. Burnet wrote with a Miltonic grandiosity of vision, imagining not only the Deluge but earth's final Conflagration, in apocalyptic language that inspired Coleridge and Wordsworth and Shelley, over a century after the book's first appearance.

At the conscious level, Burnet meant to destroy admiration for a Nature so ravaged as our postdiluvian wreck. But in fact he gave Augustan artists a twofold excuse for attention to the oddest landscapes. As signs of primordial disaster, rude scenes were symbols of dramatic conflict and loss. Yet as the remains of a prior order, they tempted men to find evidences of a glory not quite effaced even now. The whole world became a "gothic" ruin of God's "classical" masterpiece. Burnet himself succumbed to the fascination he denounced. While arguing that art's structures had been razed in this leftover world, he made it impossible to talk outside art's categories. After all, a damaged artifact is still an artifact. Besides, Burnet's prose responded to ruins in ways that inspired "gothic" taste all through the eighteenth century. Longinus had taught men of Burnet's generation that the sublime causes momentary stultification (*ekplēxis*), an idea Addison domesticated as "transport." Burnet made the dizzying effect of mountain heights a standard example of ekplēxis:

But suppose a man was carried asleep out of a plain country amongst the Alps, and left there upon the top of one of the highest mountains. When he waked and looked about him, he would think himself in an enchanted country or carried into another world, everything would appear to him so different to what he had ever seen or imagined before. To see on every hand of him a multitude of vast bodies thrown together in confusion, as those mountains are, rocks standing naked round about him, and the hollow valleys gaping under him; and at his feet, it may be, an heap of frozen snow in the midst of summer. He would hear the thunder come from below, and see the black clouds hanging beneath him. Upon such a prospect it would not be easy to him to persuade himself that he was still upon the same earth; but if he did, he would be convinced, at least, that there are some regions of it strangely rude and ruin-like, and very different from what he had ever thought of before (*Theory*, i, 12).

Though Burnet represents such mountain scenery as "ghastly and frightful," as "placed in no order," his own impression is of artifacts —broken up indeed, but retaining traces of a shattered majesty:

And yet these mountains we are speaking of, to confess the truth, are nothing but great ruins—but such as show a certain magnificence in nature, as from old temples and broken amphitheaters of the Romans we collect the greatness of that people (ibid.).

Still, Burnet must go on from awe and admiration to explanation:

After this general survey of the mountains of the earth and their properties, let us now reflect upon the causes of them. There is a double pleasure in philosophy [i.e., science]—first that of admiration whilst we contemplate things that are great and wonderful, and do not yet understand their causes; for though admiration proceed from ignorance, yet there is a certain charm and sweetness in that passion. Then the second pleasure is greater and more intellectual, which is that of distinct knowledge and comprehension, when we come to have the key that unlocks those secrets, and see the methods wherein those things come to pass that we admired before (ibid.).

The admiring ignorance of one's ekplēxis is not at odds with scientific inquiry—on the contrary, it catches the attention, it acts as an immediate motive for investigation:

There is nothing doth more awaken our thoughts or excite our minds to inquire into the causes of such things than the actual view of them, as I have had experience myself when it was my fortune to cross the Alps and Appennine mountains, for the sight of those wild, vast, and indigested heaps of stones and earth did so deeply strike my fancy that I was not easy till I could give myself some tolerable account how that confusion came in nature (ibid.).

Burnet is merely the best-known early writer of the "sublime" period to move from awe and terror, through aesthetic judgment, to scientific conclusions, while describing mountains. Jefferson's description of his own favorite natural wonder is therefore couched in an accepted mountain "language"—as we should expect from his report drawn up for French readers.

But what of the headache he mentions? The fact that Jefferson did suffer from migraine—variously "explained" by psychohistorians —makes Erikson find an entirely private signal being sent us in this ostensibly public discourse. Still, how was Jefferson, in his own ekplēxis passage, to impress men with the bridge's sublimity? Others would stress giddiness, vertigo, nausea, and tell us that relief was only to be had by descent from such terrifying height. Here, for instance, is Shaftesbury, in Part Three of his dialogue, "The Moralists":

See! with what trembling steps poor mankind tread the narrow brink of the deep precipices, from whence with giddy horror they look down, mistrusting even the ground which bears them, whilst they hear the hollow sound of torrents underneath, and see the ruin of the impending rock, with falling trees which hang with their roots upwards and seem to draw more ruin after them.

Shaftesbury describes the temptation to leap as an assuagement of one's very *fear* of height—and he goes on immediately to see the ruin of the world imaged here, and to draw philosophical reflections from that.

Addison, great advocate of "the sublime," needs to find level ground again for reassurance, after his experience of the Alps:

I am just now arrived at Geneva by a very troublesome journey over the Alps, where I have been for some days together shivering among the eternal snows. My head is still giddy with mountains and precipices, and you can't imagine how much I am pleased with the sight of a plain, that is as agreeable to me at present as a shore was about a year ago after our tempest at Genoa (To Edward Wortley, December 9, 1701).

But when men of Jefferson's generation talked of sublimity—and Jefferson twice calls his bridge "sublime"—they were bound to think of one man's theory. Edmund Burke's 1757 *Philosophical Enquiry into the Origin of Our Ideas of the Sublime and Beautiful* was as successful as it was original. It won the admiration of men as different as David Hume and Dr. Johnson. W. J. Hipple accurately describes the eighteenth-century debate on sublimity this way: "Everyone after Burke either imitates him or borrows from him or feels it necessary to refute him." It is easy to see why Burke had such impact. He took one of the major philosophical problems posed by Locke's theory of sensation and gave it a daring solution.

If the source of all our ideas is sensible pain or pleasure, then the beautiful must be a source of pleasure. Accepting that definition, Hume defines ugly *sounds* in poetry as those which cause *pain* to a person trying to pronounce them (*Essay, Morals*, v, 2). From this comes the aesthetic of smooth verse. From this, too, comes the cult of pastoral as a totally pleasing scene. Hume, in the same place, praises idyllic tranquillity and attacks pictures of rough or fearsome nature: "Sennazarius, who transferred the [pastoral] scene to the seashore, though he presented the most magnificent object in nature, is confessed to have erred in his choice. The idea of toil, labor, and danger suffered by the fisherman is painful by an unavoidable sympathy which attends every conception of human happiness or misery."

But if one cannot show challenge and the terrifying, how admit the *sublime* to one's art, since it stultifies and overpowers? Burke met the problem head on, arguing that certain kinds of pain contribute to pleasure. First he isolates a subordinate mode of pleasure, "delight," defined as cessation of pain. We are delighted at the spectacle of tragedy because *we* are not undergoing that pain—it is a kind of cessation, or escape, from pain seen as imminent but not present to us. (There is also a subordinate mode of pain, "grief," the cessation of pleasure—we sometimes entertain grief because memory of the pleasure is sweet even though its loss is bitter.) The image Burke dwells on in the latter part of his book is that of athletes who undergo the pain of training and competition, not merely for the delight of cessation at the goal, but for the positive pleasure of winning. The sublime exercises our athletic joy in challenge, lifting up our powers to encounter grander ideas and aspirations (iv, 7). Burke dwelt on the importance of pain to a proper aesthetics because, like most of his contemporaries, he thought human pains more intense and durable than human pleasures (i, 6). If reaction to the sublime could *incorporate* pain within pleasure, it would lift man's powers to a new and more lasting pitch. That is why the sublime is harsh, stunning, difficult, and terrifying, while beauty is soft, calm, and reassuring.

Burke is rigorous in his logic and reductionism. The mechanics of sensible pain are explored in detail, and Lockean associationism is carried to new extremes: Burke even says we derive ideas of virtue and vice from the tones of voice—soft for virtue, menacing for vice

—used by our parents and nurses when we were children. This was Burke the young philosophe who had mixed with the savants of Paris. His treatise leads more naturally to the works of Sade than toward Burke's attack, in his later years, on the French Revolution. Just as the eighteenth century knew Locke of the *Essay* rather than Locke of the *Treatises*, so Burke was for most of his life the author of the *Sublime and Beautiful*, not of the *Reflections*.

Jefferson's attitude toward Burke's treatise is easily established. He not only owned and read the book in his prepolitical years, he included it in the select list of recommended books he sent to Robert Skipwith in 1771. Burke's volume is included in the seven on "fine arts," along with Lord Kames, Adam Smith on moral sentiments, and—surprising in this category—Johnson's Dictionary. Burke made the basic response to sublimity a painful "astonishment" (ekplēxis) caused by vastness, irregularity, menace. He included in this the menace of height, and noted that this is more terrifying when seen from the top than when looked at from the bottom (ii, 7). Wondering why vastness causes pain, he suggests two explanations—the eye's strain at taking in all the points of vision simultaneously; or, if it takes in only one point at a time, the strain of *traversing* all the points of a vast object. In either case, there is a painful exercise of the retina, or last nervous part of the eye (iv, 6). Burke even challenges the master, Locke himself, in maintaining that darkness is by nature terrifying—it too produces pain in the eye; produces, in fact, a *convulsion* like muscular cramp:

Some, who allow darkness to be a cause of the sublime, would infer, from the dilation of the pupil, that a relaxation may be productive of the sublime, as well as a convulsion; but they do not, I believe, consider that although the circular ring of the iris be in some sense a sphincter, which may possibly be dilated by a simple relaxation, yet in one respect it differs from most of the other sphincters of the body, that it is furnished with antagonist muscles, which are the radial fibres of the iris: no sooner does the circular muscle begin to relax than these fibres, wanting their counterpoise, are forcibly drawn back, and open the pupil to a considerable wideness (iv, 16).

If this "mechanical effect of darkness" explains the power of foul weather and gloomy pictures and night, the *soft* glow of daylight is relaxing to the eye and calls up notions of beauty, not sublimity. Beauty is a matter of gradations, of soothing transition:

> Another principal property of beautiful objects is that the line of their parts is continually varying its direction; but it varies it by a very insensible deviation; it never varies it so quickly as to surprise, or by the sharpness of its angle to cause any twitching or *convulsion* of the optic nerve (iv, 23).

Reminded of this, the reigning theory of the sublime, we must return to the passage where Jefferson uses the word "sublime" twice in a single description. Burke has taught us 1) that the sublime gives pain; 2) that vast height is a source of sublimity; 3) that it is more painful when seen from the top than from the bottom; and 4) that beauty looks to varied and gently altering scenes.

Jefferson on top of the bridge suffers a measurable pain. It is typical of him to give us the measured time it took for the bridge to give him a headache (about a minute). Then we are transferred from top to bottom of the bridge: "If the view from the top be painful and intolerable, that from below is delightful in an equal extreme." I do not know whether Jefferson is using *delight* here in its technical Burkean sense, of surcease from pain; but the general pattern is surely Burkean. Jefferson talks of a "short but very pleasing view" opened to the eye from its lower vantage point. Burke had made smallness of object (and shortness of contemplation) a note of beauty, as relaxing the eye with things easily comprehended and passed over (iv, 24). Jefferson has arranged his description into the two categories of his aesthetic. From the top, the Bridge is mainly sublime; from the bottom, mainly beautiful. He has even let this distinction falsify his memory, putting the view of distant mountains at the *bottom* of the Bridge, though a later visit made him realize it is available only at the top. He did not want to mix the painful and the pleasant, but to keep them separate. This is confirmed by the fact that he manages to keep the distinction even when he is required to correct the description of fact. His revised text runs: "this painful sensation is *relieved* by a short, but pleasing view of the Blue ridge. . . ."

Return, now, to our starting point, to Erik Erikson. With an "Ahah!" for its private meanings, Erikson pounced on this passage of Jefferson's book and said: "Note, if you please, for future reference the juxtaposition of height and downfall, of sublime emotions —and the violent pain in the head." Well, all these have been noted —and have been traced to their proper loci in the discourse of Jefferson's time. He was a scientific observer of man's reactions, talking an understood language with his peers. He is nowhere more technical in this description than when sorting out his pains and pleasures—those immediate sensations that, by way of ekplēxis, motivate a man of sensibility to investigate nature. Chastellux said, toward the end of his own treatment of the Bridge, that it was an object deserving the attention of *"les savants des deux mondes."* Jefferson took the most effective measures for presenting the Bridge to fellow savants in the Old World.

This is one comparatively simple instance of the way Jefferson can be misread when he is read anachronistically. There are many other instances, touching more important things than the Natural Bridge. And the gravest misreadings are of the Declaration of Independence.

"... *agonizing affection* ..."

> I write a careless kind of a civil, nonsensical, good-
> humoured Shandean book, which will do all your hearts
> good—And all your heads too,—provided you under-
> stand it.
>
> —*Tristram Shandy* (6, xvii)

Jefferson owned the works of Laurence Sterne in several editions.
He persistently sought smaller versions, so he could keep this favorite author with him when he traveled. As President, he ordered a
smaller copy of the *Sentimental Journey*. (See Sowerby 4:446 for his
various attempts to order smaller copies.) In 1815, he reordered the
Sermons of Mr. Yorick when he found he was without it. His first
purchase of the *Sermons*, in 1765, is one of the earliest book transactions recorded in Jefferson's life (Peden, 230). In 1771, Jefferson
used the *Sentimental Journey* to prove the moral effect of literature;
and sixteen years later he wrote that "the writings of Sterne particularly form the best course of morality that ever was written"
(*Papers*, 1:77, 12:15). When his wife was dying she wrote out an
affecting passage on death from *Tristram Shandy* (*Papers*, 6:196).
Jefferson finished the passage in his own hand and preserved the
paper with a lock of her hair.

It may surprise some that Jefferson, known neither for his humor
nor (later in his life) for much interest in fiction, should have maintained a lifelong enthusiasm for Sterne. But Sterne was taken far
more seriously as a moral guide in the eighteenth century than we
can readily believe at present. The sentimental didacticism of Richardson is understandable, since there is comparatively little to
distract from his narrative sermonizing. But the sparkle and naugh-
tiness of Sterne seem to undercut his moral lesson for modern
readers (who love him the more for that). We have lost the taste

for blended earthiness and didacticism that explains an eighteenth-century character like Benjamin Franklin's.

Jefferson no doubt enjoyed the humor as well as the philosophy of Sterne. Indeed, his rare attempts at levity tend to echo Sterne's tone. With a rueful air of confession, Jefferson remarked that "architecture is my delight, and putting up and pulling down one of my favorite amusements." This recalls Mr. Yorick's mockery, in his first sermon, of the worldly hedonist who "withdraws himself from the busy part of the world—realises—pulls down—builds up again."

In 1814 Jefferson wrote to John Adams:

> Our machines have now been running for 70. or 80. years, and we must expect that, worn as they are, here a pivot, there a wheel, now a pinion, next a spring, will be giving way: and however we may tinker them up for a while, all will at length surcease motion (Cappon, 2:431).

Sterne likes to exaggerate the "mechanical" approach to man so fashionable in his time:

> Though man is of all others the most curious vehicle, said my father, yet at the same 'tis of so slight a frame and so totteringly put together that the sudden jerks and hard jostlings it unavoidably meets with in this rugged journey would overset and tear it to pieces a dozen times a day—was it not, brother Toby, that there is a sacred spring within us . . . [*Toby mistakes spring for a fountain of faith, and Walter corrects him*] . . . but the spring I am speaking of is that great and elastic power within us of counterbalancing evil, which like a secret spring in a well-ordered machine, though it can't prevent the shock—at least it imposes upon our sense of it (*Tristram Shandy*, 4, viii).

Jefferson gently mocked his own computing habits when he wrote Abigail Adams: "I have compared notes with Mr. Adams on the score of progeny, and find I am ahead of him, and think I am in a fair way to keep so. I have 10½ grandchildren, and 2¾ great-grand-children; and these fractions will ere long become units" (Cappon, 2:367). This resembles Tristram's attitude toward his father's computations:

> My father, as I told you, was a philosopher in grain—speculative,—systematical;—and my aunt Dinah's affair was a matter of as much consequence to him as the retrogradation of the planets to Copernicus:—The backslidings of Venus in her orbit fortified the Copernican system, called

so after his name; and the backslidings of my aunt Dinah in her orbit did the same service in establishing my father's system, which, I trust will forever hereafter be called the *Shandean System*, after his (*Tristram Shandy*, 1, xxi).

Jefferson's habit of casually referring to Sterne's work combines with these comic half-echoes to suggest how close was the mental companionship between the two (cf. *Papers*, 13:104, 14:350). But the depth of Jefferson's appreciation for Sterne as a moral teacher comes out in a far more serious piece of imitation. We know that one sequence in Sterne's works had special meaning for him. When trying to establish the moral effect of literature, he wrote to Robert Skipwith:

We neither know nor care whether Laurence Sterne really went to France, whether he was there accosted by the poor Franciscan, at first rebuked him unkindly, and then gave him a peace offering; or whether the whole be not a fiction. In either case we are equally sorrowful at the rebuke, and secretly resolve we will never do so; we are pleased with the subsequent atonement, and view with emulation a soul candidly acknowledging its fault, and making a just reparation (*Papers*, 1:77).

Jefferson is referring to the series of events which, connecting the opening chapters of the *Sentimental Journey*, became the perfect type of an action performed from moral sentiment. In those episodes, Sterne plays the head against the heart. The heart is ready for generosity when the friar enters the inn; but it is checked by the head, which produces the standard antimonastic arguments of the Enlightenment. Still: "My heart smote me the moment he shut the door" (Stout, ed., 75). When Sterne meets the friar again, he reflects that "When the heart flies out before the understanding, it saves the judgment a world of pains" (91). And amends are made when Sterne gives the friar his "peace-offering of a man who once used you unkindly, but not from his heart" (99).

It is not surprising that, when Jefferson wrote his letter on the Head and the Heart, the model of benevolent action he offered was a simple variation on Sterne's rebuke of the friar and effort to make amends:

When the poor wearied souldier, whom we overtook at Chickahominy with his pack on his back, begged us to let him get up behind our chariot, you [the head] began to calculate that the road was full of souldiers, and that if all should be taken up our horses would fail in their journey. We drove on therefore. But soon becoming sensible you had made me [the heart] do wrong, that tho we cannot relieve all the distressed we should relieve as many as we can, I turned about to take up the souldier; but he had entered a bye path, and was no more to be found; and from that moment to this I could never find him out to ask his forgiveness. Again, when the poor woman came to ask a charity in Philadelphia, you whispered that she looked like a drunkard, and that half a dollar was enough to give her for the ale-house. Those who want the dispositions to give, easily find reasons [like Sterne rejecting the friar] why they ought not to give. When I sought her out afterwards, and did what I should have done at first, you know that she employed the money immediately towards placing her child at school (*Papers*, 10:450–51).

We must take Sterne as seriously as Jefferson did if we are to avoid the very widespread misreadings of Jefferson's Head and Heart letter. It was written in 1786 to Maria Cosway, the painter-wife of the famous miniaturist, Richard Cosway. Jefferson had met them through the American artist, John Trumbull, and made with them a "sentimental journey" of his own through the sights and sounds of Paris and its environs. He indulged romantic gallantries before Maria—in his gambols, he vaulted a stile and broke his right wrist (so badly that he never played the violin again). On the night when Maria left Paris, Jefferson painstakingly wrote, with his left hand, a long letter in dialogue form.

Some of the most eminent Jeffersonians—e.g., Julian Boyd and Merrill Peterson—claim that the Head wins the argument conducted in this letter. For them, the Head is the ruling voice of reason, which always had the last word with Jefferson. As Boyd puts it, Jefferson was a "man to whom reason was not only enthroned as the chief disciplinarian of his life but also, as revealed in the nature of his response to its commands, was itself a sovereign to whom the Head yielded a ready and full allegiance, proud of its monarch and happy in his rule" (*Papers*, 10:453). Oddly enough, some of those who say the Heart wins the debate agree that the Head speaks for duty; they think the Heart successfully rebels.

To reach such conclusions, these readers had to ignore the fact that all the arguments for duty and virtue come from the Heart; that the Head speaks only for a narrow, selfish interest; and that the Head lapses into ineffectual silence, with over a third of the entire dialogue left, to hear the Heart's concluding and triumphant argument.

Part of the game in such lighthearted debate is to be precise about the thing proposed and attacked. The proposition to which both Head and Heart address themselves is this: Should we see the Cosways again? The Heart wins, of course, or this letter would not have been sent, looking forward to further meetings and even inviting the Cosways to America. The subject of the debate is first sounded, from a distance, in the Head's opening complaint, that the Heart should not have made friends with the Cosways in the first place. For "we had no occasion for new acquaintance" (444). Heart answers that the Head has no one to blame but itself, since they went out, originally, to study architecture (the Head's province). The two quibble back and forth, remembering scenes traversed with Maria (for Mr. Cosway is included only as a gesture to propriety).

The Head concludes this squabble with the proposition it has been defending all along: "you should abandon the idea of ever seeing them again" (446). Parting is painful, as the Heart just found out, and it will just get more painful every time the experience is renewed. The Head wants to "make you sensible how imprudent it is to place your affections, without reason, on objects you must so soon lose, and whose loss when it comes must cost you such severe pangs . . . The art of life is avoiding pain" (1:448).

That last sentence is the supreme heresy for the lachrymose (*larmoyant*) genre of writing that Sterne partly satirizes but ultimately endorses. Tears—of compassion, regret, or tenderness—were the sign of a heart not "senseless" of true feeling. Diderot wrote Voltaire that if people but weep, they cannot be wicked (*Correspondence*, 3:292) and said his orgasmic nun must be good because sensible (*La religieuse*, Pléiade, 345). In Marmontel's story, "La bonne mère," a mother chooses the more virtuous of two men for her daughter to marry by observing which one cries more at the theater. Voltaire judged the merit of his own plays by the tears they caused, and made the converted Gusman say in *Alzire*, "*Tout vous est pardonné puisque je vois vos pleurs.*" So Jefferson's Heart begins its long last answer with that Enlightenment topos, "*la douceur de pleurer*":

And what more sublime delight than to mingle tears with one whom the hand of heaven hath smitten! To watch over the bed of sickness and to beguile it's tedious and it's painful moments! To share our bread with one to whom misfortune has left none! This world abounds indeed with misery: to lighten it's burthen we must divide it with one another.

It is the world of Greuze we enter here, of refined sensitivity that mingles pain with pleasure and teaches men through tears. Jefferson calls this delight "sublime," and had learned from Burke that sublimity includes pain in one's joy—as does a view from the Natural Bridge. So the Heart goes on to say, of this compassionate weeping: "Grief, with such a comfort, is almost a luxury!"

The Heart attacks the Head's "mathematical balance" (449), which tries to trade off pain against pleasure on a calculus—just the effort we saw exemplified in the moral syllogisms of William Wollaston (see chapter Ten). That, says the Heart, is a "miserable arithmetic," the product of "frigid speculations" which can "mistake for happiness the mere absence of pain" (450). This is the *vil intérêt* Voltaire presents as the enemy of virtue in *Mérope*. It is a misapplication of science, where the Head should serve the Heart.

The doctrinal center of this rebuttal by the Heart repeats the technical exposition of moral-sense philosophy:

Respect for you has induced me to enter into this discussion, and to hear principles uttered which I detest and abjure. Respect for myself now obliges me to recall you into the proper limits of your office. When nature assigned us the same habitation, she gave us over it a divided empire. To you she allotted the field of science, to me that of morals.

The Head cannot speak of duty or virtue, for the reasons we looked at in Part Three of this book. It is not a principle of action, but only of reflection. It weighs the means; it cannot determine the end—to use the distinction of Hume, who wrote in the *Treatise,* "Reason is, and ought only to be, the slave of the passions; and can never pretend to any other office than to serve and obey them" (Selby-Bigge, 415). The Head is told to limit itself to matters of technique, of perfecting the means toward higher ends (which must be chosen by a higher faculty):

When the circle is to be squared, or the orbit of a comet to be traced; when the arch of greatest strength, or the solid of least resistance is to be investigated, take you the problem: it is yours: nature has given me no cognisance of it.

When the Heart speaks of its own higher office, it lists the classical moral-sense virtues—sympathy (as in Smith), benevolence (as in Hutcheson), gratitude (as in all the moral-sense philosophers), justice (as in Kames), love and friendship (aspects of benevolence):

> In like manner in denying to you the feelings of sympathy, of benevolence, of gratitude, of justice, of love, of friendship, she has excluded you from their controul. To these she has adapted the mechanism of the heart.

Hutcheson had popularized the mechanical view of virtue as a momentum acquired by the impact of benevolent deeds on the spectator. And that mechanics is automatic in everyone, not dependent on theory:

> Morals were too essential to the happiness of man to be risked on the incertain combinations of the head. She laid their foundation therefore in sentiment, not in science.

That last sentence reverses our normal way of looking at things—which explains why it is so often misread. We think of science as comparatively stable, objective, and normative; while sentiment is considered light, trivial, and shifting. The misreading of this letter can be seen as part of a larger pattern of misunderstandings. Boyd misinterprets the Head's role here, just as Winthrop Jordan misread the slavery passage in *Notes on the State of Virginia* and Erik Erikson misread the same text's treatment of the Natural Bridge. In all three cases—to which, in time we must add the Declaration—modern men are not able to believe that Jefferson considered "sentiment" the superior faculty in man. The Heart's superiority to the Head explains the blacks' equality of moral sense with white men and the proper response to sublime sights like the Natural Bridge.

Jefferson was a "sentimentalist" in Sterne's meaning of the term —a meaning common in the Parisian circles of Jefferson and Mrs. Cosway when this letter was written. The development of French "*sensibilité*" roughly paralleled (and cross-pollinated) Scottish thought on the moral sense. The model was the same—a mechanics of external sensation as expounded by Locke. (Condillac had established in France an authentic Lockean sensationalism.) The Abbé de Saint-Pierre invented a word, "*bienfaisance*," that played the same role Shaftesbury's "moral sense" played in Scottish thought after Hutcheson had specified it as benevolence—as the aesthetics of sensibility in Jean-Baptiste Dubos' *Réflexions* (1719) resembled that of Shaftesbury's *Characteristics*. The Enlightenment Jesuit Claude Buffier gave *"sens commun"* a meaning that anticipated (and later influenced) Reid's treatment of the same subject. And Buffier's very language, as well as his thought, went into the Encyclopédie article on "Sens commun" (written by the Chevalier de Jaucourt). Jaucourt gave credit to Hutcheson for the doctrine that had influenced Burlamaqui and others in the article on *"Sens moral"* as *"un sentiment de bienveillance . . . toujours plus vif et plus prompt qui n'est le raissonement"* because it works *"par une sorte de sensation et par goût."*

All the related 1765 Encyclopédie articles on the senses reflect an overwhelming consensus among the philosophes that *"sensibilité"* was the highest moral guide for man. Thus Jaucourt's article on *"Sensibilité"* proclaims the heart's superiority to the head:

> SENSIBILITÉ, (*Morale*) *disposition tendre et delicate de l'ame, qui la rend facile à être émue, à être touchée.*
>
> *La sensibilité d'ame, dit très-bien l'auteur des moeurs* [Voltaire], *donne une sorte de sagacité sur les choses honnêtes, et va plus loin que la pénétration de l'esprit seul. . . . La réflexion peut faire l'homme de probité; mais la sensibilité fait l'homme vertueux.*

Jaucourt defines "Sentiment" as another word for *"la sensibilité du coeur."*

Voltaire was referred to, in the *"Sensibilité"* article, as holding to the heart's superiority. Voltaire's plays and poems reflect the aesthetic of Dubos and turn often on the conflict between *"coeur"* and *"l'esprit."* Thus the moral of *Charlot* is put in these lines:

> *Les vices de l'esprit peuvent se corriger;*
> *Quand le coeur est mauvais, rien ne peut le changer.*

And *Mérope* is meant to teach that *"il ne faut consulter que le ciel et son coeur."* The conflict of the head and heart was endlessly explored, as in Antoine Pecquet's *Parallèle du coeur et de l'esprit* or the Marquis de Charost's *Réflexions sur l'esprit et le coeur* (cf. Mauzi, 514 ff.). The idéologues continued the moral emphasis on *"sensibilité"* despite their increased sophistication of social analysis (cf. Moravia, 158, 187); and Jefferson's own friend, Dupont de Nemours, wrote *"En médecine, suivez la nature. En philosophie, écoutez l'instinct"* (*Philosophie de l'Univers*, 205–6). Just as Hutcheson came back to Bentham by way of Beccaria, so moral-sense philosophy came back into English poetry by way of books expressing French *sensibilité*—e.g., in Hannah More's 1782 poem, *Sensibility:*

> Sweet sensibility! thou keen delight!
> Thou hasty moral! sudden sense of right!
> Thou untaught goodness! Virtue's precious seed!
> Thou sweet precursor of the gen'rous deed!
> Beauty's quick relish! Reason's radiant morn,
> Which dawns soft light before Reflexion's born.

Jefferson would in any event have been receptive to this French teaching, since he was trained to its basic tenets by the Scots. But it was kept vividly before him in his regular reading of Sterne. The relation of Walter and Toby in *Tristram Shandy* is often presented as a struggle between head and heart—with Walter undergoing periodic conversions (e.g., at 3, xxiv) to the "higher sense" represented unwittingly by Toby. (When this occurs, the play of knowledge and virtue becomes more complex, Tristram standing for the cool narrative head, Toby for the heart, and Walter for the integration of the two.) The real aim of the later *Sermons* is spelled out by the rueful Yorick's comment on the sample he has with him in the book:

> I was delivered of it at the wrong end of me—it came from my head instead of my heart. . . . To preach, to show the extent of our reading, or the subtleties of our wit . . . 'tis not preaching the gospel—but ourselves—For my own part, continued Yorick, I had rather direct five words point-blank to the heart (4, xxvi).

Thus, in attacking the human disorder that gives men heads like pumpkins and hearts like pippins (5, ix), Sterne was preaching with earthy laughter the moral Crébillon *fils* reached by way of bitter disillusion in *Les Égarements du coeur et de l'esprit* (second part, 1738): *"s'il est presque impossible de se corriger du vices du coeur, on revient des erreurs d'esprit."*

One of the more interesting aspects of Jefferson's letter is that he attributes the American Revolution itself to the moral guidance of the Heart:

> If our country, when pressed with wrongs at the point of the bayonet, had been governed by it's heads instead of it's hearts, where would we have been now? hanging on a gallows as high as Haman's. You began to calculate and to compare wealth and numbers: we threw up a few pulsa-

tions of our warmest blood: we supplied enthusiasm against wealth and numbers: we put our existence to the hazard, when the hazard seemed against us, and we saved our country: justifying at the same time the ways of Providence, whose precept is to do always what is right, and leave the issue to him (451).

This was written on the eve of the French Revolution, which came as a patriotic outburst of feeling, to glorify emotions like *"gloire"* and *"fraternité."* The American Revolution is sometimes contrasted with the French, as a more calculating and legally re-formist series of acts. But Jefferson gives, here, a very different pic-ture of the first Revolution of the modern world; he makes it the re-sult of American "hearts" throwing up "a few pulsations of our warmest blood." It might be thought Jefferson was altering his memory of the prior decade because of the atmosphere in Paris. But the Declaration as he wrote it mentions "the last stab to ago-nizing affection"; and we shall weigh reasons, later, for consider-ing the Declaration's real point "sentimental"—i.e., grounded upon *"sensibilité."*

Meanwhile, Jefferson's picture of the Revolution allows us to date from an early time—well before his presidency—his "geographical" reading of the Revolution's history. It is well known that he de-spised New Englanders when he was President. But in 1785, the year before his letter to Mrs. Cosway, he had pictured Northerners and Southerners in America as representing, collectively, the na-tion's head and heart. He was writing to the Marquis de Chastellux, correcting the latter's book on America.

In the North they are	In the South they are
cool	fiery
sober	voluptuary
laborious	indolent
persevering	unsteady
independant	independant
jealous of their own liberties, and just to those of others	zealous for their own liberties, but trampling on those of others [i.e., the slaves]
interested	
chicaning	generous
superstitious and hypocritical in their religion	candid
	without attachment or pretensions to any religion but that of the heart

The faults and virtues of the North are those of the head—it is "interested," out for gain, calculating and "chicaning." It does just what Jefferson's letter to Mrs. Cosway attacks the Head for doing at the Revolution's opening: "You began to calculate and to compare wealth and numbers" (451). The South, by contrast, is warm and impulsive, generous and fiery—just what makes the Heart win the Revolution by "pulsations." Most important, the South is directly credited with a religion of the heart—the title often given to Voltaire's brand of deism, by contrast with that of Englishmen like Toland. The warm and optimistic love of Providence better expresses Jefferson's religious and moral views than does the ordinary "deist" picture of a cold regard for the Great Watchmaker. It is natural, therefore, for Jefferson to move from the duties of friendship, in his letter to Mrs. Cosway, through those of patriotism, to an emotional trust in Providence. That *is* Voltaire's religion of the heart; and it was always the worldview of Jefferson.

TWENTY-ONE

"... bands which have connected ..."

> The whole system of the mind, especially our moral
> faculty, shows that we are under natural bonds of
> beneficence and humanity toward all, and under many
> more special ties to some of our fellows, binding us to
> many services of a higher kind than what the rest can
> claim.
>
> —Francis Hutcheson (5:281)

The importance of *"sensibilité"* to the philosophes explains the force of one argument made by Buffon against the American continent. Jefferson quoted that charge before laboring to refute it in his *Notes on the State of Virginia:*

Although the savage of the new world is about the same height as man in our world, this does not suffice for him to constitute an exception to the general fact that all living nature has become smaller on that continent. The savage is feeble, and has small organs of generation; he has neither hair nor beard, and no ardor whatever for his female; although swifter than the European because he is better accustomed to running, he is, on the other hand, less strong in body; he is also less sensitive, and yet more timid and cowardly; he has no vivacity, no activity of mind; the activity of his body is less an exercise, a voluntary motion, than a necessary action caused by want; relieve him of hunger and thirst, and you deprive him of the active principle of all his movements; he will rest stupidly upon his legs or lying down entire days. There is no need for seeking further the cause of the isolated mode of life of these savages and their repugnance for society: the most precious spark of the fire of nature has been refused to them; they lack ardor for their females, and consequently have no love for their fellow men: not knowing this strongest and most tender of all affections, their other feelings are also cold and languid; they love their parents and children but little; the most intimate of all ties, the family connection, binds them therefore but loosely together; between family and family there is no tie at all; hence they have no communion, no commonwealth, no state of society. Physical love constitutes their only morality; their heart is icy, their society cold, and their rule harsh.

To grasp the import of that passage, we should compare it with Jefferson's analysis of Negro disabilities. Jefferson denied the Negro talent, beauty, and intellect; but recognized in him the greater gifts of the heart, moral sense, and the virtues. Buffon, by contrast, stresses precisely the lack of such sociability among Indians—"their heart is icy." For him, the Indians are weak not only in body and head, but especially in the highest faculties of benevolence. If this analysis were validated, then Indians would indeed be an exception to the proposition that all men are created equal—and Buffon understood these implications. He goes on, in the passage quoted, to conclude: "Nature, by refusing him the power of love, has treated him worse and lowered him deeper than any animal."

The challenge to Jefferson was even greater, therefore, than has been generally thought. He was not only defending the honor of the continent, as he did when arguing that other animals were as large in America as in Europe. He was defending the basis of his whole political creed, the belief that all men possess an equal and automatically functioning moral sense, to serve as the ground for rights and self-rule. He had strenuously countered objections to this belief, based on the black slaves' thieving habits, even when the honor of the continent was not at stake. Now he had an overlap of motives to make him muster all his forces of argument against Buffon. Buffon's view was menacing precisely because it took the Enlightenment approach of judging men on the basis of their "bienfaisance," which Voltaire called the entirety of virtue. Buffon struck at the basis of all social bonds, the Indian family. All the Scottish school had made the mutual love of family members the highest manifestation of benevolence, and Hume was very precise in identifying sexual attraction as the principal social force:

But in order to form society, 'tis requisite not only that it be advantageous, but also that men be sensible of these advantages; and 'tis impossible, in their wild uncultivated state, that by study and reflection alone they should ever be able to attain this knowledge. Most fortunately, therefore, there is conjoined to those necessities, whose remedies are remote and obscure, another necessity which, having a present and more obvious remedy, may justly be regarded as the first and original principle of human society. This necessity is no other than that natural appetite betwixt the sexes, which unites them together and preserves their union until a new tie takes place in their concern for their common offspring. This new concern becomes also a principle of union betwixt the parents and offspring, and forms a more numerous society . . . (*Treatise*, 3, ii, 2).

The highest form of benevolence was not, for the philosophes, the least "interested" but the most necessary—since they sought the elements of predictable and automatic attraction in human society. Mother love is certainly self-sacrificing in the vulgar sense, but it is also a compulsion *of* the self. This explains the philosophes' interest in the bourgeois family drama—in the plays of Diderot, in the paintings of Greuze.

Thus, to establish a moral sense in the American Indian, Jefferson had to prove he was capable of sexual and parental love: "his sensibility is keen, even the warriors weeping most bitterly on the loss of their children, though in general they endeavour to appear superior to human events" (60). The slow increase of Indian population was an embarrassment to Jefferson's thesis; but he argues this is not for lack of sexual ardor. Since Indian women must attend their men in war and on hunts, they practice abortion "by the uses of some vegetable" (60). Besides, their women's hard labor leads to frequent miscarriages and accidental infertility (61).

Buffon argued that, without strong families, the Indians can have no commonwealth or state at all. Jefferson admits the scarceness of positive law or the machinery and offices of state—but turns that argument on its head by saying this proves the force of social ties:

The principles of their society forbidding all compulsion, they are to be led to duty and to enterprize by personal influence and persuasion. Hence eloquence in council, bravery and address in war, become the foundations of all consequence with them. To these acquirements all their faculties are directed (62).

Jefferson says the colonists learned to their cost how brave the Indians could be in war—which involves not only the warriors' co-operation with each other, but the force of shame and benevolence making a man fear to show respected fellows any cowardice or expose his family to peril. This proves the essential point—the existence of moral sense, in Indians as in blacks: "Their only controuls are their manners, and that moral sense of right and wrong, which, like the sense of tasting and feeling, in every man makes a part of his nature (93).

Oratory is an even greater proof of sensibility, since eloquence can only sway people by reaching their feelings, by presenting shared ideals, shaming, challenging, inspiring (cf. Shaftesbury, *Characteristics*, misc. 3, ch. 1). The Mingo (Iroquois) chief Logan was thus able to equal, or even excel, a Demosthenes or Cicero, despite the primitive civilization he grew up in.

Admittedly the Indian looks hard and hostile to an outsider, whom he fears. But one must grant:

that he is affectionate to his children, careful of them, and indulgent in the extreme: that his affections comprehend his other connections, weakening, as with us, from circle to circle, as they recede from the center: that his friendships are strong and faithful to the uttermost extremity (60).

Jefferson is stating a very important doctrine of moral-sense theory in this passage—that benevolence is not "universal" if that means *equally* exerted among all men, whoever they are or wherever encountered. Benevolence is an organizing principle in society, much as gravity is the binding force of the universe; and as gravity differs according to mass and distance, so benevolence is a matter of cohering social *systems*. Hutcheson used the comparison, in his first work, that would be repeated by all the moral-sense theorists:

This universal benevolence toward all men we may compare to that principle of gravitation which perhaps extends to all bodies in the universe. But, like the love of benevolence, [it] increases as the distance is diminished; and is strongest when bodies come to touch each other. Now this increase of attraction upon nearer approach is as necessary to the frame of the universe as that there should be any attraction at all—for a general attraction, equal in all distances, would by the contrariety of such multitudes of equal forces, put an end to all regularity of motion and perhaps stop it altogether. This increase of love toward the benevolent, according to their nearer approaches to ourselves by their benefits, is observable in the high degree of love which heroes and law-givers universally obtain in their own countries, above what they find abroad, even among those who are not insensible of their virtues—and in all the strong ties of friendship, acquaintance, neighborhood, partnership, which are exceedingly necessary to the order of human society (1:198–99—cf. Adam Smith, *Moral Sentiments*, 6, ii, 1).

For thinkers of the moral-sense school, even war and hatred were manifestations of affection and benevolence. Connection with one's own system of social ties makes for enmity toward an alien system threatening it. Thus the mother will die for her child, the patriot for his country. Though the mind may mistake the grounds for conflict, or misinterpret a menace, response to the menace is automatic and powerful because the bonds of affection are so strong (cf. Adam Ferguson, *Civil Society*, 28–45). The stronger the family ties, the stronger will civil ones be; and this is a necessity without which there would be no binding order in human life. Hume put it this way:

In proportion to the station which a man possesses, according to the relations in which he is placed, we always expect from him a greater or less degree of good and, when disappointed, blame his inutility; and much more do we blame him if any ill or prejudice arises from his conduct and behavior. When the interests of one country interfere with those of another, we estimate the merits of a statesman by the good or ill which results to his own country from his measures and counsels, without regard to the prejudice which he brings on its enemies and rivals. His fellow citizens are the objects which lie nearest the eye while we determine his character. And as nature has implanted in everyone a superior affection to his own country, we never expect any regard to distant nations where a competition arises. Not to mention that while every man consults the good of his own community, we are sensible that the general interest of mankind is better promoted than by any loose indeterminate views to the good of a species, whence no beneficial action could ever result for want of a duly limited object on which they could exert themselves (*Enquiry, Morals*, 5, ii).

The principles of social "gravity" were explored in Newtonian terms. Hutcheson even suggested that "interest," which other philosophers misname self-love, serves the benevolent system: It plays the role of *cohesion* within a mass to make the *movement* of masses possible under the forces of attraction (1:263). Lord Kames noted how unfamiliar human systems, though distant from us, exert an attraction by their cumulative immensity, making it possible to love all mankind in a vague way, at least (*Principles*, 78–82).

Gravity is a single force with multiple manifestations. In the same way, benevolence was used to explain all the systems-within-systems of social organization. Not only did society exist in counterpoise with society, but interests and groups within a society formed countervailing clusters. The principles of mechanical balance were manifested even within the individual, for whom Hutcheson framed his algebraic formulae to find the "moment" of virtue produced by the counteraction of Interest and Benevolence. Then there was the play of public against private benevolence:

> With this balance of public passions against the private, with our passions toward honor and virtue, we find that human nature may be as really amiable in its low sphere as superior natures endowed with higher reason and influenced only by pure desires—provided we exercise the powers we have in keeping this balance of affections . . . (Hutcheson 2:54).

We find here the real source of that concept of balanced social interest that informs the American Constitution. It has been assumed in the past that a Lockean individualism and Adam Smith competitiveness explain the mechanics of our Constitution as expounded in the *Federalist* papers. But Smith believed in competing *systems* (formed by a co-operative division of labor) rather than individualism. And moral sympathy drove society's whole machinery in his theory. Social mechanics were developed in a subtle and thorough way by the Scots, who taught a whole generation of the founding fathers. Dr. Witherspoon at Princeton especially loved the principle of social "overpoise," as he called it; and his student James Madison drew on Hume's essays in writing *Federalist* 10, the classic exposition of social mechanics (see Adair's "That Politics May Be Reduced to a Science," *Huntington Quarterly*, 1957).

Jefferson, in his answer to Buffon, was thus using the Ferguson paradox—he proved that Indians love by showing that they hate. If they are powerful in war against others, they must cohere among themselves. We have already seen that the principle of social homogeneity within smaller systems was supported by Jefferson in the *Notes;* that is why he opposed wholesale immigration, which would

loosen the social bonds by destroying the common ethos and republican character of Virginian society (*Notes*, 84–85).

Language of tightening or loosening the social bonds was the
special currency of moral-sense philosophers. The necessary action
of benevolence becomes a "tie" or "bond" or "chain" linking the
parts of each system. To take just one work of Hutcheson, the
seminal 1725 *Inquiry*, we find this language running through the
book:

Whence this secret chain between each person and mankind? How is
my interest connected with the most distant parts of it? (111)

You shall find a bond of benevolence further extended than a family
and children, although the ties are not so strong (146).

The highest benevolence possible would not lead a wise man to prefer
another to himself were there no ties of gratitude . . . (162).

. . . overpower benevolence in its strongest ties . . . (185).

. . . who should be dear to him by the ties of nature . . . (192).

. . . all the strong ties of friendship, acquaintance, neighborhood,
partnership . . . (199).

. . . the stronger ties of benevolence . . . (263).

The stronger ties of benevolence, in equal abilities, must produce a
greater moment of good in equally good characters than the weaker ties.
Thus natural affection, gratitude, friendship have greater effects than
general benevolence (269).

. . . the good offices of the stronger ties (270).

My point is not merely that Hutcheson, here as elsewhere, used a
common metaphor of binding or tying to express social connection,
but that the bond referred to is *always* one of *affection*. Others
speak of political bondage as submission or oppression or sovereignty or duty. The moral-sense school gives the terms bond and tie
a technical sense to parallel the action of gravity in the physical
order. Benevolence supplies all "the bands of society" (Ferguson,
Civil Society, 79).

A question naturally arises here: Was Jefferson using "political
bands" in the preamble to the Declaration as Ferguson used "the
bands of political union" (ibid., 395, 435), referring to the bands of

affection in the moral-sense terminology? Fortunately, we can give that question a certain answer. There are three arguments, of increasing force, to lead us to this conclusion.

First, Jefferson's bands are not those of subjection to King or Parliament, but the kind that bind "one people . . . with another." The bands, in other words, have united Americans to "our British brethren," as they are later called in the Declaration. These cannot be bands of subservience, of obedience to superiors. British subjects living in England and in America are equal, Jefferson has argued all along (*Papers*, 1:126), and the bond between equals is one of brotherhood. In *A Summary View*, Jefferson said the British and American peoples were connected by "fraternal love and harmony" (ibid., 1:135).

That argument from the very phrasing is confirmed by Jefferson's only recorded prior use of "bands" to express political connection. In the draft for Virginia's answer to Lord North, he speaks of "those bands of amity with our fellow subjects which we would wish to remain indissoluble" (1:171). In the Declaration, the hope for such indissoluble bands gives way to the necessity for dissolving them. The same bands are obviously at stake in both passages.

Aside, even, from such verbal concinnities, there is ample evidence for Jefferson's belief, in the 1770s, that government is based on ties of affection. We looked, earlier, at Jefferson's contention that expatriation had made the colonists independent at the time of their departure from the motherland. But the colonists, once established in America, recontracted for a common executive; and Jefferson makes the motive for this new charter explicit in several places. In his Declaration of the Causes and Necessity for Taking Up Arms, Jefferson wrote: "To continue the connection with their friends whom they had left, they arranged themselves by charters of compact under one common king" (ibid., 1:199). At first he wrote "whom they had left and loved" (ibid., 1:193). He removed "loved"; and there were several good reasons for doing that. The past tense would suggest a love *already* discontinued, while Jefferson was still arguing in 1775 that America's love could be maintained if grievances were redressed. Besides, the note of love was already expressed in calling the English "friends." And a few sentences later, Jefferson says that certain past grievances were borne "through warmth of affection" (1:199). In his earlier resolution,

Jefferson welcomed Lord North's "benevolent tender" because he professed the wish for "perpetual continuance of that brotherly love we bear to our fellow subjects" (1:170).

In the deleted part of the Declaration itself, Jefferson describes again the adoption of "one common king, thereby laying a foundation for perpetual league and amity with them" [i.e., with the "British brethren"]. This mention of amity, looking back to the "bands of amity," shows that the whole verbal cluster expressed in these early documents was taken from the moral-sense philosophy of government. The political bands are those of benevolence, formalized by compact to continue an existing affection.

Jefferson's treatment of Indian society gives us an insight into his understanding of government and makes it possible to correct one common view of his politics. Several of Jefferson's dicta are sometimes paraphrased to say that governments govern best when they govern least. That has been taken as an expression of extreme individualism verging on anarchy; it seems at the farthest pole from Scottish belief in government as an expression of man's basic sociability. But Jefferson praises the Indians for needing few positive laws since their social ideals are so shared and binding that little coercion is needed to enforce them. They need little government, not because the individual is self-sufficient and divided from his fellows, but because they are such a compact society, swayable by admiration of the same things and desire for each other's respect. Government, though based on the social affections, must at times supply their partial defect—as Hutcheson taught (6:212 ff.), along with Hume (*Treatise*, 537–38). Jefferson's admiration for social cohesion appears not only in his comments on the Indians, but in his desire to preserve homogeneity in America by controlling the influx of immigrants. That is not the stance of a pure individualist, of the sort Albert Jay Nock tried to make of his hero. It is the teaching of the Enlightenment as that was understood (for example) by Diderot:

Man is born for society. Separate him, strand him, you scramble his thoughts, pervert his character. Silly urges rise in his heart. Wild thoughts burgeon in his mind, like thorns in a wilderness (*La religieuse*, Pléiade, 342).

TWENTY-TWO

" . . . *one people* . . . "

> This is not inflaming or exaggerating matters, but trying
> them by those feelings and affections which nature
> justifies, and without which we should be incapable of
> discharging the social duties of life. . . .
>   —Thomas Paine

The idea that different social systems cluster and counterbalance, all under the driving force of benevolence, raises the problem of different cultures and how they might live together. Locke's limited defense of slavery (*Treatise*, 2:23–24, 85, 172) was a recognition that some cannot live together on an equal basis. The conqueror in war can take the life of one who tried to take his. But he can also spare it, and demand war reparations in the form of penal servitude, for a certain period or a whole lifetime. Such slaves are, in effect, dead to the law, slavery being "but the state of war continued," where no containing social compact is possible (ibid., 2:24). The slaves' lives were forfeit once, and remain at the disposal of the sparing conqueror.

In the earliest indication left us of Jefferson's attitude toward slavery, this Lockean argument is rejected. Jefferson inserted a passage running across the bottom of three pages in his copy of Lord Kames's *Essays on the Principles of Morality*. The handwriting is very young, so Sowerby (2:11–12) argues the book must have escaped the Shadwell fire:

This is a remarkable instance of improvement in the moral sense. The putting to death captives in war was a general practice among savage nations. When men became more humanized the captive was indulged with life on condition of holding it in perpetual slavery; a condition exacted on this supposition, that the victor had right to take his life, and consequently to commute it for his services. At this stage of refinement were the Greeks about the time of the Trojan war. At this day it is perceived we have no right to take the life of an enemy unless where our own preservation renders it necessary. But the ceding his life in commutation for service admits there was neither necessity nor right to take it, because you have not done it. And if there was neither necessity nor right to take his life then is there no right to his service in commutation for it. This doctrine is acknowledged by later writers, Montesquieu, Burlamaqui, etc., who yet suppose it just to require a ransom from the captive. One advance further in refinement will relinquish this also. If we have no right to the life of a captive, we have no right to his labor; if none to his labor we have none to his absent property which is but the fruit of that labor. In fact, ransom is but commutation in another form.

Though the passage speaks of advances in "the moral sense," Adrienne Koch uses it in her effort to play down the Scottish influence on Jefferson. She says the concept of a *developing* moral sense was foreign to orthodox Hutchesonians. We have seen that is not true. Hutcheson explains the differences between men all possessing an equal moral sense by the refinements of their nurture and education. Besides, the moral sense is closely related to the aesthetic "inner sense" that civilizes man in Hutcheson's scheme of things. (Koch, it will be remembered, used another passage copied into Jefferson's books to prove he was not a Humean—and then Lucia White found the passage came from Hume himself!)

There is more than the mention of "moral sense" to connect this passage with Hutcheson. It was Hutcheson who penned the most complete early refutation of Locke's case for slavery—cf. Wylie Sypher, *Journal of Negro History*, 1939. Hutcheson attacked the capture-thesis of enslavement in his *System of Moral Philosophy* (1755), the principal textbook of America's colleges on the eve of our Revolution. And it should be noticed that one of the authors cited in the passage Jefferson put in his copy of Kames was Burlamaqui, Hutcheson's Swiss disciple. Jaucourt, who was a student of Hutcheson by 1765 at the latest, credited him as *"un homme anglois* [sic] *moderne plein de lumière et d'humanité"* with refuting the capture theory (Encyclopédie, s.v. *"Traité des nègres"*). Earlier, in the article on *"Esclavage,"* he had referred to Montesquieu's attack on this theory (*L'esprit*, 15); but he must have learned in the interval that Hutcheson's refutation was more thorough and detailed. (It was also written before Montesquieu's, though published later.)

Hutcheson connects the rejection of the captive theory to re-finements in the moral sense, the very thing Koch thought non-Hutchesonian: "Must not all the sentiments of compassion and hu-manity, as well as reflection upon the general interest of mankind, dissuade from such usage of captives, even though it could be vin-dicated by some plea of external right?" (6:203). Jaucourt, at "*Es-clavage*," 938, said no modern people but the Tartars practice en-slavement by war, since that takes the suppression of "*tout senti-ment généreux.*" Montesquieu had said only cannibals now enslave by capture.

Locke was still open to an argument for slavery because he began with a basic view of man as property. Hutcheson's starting point was very different: "No damage done, or crime committed, can change a rational creature into a piece of goods . . ." (ibid., 202–3). Hutcheson denies the right, even in a just war, to enslave conquered combatants (208), much less civilians (203 ff.). In an in-teresting anticipation of Nuremberg principles, he admits the possi-bility of punishment only for "unjust governors, and their coun-sellors and ministers" (207)—and even they must not be treated as "a piece of goods." (Such a small group would not tempt men to war as a means of acquiring hordes of slaves.)

Hutcheson denies the whole argument that a life can be "owned" by another because that other spared it: "At this rate, one would be obliged to become a slave to any powerful pirate or robber who had spared his life" (210). Jaucourt, in his 1765 article, says of the "sparing" conqueror: "*On a comprit que cette prétendue charité n'est que celle d'un brigand.*" By a *reductio ad absurdum*, Hutche-son shows that such a principle would make most of us somebody else's slave. Even "princes may thus owe their lives to midwives, surgeons, or physicians, who might have murdered them with im-punity" (210).

So Jefferson copied into his copy of Lord Kames—into a book that itself illustrated the progress of moral refinement—a view of enslave-ment quite at home in the moral-sense school, as that was taught to Americans in New York, Princeton, Philadelphia, and Williams-burg. His very choice and writing out of the passage shows that, from an early age, he knew enslavement was wrong, no matter what Locke or others said on the matter.

But enslavement, and the slave trade, were one thing. Retaining slaves, within a system already established, was another. Jefferson thought this was defensible, and even a duty, under certain circumstances. For one thing, he thought wholesale manumission in the Virginia of his day would lead straight to race war, ending in genocide—since the whites had all the wealth and weapons and outside support.

To weigh his argument properly, we must begin with a recognition that manumission was not always desirable. Slaveholders were not allowed to free anyone they wanted to. The result, with evil masters, would have been the "freeing" of the old, the sick, the crazy, the troublemakers, the disabled—to starve or steal, to prey on or be the prey of a hostile society. Virginia's laws made this impossible.

Even to release a slave of sound mind and body was not possible without provision for his later sustenance. Where would he go? How would he live? Colonial Virginia was organized around the great plantations. It had no major ports or urban centers, into whose proletariat freedmen might be absorbed (a difficult enough thing even in Boston or Philadelphia). There was no natural place, off the plantation, for the acculturation of free blacks in any number. Small planters feared and hated even more than large ones the thought of free blacks going armed in their midst.

Thus the master who took his slave to the county court to certify his manumission had to produce evidence that the slave had a skill and a place to use it, or the means to leave the state. In this way, a lawyer like George Wythe could free his few slaves, which were not necessary to his income. But how was the owner of a large plantation to free his work force? Most such owners were in debt, and their only wealth was in their land. But the land itself was useless without cheap labor. Without their slaves, most owners did not have the resources necessary for freeing their slaves—a vicious circle. This explains the elaborate arrangements even a successful planter like George Washington had to make in order to free part of his work force, the unentailed non-Custis part, at his wife's death (Flexner, 4:112–25, 432–47). It was legally impossible for Jefferson, who was always in debt, to free any but a few of his slaves.

In these circumstances, Jefferson thought individual manumission a disservice to the community and to the freedmen themselves. Any but a very rare freedman was resented or unwanted on most plantations. If part or all of his family was freed with him, it became an even greater burden on his already precarious existence. If part or all of his family was not freed with him, he might remain or return wherever they were, making him a threat to the owner or his overseer. If the freedman was unmarried, where would he find a free mate or bring up his free children? Or would he seek some woman still enslaved, whose owner would resist him?

In a world where guns were a virtual necessity for the free man, a freed black could not own a gun unless he became a householder —which was one reason much of the white population tried to prevent him from becoming one. Edmund Morgan has demonstrated, in *American Slavery, American Freedom,* how much of Virginia's history and mentality was shaped by the urgency to keep weapons from the blacks. (Even in the hands of poor white men they had proved a very real danger.)

Jefferson also thought individual manumission would distract men from the larger effort necessary in the long run—a general manumission accompanied by deportation. That is why Jefferson freed only mulattoes light enough to "pass" as white, most of whom he did not consider truly black any more, so not legally subject to slavery: "You asked me in conversation, what constituted a mulatto by our law. . . . Our canon considers two crosses with the pure white and a third with any degree of mixture, however small, as clearing the issue of negro blood." As usual, he tried to put mathematics to the service of enlightenment:

Let us express the pure blood of the white in the capital letters of the printed alphabet, the pure blood of the negro in the small letters of the printed alphabet, and any given mixture of either, by way of abridgement in MS. letters.

Let the first crossing be of a, pure negro, with A, pure white. The unit of blood of the issue being composed of the half of that of each parent will be $\frac{a}{2} + \frac{A}{2}$. Call it, for abbreviation, h (half blood).

Let the second crossing be of h and B, the blood of the issue will be $\frac{h}{2} + \frac{B}{2}$, or substituting for $\frac{h}{2}$ its equivalent, it will be $\frac{a}{4} + \frac{A}{4} + \frac{B}{2}$, call it q (quarteroon) being $\frac{1}{4}$ negro blood.

Let the third crossing be of q and C, their offspring will be $\frac{q}{2} + \frac{C}{2} =$

$\frac{a}{8} + \frac{A}{8} + \frac{B}{4} + \frac{C}{2}$, call this e (eighth), who having less than $\frac{1}{4}$ of a, or of pure negro blood, to wit $\frac{1}{8}$ only, is no longer a mulatto, so that a third cross clears the blood.

From these elements let us examine their compounds. For example, let h and q cohabit, their issue will be $\frac{h}{2} + \frac{q}{2} = \frac{a}{4} + \frac{A}{4} + \frac{a}{8} + \frac{A}{8} + \frac{B}{4} = \frac{3a}{8} + \frac{3A}{8} + \frac{B}{4}$, wherein we find $\frac{3}{8}$ of a, or negro blood.

Let h and e cohabit, their issue will be $\frac{h}{2} + \frac{e}{2} = \frac{a}{4} + \frac{A}{4} + \frac{a}{16} + \frac{A}{16} + \frac{B}{8} + \frac{c}{4} = \frac{5a}{16} + \frac{5A}{16} + \frac{B}{8} + \frac{c}{4}$, wherein $\frac{5}{16}$ a makes still a mulatto.

Let q and e cohabit, the half of the blood of each will be $\frac{q}{2} + \frac{e}{2} = \frac{a}{8} + \frac{A}{8} + \frac{B}{4} + \frac{a}{16} + \frac{A}{16} + \frac{B}{8} + \frac{C}{4} = \frac{3a}{16} + \frac{3A}{16} + \frac{3B}{8} + \frac{C}{4}$, wherein $\frac{3}{16}$ of a is no longer a mulatto, and thus may every compound be noted and summed, the sum of the fractions composing the blood of the issue being always equal to unit . . . (LB, 15:452).

(This looks like a page of Hutcheson's formulae for the moment of virtue.)

His opposition to turning individual freedmen loose in Virginia society made Jefferson draft slave laws for the state so harsh that his countrymen would not pass them. Among the measures deleted from his bill were these:

Freedmen must leave the commonwealth within a year.

Those coming into the commonwealth of their own accord "shall be out of the protection of the laws"—to be killed with impunity by anyone.

Freedmen who do not leave within a year shall equally be outlaws.

A white woman bearing a child to a black or a mulatto must leave the commonwealth within a year, taking her issue, or be outside the laws (*Papers*, 2:471).

We have seen that Jefferson opposed large-scale immigration, even of whites, into Virginia, as a threat to the social bonds and homogeneity of the place, to the genius of the people. He was even more strict in wanting to exclude the turmoil caused by any more black freedmen in the state.

Jefferson wrote these fierce laws inhibiting individual manumission at the same time he was conceiving his scheme for general emancipation. That scheme, offered in the *Notes on the State of Virginia* to French philosophes as a sample of American enlightenment, was to take place in four careful steps, all connected, each necessary to the other. It was an intricate "invention"—more so than Jefferson's rotation scheme for his own farms, or the education program for sifting the best "geniusses" out of the free white population. It was complex, but only from necessity. There were many problems to be handled all at once. These are the four steps (*Notes*, 137–38):

1) All slaves born after a legislated date would be raised and educated with a view to being freed. They would be removed from their parents at "a certain [fixed] age" and brought up at public expence "to tillage, arts or sciences, according to their geniusses."

2) On reaching their majority (twenty-one for males, eighteen for females) "they should be colonized to such a place as the circumstances of the time shall render most proper" and given a stake there of tools, seeds, animals sufficient to support them. Only on arrival at the colony would Virginia declare them "a free and independent people," but their government would still be under Virginia's protection until they had time to become self-sufficient.

3) During this deportation out, the state must arrange to bring cheap white labor in (presumably in the form of indentured servants). These new laborers would be freed in time and enter into citizenship with the free white people, after the remaining blacks—those born before the legislated date—died off in Virginia.

4) The black colony would be severed entirely from dependence on Virginia.

Quotes and snippets from Jefferson have been used to suggest that he altered his views on slavery, or that these were inconsistent with each other. He can be quoted to sound like an ardent abolitionist, or to sound like the most oppressive of masters. But everything he wrote on the subject is consistent with the complex treatment he gave to slavery in his *Notes*. He always opposed enslavement in general and further slave imports to Virginia in particular. He always supported the freeing of slaves en masse, *but always and only in connection with a scheme of deportation* (see, for instance, Ford, 9:478, 10:157–58). In Paris, he indulged a brief hope

—it was no more than that—to find a one-plantation equivalent of his scheme, bringing in "Germans" and sending slaves off to learn freedom and skills on separate farms (*Papers*, 14:492–93); but it was a plan even less realistic than the state-wide scheme, and we hear no more of it after the first wish.

Jefferson opposed partial or individual manumission on principle; and thought the owner's duty, up to the time when his scheme could be effected, was to hold his slaves humanely while seeking ways to advance the scheme. As he wrote in 1814:

> My opinion has ever been that, until more can be done for them, we should endeavor, with those whom fortune has thrown on our hands, to feed and clothe them well, protect them from ill usage, require such reasonable labors only as is performed voluntarily by freemen, and be led by no repugnances to abdicate them, and our duties to them. The laws do not permit us to turn them loose, if that were for their own good; and to commute them for other property is to commit them to those whose usage of them we cannot control (Ford, 9:479).

Once, he even compared freeing a slave to abandoning a child (*Papers*, 14:492).

In an earlier chapter (Fifteen) I have argued that Jefferson's strictures on Negro disability did not make him insincere in his claim that "all men are created equal." It is easy to ignore the moral-sense basis for that claim, or to consider it trivial. But we have seen parallel misunderstandings of his stand, based on that theory of moral sense, in areas where interest could not have dictated his views—e.g., in his emphasis on the heart's insights at the Natural Bridge or in the Cosway dialogue.

I would now like to ask if moral-sense theory can free his deportation scheme of any charge that blacks are inferior, are unworthy of living with whites. My aim is not to defend Jefferson's views on slavery—which, in any case, some people think impossible; but to understand them, if *that* is possible.

One of the most interesting points in Jefferson's scheme is the separation of those destined for freedom from their parents. This might seem cruel to parents or children, or both. But it could not be motivated by the owners' interest. In the first place, removing the young would deprive their masters of teen-age labor combined with their training and apprenticeship. The state schools would presumably use that teen-age labor, at crafts and in fields, to support the importation of white workers—so the master could look to ultimate recompense. But he would meanwhile be supporting the state schools with his taxes, while losing the immediate labor of his youngest slaves.

The remaining parents would provide a marginal work force during the transition scheme; but as they aged they would become drones or a drain on the plantations where they must be left to die out. The scheme does not look to the whites' advantage, but to the blacks', as we can see from another section of these *Notes*. Jefferson opposed (84–85) large immigrations to Virginia, since those arriving would have an insufficiently republican ethos, instilled in them by their upbringing. One of the trade-offs of his own emancipation scheme—a lesser evil purchased to rid men of the greater—is the new white work force brought in on a fairly large scale.

By recognizing that there was an instilled slave mentality, and trying to protect those born for freedom from its contamination, Jefferson was implying what he would shortly assert in these *Notes* —that the slave's moral sense was damaged by wrongs done him (e.g., in his attitudes toward property) but would be restored to equal alertness when those damages ceased and their effects were allowed to wear off.

Jefferson felt that a certain homogeneity was necessary in any society of men contracting with each other on the basis of mutual affection. This is as apparent in his treatment of Indian society as in his effort to keep the bonds close in Virginia by limiting the number of white immigrants. That is why he has the new black society prepared from youth up to be declared "a free and independent *people*" (emphasis added) on arrival in their new home.

Many strands of moral-sense thought come together here, to show how far was Jefferson from the belief that the individual is atomistic in a Lockean state of nature—Reid's belief that all good sense is a *common* sense, and that man in isolation is man insane; Ferguson's belief that man is fully human only "in groups"; Smith's belief that morality arises only from sympathy with others; Hutcheson's belief that language and thought arise together; Diderot's dictum (in his *Fils naturel*) that "*l'homme seul est l'homme méchant*"; Voltaire's even more radical assertion that "*Tant qu'il est seul, il*

n'est ni bienfaisant ni malfaisant; il n'est rien pour nous" (Dictionnaire philosophique, s.v. *"Vertu"*). The theory of individual *"sensibilité"* was meaningless except within a theory of *"sociabilité."*
Benevolence spread by a mechanics (Hutcheson), a contagion
(Hume), or a kindling (Ferguson). Men only become men in the
company of men—free men in free company. The figures in a
Greuze family scene are sometimes literally "bound" together by
their intertwining clothes.

We discover Jefferson's thoroughgoing consistency even in little-
noticed things like his attempt to save the new society of freeborn
blacks from the old slave ways—precisely as he wanted Americans
to be separated from the feudalism and superstition of monarchical
Europe. His stand here is not racial: what is needed for the blacks
is exactly the same thing whites need. Jefferson felt European whites
were often sheepish or servile, and wanted America to escape the
stultifying nurture that inhibited refinement of the moral sense for
European whites.

The belief in the need for a shared ethos—for *"fraternité"*—is
what made Jefferson doubt that blacks could ever be incorporated
into Virginia society. His reasons for this are clearly stated and are
clearly nonracist:

It will probably be asked, Why not retain and incorporate the blacks
into the state, and thus save the expence of supplying, by importation of
white settlers, the vacancies they will leave? Deep rooted prejudices entertained by the whites; ten thousand recollections, by the blacks, of the
injuries they have sustained; new provocations; the real distinctions
which nature has made; and many other circumstances will divide us
into parties, and produce convulsions which will probably never end but
in the extermination of the one or the other race (138).

The result, that is, would be genocide—with the whites the probable winners.

Take the reasons given, one by one:

1) *"deep rooted prejudices entertained by the whites"*: Jefferson
was no Burke for defending prejudices. His ideal was always the
candid mind, open to evidence, unswayed by prior bias. He tried to
let facts speak to him unimpeded, as he thought Newton had. But
precisely because he set himself that pure ideal, he realized how
hard it was to attain, and how little shared by men at large. All

men are not scientists; yet the social bond must include all men within any society. Prejudice cripples the moral sense in some measure, and Jefferson clearly states that the prejudice involved here is that of whites. They have a stunted moral sense, like the Negro who steals because of his upbringing. Insofar as any social inferiority is asserted in this reason, it is that of the whites.

2) *"ten thousand recollections, by the blacks, of the injuries they have sustained"*: Again, the whites are in the wrong here. They cannot expect a brotherhood to spring up and be revered after generations of wrongs inflicted, not only on the slave himself but on his dear ones. The very principle of benevolence, which should bind men, leads to opposition where mutual kind offices of the family have been disrupted—just as Indians were harsh toward advancing white men who menaced their children and wives.

The nonracial character of this observation is proved by the fact that Jefferson claimed Americans could no longer maintain political bands with their British "brethren," because the latter had wronged other Americans too deeply and too long. This it was that made Americans "one people" separable, of necessity, from "another." Nor was Jefferson alone in seeing the Revolution as a matter of shattered affections. The key paragraphs in Thomas Paine's *Common Sense* (a Scottish title given to the pamphlet by Edinburgh-trained Benjamin Rush) contain the argument from sensibility-sociability:

Men of passive tempers look somewhat lightly over the offences of Britain and, still hoping for the best, are apt to call out, "Come, come, we shall be friends again, for all this." But examine the passions and feelings of mankind. Bring the doctrine of reconciliation to the touchstone of nature, and then tell me whether you can hereafter love, honor, and faithfully serve the power that hath carried fire and sword into your land? If you cannot do all these, then are you only deceiving yourselves, and by your delay bringing ruin upon posterity. Your future connection with Britain, whom you can neither love nor honor, will be forced and unnatural; and, being formed only on the plan of present convenience, will in a little time fall into a relapse more wretched than the first. But if you say you can still pass the violations over, then I ask, Hath your house been burnt? Hath your property been destroyed before your face? Are your wife and children destitute of a bed to lie on, or bread to live on? Have you lost a parent or a child by their hands, and yourself the ruined and wretched survivor? If you have not, then are you not a judge of those who have. But if you have, and still can shake hands with the murderers, then are you unworthy the name of husband, father, friend, or lover, and whatever may be your rank or title in life, you have the heart of a coward, and the spirit of a sycophant.

What could not be asked of whites, Jefferson will not expect from blacks. Indeed, to ask men to overlook the kinds of wrong inflicted by slavery, to enter into true brotherhood with the oppressor, would be an insult to the very feelings of humanity that bind societies together.

But there is no reason to think that, because Jefferson felt blacks could not live with whites, he thought blacks inferior. He thought Americans could no longer live with the British, and clearly did not think Americans inferior. He was very sympathetic to the Indians, admiring of them in many ways; but it never entered his head that they could become part of the white man's government. They were so clearly "one people," different from the whites, that they must be self-governing as separate nations.

3) *"fresh provocations"*: The very attempt at acculturation among whites would lead to new wrongs against the blacks. Jefferson saw this as the result of individual manumission; and general emancipation without deporting would just magnify the problems. How could the individual freedman achieve fraternity with the whites, so long as any blacks were being mistreated? To profess one form of benevolence would be to deny the other and deeper one. Whites could not trust such affection, even if it were felt. Remember that Jefferson had defended slave thefts by saying the blacks were outside all compact with the whites. He could foresee no way to bring them inside a compact whose whole basis was the natural and necessary bond of affection.

4) *"the real distinctions which nature has made"*: These are the distinctions already considered in chapter Fifteen—those of head and body, not of heart; not of the affective basis for all equality, the moral sense. That Jefferson could talk of natural distinctions without implying moral inferiority is proved, once again, by his treatment of the Indians. He says there, "I do not mean to deny, that there are varieties in the race of men, distinguished by their powers both of body and mind" (*Notes*, 63)—not, you notice, of heart. He goes on, in fact, to say: "Their controuls are their manners, and that moral sense of right and wrong, which, like the sense of tasting

and feeling, in every man makes a part of his nature" (93). Having said they are equal in moral sense, he has said everything he can to assure them all the rights of self-rule. *And he has said exactly what he said of the blacks.* The "natural distinctions" that exist between whites and blacks, or between whites and the Indians, are of the same kind that exist between any two peoples that are different— e.g., between Americans and the British at that point where Americans felt it necessary to dissolve the bands connecting them with *another people.*

5) *"many other circumstances will divide us into parties":* The fear of party faction was famous among the framers of our Constitution, but Jefferson has normally been absolved of that fear. James MacGregor Burns even built his book *The Deadlock of Democracy,* around a contrast between Jefferson's thought and Madison's treatment of faction in the *Federalist Papers.* It is true that Jefferson would (like Madison) later be a partisan and help found the first party system; but he thought, even as he was helping frame that system, that he was making partisanship unnecessary, as scholars like Noble Cunningham and Richard Hofstadter have demonstrated.

Besides, Jefferson's thought at the time of composing his *Notes* (1781) was part of the complex of attitudes belonging to the moral-sense school; and that is precisely where Madison picked up his teaching on faction, as Douglass Adair proved by parallel quotes from *Federalist* 10 and Hume's essay "Of Parties in General." Factionalism was a matter of special concern to the moral-sense philosophers. They would admit the usefulness of balanced interests in the mechanics of society; but real animosity tore at the very basis of their contract, grounded as it was in affection. Thus, in the second edition of his 1725 *Inquiry,* Hutcheson inserted a long refutation of the idea that "various sects, parties, cabals, factions of mankind" can be an expression of public spirit. With people of their own society men should foster "friendships, trust, and mutual confidence" (1:296–99). It is just that mutuality of trust, so necessary in his scheme of things, that Jefferson could not believe blacks and whites capable of manifesting as fellow citizens. Their "parties" would lead to "convulsions," which would lead in turn to "extermination."

The bad habit of partial quotation where Jefferson's views are concerned reached a climax when the Jefferson Memorial was built. One of the key quotations carved inside the monument, and therefore made a part of our general wisdom on the man, is misleadingly truncated. It begins, "Nothing is more certainly written in the book of fate, than that these people are to be free . . ." But it continues, immediately: "nor is it less certain, that the two races equally free, cannot live in the same government" (Ford, 1:49). And then he gives a summary of the reasons for the view expressed more at length in his *Notes on Virginia:* "Nature, habit, opinion have drawn indelible lines of distinction between them."

To speak as Jefferson did was not simply to express a Virginia slaveholder's interest. The Marquis de Chastellux, an ardent opponent of slavery with no personal stake in slaveholding, offered as one mitigating factor in modern slavery the consideration that "*la grande dissemblance de ces malheureux avec nous rappelle moins les sentiments d'humanité*" (1:48). It was less an infringement on nature to enslave those with whom one has no natural ties of sympathy. If even Chastellux could speak thus, in the safe precincts of the French Enlightenment, it is no wonder Jefferson felt that, even though slaves should be freed, they could not enter into comity with their natural and ancient enemies.

It is erroneous to say that Jefferson denied either equality or self-rule to the blacks as a matter of right. But he thought they had, what all men have, the right to self-rule *as a people*. Deportation was necessary so they could exercise that right. He talks in the Declaration of the "right of *the people*" to form, alter, or abolish governments for their safety and happiness. He never envisioned the assertion of these basic rights by *individuals*, outside a context of mutual affection and benevolence. For Americans, he asserted the right of "one people" to "assume among the powers of the earth the separate & equal station to which the laws of nature and nature's god entitle them." His deportation scheme was meant to assure for blacks the same right Americans were asserting. But the blacks had first to have a *separate* station, for that to become an *equal* one.

"... unfeeling brethren ..."

> I wish sincerely, as well for the honor of Congress as for
> that of the states, that the manuscript had not been
> mangled as it is. It is wonderful, and passing pitiful,
> that the rage of change should be so unhappily applied.
> —Richard Henry Lee

I believe we now have in hand all the materials necessary for understanding Jefferson's disappointment at the treatment of his Declaration by Congress. First, though, we should remind ourselves
how deep that disappointment was, and how inexplicable it remains if looked at from the scholarly consensus on the merits of the
two versions of the Declaration.

I have found no scholar who argues that the congressional
changes altered Jefferson's message in any substantial way. In fact,
most critics think that Congress—with the possible exception of
the paragraph on slavery—improved his draft, sharpened its meaning, trimming nothing but rhetorical excess or exaggerated claims.
We can let Dumas Malone, the dean of Jeffersonians, phrase the
learned consensus: "Jefferson and some of his Virginia friends
believed that Congress weakened the Declaration, but there can
now be little doubt that the critics strengthened it" (Malone,
1:222).

If that is the case, then Jefferson is made to seem morbidly sensitive. After all, he suffered so obviously under changes being made
that Franklin had to come over and comfort him with a joke (Ford,
10:20). Nor was this a passing moment of pique or writer's pride.
On the very evening of July 3, after the first full day of debate on
the Declaration's phrasing, Jefferson sat down and copied his draft
at least twice, to send off to friends, lest they think the version
printed in broadsheet was his (Boyd, *Evolution*, 35). He continued

his copying labors over several days or nights, and eventually sent copies of the original draft to Richard Henry Lee, George Wythe, Edmund Pendleton, Philip Mazzei, and his old school friend John Page. Lee replied as the author wished, regretting the "rage of change" that had "mangled" his manuscript (*Papers*, 1:471).

Seven years later, Jefferson was still working to keep his original draft before the men he respected. At that time he sent James Madison a reworked copy of his notes on the debates surrounding the Lee resolutions. In those notes he printed his original text side by side with the text as adopted by Congress. In the original, deleted passages were underlined and alterations put in the margin, to make comparison easier. Then, late in his life, Jefferson incorporated these "Notes" in his *Autobiography*, retaining the marks to signal each point where the documents diverge. Julian Boyd thinks the Notes were included in the *Autobiography* to answer charges that Jefferson was not the author of the Declaration, and this may have been part of his motive. But including the whole lengthy treatment of all the debates from that time did not address directly the question of his authorship of the one document. Besides, he could have established his claim just by printing his draft, without the complex scheme of comparison. Another aspect of his motivation must have been the desire to keep his original text alive in its own right, to be studied with the congressional Declaration, and contrasted with it—to the advantage of the first author. Boyd remarks that the inclusion of the "Notes" makes the *Autobiography* lack proportion—they contrast so sharply in bulk with all other events referred to in the *Autobiography*. But their inclusion reflects Jefferson's opinion, toward the end of his life, that the events around the Lee resolutions—including his own drafting of the Declaration—deserved prominent attention. Indeed, Jefferson's inclusion of the Declaration of Independence in the brief list of achievements for his tombstone should be read in conjunction with the decision to include the draft-and-comparison in his *Autobiography*. When Jefferson calls himself in the epitaph "author of the Declaration of American Independence," he is referring precisely to *his* act of authorship—to the Declaration printed as his in the *Autobiography* and set off for contrast with the official document.

Of course, being the principal author of the Declaration accepted by the whole Congress is a more weighty achievement in official

terms—the proper stuff of epitaphs. But Jefferson's epitaph is famous for its semiprivate character, for its exclusion of official things
like the presidency (twice held). He affected American history in
many official ways, perhaps most by doubling the young nation's
territorial holdings. He was governor of Virginia, Secretary of State,
and minister to France. None of these things are recorded for posterity at his gravesite. The three things noted there had close personal meaning for him; and we know he continued to think his first
draft the one most significant to him personally. The other two
achievements were his sole accomplishment. He presents himself as
the "*father* of the University of Virginia," the only begetter and
name-giver; and as the author of "the statute of Virginia for religious freedom," a statute that was more his personal document than
his other revisions of Virginia law. In a list that leaned away from
the public, official, and national, toward the single, the local (both
other achievements were actions in and for Virginia), and the personal, Jefferson's own Declaration fits better than the congressional
one. It was for him *the* Declaration, the one not tampered with.

But, considering the almost universal judgment of posterity on
the comparative merits of the documents, one is forced to ask: How
could Jefferson be so wrong? Why did he try to keep before men's
eyes an inferior product? Even if we do not go so far as most critics
—even, that is, if we do not claim Congress improved the draft—
there are many reasons for preferring the signed parchment on display in the National Archives to the paper of Jefferson's "rough
draft" in the Library of Congress. If the two versions were only
equal in merit, or roughly equal—with no preponderant superiority
for either—the document passed by Congress, accepted by the nation, and passing into legend, would have the greater claim on our
attention. That is the document Lincoln revered and praised. That
is what we have read on the Fourth for many years. That is what so
many great men put priceless signatures to, in an act that made
"Signers" become for this continent what "Revolutioners" were to
seventeenth-century England.

Jefferson himself made an argument against giving his own draft
prior consideration. He said he was expressing "the common sense
of the subject" (Ford, 10:343). Then why should we not prefer the
common expression of that common sense—the expression of the
whole Congress, not his (merely personal) version? If he was say-

ing what everybody said at the time, why not give first rank to the form of that statement everybody has read in succeeding times?

But we have seen that Thomas Reid's "common sense" demanded uncommon presentation if it was to reach the candid mind. And all the Jefferson scholars have worked on an assumption that the excisions from Jefferson's draft worked no doctrinal change in the Declaration. They think it was a Lockean document before the excisions, and remained a Lockean document afterward. They do notice, either to praise or regret, the loss of something a little different in the slavery count (though most of them fail to remark that the central charge in that paragraph was retained by an earlier insertion). In other words: They think nothing but a rhetorical fillip or two was cut out when over three hundred words were dropped toward the end of the document.

The slave clause is often called the major excision, and it is, indeed, the longest of the *grievances*. It had to be, because of the preliminary maneuvers Jefferson made to call *freeing* slaves a war crime. Yet this long clause comes to only 168 words; and the later cut runs over 300 words. The slavery clause is, admittedly, emphatic by its position—last in the war-atrocities list, penultimate in the whole list of grievances (followed only by the summary charge of not redressing the grievances).

But the late passage occurs at the climax and conclusion of the *whole* document; and it was more emphatic in the original draft than one might gather at a glance back from the final Declaration, since Congress inserted the Richard Henry Lee resolution ("that these United colonies are & of right ought to be free & independent states; that they are absolved from all allegiance to the British crown, and that all political connection between them and the state of Great Britain is, and ought to be, totally dissolved") for the climax of its paper. Jefferson's own final declaring of a separation was thus lost, with the special twist he gave to that.

The large final excisions of the Congress accomplished five things, all of which have hitherto been treated as unimportant, receiving little notice or none at all.

1) Congress cut out Jefferson's special theory of expatriation followed by a new compact at the foundation of the various colonies. We have already considered (chapter Six) how Jefferson tried, again and again, to insert this theory into congressional papers and

failed. We also looked (chapter Twenty-one) at how Jefferson grounded the new contract on a moral-sense theory of the state's basis in mutual benevolence—"laying a foundation for perpetual league & amity with them [the British brethren]." Those who believe this excision is unimportant must find Jefferson's theory of the American expatriation and fresh compacts not worth considering. Given the normal treatment of the *Summary View*, where Jefferson first expressed his theory, we should not, perhaps, be surprised that scholars have not wanted to discuss that theory in connection with the Declaration of Independence. Even in the earlier document, they found it an embarrassment. And once this excision is made, the later ones, connected with this, seem to follow naturally.

2) The next excision obscured the real "target" of Jefferson's paper. It is customary to say that Jefferson shifted the assault from Parliament to the King. I have discussed some difficulties with that view (in chapter Five), even in the Declaration as Congress passed it. But that is a view that could not arise from the original draft, which has two sentences expressly excluding *both* King *and* Parliament as the real culprits. Grant that Parliament made uncongressional usurpations, and the King supported these moves. Still, under the constitutional theory to which Americans have all along been appealing, and which Jefferson repeats in his document, "the people" have the right to alter or abolish governments. Americans have been arguing that they were not consulted as part of this people. They did not make that claim for their British brethren across the sea. King and Parliament were at least answerable to *that* people. If King *or* Parliament committed wrongs with impunity, it was because that people did not call them to account. The draft makes this clear as it mounts to its conclusion—first noting the people's inaction against Parliament:

and when occasions have been given them, by the regular course of their laws, of removing from their councils the disturbers of our [i.e., the British and American brethrens'] harmony, they have, by their free election, re-established them in power.

And then the people's inaction against its King:

At this very time too they are permitting their chief magistrate to send over not only souldiers of our common [British and American] blood, but Scotch & foreign mercenaries to invade & destroy us.

Not only did this deletion lead to the false issue of deciding whether Parliament or the King was being blamed for the final break. It has lent color to those who said Jefferson advanced a new theory of government in the second paragraph of the Declaration—the right of the people to alter or abolish governments that do not serve the common good. We have already seen (in chapter Three) that this was simply good doctrine from the Glorious Revolution, voiced in the early petitions to recall the circumstances of Hanoverian succession to the reigning monarch. In this deleted section, Jefferson blames the British brethren for not acting on their *own* theory of government, which he expressly says they had the power to do. They could not be blamed here for neglecting their duty, if he thought they were simply *unable* to perform it. The preamble does not contain a new theory of revolution. What was new in it has not been noticed—mainly because of the next excision.

3) The next cut sweeps away the climax of the whole document, as Jefferson has been shaping it from the beginning—the last break with that other people to whom Americans were joined by the political bands here being dissolved:

These facts have given the last stab to agonizing affection, and manly spirit bids us to renounce for ever these unfeeling brethren. We must endeavor to forget our former love for them, and to hold them as we hold the rest of mankind enemies in war, in peace friends. We might have been a free and a great people together; but a communication of grandeur & of freedom it seems is below their dignity. Be it so, since they will have it.

This deleted passage is the earliest part we have of the Declaration itself (considered as separate from the list of grievances shared with the Virginia constitution's draft). In the fragment of composition draft (*Papers*, 1:420–22), the key sentence on agonizing affection is written separately, then reworked—"unfeeling" being inserted for "unjust" brethren, to strengthen a passage that originally ran: "This is too much to be borne even by relations." The passage is worked carefully to express deeper emotion. "We do renounce these unfeeling brethren" gives a solemnity and finality to what started as "Enough then be it to say, we are now done with them."

It is easy to see why those who think of Jefferson and his time as hard bargainers into the individualistic contract of John Locke should be simply impatient with all this talk of "affection," the feelings of "brethren," and "former love." What kind of revolution begins with the recollections of a jilted lover? But we should not be too quick to think this is romantic drivel spouted oddly from a man of the Enlightenment in the most important part of what became his most important public paper.

I have suggested, in earlier parts of this book, that the phrase in the congressional Declaration most often attacked for vagueness— "the pursuit of happiness"—had meanings for Jefferson that were hard and scientific (chapter Ten), moral (Seventeen), and political (Eighteen). We should at least entertain the possibility that this rejected passage of the Declaration had the same kind of specificity in Jefferson's mind, if we can only penetrate that mind.

Take it phrase by phrase. The British brethren have delivered a *last stab* to affection Americans felt for them. This implies, of course, former stabs. And Jefferson had given that prior history of affront in his Declaration of Causes in 1775:

Some occasional assumptions of power by the parliament of Great Britain, however unacknowledged by the constitution of our governments, were finally acquiesced in thro' warmth of affection. Proceeding thus in the fulness of mutual harmony and confidence, both parts of the empire increased in population & wealth with a rapidity unknown in the history of man (*Papers,* 1:199).

This mention of "mutual harmony" parallels the description of Parliament as "disturbers of our harmony" in the rejected section of the Declaration. The earlier affronts were like the grievances the Declaration lists. So re-election of a Parliament intent on disturbing the harmony of brothers delivered a penultimate stab to affection. The ultimate stab was popular acceptance of the King's military scheme to use foreign mercenaries on "brethren."

The stab was delivered to an *agonizing* affection. Affection had overcome earlier affronts only after some hesitation (*"finally* acquiesced in thro' warmth of affection"). Americans had struggled with their feelings all through the petitioning process, Jefferson himself professing as late as 1775 that he wanted no separation from England. Jefferson's use of the term "agonizing" is not mere hyperbole for pain, but shows a nice feeling for the Greek word that meant to compete in a contest (*agon*). Johnson's Dictionary economically caught that meaning in the definition of agonistes as "a prizefighter," and Johnson cited for the verb Rowe's *Jane Shore:*

> Dost thou behold my poor distracted heart,
> Thus rent with agonizing love and rage . . .

Jefferson may have remembered Lord Shaftesbury's sentence in the *Characteristics:* "He agonizes, and with all his strength of reason endeavors to overcome himself." Just so had American affections struggled to maintain themselves through blow after blow, until the final one was at last delivered.

It is *manly spirit* that bids Americans renounce their British brethren. We saw in the last chapter how Paine put the same thought: If Americans could see their dear ones wronged and still shake the hand of their assailant, they would have lost their manly spirit and become cowards. Jefferson's own interpretation of the act declaring independence lies in that phrase, to "renounce forever these unfeeling brethren." Since the compacts formed after expatriation had been based on a desire "to continue their connection with the *friends* whom they had left" (1:199), to strengthen "those bands of *Amity* with our fellow subjects" (1:171), to maintain "perpetual league & *amity*" (1:318), the one thing that could dissolve the bands was the destruction of the affection on which they were based—and this the British have accomplished by becoming *unfeeling* brethren.

The necessity for social homogeneity in a government based on benevolent affections made Hutcheson see that long absence from one set of brothers and the knitting of daily ties among others would make a man move naturally into another social cluster:

> Whatever place we have lived in for any considerable time, there we have most distinctly remarked the various affections of human nature. We have known many lovely characters; we remember the associations, friendships, families, natural affections, and other humane sentiments. Our moral sense determines us to approve these lovely dispositions where we have most distinctly observed them, and our benevolence concerns us in the interests of the persons possessed of them. When we come to observe the like as distinctly in another country, we begin to acquire a national love toward it also. Nor has our own country any other preference in our idea, unless it be by an association of the pleasant ideas of our youth, with the buildings, fields, and woods where we received them (1:148).

As always, Hutcheson is thinking of the affections in terms of gravitational force. When one goes far enough out from his own system, enters the pull of another cluster, the tug backward weakens and then disappears. This is true, even if the two systems show an equal benevolence and charm. But what if the former body wrongs the departed man, and harms his new associates needlessly? Then the attack on benevolence makes him defend the attacked, out of benevolence. The feelings are wounded, bonds loosened, the social contract undermined. This was Paine's reading of the course of events, as well as Jefferson's. *Common Sense* also contains a renunciation of unfeeling brethren:

Nature hath deserted the connection, and Art cannot supply her place. For, as Milton wisely expresses, "Never can true reconcilement grow, where wounds of deadly hate have pierc'd so deep. . . ." To talk of friendship with those in whom our reason forbids us to have faith and our affections, wounded through a thousand pores, instruct us to detest, is madness and folly. Every day wears out the little remains of kindred between us and them; and can there be any reason to hope that, as the relationship expires, the affection will increase; or that we shall agree better when we have ten times more and greater concerns to quarrel over than ever?

Ye that tell us of harmony and reconciliation, can ye restore to us the time that is past? Can ye give to prostitution its former innocence? Neither can ye reconcile Britain and America. The last cord now is broken, the *people* [emphasis added] of England are presenting addresses against us. There are injuries which nature cannot forgive; she would cease to be nature if she did. As well can the lover forgive the ravisher of his mistress, as the continent forgive the murders of Britain. The Almighty hath implanted in us these unextinguishable feelings for good and wise purposes. They are the guardians of his image in our hearts. They distinguish us from the herd of common animals. The social compact would dissolve, and justice be extirpated the earth, or have only a casual existence, were we callous to the touches of affection.

The last cord now is broken: the necessary dissolving of political bands is expressed by Paine in terms nicely paralleling Jefferson's. For Paine, too, the social contract is based on feelings. Spotty as Paine's education was, he caught well what was in the air. And the air of enlightened America was full of Hutcheson's politics, not Locke's.

It is now the Americans' duty to work at forgetting former love. To remember it would be to betray nearer loves, so the league of perpetual amity yields to the relation between any nations of free and equal station, "enemies in war, in peace friends" (a chiastic play on the language of treaties). We might have been "*a* great *people* together" (emphasis added). Here Jefferson spells out what was implicit in the Declaration's opening sentence, which spoke of "one people" in America severing the bands with another, an alien people in England. The severance had taken place in the hearts of men—the Declaration is just a recognition of this fact of history, this necessary occurrence in the course of human events. Social necessity is as inexorable as the law of gravity. Two peoples at odds cannot be made one, on the basis of mutual benevolence—as Jefferson had said of the blacks and white Americans, or of those whites and American Indians.

"A *communication* of grandeur & of freedom it seems is below their dignity." Hutcheson founded society on the intercourse of kindnesses (chapter Sixteen). As Voltaire put it in his Dictionnaire philosophique (s.v. "*Vertu*"): "*La vertu entre les hommes est un* commerce *de bienfaits*." The mention of grandeur brings us to a fourth note omitted when this whole passage was struck out.

4) Frenchmen sang, in their Revolution, of "*le jour de gloire*." It is a note some find missing in America's more legalistic war of colonial secession. But it was not missing from the Declaration until Congress struck this passage, which talks of "grandeur" and goes on:

The road to happiness and to *glory* is open to us too. We will tread it apart from them.

This accords with another passage, struck out earlier from the preamble, one that pledged "a faith yet unsullied by falsehood."

We must recall the meaning of "fidelity," or faith, in Hutchesonian morals. It is the virtue of honoring contracts. It lies at the basis of all mankind's intercourse of kindnesses—the marriage contract, the patriot's loyalty, the bond of friends. It is a deliberate paradox for Jefferson to advance a revolution in the name of "faith." Rebels are perfidious, the enemies of fidelity. But of course Jefferson did not think the Revolution was a rebellion. If he could prove that real stabs to affection came from the British, then fidelity in the deepest sense—under the all-inclusive and guiding virtue of benevolence—demanded a resistance to people threatening one's friends.

It was important for Enlightenment thinkers to clarify the role of honor in republican ethics. Honor no longer hedged nobility or mere class, thus Hutcheson attacked the aristocratic basis of a dueling code (4:239, 6:97). Honor was a guard to virtue. It held men's opinion in high esteem, and felt shame to be caught in less than virtuous action before mankind (2:146, 4:26). Even more to the point, it increased pleasure in the benevolence that propels men into social concord: "When honor is thus constituted by nature pleasant to us, it may be an additional motive to virtue, as—we said above—the pleasure arising from reflection on our benevolence was" (1:202).

Hutcheson had solved the problem of benevolence, in a creature reacting only to pleasure and pain, by having the *spectacle* of benevolence give pleasure. So part of virtue, an essential part, was to appear virtuous to others, giving them a motive to pass on the pleasure of doing good. Adam Smith made it clear that, since the motion begins with the pleasure of a spectator, one must *remain* a spectator of one's own benevolence, even in the act of exercising that virtue. The Enlightenment was unembarrassed to display virtue, to take obvious delight in one's own virtue. For Voltaire, the idea of private virtue was contradictory: Private virtue would be vice. So honor became the satisfaction given one by acts of virtue—e.g., in Hume:

This constant habit of surveying ourselves, as it were in reflection, keeps alive all the sentiments of right and wrong, and begets in noble natures a certain reverence for themselves as well as others, which is the surest guardian of every virtue (*Enquiry, Morals*, 9, i).

Lord Kames, that early hero of Jefferson, wrote:

When we consider our own character and actions in a reflex view, we cannot help approving of this tenderness and sympathy in our nature. We are pleased with ourselves for being so constituted, we are conscious of inward merit, and this is a continual source of satisfaction (*Principles*, 17).

Thus Jefferson's language of unsullied faith, and sacred honor, and the path to glory, is a sign of his document's deepest intent. He does not offer the American Revolution as something permissible, merely. It is *necessary* in nature; and the recognition and co-operation with nature is the essence of human virtue. Seeing the impulse to happiness, and co-operating with it, is man's highest calling.

It has often been denied that America, at the outset of its independent life, offered its Revolution as an example for all the world to follow. But Jefferson surely wanted to impress others with the spectacle of American virtue; and that was the way to motivate others toward virtue in Hutcheson's system. The action of benevolence, even wounded benevolence, which casts off unfeeling brethren to defend those still feeling and acting together, presents a spectacle that pleases others, who are led to imitate such virtuous action. It seems odd to us to call acts of war the result of benevolence; but that is precisely the way Adam Ferguson explained hostilities. It is the way Jefferson explained Indian resistance to white colonizers.

Honor maintains respect for oneself and "a decent respect to the opinions of mankind." It would be dishonorable for a man of the Enlightenment to address the candid world in any *but* a pose of conscious virtue. For the greatest happiness a moral-sense theorist can bestow on others is the sight of virtue inciting to virtue, the intercourse that alone makes all parties truly happy.

5) A final omission, after the great cut, was made to clear space for including Richard Henry Lee's resolution in the text. Lee declared Americans free of all political connection with "the state of Great Britain." Jefferson characteristically severs all political bands, not only with King and Parliament but especially with the British people as well (since that was always the heart of the contract in his view):

[We] reject & renounce all allegiance & subjection to the kings of Great Britain & all others who may hereafter claim by, through or under them: we utterly dissolve all political connection which may heretofore have subsisted between us & the people or parliament of Great Britain. . . .

Jefferson is precise, as ever. He renounces allegiance and subjection to the King—"federal" or treaty ties, as he put it earlier in his notes (*Papers,* 1:311), or the subjection to an executive coming from embodiment in the people represented by a legislature. But the primary political *connection*—what he called in the preamble "political bands"—was what subsisted between the American colonies and the people of Great Britain (or the Parliament insofar as that spoke for the people). Jefferson's declaration of independence is a renunciation of unfeeling brethren. His whole document was shaped to make that clear. Even after Congress removed the heart of his argument, at its climax, traces of it remained, looking vague or misleading in the official version. The "one people" and "political bands" of the preamble—along with the affective base for things like the right of pursuing happiness—sit uneasily in Congress's paper. No wonder Jefferson preferred his version till the very end of his life.

PART FIVE

NATIONAL SYMBOL

"... *opinions of mankind* ..."

If by the Declaration of Independence we mean the document itself, or the actual language that was written in Philadelphia and published in July, 1776, then I do not think it was ever well-known in France, or had any particular influence in that country. In contexts where we might expect the Declaration to be referred to, that is when Frenchmen were discussing the ideas of the American Revolution, we seldom find the Declaration quoted or even mentioned. In the Constituent Assembly, in August 1789, during the debates on the Declaration of the Rights of Man and the Citizen, the speakers often referred to American precedents, but not to the Declaration of Independence. Almost half a century later Alexis de Tocqueville, in writing *Democracy* in America, thought that "equality" was the one most fundamental idea in the United States; but he also thought that the American Revolution had been of little importance in producing this spirit of equality, and unless I am mistaken he never in two volumes even mentioned the Declaration of Independence. ... In the strict sense, then, there is no such subject as the "Declaration of Independence in France."

—R. R. Palmer

One of the problems with the early history of the Declaration is that there is so little of it. The Fourth International Conference on the Enlightenment scheduled a panel session on the Declaration's influence abroad, and the panelists embarrassed each other, a bit, by finding practically no influence. A year after that, Howard H. Peckham studied the Declaration's career in England, and found "the beam of light which the Declaration cast on a new order of government for the empire was never perceived" (*Declaration of Independence*, American Antiquarian Society, 1976).

Far more surprising is the lack of initial attention to the document in America. Although the *act* of declaring independence was celebrated—and celebrated, by an accident, on the Fourth—the document was not an important part of the earliest festivities. Philip F. Detweiler showed (in *WMQ*, 1962) that "little attention was given to the political language of the Declaration even on those infrequent occasions during the [Revolutionary] war when the Declaration itself was the featured topic" (559). Early Independence Day orators made little use of the Declaration's language; and they almost totally ignored the preamble (559). During the 1780s "in neither the orations nor the toasts [of the Fourth] was the Declaration substantially more than the act of independence" (560). State constitutions did not imitate the Declaration, any more than the federal one was to do, even though eight of the original constitutions included a bill of rights—modeled for the most part on Virginia's, penned by George Mason. Not until 1848 did a state constitution, Wisconsin's, adopt the language of the Declaration. After that, seven more states included key phrases of the preamble—which allowed Howard Mumford Jones to study treatment of those phrases in state courts (*The Pursuit of Happiness*, 1953)—an effort that throws no light, of course, on the sense of the term in Jefferson's time.

The Declaration played almost no part in the debates over ratification of the Constitution (Detweiler, 563), and the *Federalist Papers* quoted only the phrase about altering or abolishing governments—Glorious Revolution doctrine. The first American histories of the Revolution did not find the Declaration an important part of the process. By the last decade of the eighteenth century, the Declaration emerged as a partisan issue and symbol for the nascent Federalist and Republican factions, but Detweiler thinks it did not become a generally accepted "national charter" till after the War of 1812. Indeed, he says "historical interest in the Declaration [only] became clearly evident in 1817" (572). John Fitzpatrick, in his *Spirit of the Revolution* (1924), thought "the discovery of the Declaration of Independence by the people of the United States" could be dated from the engravings of the text in 1818 and 1819 by Benjamin Owen Tyler and John Binns.

Early celebrations of the Fourth were spotty, full of anomalies, wavering in their symbolism (Charles Warren, *WMQ*, 1945, 254 ff.). We shall see, in later chapters, that the memory of those involved in drafting, amending, voting on, and signing the Declaration proved to be dim, contradictory, even nonexistent. Why was that?

The beginning of wisdom in this matter is to realize that the men who debated and passed the Declaration of Independence did not think of it as one of the more important duties on their crowded agenda. They were not trying to enunciate a new theory of government, or to found a nation, or write a national charter. I do not mean simply that the document was less important than the *act* of declaring the colonies independent on July 2. Even that *act*, as it appeared to the men who had to take responsibility for it, was not important for its own sake. It was only a means to an end. And that made two other acts, interconnected with the declaring of independence, of greater immediate importance.

About the motive for declaring independence there can be no doubt. The testimony is ample and unanimous. It was not done to found a new nation—the colonies took special measures to prevent that. It was not done to make the colonies self-governing—they were already that in fact; and since the May 10 and May 15 measures for committee rule, they were almost self-governing *de jure* as well as *de facto*. It was not to bind other colonies more securely to one's own. No—there was only one motive, dwelt on repeatedly by both friends and foes of the move, that made declaring independence look attractive. It was a necessary step for the securing of foreign aid in the ongoing war effort.

The man who offered Congress the resolution on independence best explained the end it had to serve. Richard Henry Lee wrote on June 2: "It is not choice then but necessity that calls for independence as the only means by which foreign alliance can be obtained" (Burnett, 469). The colonies were in dire need of supplies and cordial relations with France, to keep their army in the field and their hopes of prevailing alive. But it was hard to get any major or continuing commitment while the colonies lacked international legal standing. They were not a corporate body that could enter into a contract. In international law they were still parts of England, engaged in a civil war. Aid to them would be an entry into England's internal affairs. Before treaties could be made, the colonies had to become a treaty-making entity. That meant not merely a declaration of independence, but the formation of a league among themselves, one that would empower Congress to commit all the colonies to a single contract with foreign governments. France could hardly be expected to negotiate thirteen different treaties with the separate little countries in America. The provisos and reservations withholding sovereign rights were meant to circumscribe the "confederacy," to hold it to the immediate purpose—the power to make a treaty with France, as well as take steps to provision armies in the field.

The instructions to delegates in Philadelphia make it clear that foreign aid was the aim of the declaration. North Carolina put the two acts as a co-ordinate single aim: "declaring independency and forming foreign alliances" (Force, *Archives*, ser. iv, 5:860). Virginia put the declaration of independence among *other* means to the real goal—granting the "assent of this colony to such declaration and to whatever measures may be thought proper and necessary by the Congress for forming foreign alliances and a confederacy of the colonies" (ibid., 6:461). New Jersey, too, put independence in this *chain* of actions aimed at French alliance: "we empower you to join with them in declaring the United Colonies independent of Great Britain, entering into a confederacy for union and common defence, making treaties with foreign nations for commerce and assistance, and to take such other measures as may appear to them and you necessary for these great ends" (ibid., 6:1726).

Against the background of these instructions, we are better able to read what Richard Henry Lee actually proposed on June 7. His motion is often reduced to one part of it, the call for independence. But he made three different motions; and the Congress set up three different committees to deal with them. Not only were the other two motions just as important as the first; they were, in fact, the real goals to which declaring independence was directed. Independence *had* to be declared to get foreign aid; and a league had to be formed to negotiate that aid. Here, then, are the interlocking three resolutions:

That these United Colonies are, and of right ought to be, free and independent states, that they are absolved from all allegiance to the British

Crown, and that all political connection between them and the State of Great Britain is, and ought to be, totally dissolved.

That it is expedient forthwith to take the most effectual measures for forming foreign alliances.

That a plan of confederation be prepared and transmitted to the respective colonies for their consideration and approbation.

We have seen from Lee's own letter, written five days before he made this motion, what he had in mind. The evidence of the delegate-instructions reinforces the terms of the threefold resolution itself, to demonstrate that independence was not sought for its own sake but as the price to be paid for help from abroad. The letters and notes of the members of Congress confirm this. Foreign aid was the real "selling point" for the resolution on independence. As Carter Braxton admitted in a letter of April 14: "It is said by the advocates for separation that France will undoubtedly assist us after we have asserted the state [i.e., constituted a political entity], and they therefore urge us to make the experiment" (Burnett, 420). The opponents of this action tried to separate the first resolution from the other two, saying aid could be bargained for and a league constituted without a formal act of separation. Edward Rutledge wrote near the eve of Lee's motion: "A declaration of independence, the form of a confederation of these colonies, and a scheme for a treaty with foreign powers will be laid before the House on Monday. Whether we shall be able effectually to oppose the first and infuse wisdom into the two others will depend in a great measure upon the exertions of the honest and sensible part of the members" (ibid., 517). The ultimate aims could no longer be opposed, only separated from the step of independence.

But the necessity of the first measure to the success of the other two had been brought home to delegates over many months of argument and experiment. John Adams wrote, as early as October 7, 1775: "What then can we offer [to France]? An alliance, a treaty of commerce? What security could they have that we should keep it?" (Burnett, 219). George Wythe put this argument to Congress: "If we should offer our trade to the court of France, would they take notice of it, any more than if Bristol or Liverpool should offer theirs, while we profess to be subjects? No, we must declare ourselves a free people" (JA, *Papers*, 2:230).

The logic of these demands had become clear to men outside the

Congress, who sent their advice to delegates. Joseph Hawley wrote to Elbridge Gerry on February 20: "If we resolve on independence, what will hinder but that we may instantly commence a trade not only with Holland, France, and Spain, but with all the world. . . . Pray consider this matter with regard to Canada and the Dutch of New York. Will they ever join with us heartily, who, in order to do it, must sacrifice their trade? . . . Whereas, the moment that we resolve on independence, trade will be free for them—for the one to France and the other to Holland" (Hazelton, 49).

There is an urgency in the later cries for independence that does not come from literary promptings to voice a theory of government. What is being cried for is aid from France. It was reported back from Washington's camp that the general believed "nothing else [but independence] will save us" (Hazelton, 41). John Page wrote a brief appeal to Jefferson on April 6: "For God's sake declare the colonies independent at once, and save us from ruin" (*Papers*, 1:287). He explained this urgency in a longer dispatch sent three weeks later, when he said Virginia's will to resist was crumbling under a lack of supplies: "Some sure means of importing them should be instantly fallen upon, and as no means can be so certain and can so fully answer our purpose as forming an alliance with France, no time should be lost in doing so" (ibid., 288). About the same time, John Augustus Washington wrote to Richard Henry Lee: "I am clearly of opinion that unless we declare openly for independency there is no chance for foreign aid" (Hazelton, 73).

John Penn wrote from Philadelphia on March 2: "The consequence [he means the condition] of making alliances is perhaps a total separation with Britain, and without something of that sort we may not be able to provide what is necessary for our defense" (Hazelton, 82–83).

Jefferson's own notes quote the use made of this argument in the June debates:

That a declaration of Independance alone could render it consistent with European delicacy for European powers to treat with us, or even to receive an Ambassador from us:

That till this they would not receive our vessels into their ports, nor acknowledge the adjudications of our courts of Admiralty to be legitimate, in cases of capture of British vessels:

That tho' France & Spain may be jealous of our rising power, they must think it will be much more formidable with the addition of Great Britain; and will therefore see it their interest to prevent a coalition; but should they refuse, we shall be but where we are; whereas without trying we shall never know whether they will aid us or not:

That the present campaign may be unsuccessful, & therefore we had better propose an alliance while our affairs wear a hopeful aspect:

That to wait the event of this campaign will certainly work delay, because during this summer France may assist us effectually by cutting off those supplies of provisions from England & Ireland on which the enemy's armies here are to depend; or by setting in motion the great power they have collected in the West Indies, & calling our enemy to the defence of the possessions they have there:

That it would be idle to lose time in settling the terms of alliance, till we had first determined we would enter into alliance:

That it is necessary to lose no time in opening a trade for our people, who will want clothes, and will want money too for the paiment of taxes:

And that the only misfortune is that we did not enter into alliance with France six months sooner, as besides opening their ports for the vent of our last year's produce, they might have marched an army into Germany and prevented the petty princes there from selling their unhappy subjects to subdue us (*Papers*, 1:312–13).

It is clear from the notes how every aspect of the motion for independence was attacked and justified in terms of one thing—aid to be won from France.

Even more interesting is the climactic argument in that pamphlet credited with bringing a crucial margin of people around to the cause of independence. Later commentaries have naturally stressed the political theory of Paine's *Common Sense;* but he seemed to know what would have practical impact on his audience, and he ended the pamphlet with arguments very similar to those rehearsed in Jefferson's notes:

To conclude, however strange it may appear to some—or however unwilling they may be to think so matters not—but many strong and striking reasons may be given to show that nothing can settle our affairs so expeditiously as an open and determined declaration for independence. Some of which are:

First.—It is the custom of nations, when any two are at war, for some other powers not engaged in the quarrel to step in as mediators, and bring about the preliminaries of peace. But while America calls herself the subject of Great Britain, no power, however well disposed she may be, can offer her mediation. Wherefore, in our present state we may quarrel on forever.

Secondly.—It is unreasonable to suppose that France or Spain will give us any kind of assistance if we mean only to make use of that assistance for the purpose of repairing the breach and strengthening the connection between Britain and America; because those powers would be sufferers by the consequences.

Thirdly.—While we profess ourselves the subjects of Britain, we must, in the eye of foreign nations, be considered as rebels. The precedent is somewhat dangerous to their peace for men to be in arms under the name of subjects. We, on the spot, can solve the paradox; but to unite resistance and subjection requires an idea much too refined for common understanding.

Fourthly.—Were a manifesto to be published, and dispatched to foreign courts, setting forth the miseries we have endured and the peaceable methods we have ineffectually used for redress—declaring at the same time that not being able any longer to live happily or safely under the cruel disposition of the British court, we had been driven to the necessity of breaking off all connections with her—at the same time assuring all such courts of our peaceable disposition towards them and of our desire of entering into trade with them, such a memorial would produce more good effects to this continent than if a ship were freighted with petitions to Britain.

Under our present denomination of British subjects, we can neither be received nor heard abroad. The custom of all courts is against us, and will be so until, by an independence, we take rank with other nations.

These proceedings may at first appear strange and difficult; but like all other steps which we have already passed over, will in a little time become familiar and agreeable. And until an independence is declared, the continent will feel itself like a man who continues putting off some unpleasant business from day to day, yet knows it must be done, hates to set about it, wishes it over, and is continually haunted with the thought of its necessity.

The extraordinary thing about this conclusion to Paine's work is that he spells out four reasons, then adds a fifth; yet they are all one and the same—the need to have independent status as a nation in order to get help from abroad. The success of the pamphlet must have been derived, in large part, from the way it hammered home this overriding consideration of the moment.

Three days after Lee offered his motion, Congress voted to delay the debate on independence (while votes for it were sought), yet to appoint a committee to draft a declaration in order "that no time be lost, in case the Congress agree thereto" (*Journals*, 5:428). On the next day (June 11), a committee was appointed "to prepare a declaration to the effect of the said first resolution." One day later still, committees were appointed to draw up documents addressing the second and third parts of the motion—i.e., to write a draft treaty with France (the real aim of this complex three-part operation) and a plan of confederation or alliance. John Adams, who did little on the declaration committee, worked very hard on the treaty operation, getting models of treaties from Benjamin Franklin. The Declaration was passed with few changes after two days of debate. The treaty was a more difficult business, and could not even be reported to the Congress until two weeks after the Declaration was passed. It was then another two months before Congress agreed to all its provisions. It was as important to make this document proper as it had been, in the first Congress, to draw up a sound Bill of Rights and Petition (the real aim of that meeting). The work was well enough done, in the words of Samuel Flagg Beamis, to "furnish the model for all, except one, of the eighteenth-century treaties of the United States, and may be regarded as a charter document of early American maritime practice." Another year and a half of negotiation passed before this important paper was signed by the French (on February 6, 1778).

The other document to be drafted raised even more ticklish problems. The treaty with France looked to one set of foreign sensibilities. The draft for an alliance or confederation had to deal with thirteen new sovereign entities, all very jealous of their prerogatives. This meant that all thirteen had to be represented on the drafting committee, which became the largest of the three bodies formed. The limits under which men worked in this area are indicated by the carefully hedged instructions given to the states that voted independence.

North Carolina, for instance, told its delegates on April 12 they could vote for independence, but only while "reserving to this colony the sole and exclusive right of forming a constitution and laws for this colony" (Force, *Archives*, ser. iv, 5:860). Virginia, the next month, passed the resolutions Lee carried to Philadelphia; but did so "provided that the power of forming government, and the regulation of the internal concerns of each colony, be left to the respective colonial legislatures" (ibid., 6:461). Others used much the same language. Pennsylvania: ". . . reserving to the people of this colony the sole and exclusive right of regulating the internal government and police of the same" (ibid., 6:735). New Jersey: ". . . always observing that whatever plan of confederacy you enter into, the regulating the internal police of this province is to be reserved to the colony legislature" (ibid., 6:1726). Connecticut: ". . . saving that the administration of government and the power of forming governments for, and the regulation of the internal concerns and police of, each colony ought to be left and remain to the respective legislatures" (ibid., 8:868).

Not one country, but thirteen separate ones, came into existence when the Declaration was at last made unanimous on July 19, 1776—the plan of future confederation was left undecided at that time. It is sometimes said that Jefferson's document set up a new form of government "by the people." That was not even true of the general basis given for popular government—that doctrine was drawn from the Glorious Revolution, to have most force in a petitioning process based on that precedent. But in a more basic sense, Jefferson could not establish any new government because all the colonies had expressly instructed their delegates *not* to do any such thing when declaring independence. Each new state would establish its own constitution, then agree on later terms of alliance with the others.

This process was bound to be slow and difficult. It is typical of men's caution in this area that John Dickinson—the drafter of the first Congress's main documents, who had fallen behind the effort to declare independence—was put in charge of drafting the terms of confederation. Men still welcomed his caution and legalism in this area. It was one thing to thunder against George III, and quite another to work out cagey terms among themselves. Dickinson went back to an even earlier stage of the quarrel with England to revive Franklin's Hartford scheme of alliance—showing, again, how the thoughts on union lagged far behind those on independence.

The Articles of Confederation were not ready to be sent to the states for ratification until November of 1777. Meanwhile, states busy forming their own constitutions co-operated with the war effort in the informal ways established before independence was declared. Even after the Articles were submitted to the states, it took four years to gather all the ratifications, and another six years to discover that the Articles were too cautious and could not be made to work.

In the midst of a war, while forming constitutions in their own provinces, men obviously felt that the treaty and the articles were more difficult projects of practical politics, and set more useful or dangerous legal precedents, than the Declaration itself. The latter was not a legislative instrument. Its issuance was a propaganda adjunct to the act of declaring independence on July 2—and that act, in turn, was just the necessary step toward the two projects men were principally wrestling with.

If it was inevitable that the treaty and the Articles (and the state constitutions) should fill men's heads more thoroughly than the Declaration, it was also inevitable, in the long run, that those other documents would become less interesting. Precisely because they were urgently tailored to the time, they suffered the changes of time. The treaty with Paris was absorbed into the course of diplomatic adjustments, new times and new wars calling for new understandings. The Articles, so long in the adoption, would be criticized and at last replaced by the federal Constitution. Even the state constitutions needed redrafting, revision, amendment, and ultimate adjustment to the federal Constitution. The Declaration, by contrast, was blessed with comparative irrelevance. Its words could stand untouched because it just explained an event already passed (on July 2); it bound men to nothing further than support of that past act. *How* they would support it had to be spelled out in the treaty and the Articles.

The Declaration had a modest objective; yet it failed to accomplish even that small object. It was an explanation, addressed to a candid world, of what had happened. It was a propaganda overture, addressed primarily to France, which the treaty was meant to follow. But we have seen that the Declaration was not read much, nor studied at all, in France. The Declaration had a loftier destiny ahead of it—but an accidental one, and one still far down the road as men busied themselves with laws and armies in the critical autumn months of 1776.

"... *decent respect* ..."

We esteem ourselves bound by obligations of respect to
the rest of the world to make known the justice of our
cause.

—John Dickinson, 1775

The general structure and strategy of argument in the Declaration
were affected by the petitioning process (see chapter Four). The language of a mutual pledge at the end, and the insertion of Lee's resolution of independence, gave the document some appearance of a
charter; yet it could not be a formal compact of government, since
the colonies had withheld the power to make such a pledge from
their delegates.

Actually, there was no confusion at the time about the document's
genre. It was a paper issued subsequent to an action in order to
explain that action. These papers were normally called Declarations
and had a long history. To go no further back than 1775, Jefferson
had drafted, Dickinson altered, and Congress passed the Declaration
of the Causes and Necessity for Taking Up Arms. The arms were
already assumed; but—as Jefferson put it in his draft—

as it behoves those, who are called to this great decision [the assumption of arms], to be assured that their cause is approved before supreme
reason, so it is of great avail that it's justice be made known to the world,
whose affections will ever take part with those encountering oppression
(*Papers*, 1:199).

Dickinson omitted this passage from the draft Congress voted on—
it was another of those omissions that tended to occur when Jefferson was voicing his theory of society as based on affection. But
Jefferson kept one element of that first Declaration in his second—
the concept that the justice of their cause should "be made known

to the world." This became: "Let facts be submitted to a candid world." Jefferson also used elements of Dickinson's draft, since the latter had spoken of "obligations of respect to the rest of the world." This became Jefferson's "a decent respect to the opinions of mankind." As he put it long after, the Declaration was intended as "an appeal to the tribunal of the world" (Ford, 10:343).

It was even more appropriate to issue a Declaration in the matter of independence than in that of taking up arms. There were two reasons for this. The Glorious Revolution had been negotiated through some famous Declarations. There was, for instance, William of Orange's Declaration of his intentions on September 30, 1688. There he said that he had decided to intervene in the affairs of Englishmen "for the securing to them the continual enjoyments of all their just rights," including their "lives and liberties." That decision was already made; and William's Declaration was issued to give "a true account of the reasons inducing Us to it." The Parliament answered with its Declaration of Rights on February 13, 1689—the model for the Bill of Rights drawn up by the First Continental Congress. This spelled out the rights of petition and redress, found James wanting in the protection of those rights, and declared the Parliament "particularly encouraged by the Declaration of His Highness the Prince of Orange, as being the only means for obtaining a full redress and remedy therein." The distinction between an act and the proclamation of that act was spelled out in the same document, which concluded with the resolution "that William and Mary, Prince and Princess of Orange, be, and be *declared*, King and Queen of England" (emphasis added).

These political declarations seem analogous to declaration in the stricter legal sense, which meant a justifying explanation for the bringing of a suit. First, one brought the action and identified its object. Then a declaration had to be filed. Thus Rastell's 1579 *Termes of Law* said: "Declaratyon is a shewing forth in writing of the griefe [i.e., grievance] and complaynt of the demaundant or pleintiffe against the tenant or defendant." Blackstone said (3:303): "As soon as the action is brought . . . the complaint must be fully stated in the declaration." Johnson's Dictionary quoted Cowell on declaration as "the shewing forth or laying out of an action personal in any suit, though it is used sometimes for both personal and real actions." Chambers Cyclopaedia used Rastell's definition and added:

"This [declaration] ought to be plain and certain, both because it impeacheth the defendant, and also compels him to answer thereto." This legal analogue was very appropriate for the Declaration of Independence; which was, nonetheless, a declaration in the looser political sense of explanation.

The very precision of the term would lead to later confusion. This was perhaps unavoidable, since *state* declaration had two quite different meanings in the legal literature familiar to Jefferson's fellows in the Congress. Declaration sometimes meant just the explanation of an act. But at other times declaring was the act itself—e.g., when a sovereign declares war. William of Orange's Declaration was just an explanation; but one of the things that led to that document was James II's Declaration for Liberty of Conscience of April 4, 1687—an instrument that *effected* the state it described. The Parliament's Declaration of Rights was both explanatory (describing the failure of petitions to James) and declaratory of an effect (the naming of William and Mary as King and Queen). Jefferson's Declaration is explanatory of an act; but that act had itself been declaratory. Declaring independence, like declaring war, is an act of state. That act was accomplished on July 2, when the Congress voted on Lee's resolution that the colonies "are [at that very moment], and of right ought to be, free and independent states." The condition of independence was declared to exist, already, at that vote.

Those immediately involved in the process understood, at the outset, the difference between declaring as an act and the Declaration as an explanation of that act. Thus Richard Henry Lee, after deploring the changes made in Jefferson's text, said: "However the *Thing* is in its nature so good, that no Cookery can spoil the Dish for the Palates of Freemen" (*Letters*, 1:210—italics in original). The Thing's own nature or essence is the act of declaring, not simply Lee's phrasing of the act—much less Jefferson's. But one could not expect the general populace to keep that distinction in mind.

Confusion was probably inevitable in any case; but Congress made sure that confusion would not only exist but spread when it incorporated the July 2 resolution in the July 4 explanation. The latter document is thus made to say that the "united colonies are and of right ought to be free and independent states." Of course the Declaration could not make the colonies independent if they were already independent; so the Declaration does not declare them independent at that moment. It merely repeats what had been declared, that they are still in the condition effected by the act of declaring on July 2. But later on, as the Declaration acquired its popularity, it became the custom to misread it as both the first enactment (contained in it) *and* the later explanation—but principally the former!

The seeds for this confusion were sown early. Palmer, Detweiler, and others have shown that almost all the early references to "the declaration of independence" denote the *act* of declaring, the formal break; but they tended from the outset to connect that *act* with the date of the *explanation's* passage (July 4), since this lent itself to public proclamation. Soon other dates (e.g., of the unanimous passage of the thirteen colonies, or of the various signings) also drifted toward that convenient day for the celebration of all things connected with the process of becoming independent. The Fourth became a convenient symbolic date, and most of what was celebrated as belonging to it had either preceded or followed the actual event of that day—i.e., the favorable vote by twelve states, already independent, to approve a statement of the causes for their prior vote.

Charles Warren described (*WMQ*, 1945) the sporadic, rather casual way celebration of the Fourth began, and the vaguely inclusive symbolism of its early years. It became a patriotic day for a people with a *patria* still undefined in constitutional terms; and when constitutions were added, that day generously included *them* in the causes for hilarity. The first annual celebration in Philadelphia was late, hugger-mugger, and unofficial; but it set a pattern by occurring on the Fourth. John Adams tells us why:

The thought of taking any notice of this day was not conceived until the second of this month [July] and it was not mentioned until the third. It was too late to have a sermon as everyone wished, so this must be deferred another year. Congress determined to adjourn over that day [the Fourth] and to dine together (Warren, 255).

The fatal displacement had taken place, by an oversight. The second of July would never be celebrated as Adams expected during the heat of events in 1776. His own letters on the subject would be altered, in the nineteenth century, up to the scholarly revision of them by his grandson, to make him speak even in 1776 of the Fourth.

In 1778, the Fourth fell on a Saturday, and Congress combined an official dinner that night with congressional attendance "in a body" at "divine worship on Sunday, the fifth day of July." In 1779, the Fourth fell on a Sunday, and was celebrated with sermons that day, followed by dinner on the fifth. Congress after that sometimes remembered, and sometimes did not, to proclaim a celebration during the rest of the war and the Confederation period.

The Fourth was early combined with other reasons for holiday. The first state celebration was in Massachusetts, the year of the war's happy conclusion. In 1783, the proclamation still celebrated both independence and victory. Celebrating the war's success was so much an aspect of the Fourth that the Society of the Cincinnati chose that day for its annual feast. In 1788 the Fourth was used by supporters of the federal Constitution to signal the ratifications of it by that date (Warren, 259). Thenceforth the Constitution, which had no single date to call its own, moved in and lived side by side with the Declaration as a cause of mutual congratulation on the Fourth.

Because the Fourth accumulated in symbol all the successes of the war, the constitutional period, and the early government, it had become before the end of the century a Federalist preserve. (See Warren, 259–71, and R. P. Hay, *Freedom's Jubilee*, University of Kentucky dissertation, 1967, pp. 31–46.) Toasts to the patriots were colored by this fact: Samuel and John Adams were publicly credited not only with inspiring or helping pass the Declaration, but sometimes with writing it as well: "While the names of Washington and Hancock, Samuel Adams and John Adams were always the subject of toasts, the name of Thomas Jefferson does not appear to have been mentioned in connection with the Declaration until he became Vice President in 1797" (Warren, 261). Thus the attempt to assert Jefferson's authorship became a narrow and partisan matter, consciously at odds with the larger tradition of celebrating the Fourth.

After Jefferson's election as President, some Federalists claimed the Republicans had not only usurped all the glorious associations of the Fourth, but wrongfully laid claim to the Declaration itself (Warren, 268–70). The Republicans who meant to challenge this effrontery had to organize themselves, in 1805, as the *Washington* Society to secure Republican orators for the Fourth. Two years after that, factional celebration of the Fourth led to riot and murder in Boston.

Even when the Era of Good Feeling brought in universal acceptance of the Declaration's importance, new disputes arose about its authorship and signing. As all kinds of patriotic meanings were attached to the Fourth, the signers themselves began, very early, to talk about having *signed* the Declaration on the Fourth. John Adams made this claim only five years after 1776, Jefferson seven years later, and Franklin ten (Warren, *WMQ*, 1945, 242–43). By 1814, Adams had even forgotten that the vote on independence took place on July 2 (Letter to Mercy Warren, January 7).

These men could not, at first, have made this claim after much reflection on the matter. The document itself, read carefully, reveals what they were forgetting. The inscribed Declaration begins, "The Unanimous Declaration of the Thirteen United States . . ." But it was known to all those who took part in the events that the thirteen states were not unanimous on the Fourth. New York's delegates were still waiting for instruction and could not vote. Their approval of the document did not reach the Congress till July 19, when at last the boast of unanimity became fact. An engrosser was commissioned to pen a formal copy of the document under its proud title. This fair copy was not ready for signing until August 2, when the delegates began to put their names to it. But by that time, not all those who had voted on the Fourth were still present. (There was intense travel and advising back and forth between Philadelphia and the efforts, at home, to draft provincial constitutions—a matter more serious to many delegates than anything the Congress was currently doing.) Some of these absentees returned, after August 2, and put their names to the parchment. But others who actually voted for the document's passage on the Fourth would never come back and be known as Signers. And some new arrivals would sign without having voted on the wording. Not only were the Signers not all present together on the Fourth. They were never together in the same room at any time—on, before, or after the Fourth.

Actually, this matters less than one might think, from the later cult of individual Signers. No individuals voted on the last ballot for the Declaration. Only the new-formed states did, one vote one state. No matter how many men were in a delegation, no matter how slim the majority within any delegation, each group voted as a block, since the larger states had lost their effort at "weighted" voting, led by Patrick Henry in the first Congress. Thus, when the signing began on August 2, the delegations were widely spaced about on the bottom of the parchment document, so that delegates arriving could put their names in the area allotted to their state. It was a memorial action by that time. The notion that putting one's name to the Declaration was an act of individual courage is a bit of genial mythologizing in the general air of inflation that was to occur all around this document. The men who signed—and even the men who voted and did not sign—were all known revolutionaries. Their very presence in the Congress after August 2 made that clear.

The signing itself had no great significance. The Congress had issued its former Declaration—on the Causes and Necessity for Taking Up Arms—with the simple validating signatures of the President and Secretary (Messers Hancock and Thomson). Other important documents like the Bill of Rights had not been signed, though both petitions to the King were. The vote of July 2, far more serious and consequential than that of July 4, had not led to a signing of any paper bearing Lee's threefold resolution. Julian Boyd claims (*Papers*, 1:307) that the phrase "mutually pledge to each other" calls, almost of necessity, for a general signing—as the pledge to the Association and other boycott schemes had. But the "we" of the Declaration is neither the "we the people" of the Constitution nor the "we as individuals" who signed as a promise of observing the embargos. The Declaration speaks for the thirteen united *states*. These new *states* pledge to each other their honor, that honor accruing to sovereignties as they take their "free and equal station" with other nations.

So the signing becomes another of those things that subtly misled later generations. The fact that different numbers of men signed for the different states leads some to overlook the fact that only states voted, and all equally.

Why was the Declaration signed at all? There was a desire to have some memorial of the complex action that took place in the months from May to August of 1776. The Lee resolutions were not a public document, but a crucial statement of the whole congressional agenda for the next months and years. They looked to the preparation of a treaty and of the Articles of Confederation. But neither of those documents would be ready for a long time, and the vital signatures for them would come from Paris and from the states' ratifying conventions.

The Declaration, precisely because it was a propaganda document, was addressed to the widest possible audience—to the whole "candid world," to that mankind whose opinion deserves a decent respect; not simply to the King (like the petitions) or the British (like the address of September 5, 1774) or one's own subjects (like a legislating instrument). Thus the large formal parchment brought into the Congress on August 2 was kept available, over the next six months, for men to sign, joining their peers and predecessors. It gave men a kind of overnight antiquity and tradition because it was already outside time's more immediate and practical challenges. The Declaration had already begun to live as a "conservative" symbol of past action, responding to the congressional desire for an at least symbolic "charter"—something signable as Magna Carta had been, though the Declaration had none of the strictly legal force of the first Great Charter.

The confusion over the dates on which the Declaration was signed continued through most of the nineteenth century. In 1884, Mellen Chamberlain proved from manuscript originals in the Department of State that the printed Journal had erred in reporting that members signed on July 4. The original Journal merely has the broadside printed on July 5 wafered into the account of events; and that was signed only by Hancock and Thomson. It was John Hazelton's great contribution, in 1906, to demonstrate once for all that the complete list of signatures on the engrossed parchment could have been collected neither on July 4 *nor* on August 2. By a thorough study of the whereabouts of all the Signers, he proves they were not there on July 4, when no signing was reported (*Declaration*, 508–31). But he goes further: Even on August 2, when there was undoubtedly a signing, certainly eight and perhaps as many as twelve of the Signers were absent. Their names had to be added subsequently. Indeed, Matthew Thornton cannot have signed before November 4, the day he first appeared in Congress and presented his credentials. This means that signatures were accumulating—from all the delegates, no matter what part they had played on July 4—for several months after August 2, and they could have been put down any time before the publication of the signed document on January 19, 1777. John Adams, who would later be certain he signed on the Fourth, wrote to Samuel Chase on July 9, 1776, "As soon as an American Seal is prepared, I conjecture the Declaration will be subscribed by all the members, which will give you the opportunity you wish for of transmitting your name among the votaries of independence." The language and the connection with the seal suggest that this was already a memorial act, one prepared as a symbol of the nation's pride and existence. Almost three weeks *after* the Fourth, Elbridge Gerry wrote back to Philadelphia: "Pray subscribe for me the Declaration of Independence if the same is to be signed, as proposed. I think we ought to have the privilege, when necessarily absent, of voting and signing by proxy" (Burnett, 2:20).

Julian Boyd notes that Jefferson, despite all the evidence to the contrary, continued to believe and affirm very strongly that there had been a signing on the Fourth. This compelled him, at last, to argue for two signings—one on paper, followed by the other on parchment. Jefferson did not fall back to this position, however, until the publication of the secret journals of Congress proved there had been a signing on August 2. He began, in the controversy, with the belief that there was only one signing; and even after he was forced to bring forward a hypothetical signing on paper, he continued to speak as if the cast of signers had been roughly the same on July 4 and August 2. (Hazelton's point, that not even August 2 will explain the presence of all the Signers' names, was not brought into the debate during Jefferson's lifetime.)

Boyd rightly observes there is practically no way of proving a negative—that men *could* not have signed something on July 4 that was lost and never referred to again (*Papers*, 1:306–8); but his attempt to vindicate Jefferson's account of the matter seems farfetched. For one thing, we should remember what the "paper" available for signing on the Fourth would have looked like. It was, presumably, the official paper reported out of committee June 28 and tabled by Congress until the July 2 vote made it necessary to debate the wording of the Declaration. The paper would have undergone all the emendations made by Congress before it was sent to John Dunlap for printing as a broadside (see Boyd himself, *Evolution*, 40–41).

This, the formal result of the debates on July 2 through 4, would not be as neat as Jefferson's copy of the document. Boyd himself showed how a phrase like "Scotch and other" before "foreign mercenaries" was at first taken by Congress from one passage and considered for another, then returned to the first passage, only to be deleted along with that whole passage (ibid., 35). The tabled document would be heavily written over with emendations, crossings-out, interlineations, and perhaps with further notes to the printer making clear which version was finally approved. Even if we assume there was room on this document for all the delegates' signatures, why would they sign a document only to add instructions telling the printer *not* to include their names? For they would have to do that to make sure Dunlap's printer put down only the two names he did—Hancock's and Thomson's. The whole thing makes no sense. The President and Secretary had to validate the final document as official; but it was not the kind of paper suitable for ceremonial signing. The Congress was busy with many things in July—why waste time signing a paper that was not even considered valuable enough to be retrieved from the printer and preserved? Even the published Journal that misled so many men for so many years stated that the Declaration was *"engrossed* and signed" on the Fourth, not imagining that delegates signed the original "paper" with all the scribblings on it. (This would assume an engrosser was available and could have done the job rapidly, before the paper was sent off to the printer. If that had been the case, the official Journal of the Congress would have used that *engrossed* copy of the text, not the broadside, when it inserted the results of the debate of July 4.)

This is a minor point, which Boyd pursues at length because he seems to think Jefferson's veracity is involved. Actually, as Hazelton argued (in a way that even Boyd had to admit was "plausible"), it was Jefferson's memory, not his veracity, that failed. And so, for that matter, did the memory of all the other Signers who remembered the event after a lapse of years—all, that is, but Thomas McKean, who raised the issue in his 1813 letter (published in 1817). Boyd himself shows how inaccurate were Jefferson's memories of the passage of that other Declaration he drafted, the one on taking up arms (*Papers,* 1:187–92). Paul H. Smith has found another error, traceable to bad memory, in Jefferson's notes on the July 4 debate: Jefferson says the Declaration was discussed all day and into the evening, but the secret Journal shows it was passed in the morning. (Smith's article is in the October, 1976, *Quarterly Journal of the Library of Congress*.)

The fact that many Signers had such poor memories of what happened in July 1776—memories distorted less than a decade after the event—reinforces my argument of the last chapter, that the men who passed the Declaration had no idea it would become as important as it did. Yet the memorial signing of the handsomely engrossed text also indicates the path this symbol would take over subsequent years, becoming a cult object whose importance was only loosely connected to its original purpose, argument, or legal standing. It became a paradoxically "conservative" symbol of a new thing's past. It would in time become doubly "radical"—both rooted and deracinating—in ways no one, even Jefferson himself, could have expected.

TWENTY-SIX

"... communication
of grandeur ..."

The painting executed by Col. Trumbull, representing
the Congress at the declaration of independence, will, I
fear, have a tendency to obscure the history of the
event which it is designed to commemorate.
—Samuel Wells, 1819

Although the Declaration of Independence was, in practical terms,
the least important of the three documents growing out of Lee's
resolutions, it was signed well before the other two. Yet, in the
twists of history, an even later signing than these three formed our
most persistent visual image of that first signing. For the Declaration soon slipped the constraints of temporal logic and sequence, to
live outside time with something of the insouciance of Tristram
Shandy (who regularly says things like "a cow broke in tomorrow
morning"). To follow the Declaration's fortunes is to enter a realm
of wild reversals.

We have seen that the signing of "the Fourth" actually took
place on a number of dates—and the Fourth was not one of them.
But our image of those later signings is derived from a different
signing altogether, one that took place in Paris on November 30,
1782. On that day, four American diplomats and two English
spokesmen brought the Revolutionary War to a formal end by signing the Preliminary Treaty. The very next year Benjamin West, the
Philadelphia artist who had become King George's favorite painter
and the head of the Royal Academy, began a painting of that event
(now in Delaware's Winterthur Museum). His sympathies still lay
with America, though he was a permanent resident in England; and
he hoped to do several paintings on the Revolution to be engraved

and sold as a series. The plan was aborted, no doubt because of the sensibilities of West's English patrons; but he completed all five American figures for his painting (the four diplomats—John Adams, Benjamin Franklin, John Jay, Henry Laurens—and their secretary, William Franklin).

The American group takes up almost three quarters of the picture, with a space at the right for one seated and one standing Englishman, never painted in. The most prominent figure is that of John Adams, taken from live sittings in London. Adams, wearing a powdered wig and brown suit, sits at the very edge of the table, nearest to us of the Americans. John Jay, standing behind him in the orator's pose, gestures to the treaty that has been spread on the table (and spills over its edge), about to state the American position.

Benjamin Franklin, in Quaker-plain black garb, is seated to Adams's left and looks almost straight out at the viewer—West took the face from a miniature based on Duplessis's frontal portrait. Laurens, in red, stands behind Franklin and leans forward to hear Jay speak. William Franklin, seated to his grandfather's left, is looking over at Jay. The massive and imposing presence of these Americans leaves little space for the British, whose backs would be toward us, accepting the terms of their defeat by former colonials.

John Trumbull, son of one Connecticut governor and brother to another, fought a bit in the Revolution, and seems to have spied a bit; but mainly he studied painting in London with West. Adams sat for West's "American Commissioners" sometime between November 1783 and January 1784—just the period when Trumbull was traveling back toward Europe for a second period of study with West. He had to know his master's attempt at an American series—a matter of great interest to Trumbull, since he was soon planning just such a lucrative series of engravings himself.

Three years later, visiting Jefferson in Paris (where he carried letters to and from Maria Cosway), Trumbull mentioned his plan and some of the subjects he proposed to cover—the battles of Bunker Hill and Trenton, the surrenders at Saratoga and Yorktown. Jefferson suggested that the Declaration be included and sketched (inaccurately) architectural details of the chamber the 1776 Congress sat in. Trumbull drew the layout for his most famous picture, which he would not complete for years.

Trumbull shows the Declaration's drafting committee presenting the Declaration to Hancock, president of the Congress, who sits with his back to us in the posture of West's intended British diplomat. Since there were five men on the drafting committee, and Charles Thomson stands by Hancock, the general grouping of the figures at the table repeats West's treatment of his seven figures. Here, too, the papers spill off the table toward the viewer.

Adams, though standing here instead of seated, is in brown, with white stockings over his prominent calves. John Quincy Adams later remembered how West measured those calves with calipers. These gaiters are the real source of John Randolph's famous gibe against Trumbull's painting: He called it a "shin piece." Most critics think he is mocking the lineup of legs around the committee tables; and Irma Jaffe calls the crack unjust, since most of the forty-seven figures have their legs hidden. But this was a time when "historical" scenes were often presented in classical garb—West himself had created a sensation by painting his "Death of Wolfe" with modern uniforms and a naked Indian. The calves of John Adams twinkle with Pickwick's own self-satisfaction in this decidedly bourgeois picture of a heroic deed.

Adams's face, seen in three-quarter profile, strikingly resembles West's portrait, as one can see by comparing all other life portraits of Adams in Andrew Oliver's collection of them (Harvard Press, 1967). The details printed by Oliver at pages 44 and 59 show that Trumbull's Adams was at first painted with a wig, like West's—then the powder was painted out, not entirely effacing the contours of the wig. The treatment of nose and mouth shows how closely Trumbull imitated his master in posing this life portrait of Adams.

In Trumbull's work, Jefferson takes the orator's position that Jay had in West; but he is not merely pointing to the document, he places it on the table. He has been moved closer to the table, therefore to Adams's left. Though all Trumbull's figures are standing, his Franklin is seen over the table in a bust-length treatment exactly like West's. He wears the same black garb and stares out toward the viewer.

This seven-man main group is placed off-center in a semicircle of delegates. Benjamin Harrison, the most prominent figure seated on the left of the semicircle, leans toward the desk as if waiting for Jefferson to speak—Laurens, with a similar oval face, leans that way in West's painting. The color scheme of the principals is similar too. Adams and Franklin wear the same clothes in West and Trumbull. The other clothes are red (West's Laurens, Trumbull's Jefferson), olive (West's Jay, Trumbull's Roger Sherman), and indeterminate (West's William Franklin, Trumbull's Robert Livingston).

Trumbull worked on his painting for about ten years, adding faces as he met Signers or came across good images of them. In 1816 Congress commissioned him to repeat his American series in life-size paintings for the rotunda of the Capitol. By that time Trumbull was a Federalist critical of Jefferson's "irreligion." His Capitol series—two military and two civil scenes—was meant to glorify Washington, the only man in both a civil and a military painting. But reproductions of the Declaration painting, in its smaller first version now kept at Yale, caught the public's fancy. Against his final will in the matter, Trumbull advanced the cult and myth of the Fourth.

The ironies are endless. The picture, modeled on a treaty-signing in 1782, was described by Trumbull himself as portraying the events of the Fourth. But his cast of characters does not represent the exact makeup of Congress on either July 4 or August 2, and in fact does not represent a signing at all. It gives us the moment when the drafting committee brought in its document on June 28, when it was tabled. (Actually, only one member of the committee would have brought it forward.)

Even if we were to imagine the committee again coming forward with the document for debate after the vote on independence, that would have occurred on July 2, when discussion of the Declaration began. And the scene depicted is not the time of voting, but of the introduction of the text. The delegates are interested, but have had no chance to see the paper. They lean and listen as Jefferson begins to describe it. The signing is a long way off.

Thus, by the time Trumbull began his composition, ten years after the events he was depicting, the Fourth had become an omnium-gatherum term including aspects of what was done on June 28, July 2, July 4, July 19, and August 2 through January—and, more generally, the victories and conclusion of the war, the drafting and passage of the Constitution.

Scholars have sorted out the actual dates and events that were merged in the mythic glow of the Fourth. But reputable historians relay John Adams's memories without sufficient skepticism. One still finds some of them believing Adams's version of the way he got Jefferson to draft the document. In an 1822 letter to Timothy Pickering, Adams claimed that Jefferson asked him to write the draft, but he answered: "I am obnoxious, suspected, and unpopular." Earlier, in his *Autobiography*, he spelled out the matter more fully: "I had been so obnoxious for my early and constant zeal in promoting the measure that any draft of mine would undergo a more severe scrutiny and criticism in Congress than one of his composition" (JA, *Papers*, 3:366).

In the same place Adams said that Jefferson was only included in the drafting committee because the Virginia faction led by Benjamin Harrison wanted to exclude Richard Henry Lee, thus depriving him of credit for the resolution on independence. That makes no sense. Harrison could have introduced the resolutions if he wanted to. Inclusion on the committee would not necessarily lead to drafting of the document; Lee had tried his hand at several documents in the first Congress, but Dickinson redrafted them (*Respect*, 22, 34). Besides, Lee was involved in what seemed a more important matter, drafting a constitution back in Williamsburg. Adams is, once more, remembering the general lines of division, the patronage of Jefferson by Lee's enemies, and applying it to a matter that became important only in retrospect.

On the question of ability to write the draft, Adams's later accounts are theatrical with self-effacement. He pictures himself expansively granting that Jefferson could write "ten times better" than Adams himself—or, in the soberer *Autobiography:* "I had a great opinion of the elegance of his pen, and none at all of my own" (JA, *Papers*, 3:336). But there was no reason for the author of the "Novanglus" papers and *Thoughts on Government* to be so abject before the author of *A Summary View*. By the time he wrote his account of the Declaration's composition, after service in the White House, Adams was the resentful author of *Discourses on Davila* exchanging praise for blame with the author of *Notes on the State of Virginia*. Not that literary skill was the primary qualification for drawing up documents at the Congress. The problem was to know the law, the course of the debate, and the common grounds of grievance. Adams certainly felt himself (with good cause) as versed in these things as Jefferson.

As to jeopardizing the Declaration with his own unpopularity, it is true that Adams underwent a period of intense dislike from John Dickinson and his friends in 1775. This was a smaller and later version of the clash, at the first Congress, of Joseph Galloway with Samuel Adams. But by the spring of 1776, Dickinson was the man being isolated with his lost cause. In May of that year, he was not even considered the real representative of his own province. In the chain of concerted actions that overthrew his power in the Assembly, John Adams took an active and open—and successful—part. If he was afraid to bring forward a controversial measure, he would not have seconded the May 10 resolution for provincial government by revolutionary committees. He certainly would not have drafted and introduced and defended the even more controversial preamble to that resolution, which passed on May 15 and became the instrument for overthrowing Pennsylvania's Assembly.

Nor did Adams let up throughout June. By the time of the climactic debate on independence (July 1), he personally stood up to refute Dickinson's futile last effort. There was nothing shrinking about the John Adams of those days. He was getting the same kind of glory Hancock reaped from earlier schemings of Samuel Adams —and he enjoyed it, if anything, even more than Hancock had.

But the final proof that Adams did not renounce the chance to write the Declaration is the active way he seized a greater opportunity, the drafting of a treaty with France. We have seen that this was the real aim of the Lee resolutions, and debate on the treaty would be longer and more difficult than that on the Declaration. What is more, Adams was less qualified than some others on the treaty committee—Benjamin Franklin, for instance, from whom he borrowed models of the former treaties, or Benjamin Harrison, who had run foreign affairs for Congress. But Adams not only secured an appointment to the committee; he took it on himself to write the treaty. If his story about the Declaration were true, he would have had far greater reason to turn down the treaty assignment. But, of course, it was not true. The Declaration, a minor matter in 1776, had become a great if vague national symbol since then, and Adams's self-pity made him remember giving up the chance to secure glory because of his noble resignation to the common good.

By the end of their long lives, Jefferson and Adams agreed on the Declaration's importance. Jefferson could even say of Adams, "I think he will outlive us all, I mean the Declaration-men" (LB, 15:330). Writing Adams himself, he spoke of the time when "you and I shall be at rest with our friends of 1776" (Cappon, 430). Indeed, the skeptical Jefferson returned to this thought with a kind of lyrical hope for the afterlife: "May we meet there again, in Congress, with our antient Colleagues" (ibid., 594). The two men kept each other informed on the number of Signers still living (ibid., 292, 296, 323, 574)—which is the point of Adams's dying words, "Jefferson still lives."

History, working its regular miracles to shove along the Declaration's fame, arranged for both men to die on the same day, the fiftieth anniversary of the Fourth. Adams's mistaken belief that Jefferson was the only Signer still alive is sometimes given a wider meaning. It would be as easy to extend Jefferson's comment on his deathbed: "Is it the Fourth?" He was happy, with the kind of superstition he rebuked in stronger moments, to have lived into that day. But we can pose the question in a much broader sense. Was it ever "the Fourth"? For Jefferson died on the anniversary of a day that never was. The Fourth includes celebration of some things that happened on different days and of other things that did not happen at all. We remember how Rittenhouse swooned when his hopes for accuracy in the transit of Venus faded in the glow of the planet's atmosphere, fuzzing the exact time, making the precisionist resort to guesses. But at least he knew the significance of what he was watching. The huge glow cast through the years from the Fourth was not visible to the men who worked and argued through the actual July 4 of 1776. It is in every way an *after*glow, drawing almost as much of its intensity from the deathbeds of these two men as from the event that took place fifty years before.

TWENTY-SEVEN

"... no part of our constitution ..."

> It is not easy to understand today why since Civil War days intelligent Americans should so strangely have confused the Declaration of Independence and the Constitution, and have come to accept them as complementary statements of the democratic purpose of America. Their unlikeness is unmistakable: the one a classical statement of French humanitarian democracy, the other an organic law designed to safeguard the minority under republican rule.
>
> —Vernon L. Parrington

Scholars long ago demolished Parrington's thesis that American history has been "largely a struggle between the spirit of the Declaration of Independence and the spirit of the Constitution, the one primarily concerned with the rights of man, the other more practically concerned with the rights of property" (*Main Currents*, 3). Yet the notion of antagonism between the documents lingers in the popular mind. I have just read a new book and a new article, both by well-known authors, trotting out this tired idea as the secret of American politics.

I mentioned in my Prologue the odd charm many Americans find in the notion that the Declaration proclaimed a revolution which the Constitution betrayed. To use Parrington's own phrase, "it is not easy to understand today" how such a notion could have grown up and attracted otherwise bright people, considering the facts that:

– the principal formulator of the Constitution's doctrine was James Madison, friend and disciple of Jefferson;

– Madison under Witherspoon, like Jefferson under Small, had shaped his politics to Scottish Enlightenment ways;

– there is not a single reference, by *participants* of either transaction, to any disparity in spirit between the passage of the Declaration and that of the Constitution;

– in fact, seven of the Declaration's Signers were at the constitutional convention;

– and, more to the point, thirty of the forty-three living Signers supported the Constitution;

– while the Signers opposed were, as we shall see, defenders of local (state) establishments;

– those at the constitutional convention were younger, poorer, and less powerful in their states than the men who met in Philadelphia from 1774 through 1776 (including the Signers);

– the ratifying procedures for the Constitution, which Parrington (following Beard) called undemocratic, were *more* democratic than those used to adopt the Articles or the state constitutions that preceded them;

– so were the amending procedures and the lack of religious test for office more democratic even than the "radical" constitution of Pennsylvania (which had not been passed by popular vote);

– George Washington, the principal symbol and vindicator of the Revolution from the outset, stood warrant for the Constitution;

– Jefferson, though he criticized some aspects of the Constitution (no more than he had the defects of the Virginia state constitution), still thought it "unquestionably the wisest ever yet presented to men" (*Papers*, 14:678);

– had Jefferson been a delegate to the convention, he would undoubtedly have voted with Madison, as did many who felt some objection to one or other parts of the document; since he wrote that —while not being of the Federalist faction—"I am much farther from that of the Antifederalists."

It is not surprising that criticism of the Constitution grew up after the Gilded Age, during the populist movement at the end of the nineteenth century, when America's plutocracy had learned so well how to hide behind constitutional provisos. Time had revealed some defects, though amendment was always possible. Yet why was it assumed that those defects were imposed on a *prior* and purer republic? If the framers of the Constitution were a selfish lot, prompted mainly by economic interests, what had happened to the nobler race of their predecessors that signed the Declaration of Independence? Had the revolutionary experience itself taught men to adopt what they had opposed in arms?

Parrington thought Beard had solved this problem by contrasting the older "Declaration men," who were landholders, with a new kind of entrepreneur formed by the war's debts—the holders of "personalties" (mainly public securities). But Robert E. Brown proved that the treasury records Beard relied on, covering the period *after* the convention, showed little about the holdings of men as they came into the convention, and practically nothing about those who had sat at the Continental Congresses a decade before that. Besides, the actual delegates did not behave the way Beard thought their interests dictated. Forrest McDonald carried further this analysis and found anomalies like this: The seven men who walked out of the Convention or refused to sign the Constitution were among the heaviest owners of public securities, while the three states that ratified the Constitution unanimously—Delaware, New Jersey, and Georgia—were controlled by agrarian interests. Sectional and state issues, even in an economic sense, did not fall into the symmetrical scheme Beard constructed.

Other attempts to create a continental division along consistent economic lines—e.g., Carl Becker's merchants versus "mechanics"—have failed for lack of evidence or because of unconscious anachronism. These were efforts to impose a theory of proletarian revolt on the essentially bourgeois scheme of eighteenth-century revolution. That kind of revolution fought the religious and monarchic establishment, along with mercantilism, in the name of free speech and free trade. To the embarrassment of some Beckerites, the "radicals" they looked for were often religious enthusiasts, like those who put the religious qualification in the Pennsylvania constitution. Moderate whig deists were philosophically more "open" in their attitudes.

The Antifederalists, as people have realized since Cecilia Kenyon made her study of them, were not the champions of democracy against privilege. They were often men of established power within their states, who did not want to yield that power to a federal apparatus. They talked of defending the individual by interposing the state's power against any rival. Patrick Henry began his speech against the Constitution by arguing for the status quo—the new

Constitution would upset the web of treaties established with other countries in the name of the Confederation. He went on: "Give me leave to demand what right had they to say, We the people? My political curiosity, exclusive of my anxious solicitude for the public welfare, leads me to ask who authorized them to speak the language of We the people instead of We the States? States are the characteristics and soul of a confederation" (Grigsby, *Virginia Convention*, 81).

The idealization of agrarian virtue by progressive historians overlooked the way plantation owners were bound by tradition as well as by slaveholding, by rural isolation and the desire to retain local autocracies of various sorts. Stanley Elkins and Eric McKitrick have argued that it was the younger generation—formed almost entirely in the revolutionary experience, and with little stake in the old ways—that made up the federalist vanguard, willing to risk and innovate at Philadelphia. A number of them had fought with Washington and knew how much his efforts had been hampered by local pride and obstructionism. They had served in the Confederation congresses, while many of the Antifederalists stayed home, exercising the familiar powers of their provincial legislatures. Even Merrill Jensen, in fighting his rearguard action for Beardism, came up with lists of Federalists and Antifederalists that showed the leaders separated by an average of eleven years. Four of the nine Federalist leaders were still in their twenties. Of the Antifederalists, only three were under forty (and one of those was the anomalous sixteen-year-old son of George Bryan).

The Constitution has, at various times, been attacked as "conservative" on grounds not only anachronistic in themselves but mutually contradictory. It is attacked by Jensen for dangerously concentrating power, yet attacked by James McGregor Burns for inefficiently dividing and checking power.

Did the Constitution concentrate power? It created new powers, not so much over individuals as over these old loci of power, the states. Indeed, the main task was to get those old centers to surrender certain prerogatives; and the effort at reassuring them led to lingering ambiguities in our use of the very term "federalism." In itself, this has to do with treaties (*foedera*) or alliances—the neutral use at, e.g., Jefferson, *Papers*, 1:311. But there was an emphasis, in the 1780s, on the ties that connect those under treaty—on *union* and

united force, as in the term "federal [i.e., covenant] theology."
Federalists were, therefore, thought to stand for federal power over
against the states. But in explaining their position, Madison and
Hamilton labored in the *Federalist Papers* to show the states they
had nothing to fear from this central (federal) power. Thus federalism has come, in modern parlance, to mean the division or *dis-
persal* of central power.

Gordon Wood has shown that the framers tried to muster popular support by calling for freshly elected conventions, not the sitting
legislatures, to ratify the Constitution. This was more "democratic"
than the procedure used in ratifying the state constitutions themselves. Even the issue of a bill of rights was not the simple battle
between democracy and privilege often presented to us. Having a
bill of rights was, of course, a whig tradition, harking back to
Magna Carta through the 1689 Bill of Rights. In that sense it was
"conservative" and represented concessions wrung from an executive by a legislature. Most states put bills of rights in their constitutions as a matter of course. Those who opposed a bill of rights at
the Constitutional Convention—including, at first, Madison himself,
who drafted and steered through the final bill—were assuming that
the individual was already protected by the states' bills; that the
central government could not reach the individual except through
the states, which had put impenetrable barriers around individual
rights. Would it not be an act of usurpation to imply that the federal power could go around those barriers? The growth of the Bill
of Rights was nudged along by antithetical developments. On the
one hand, the states used the Bill of Rights as a further statement
of limit on the central power; while, on the other, the effort to solicit
popular support against state establishments made the framers
themselves see their instrument as reaching individuals in new
ways, who must therefore be assured of the customary exemptions.

As the progressive era gave way to the New Deal, liberal support
for an active executive made some people look at the constitution in
an entirely different way. "Concentration" of power was no longer,
in itself, the issue. Concentration was benign so long as it was democratic. After all, the radical Pennsylvania constitution had what
John Adams called a dangerous concentration of power in its uni-
cameral legislature.

The Constitution was an ingeniously constructed Enlightenment machine of "counterpoises"; and it was recognized as such in Europe. The Declaration, which more recent celebrants have thought a pure voice of the Enlightenment, had no impact at all on the European continent. But the state and federal constitutions were studied with enthusiasm and much debate; it was to explain their novelties that John Adams launched his three-volume *Defense* toward a foreign audience. Constitution-making was a favorite Enlightenment exercise, as Rousseau showed with his plans for Geneva and Poland. Jefferson was himself engaged in this pastime, while the convention sat in Philadelphia, discussing amendment procedures with Lafayette and Condorcet in Paris. Intricate mechanics were "progressive," not inhibiting, to these men. Frenchmen thought they saw how to tie the *"parlements"* to a central government as they watched Americans combine local government with a central power neither monarchic nor merely symbolic. Washington was almost as much a hero in France as in America, and his presence at the helm meant the Revolution was steering forward true to its origins.

The Constitution had the virtue, for its contemporaries, of specificity. They liked their machinery well-made. The propaganda effort of Madison and Hamilton stressed the Constitution's complexity and predictability of function. But that first strength became a later liability. When things did not work well, or did not work as expected, the Constitution could be blamed for causing things it merely countenanced. The problem of slavery, for instance, had to be deferred to accomplish any kind of constitution. But then it was used as a bulwark for state authority to enslave. Its powerlessness looked like complicity.

The Declaration did not labor under those particular disadvantages. It did not (any more than the Constitution would) express a desire or form a plan to end slavery in America. That was even less thinkable to the delegates in 1776 than in 1789 (and it would have run up against just that *agrarian* power Beard tried to call the source of democracy). But the Declaration did say "all men are created equal," and that could be used as a pledge of future actions—just the use we saw Lincoln put it to in the Prologue of this book.

The Declaration, as it was passed and as it is generally read, looks just as vague as the Constitution looks concrete. Even its defenders and admirers think there is some virtue to its vagueness, its idealism, its general statement of nice goals, unencumbered by too precise and transient instructions over the means to be taken to such ends. Liberal apologists for an active presidency saw in "the pursuit of happiness" a general mandate for strong government measures that could promise happiness to those affected. "Self-evident truths"—ill-defined as their grounds might be—conveniently became any speaker's favorite truths of the moment.

In time it became psychically important for men to keep the Declaration vague. When the Constitution or some part of the actual government had to be criticized, this reality could be contrasted with the ideal. One could oppose the American government without becoming un-American. After all, what is more American than the Declaration of Independence? So radicals of the 1960s read the Declaration at gatherings meant to end in acts of civil disobedience. One could repudiate the mere *letter* of the law, the Constitution, in the name of a higher law, containing the *spirit* of America.

And what was true of Jefferson's document was also true of his person. There was a vested interest in keeping him vague. The Jefferson cult offers endless cases of vagueness in the service of anachronism. At times he seems to sidle through our history in odd dance steps that keep pairing him with another man to belittle that man's achievements—Jefferson versus Hamilton, or Adams, or Washington, or even Madison. When earth was to be rebuked by heaven, men brought the Declaration to sit in judgment on the Constitution. In the same way would Claude Bowers bring Jefferson to the condemnation of Hamilton.

The conflict between Jefferson and Hamilton was real, almost as much a matter of personality as of principle. Jefferson, a gentleman farmer, disliked the professional politician, the man without independent land to stand on, one who must live by serving a constituency. Neither position is, in itself, "democratic." It is said that Hamilton loved power, and he certainly admired efficiency—a spirit that was necessary to the Revolution, and one that always needs watching. Jefferson's own dreams would have come to nought if Washington had been forced to depend on soldiering no more efficient than his fellow Virginian's. Hamilton fought the revolution that Jefferson, as war governor, could barely bring himself to attend. In the first administration, Hamilton's kind of efficiency, expertly used by Washington, helped stave off that chaos from which dictatorships are bred. The highest aims can lead to disaster if one is unwilling to adopt the necessary means for their attainment. Jefferson could not even run his own plantation profitably—which meant, among other things, that he could not free his slaves, nor escape the necessity of selling some of them at times, which broke up families. Washington could free his own slaves because he made Mount Vernon pay.

This is not said to disparage Jefferson, but to show how unfair it is to use his quite different gifts to denigrate a man like Hamilton. Jefferson was in some ways as nationalist as Hamilton. He wanted an American ethos protected from European ways. It was he, not Hamilton (as Woodrow Wilson and others have said), who warned against "entangling alliances." Many of his finer schemes would have called for extensive state powers he was unwilling to envisage —e.g., the effort to secure control of the whole continent for America, from Cuba to Canada; his plan for allotting free acreage to citizens; his slave-deportation scheme. Hamilton is vulnerable to "idealistic" criticism because he realistically saw what was necessary when vague schemes and ideals were discussed. But even where Jefferson was not vague in fact, his defenders try to keep him mercifully unspecific.

Since Adams died on the same day as Jefferson, it has been customary to pair them. Their very reconciliation brought their final letters together in a way that made for convenient contrast between the Federalist President and the Republican one. James MacGregor Burns presents them as the type of the fearful aristocrat and the democrat who trusts the people. Adams makes an odd-looking aristocrat; and he collaborated in one of the most radical actions of the struggle for independence, the Philadelphia coup of May 1776. With his cousin Samuel, he had deeper experience of the democracy of town meetings and the presence of mobs than did Jefferson in his deferential Virginia society. One of the things that caused Jefferson to dislike New England so much during his second term was precisely the tradition of direct action on matters like his embargo, a tradition that had helped bring on the Revolution in the first place.

Some of the differences between the two men ran deep. Jefferson *was* always more optimistic, almost eerily so; he felt the Revolution's outcome was foreordained when there was no very solid evidence for thinking so. Adams, though he ended fully as rationalist in his theology as Jefferson, retained a Calvinist vision of fallen man's limitations. Adams can be condescended to. Jefferson could be hated, but never dismissed. Perhaps that explains why so many tend to think the failings of Adams's presidency an *expression* of the man's character, while President Jefferson's faults are considered an *exception* to his general virtue—though the Alien and Sedition Acts were less personal efforts for Adams than were the embargo and the pursuit of Burr on Jefferson's part. Once again, comparison does not generally enlighten us—it just reduces Adams, while fuzzing the Jefferson image in aureole.

Jefferson has even been played off against Madison, his friend and student. Madison's political thought was more earthbound, as we saw from his reaction to Jefferson's scheme of letting contracts run nó longer than twenty years. Madison was perhaps the best political thinker this country has produced; but he is forced to play second fiddle to his mentor, even in this one matter of his supremacy. As the author of the basic draft for the Constitution, he is felt to have betrayed his master's Declaration in some unspecified way, and he is made the more partisan leader in forming the first party system. It was hard to be Jefferson's friend. Madison shows it could be, in the long run, hurtful.

The two greatest Virginians of their day were clearly Washington and Jefferson. But no contemporaries thought they had even roughly similar stature. Dazzling as was the galaxy of founders and framers, there was no doubt in their midst who was pre-eminent among them. It was impossible to think there could be another man than Washington at the helm of the Constitutional Convention or of the first administration. Washington was Cincinnatus, the world hero as famous for his surrender of power as for his achievement of it. He took the lead at each crucial moment, in the war, in the framing and passage of the Constitution, in the governing of the country through its precarious first experiments—without Napoleonic excess, yet without weakness or pettiness.

One of the most astonishing reversals in public attitudes toward American history is the one that makes it possible for people, now, to think Jefferson was a greater man than Washington himself. The process of this change was a complex one; a full account of it would involve most major changes that took place in our politics over the last century and more. But the result of that process gives us still another use for Jefferson's putative vagueness. Washington was "merely" practical, "just" a general and good manager. Not a thinker. He worked out some details for the ideals Jefferson formulated. He was a man of the day-to-day; of compromise; of the Constitution. Chance removed him from the scene of the Declaration (where he would certainly have been a signer if he had not been on the battlefield), just as chance removed Jefferson from America when the Constitution was being drafted. A fortuitous symmetry was thus established—Jefferson as the man of the Declaration, the ideal, the dream; Washington the man of the Constitution, of the real, of power.

Jefferson did not share the ideals some of his defenders use to enhance his stature. They say Washington, for all his restraint in power, was still in love with glory and honor. True. But so was Jefferson. The ideal of earned public honor was posed to all men of the Enlightenment. Jefferson held honor sacred, and arranged for the glorification of American heroes, including himself. He made sure that Houdon and Trumbull would make his features imperishable, along with Franklin's and Washington's. Nor would Jefferson have scorned the "merely practical" work of making a constitution, and making it work—as we see from his labors on the Virginia constitution and the revision of Virginia's laws. Those laws —including the harsh ones against freed slaves—are not a high point in Jefferson's work, nor are some of his measures as President. But the cult of Jefferson looks only briefly, if at all, toward his "practical" problems as governor or politician. It prefers to linger in his study, pronouncing self-evident truths.

Douglass Adair reminded us that the Enlightenment's highest ideal was the law-giver, who had been the supreme hero since Bacon's time. Though Jefferson called the three greatest men Bacon and Newton and Locke, he would not have denied Bacon's praise for the "founders of states and commonwealths, such as were Romulus, Cyrus, Ottoman, and Julius Caesar" (*Fame and the Founding Fathers*, 14–15). A much later concept of democracy than Jefferson's had to develop before men would question Washington's greatness as recent decades have.

Jefferson has been made a vague idealist despite himself, despite his empiricism and love of precision. This has made him hard to understand but easy to use. It has made him and his Declaration a touchstone by which other men and ideas are found wanting. I mentioned in the Prologue some of the uses Lincoln put him to. And reverence for the one man rubs off on the other. Jefferson and Lincoln are the twinned saints of our politics. The Gettysburg Address, another piece of war propaganda with no legal force, has entered the empyrean with the Declaration, bathed in a light that makes them easy to see but hard to read.

Epilogue

No uniform Monticello image of Jefferson emerged.
Monticello predicated culture, but in what precise sense
it was difficult to say. The dominant recognition, however, was the one which shocked political preconceptions the most. The poetry of Monticello, in landscape,
architecture, and interior decor, was more persuasive
than its practical mechanism; the sense of the archaic
more powerful than the sense of the modern; the impression of Old World order and refinement more compelling than the impression of New World life. But the
portico, after all, faced the wilderness. There was the
riddle.

—Merrill Peterson, 1959

My impression, gained from going through Jefferson's home many
times with tourists, is not quite the same as Professor Peterson's.
What impressed the visitors, and led to most comment, was the
"Yankee" ingenuity of various tricks and utensils about the place,
rather than the place itself. Doors opening by "magic" if you touch
but one of them. Other doors swinging food in, as the mantle
quietly slips wine bottles up. The two-pen copier and swivel chair,
the bed-in-an-open-wall articulating a room without commanding
it, recessed but open. All these things seemed to point to Jefferson
as a cleverer Benjamin Franklin, and to impress Americans most.
He had a Connecticut Yankee's engineering mind inside a Southern
gentleman's frock coat. This superficially clashes with the popular
image of him as a vague idealist. But that is what saves the image.
He is the idealist as practical man—one who can make a plow or
play a fiddle, though he was not "practical" in the tawdry and capi-
talist sense: He had the good taste not to be a good businessman,
even in the plantation that was his agrarian business.

Actually, most of Jefferson's inventions were just copied from European models. And most cost him more time and effort than they saved. The dittographer was always breaking down. The way he made his home "convenient" left his daughter and her children roofless, living under canvas for long periods of remodeling. Too much attention to the house's gimmicks can distract one from the home itself, which is perhaps Jefferson's most truly original work.

Of course, the eighteenth-century use of "invention" could apply to Jefferson's mere discovery of his models in Europe. To invent was, first of all, to *find*. Dr. Johnson's Dictionary quotes Spenser on finding some wine—

> Or Bacchus' merry fruit they did invent—

and quotes Bacon on Columbus as the "inventor" of America. That latter reference should remind us of Edmundo O'Gorman's play on the two senses of "invent" in his book, *The Invention of America* (1961). O'Gorman argues that America was not truly found in 1492 by Columbus, since he thought till his dying day he had come upon the coast of Asia. O'Gorman would place the real discovery in 1507, when the Waldseemüller map appeared and pictured America as a fourth continent, on a level with the other three. Columbus, he says, supplied the provocation, the raw material, which allowed men to invent (contrive) a new concept of the world. It was that concept which first accounted adequately for the mysterious facts turned up ("invented" only in that sense) by Columbus. Columbus did not think what he found was mysterious; so he could not solve the mystery.

Americans have felt for some time that Jefferson invented America—the country, not the continent. He put it on our conceptual map, as it were; recognized and named that new thing we are. The Declaration drew a new plan of the world, with a Presence theretofore unsuspected. The nation is not, in this view, simply a found object, but a contrived thing, a product of the mind.

A glance at O'Gorman's view of the earlier "invention" shows how extraordinary Jefferson's act is thought to be. Columbus at least gave others some new material for fashioning their concept. But in Jefferson's case the map is made to *precede* the landfall. Before Independence—indeed for some time after it—there was no unifying idea or machinery of government. Yet Jefferson is credited with a vision of that government before it took actual shape. Here the Idea precedes a reality that only partly measures up to It.

The sequence is religious, not scientific; Jefferson's work becomes demiurgic. The upper room in Philadelphia is an Eden of the mind where Jefferson is both Adam and Eve, begetting America in a parthenogenic act upon the little writing stand of his own design. Americans have only been able to "invent" an America after their heart's desire—to find what they want to contrive—by inventing the notion that Jefferson invented us.

I have written this book with the heretical idea that Jefferson was right in considering himself a scientist rather than a theologian. It is true that he was a designer—and a very good one, as one sees in the patient beauty of his architectural drawings. He did not sketch to convey the *effect* of his buildings, as Godefroy and even Latrobe often did. In fact, Jefferson rarely drew sections, one third of the architect's basic arsenal of indicators (but depending in part on a recognized illusion). Plan and elevation were the only tools for Jefferson.

Jefferson was not an experimentalist like Franklin. Franklin elaborated his stove by tests, but Jefferson's one practical invention—the moldboard of least resistance for a wooden plow—was worked out as a problem in pure solid geometry. There is no evidence Jefferson ever put his hand to any plow, including his own. He thought he could solve the essential problem in his study. (By an irony of history, this one truly useful contribution came too late. The day of wooden plows was ending by the time Jefferson polished his formulae.)

Jefferson's procedure with the plow could be considered a confirming parallel for his invention of America. He solved a theoretical difficulty before the time came for practical use. But Jefferson did not consider invention an *original* act. Though not an experimentalist, he was an empiricist. You can only find what is already there. The highest art is copying—that is why he loved to extravagance the Rittenhouse orrery, which (he thought) copied the universe so exactly. Each new gadget just re-exemplifies the great Newtonian laws. In that sense all "curious" mechanisms are little orreries, working models of the laws that make us work. This explains Jefferson's opposition to long or rigorous patent rights. No one can truly "own" the "invention" of things that work, since no one can own Nature, and all things work by the laws of Nature and of Nature's God. Jefferson was opposed to the individualist vision of private enterprise. All enterprise is public, is common. Not only does the earth belong to the living. So do all the forces driving the earth.

Merrill Peterson finds a twofold riddle posed by Monticello—the "practical" inventions contained in an architectural casing of impractical beauty; and the ancient style of the house fronting a primitive woodland. These are contrasts Jefferson would not have felt, any more than he thought his "sensitive" headache at the Natural Bridge was at odds with the scientific nature of his account. For him, Palladio was Rome, and Roman antiquity was Nature. He admired the Villa Rotonda for the same reasons he admired the orrery. Palladio had fixed the ratios for stable beauty in as final and mathematical a form as Newton fixed the rules for motor efficiency. The two could not be at odds. Newton moved things, by law, around poles. Palladio fixed them, by law, upon columns. Jefferson wanted to measure everything with Newton's pendulum. And one of the first things he would have measured, for his own delight, would be a Roman pillar.

Some of Jefferson's scientific aesthetic was based on simple error or accident. Palladio himself is a prime example of the way mistakes can be fruitful. He thought ancient Roman farms had pedimented porticoes, like temples. Indeed, he thought temples were merely more ornate and public copies of the basic human home. Thus Jefferson came to believe in the "ornamented farm" as a basic form in nature. To this he added the Horatian ideal of the farm as an independent landowner's place of learned retreat. When Jefferson referred to himself as a farmer, he was not indulging false modesty. "Letters of a Farmer" was a basic literary form in his time— the voice of an independent and reflective man, of the Country Party in England; in America, of John Dickinson attacking the Stamp Act or Richard Henry Lee attacking the Constitution.

Jefferson did not see conflict, or even contrast, in the juxtaposition of Nature and Antiquity, of the woods and his portico. This is exactly how ordered nature and the ordering mind should communicate, once gothic and baroque superstitions and antinatural forms are swept away. He was delighted that Rittenhouse could learn equally from Newton and from nature in an unspoiled new land. He saw, as many others did, the Indians as antique Romans in their oratory, simplicity, and freedom from that grave Enlightenment disease, "le luxe." Benjamin West won his first fame when he combined his American background and Roman study by putting the war scars and paint of an Indian chief on the body of the Belvedere Apollo in his "Death of General Wolfe."

Some try to preserve the vague Jefferson by seeing contradiction where there is none. They can admire the goals or ideals he expressed while dismissing the means he chose to reach those goals. They can ignore the fact that measurement of the means often defined the possible goals. His admirers like his agrarianism, but not his attempt to rule the fields by number—yet the thing that made farming so noble for him was its nature as a science. They like his desire for universal education, but not the sifting procedure at the heart of it. They admire his peculiarly American scheme of weights and measures, but not his way of deriving it from nature. They quote his claim that earth belongs to the living, but not the mathematics that made this proposition compelling for him. They especially like to remind others that he thought all slaves should be freed, while forgetting the one method he thought must be adopted in order to free them.

Given his methodological presuppositions, Jefferson was not only consistent within all these schemes, he was also undeviating in his adherence to them, once he had worked each out in his own mind. No criticism, even from a Rittenhouse or Madison, could shake his confidence in these "inventions," because he was convinced he *had* invented them—i.e., discovered them, already there, in the patterns of nature. He was not expressing a proprietary vanity when he clung to such views. He showed the same adherence to Palladio, his "bible" of building proportions. He opposed Latrobe's brilliant designs for the Capitol because they lacked Roman authority, the authority of nature.

One of the schemes Jefferson adhered to despite almost universal disagreement is enshrined in his own draft of the Declaration. This is the concept that expatriation led to independence, followed by a new contract at the founding of the American colonies. He admits he never persuaded another man of this theory except George Wythe, that other friend of William Small (from whom, in part, the theory may have been derived). This new contract was based on brother-feeling with the British; so the contractarian theory of the Scottish Enlightenment lies at the very heart of the Declaration. Once that is perceived, the assumptions of vagueness or contradiction disappear from the document. Even the phrase considered most vulnerable or indefinable—the pursuit of happiness—acquires a rich background of specificity, as a scientific concept for measuring distributable quanta of public happiness (chapter Ten), as a moral concept based on the benevolence-thinking of Francis Hutcheson (chapter Seventeen), as a political concept making for predictable laws of human behavior (chapter Eighteen), and as a "sentimental" basis for social life (chapter Twenty-three).

These connections have not, generally, been perceived in the past; there was a reluctance to part with the useful vagueness of Jefferson, as his image had been shaped for polemic or adulation. He has been too long the idealists' weapon against the real, despite his own insistence on literal and measurable fact, his fear of abstraction and mere theory. He has been separated from his contemporaries and colleagues—with whom he did, indeed, have conflicts. But it was a proud company he belonged to, and it makes no sense to use him against his peers. He should be seen as their collaborator in the Revolution, not as sharing with Lincoln a contrived pantheon of the mind's suffering servants.

In fact, Lincoln was in many ways the type of things that Jefferson opposed in those around him. Like Hamilton, Lincoln was a professional politician, a full-time master of that necessary and dangerous craft, who enjoyed it as much as his melancholy nature let him enjoy anything. He was also a seductive rhetorician, not theatrical in delivery like Patrick Henry, but using phrases whose power is almost entirely emotional. (There is little constitutional theorizing in Lincoln's incantatory shaping of Union as a transcendent value.) And, like Washington, Lincoln knew war lays certain inescapable necessities on men, calling for ruthless determination. Point after point that put Jefferson slightly at odds with his fellows must separate him far more deeply from that man of very different greatness, Abraham Lincoln.

This is not simply a matter of temperament. Time itself sunders them. One was quintessentially a man of the Enlightenment; he lived in the world of Catherine and Diderot. The other lived in the time of Victoria and Tennyson, of Thoreau and Edgar Poe. Of course, both speak to us in some way across the ages. But neither can speak clearly till we receive his message ungarbled by intervening quarrels of sons with their fathers' language. The men who are truly "for all times" were also fully of their own time. We ought, then, to restore Jefferson to the world he helped make, and which helped make us; to the course of an American Revolution that was not, finally, a betrayal of his ideas but their complement. Jefferson himself came to hope, after all, for an immortality, "at rest with our friends of 1776 . . . in Congress, with our antient Colleagues" (Cappon, 430, 594).

Paraphernalia

Parts of this book were delivered in different form as the Christian Gauss lectures at Princeton, the inaugural Washington Irving lectures at Union College, a Silliman College seminar at Yale, a National Endowment Fellows lecture at Yale, and several seminars on the eighteenth century at the Johns Hopkins University. I thank faculty and student challengers at each place. Friends and colleagues lent expertise—Jack Greene to Part One, Harry Woolf to Part Two, Benjamin Quarles to the slavery sections.

The eighteenth century always poses problems of orthography and text. The main one here is suggested in my subtitle. We do not know what Jefferson's original draft of the Declaration looked like. Apart even from the drafts of grievances for the Virginia constitution, his fragment of a composition draft (*Papers*, 1:420–23) proves that the "original rough draft" on display in the Library of Congress is misnamed. Yet we must go to an even later draft to find the text for this book's purposes—to the version Jefferson included in his "Notes of Proceedings in the Continental Congress" (ibid., 1:315–19). This version includes changes made by the drafting committee, yet this is the one Jefferson contrasted with the final document—in his notes, in his 1823 letter to Madison, and in his *Autobiography*. This is the text he lived with and wanted known; I include it in an appendix.

Whenever I quote Jefferson's Declaration, without further qualification, I am using that text. This leads to some inconvenience. Normal English usage of Jefferson's time—e.g., in the work of Francis Hutcheson—was "unalienable" rights. This is what either Congress or the broadside's printer substituted for Jefferson's "inalienable." Jefferson may have had French usage (e.g., by Burlamaqui) in mind, or the Latin root. When I quote Jefferson's Declaration, I shall stick to "inalienable." Elsewhere, though, un-.

I would prefer to quote all eighteenth-century texts in their first printed form, with all the vagaries of italics, punctuation, spelling, and capitals—simply to keep reminding myself and the reader that we are eavesdropping, across the ages, on men whose arguments had a different background from our own. But it was difficult, even when working mainly from the Library of Congress, to get the original printing of many books; and editors tell me such unfamiliar and shifting usage raises more barriers than it dissolves.

I settle, then, for modernization everywhere but in Jefferson. His words are so crucial to the argument that they are worth confronting in all their peculiarity. Julian Boyd's great text should be the standard, for the years it has so far covered, though even it fluctuates in one significant way. Jefferson, through all his mature life, avoided the initial capital when beginning sentences. It gives his hand an evenness that recalls the chaste order of his architectural plans. Yet this so nags at current expectation that Boyd opts for higher case as a general rule. Then, unfortunately, he abandons his rule for certain texts considered very important (including the "Notes" version of the Declaration). I hold to his rule, rather than the exception.

Things available only in other editors' work vary in the degree of their modernization. I follow their text, with preference given to Ford's edition of the writings where it has material also contained in the Lipscomb and Bergh edition.

Some things touched on in this book I have treated in greater or different detail for the *New York Review of Books*, in a series of essay-reviews on eighteenth-century subjects—the *"sensibilité"* of Diderot (Sept. 18, 1975), Greuze (Feb. 17, 1977), and Adam Smith (Feb. 23, 1978); the element of *"gloire"* in the American Revolution (Nov. 11, 1976), the background for Trumbull's painting of the Fourth (Oct. 14, 1976), and the problems of Jefferson biographers (April 18, May 2, May 16, July 18, 1974).

Key to Brief Citations

Boyd, *Evolution*   Julian P. Boyd. *The Declaration of Independence, The Evolution of the Text*[2]. Princeton, 1945.

Burlamaqui, *Droit naturel*   Jean-Jacques Burlamaqui. *Principes du droit naturel*. Genève, 1747.

Burlamaqui, *Droit politique*   – *Principes du droit politique*. Genève, 1751.

Burnett   Edmund Cody Burnett. *Letters of Members of the Continental Congress*, vol. 1. Washington, 1926.

Cappon   Lester J. Cappon. *The Adams-Jefferson Letters*. Chapel Hill, 1959.

Chastellux, *Félicité*   François-Jean Marquis de Chastellux. *De la félicité publique, ou considérations sur le sort des hommes dans les différentes époques de l'histoire*, 2 vols. Amsterdam, 1772.

Ford   Paul Leicester Ford. *The Writings of Thomas Jefferson*, 10 vols. New York, 1892–99.

Friedenwald   Herbert Friedenwald. *The Declaration of Independence, An Interpretation and an Analysis*. New York, 1904.

Hazelton   John H. Hazelton. *The Declaration of Independence, Its History*. New York, 1906.

Hutcheson   Francis Hutcheson. Georg Olms facsimile reprint of Collected Works. Hildesheim, 1971:

– Hutcheson, 1   *An Inquiry into the Original of our Ideas of Beauty and Virtue*, 1725.

– 2   *An Essay on the Nature and Conduct of the Passions and Affections*, 1728.

– 3   *Philosophiae Moralis Institutio Compendiaria*, 1745.

– 4   *A Short Introduction to Moral Philosophy*, 1747.

– 5   *A System of Moral Philosophy*, 1755.

– 6   *A System of Moral Philosophy*, Vol. II, 1755.

–	7	*Opera Minora*, 1735–56.
LB		A. A. Lipscomb and A. E. Bergh. *The Writings of Thomas Jefferson*, 20 vols. Washington, 1903.
Mauzi		Robert Mauzi. *L'idée du bonheur dans la littérature et la pensée française au XVIIIᵉ siècle*[4]. Paris, 1969.
Moravia		Sergio Moravia. *Il Pensiero degli Idéologues*. Firenze, 1974.
Notes		Jefferson, *Notes on the State of Virginia* (William Peden, editor). New York, 1972.
Papers		Julian P. Boyd et al. *The Papers of Thomas Jefferson*, 19 vols. Princeton, 1950–74.
Petty, Correspondence		Sir William Petty. *The Petty-Southwell Correspondence 1676–1687*. London, 1928.
Petty, Papers		*The Petty Papers*, 2 vols. London, 1927.
Randall		Henry S. Randall. *Life of Thomas Jefferson*, 3 vols. New York, 1858.
Respect		James H. Hutson, editor. *A Decent Respect to the Opinions of Mankind. Congressional State Papers 1774–1776*. Washington, 1975.
Ryerson		Richard Alan Ryerson. *Leadership in Crisis: The Radical Committees of Philadelphia and the Coming of the Revolution in Pennsylvania, 1765–1776*. Johns Hopkins dissertation, 1973.
Sowerby		E. Millicent Sowerby. *Catalogue of the Library of Thomas Jefferson*, 5 vols. Washington, 1952.
WMQ		*William and Mary Quarterly*.

The Declarations of Jefferson and of the Congress

(Taken from Jefferson's Notes of Proceedings—*Papers*, 1:315–19)

I will state the form of the declaration as originally reported. The parts struck out by Congress shall be distinguished by a black line drawn under them; & those inserted by them shall be placed in the margin or in a concurrent column:

A Declaration by the representatives of the United states of America, in [General] Congress assembled

When in the course of human events it becomes necessary for one people to dissolve the political bands which have connected them with another, and to assume among the powers of the earth the separate & equal station to which the laws of nature and of nature's god entitle them, a decent respect to the opinions of mankind requires that they should declare the causes which impel them to the separation.

We hold these truths to be self evident: that all men are created equal; that they are endowed by their creator with ∧ [inherent and] inalienable rights; that among ∧ certain these are life, liberty & the pursuit of happiness: that to secure these rights, governments are instituted among men, deriving their just powers from the consent of the governed; that whenever any form of government becomes destructive of these ends, it is the right of the people to alter or to abolish it, & to institute new government, laying it's foundation on such principles, & organising it's powers in such form, as to them shall seem most likely to effect their safety & happiness. Prudence indeed will dictate that governments long established should not be changed for light & transient causes; and accordingly all experience hath shewn that mankind are more disposed to suffer while evils are sufferable than to right themselves by abolishing the forms to which they are accustomed. But when a long train of abuses & usurpations [begun at a distinguished period and] pursuing invariably the same object, evinces a design to reduce them under absolute despotism it is their right, it is their duty to throw off such government, & to provide new guards for their future security. Such has been the patient sufferance of these colonies; & such is now the necessity which constrains them to ∧ [expunge] their former systems of government. The history of the present king of Great Britain is a history of ∧ [unremitting] injuries & usurpations, [among which appears no solitary fact to contradict the uniform tenor of the rest but all have] ∧ in direct object the establishment of an absolute tyranny over these states. To prove this let facts be submitted to a candid world [for the truth of which we pledge a faith yet unsullied by falsehood.]

∧ alter

∧ repeated

∧ all having

He has refused his assent to laws the most wholsome & necessary for the public good.

He has forbidden his governors to pass laws of immediate & pressing importance, unless suspended in their operation till his assent should be obtained; & when so suspended, he has utterly neglected to attend to them.

He has refused to pass other laws for the accommodation of large districts of people, unless those people would relinquish the right of representation in the legislature, a right inestimable to them, & formidable to tyrants only.

He has called together legislative bodies at places unusual, uncomfortable, and distant from the depository of their public records, for the sole purpose of fatiguing them into compliance with his measures.

He has dissolved representative houses repeatedly [& continually] for opposing with manly firmness his invasions on the rights of the people.

He has refused for a long time after such dissolutions to cause others to be elected, whereby the legislative powers, incapable of annihilation, have returned to the people at large for their exercise, the state remaining in the mean time exposed to all the dangers of invasion from without & convulsions within.

He has endeavored to prevent the population of these states; for that purpose obstructing the laws for natu-

ralization of foreigners, refusing to pass others to encourage their migrations hither, & raising the conditions
of new appropriations of lands.

He has ∧ [suffered] the administration of justice [to-
tally to cease in some of these states] ∧ refusing his assent to laws for establishing judiciary powers.

∧ obstructed
∧ by

He has made [our] judges dependant on his will alone,
for the tenure of their offices, & the amount & paiment
of their salaries.

He has erected a multitude of new offices [by a self
assumed power] and sent hither swarms of new officers
to harrass our people and eat out their substance.

He has kept among us in times of peace standing armies [and ships of war] without the consent of our
legislatures.

He has affected to render the military independant of,
& superior to the civil power.

He has combined with others to subject us to a jurisdiction foreign to our constitutions & unacknoleged by
our laws, giving his assent to their acts of pretended
legislation for quartering large bodies of armed troops
among us; for protecting them by a mock-trial from punishment for any murders which they should commit on
the inhabitants of these states; for cutting off our trade
with all parts of the world; for imposing taxes on us
without our consent; for depriving us ∧ of the benefits
of trial by jury; for transporting us beyond seas to be
tried for pretended offences; for abolishing the free system of English laws in a neighboring province, establishing therein an arbitrary government, and enlarging
it's boundaries, so as to render it at once an example and
fit instrument for introducing the same absolute rule
into these ∧ [states]; for taking away our charters, abolishing our most valuable laws, and altering fundamen-
tally the forms of our governments; for suspending our
own legislatures, & declaring themselves invested with
power to legislate for us in all cases whatsoever.

∧ in many cases

∧ colonies

He has abdicated government here ∧ [withdrawing his
governors, and declaring us out of his allegiance & protection.]

∧ by declaring us
out of his protec-
tion & waging
war against us.

He has plundered our seas, ravaged our coasts, burnt
our towns, & destroyed the lives of our people.

He is at this time transporting large armies of foreign

mercenaries to compleat the works of death, desolation & tyranny already begun with circumstances of cruelty and perfidy ∧ unworthy the head of a civilized nation.

∧ scarcely paralleled in the most barbarous ages, & totally

He has constrained our fellow citizens taken captive on the high seas to bear arms against their country, to become the executioners of their friends & brethren, or to fall themselves by their hands.

∧ excited domestic insurrections amongst us, & has

He has ∧ endeavored to bring on the inhabitants of our frontiers the merciless Indian savages, whose known rule of warfare is an undistinguished destruction of all ages, sexes, & conditions [of existence.]

[He has incited treasonable insurrections of our fellow-citizens, with the allurements of forfeiture & confiscation of our property.

He has waged cruel war against human nature itself, violating it's most sacred rights of life and liberty in the persons of a distant people who never offended him, captivating & carrying them into slavery in another hemisphere or to incur miserable death in their transportation thither. This piratical warfare, the opprobrium of *infidel* powers, is the warfare of the *Christian* king of Great Britain. Determined to keep open a market where *Men* should be bought & sold, he has prostituted his negative for suppressing every legislative attempt to prohibit or to restrain this execrable commerce. And that this assemblage of horrors might want no fact of distinguished die, he is now exciting those very people to rise in arms among us, and to purchase that liberty of which he has deprived them, by murdering the people on whom he also obtruded them: thus paying off former crimes committed against the *Liberties* of one people, with crimes which he urges them to commit against the *lives* of another.]

In every stage of these oppressions we have petitioned for redress in the most humble terms: our repeated petitions have been answered only by repeated injuries. A prince whose character is thus marked by every act which may define a tyrant is unfit to be the ruler of a ∧ people [who mean to be free. Future ages will scarcely believe that the hardiness of one man adventured, within the short compass of twelve years only, to lay a foundation so broad & so undisguised for tyranny over a people fostered & fixed in principles of freedom.]

∧ free

Nor have we been wanting in attentions to our British brethren. We have warned them from time to time of attempts by their legislature to extend ^ [a] jurisdiction over ^ [these our states.] We have reminded them of the circumstances of our emigration & settlement here, [no one of which could warrant so strange a pretension: that these were effected at the expence of our own blood & treasure, unassisted by the wealth or the strength of Great Britain: that in constituting indeed our several forms of government, we had adopted one common king, thereby laying a foundation for perpetual league & amity with them: but that submission to their parliament was no part of our constitution, nor ever in idea, if history may be credited: and,] we ^ appealed to their native justice and magnanimity ^ [as well as to] the ties of our common kindred to disavow these usurpations which ^ [were likely to] interrupt our connection and correspondence. They too have been deaf to the voice of justice & of consanguinity, [and when occasions have been given them, by the regular course of their laws, of removing from their councils the disturbers of our harmony, they have, by their free election, re-established them in power. At this very time too they are permitting their chief magistrate to send over not only souldiers of our common blood, but Scotch & foreign mercenaries to invade & destroy us. These facts have given the last stab to agonizing affection, and manly spirit bids us to renounce for ever these unfeeling brethren. We must endeavor to forget our former love for them, and to hold them as we hold the rest of mankind enemies in war, in peace friends. We might have been a free and a great people together; but a communication of grandeur & of freedom it seems is below their dignity. Be it so, since they will have it. The road to happiness & to glory is open to us too. We will tread it apart from them, and] ^ acquiesce in the necessity which denounces our [eternal] separation ^ !

ᴧ an unwarrantable
ᴧ us

ᴧ have
ᴧ and we have conjured them by

ᴧ would inevitably

ᴧ we must therefore

ᴧ and hold them as we hold the rest of mankind, enemies in war, in peace friends.

We therefore the representatives of the United states of America in General Congress assembled do in the name, & by the authority of the good people of these [states reject & renounce all allegiance & subjection to the kings of Great Britain & all others who may hereafter claim by, through or under them: we utterly dissolve all political connection which may heretofore have subsisted between us & the people or parliament of Great Britain: & finally we do assert & declare these colonies to be free & independant states,] & that as free & independant states, they have full power to levy war, conclude peace, contract alliances, establish commerce, & to do all other acts & things which independant states may of right do. And for the support of this declaration we mutually pledge to each other our lives, our fortunes & our sacred honour.

We therefore the representatives of the United states of America in General Congress assembled, appealing to the supreme judge of the world for the rectitude of our intentions, do in the name, & by the authority of the good people of these colonies, solemnly publish & declare that these United colonies are & of right ought to be free & independant states; that they are absolved from all allegiance to the British crown, and that all political connection between them & the state of Great Britain is, & ought to be, totally dissolved; & that as free & independant states they have full power to levy war, conclude peace, contract alliances, establish commerce & to do all other acts & things which independant states may of right do.
And for the support of this declaration, with a firm reliance on the protection of divine providence we mutually pledge to each other our lives, our fortunes & our sacred honour.

Index to Proper Names

Index to Phrases

accordingly all experience hath shewn that mankind are more disposed to suffer while evils are sufferable than to right themselves by abolishing the forms to which they are accustomed: 238–39

But when a long train of abuses & usurpations [*begun at a distinguished period and*] pursuing invariably the same object, evinces a design to reduce them under absolute despotism: 64, 239, 245, 316–17

it is their right, it is their duty to throw off such a government, & to provide new guards for their future security: 239

Such has been the patient sufferance of these colonies; & such is now the necessity which constrains them: 94

to [*expunge*] their former systems of government: 38, 47

The history of the present king of Great Britain is a history of [*unremitting*] injuries & usurpations, [*among which appears no solitary fact to contradict the uniform tenor of the rest but all have*] in direct object the establishment of an absolute tyranny over these states. To prove this let facts be submitted: xxi, 334–35, 362

to a candid world: 191, 302, 309, 341

[*for the truth of which we pledge a faith yet unsullied by falsehood*]: 225–27, 235–37, 316–17

1 He has refused his assent to laws the most wholsome & necessary for the public good: 69

2 He has forbidden his governors to pass laws of immediate & pressing importance, unless suspended in their operation till his assent should be obtained; & when so suspended, he has utterly neglected to attend to them: 69

3 He has refused to pass other laws for the accommodation of large districts of people, unless those people would relinquish the right of representation in the legislature, a right inestimable to them, & formidable to tyrants only: 69

4 He has called together legislative bodies at places unusual, uncomfortable, and distant from the depository of their public records, for the sole purpose of fatiguing them into compliance with his measures: 69

5 He has dissolved representative houses repeatedly [*& continually*] for opposing with manly firmness his invasions on the rights of the people: 69

6 He has refused for a long time after such dissolutions to cause others to be elected, whereby the legislative powers, incapable of annihilation, have returned to the people at large for their exercise, the state remaining in the mean time exposed to all the dangers of invasion from

About the Author

Garry Wills is a journalist, trained as a classicist (Ph.D. Yale), who wrote *Nixon Agonistes*. He is Adjunct Professor of Humanities at the Johns Hopkins University. He lives in Baltimore with his wife and three children.

VINTAGE HISTORY—AMERICAN